Mary de Witt Freeland

The Records of Oxford, Mass.

including chapters of Nipmuck, Huguenot and English history from the earliest

date, 1630

Mary de Witt Freeland

The Records of Oxford, Mass.
including chapters of Nipmuck, Huguenot and English history from the earliest date, 1630

ISBN/EAN: 9783337288310

Printed in Europe, USA, Canada, Australia, Japan

Cover: Foto ©Andreas Hilbeck / pixelio.de

More available books at **www.hansebooks.com**

THE

Records of Oxford, Mass.

INCLUDING

CHAPTERS OF NIPMUCK, HUGUENOT AND ENGLISH HISTORY FROM THE EARLIEST DATE, 1630.

WITH

Manners and Fashions of the Time.

BY

Mary de Witt Freeland.

ALBANY, N. Y.
JOEL MUNSELL'S SONS, PUBLISHERS.
1894.

CHAPTER I.

Chapters of "Nipmuck History."

Lady Mary Armine [Armyne] of England, by her benefactions to the natives of the Nipmuck country for their education and christianization, became so interested in her life as to become a part of their history, as she was their patroness.

From an old record:

"Lady Armyne gave large yearly contributions to promote the carrying on of the work begun in New England, for the conversion of the poor Indians in those parts. And this she continued even to her dying day. And of the success of that undertaking she had an annual Account to her rejoicing."

Lady Armyne gave twenty pounds per annum to Rev. John Eliot for his Indian schools in the Nipmuck country at Natick and Hassamanessit, now Grafton.

Lady Armyne, though so devoted in her charities to the heathen in the "far off Nipmuck country," was not unmindful of doing good at her own home in Lincolnshire, England. "No one followed more closely in the footsteps of her Divine Master, for like Him she went about doing good, for she took the height of her religion to consist in the height of love to God and man, and in close obedience to Christ and reliance on His Mediation."

In 1662, when so many clergymen in England were ejected from their livings, Lady Armyne, though devotedly attached to the Church of England, came to Dr. Edmund Calamy of London, and brought five hundred pounds to be given to those dissenting clergymen and their families.

During her last illness, hearing of the Rev. Richard Baxter's troubles as a dissenter from the Church of England, though the Lord Chancellor had proffered to him a Bishopric, Lady Mary sent her servant to him to hear of his case, before whose return to her, she had died.*

The quaint historian narrates of the life and time of **Lady Armyne** :

"This Honorable and Excellent Lady, was a branch of one of the most Antient, Noble, and Illustrious Families in England, whether we look to Descent, Degree, or Actings.

"The Family of the Talbots, for a long Tract of time, Earls of Shrewsbury, whose Heroick performances both in Civil and Millitary Affairs, done by them in their Native Country, are upon Record to the perpetuating of their Names and Renown. But especially their Conquests and Tryumphs in France were so signal, that the Memory of them continues until this day, and

---

* The life of Lady Armyne is found in an ancient book, with the title, " The Lives of Sundry Eminent Persons in this Later Age, Divines, Nobility and Gentry of both Sexes, by Samuel Clark, London (Printed for Thomas Simmons at the Princes Arms, Ludgate Street) 1682-3."

The introductory to the above volume closes with these words:

"It's a great work to learn to die safely and comfortably; even the work of all our lives; my turn is near, and this preparation is my daily Study; But it's the Communication of life, light and love, from Heaven, that must make all effectual and draw up our Hearts and make us ready, For which I daily wait on God. At the brink of the Grave and the door of Eternity. Jan. 16, 1682-3. "RICHARD BAXTER."

Rev. Richard Baxter writes:

"I have not read over this Book being desired suddenly to write this Preface, and, therefore, undertake not the Justification of what I have not read. But I know so many of the Persons and Histories myself as makes me not doubt the Historical truth, Judge Hales and the Countess of Warwick (my great Friends) need no testimony of mine. I have desired the Book-seller to reprint the life of the Countess of Suffolk the daughter to the Earl of Holland, written by Bishop Rainbow, as an excellent pattern to Ladies."

withal so dreadful, that Mothers quieted their crying Children by telling them that Talbot came." *

* Talbot, Earl of Shrewsbury with Henry V, left England and landed in France with an army of 6,000 men-at-arms and 24,000 foot, chiefly archers. After a furious battle the English took possession of Harfleur, August 14, 1415. Henry expelled the French inhabitants in order to people it with English.

Henry soon after finished his campaign by the victory of Agincourt Oct. 25, 1415, which the English said, "shed everlasting glory on his head." No battle was ever fought more fatal to France; the killed are said to have amounted to 10,000 and 14,000 prisoners.

Talbot, Earl of Shrewsbury, was in command at both of these battles, being styled "the greatest captain of his age."

The Earl of Shrewsbury was a great favorite at the court of Henry VI. He presented Queen Marguerite of Anjou, the last of the provençal queens, a volume of sketches executed by himself. On the title page Henry VI and Marguerite are represented as seated upon a low divan, ladies in attendance are pictured in the background. Talbot kneels before the Queen presenting his volume. Henry and Marguerite are again represented in an allegorical picture, Marguerite and the ladies of her court as the Virtues. Marguerite as Faith and King Henry as Honor. As an embellishment daisies are painted in clusters, for every lady had her emblem flower, the fashion of the time, and the queen's cipher is surrounded by the garter and its motto.

On the King's marriage all the knights and nobles wore Marguerite's emblem flower, the daisy, in their caps, when they came on horse-back in a body to receive her as her escort into London. This must have been a very flattering compliment, and the King carried it still farther by having "Marguerites" engraved on his silver. In the reign of Henry VI, during the "Wars of the Roses," Talbot, Earl of Shrewsbury, who was most loyal to the house of Lancaster, was killed in battle and was mourned by all classes of people.

AN EPITAPH

"UPON THE MUCH-LAMENTED DEATH OF THE TRULY HONOURABLE, VERY AGED, AND SINGULARLY PIOUS LADY,

THE LADY MARY ARMINE,

WHO DYED ANNO CHRISTI 1675."

"Hail Mary full of Grace, 'bove women blest;
A Name more rich in Saints than all the rest;
An Army of them fam'd in sacred Story:
All good, none bad, an unparallel'd Glory!
The blessed Virgin well may lead the Van;
Next follows Mary the Bethanian;
Next Mary, Wife of Cleophas; Another
Mary was of James and Joses Mother
How much is spoke of Mary Magdalen?
Of Mary, John Mark's Mother, we read agen.
At Rome a Mary commended by St. Paul;
All Saints; yet not to pray unto at all."

"A Mary was the Mother of our Lord.
A Mary 'twas laid up in heart his word.
A Mary 'twas that chose the better part.
A Mary 'twas that wept with broken heart.
A Mary 'twas that did anoint Christ's feet;
A Mary pour'd on's Head the Spicknard sweet.
At Christ's Cross standing Maries three I find.
When others fled, they were not so unkind.
Christ dead, interr'd, at the Sepulchre door
Two Maries stand, I find no Women more."

"So that from Cradle to the Passion;
From Passion to the Resurrection;
From Resurrection to the Ascention,
Observe you may a Mary still was one,
The Army of such Ladies so Divine,
This Lady said, I'le follow they all Ar-mine."

"Lady Elect! in whom there did combine
So many Maries, might'st say all Ar-mine.
Thou Mother Sister, Spouse wa'st of the Lord,
In that in Heart and Life thou kept'st his Word,

With th' other Mary chose the better part;
With Mary Magd'len had'st a most tender heart."

" On Christ a Mary spent all that she could;
Tho' others grudg'd, more if she had she would,
To th' Head above could'st not, on the feet below
Thou did'st not spare much cost for to bestow.
Thy name a precious Ointment, and the Armies
Of Saints, and Angels are the Lady Armiues."

" Now God and Christ are thine, and what's Divine
In Heaven's enjoyment, Blest Soul! Now All are thine."
Jo. Sheffield.

A Sketch of the Nipmuck Country.

Governor Winthrop writes of a "journey" made by himself, and in company with others, to a place now supposed to be Sudbury, Mass.

January 27, 1632 (old style), Winthrop in his journal writes: " The Governor and some company with him went up by Charles River about eight miles above Watertown (after naming certain hills and streams presented to their view).

" On the west side of Mount Feake, they went up a very high rock, from whence they might see all over Neipnett and a very high hill due west about forty miles off."—Winthrop's Journal, Vol. 1, 68.*

It is stated in the year 1631 "a Sagamore from the river Qonchtacut which lies west of the Naragancet, had visited Boston and had offered the Governor inducements in a promised tribute of corn and beaver skins to send some Englishmen to settle his country. As the Dutch had already made a settlement on the Quinnehtuck river known as the lands of the ' Dutch House of Good Hope ' " (now Hartford, Ct.).

---

* This, it would appear, was the first view of Wachusett mountain by the English, it being the first mention of the Nipmuck country by the colonists.

It also appears " there was an Indian trail of the Agawams, Woronoaks, and other small tribes on the Quonehticut (the long tidal river) who were on friendly terms with the powerful Nipmogg or Nipmuck Indians and came into their country either to pay tribute or to pass through their wide domains."

The Neipnet, Neepmug or Nipmuck Indians, inhabited the country between the sea-coast and the towns about the Massachusetts bay eastward, and the Connecticut river westward. It is said the name Neipnet or Nipmuck in the Indian language signifies " fresh water," which caused the Indians of this interior portion of the country to be thus distinguished from those upon the sea-coast. The Nipmuck country extended beyond the limits of Worcester county;. as delineated on some ancient maps it was shown as extending westward beyond the Connecticut river, and on the north into New Hampshire. There is no doubt that the territory of this tribe of Indians was originally very extensive, stretching over the entire country between the Merrimac and Connecticut rivers.*

According to Rev. John Eliot " Nipmuck or Neipnet was a great country lying between the Conactocot and the Massachusetts."

From Major Gookin's account "The Neipnet region extended from Marlborough to the south end of Worcester county, and around by the Brookfields through Washakins (Nashua) to the northern boundary of the state."

Col. Church states " the Nipmuck country was the country about Dudley and Oxford."

" These Nipmuck Indians were seated upon less rivers and lakes, or large ponds where Oxford now is and towns near it."—Governor Hutchinson.

---

* The Nipmuck country included all of what is now Worcester county.
In an ancient edition of Hubbard's " Narrative of the Indian Wars," published in 1677, is prefixed a map of New England, being as the title expresses " The first map here cut."

In 1647 there is the following record of the Nipmuck Indians:

"The Nopmat (Nipnet or Nipmuck) Indians, having noe Sachem of their own, are at liberty, part of them, by their own choice, doe appertaine to the Narragansett Sachem and parte to the Mohegens."*

"The Nipmuck Indians included several tribes. The Naticks, Nashaways, Pegans, Pawtuckets, Quaboags, Wamesits, Hassanamesits and Pennakooks.

"The Hassanamesits were in Grafton, a part of the territory of Sutton. The Naticks were located at Natick; the Nashaways were on the Nashua river, from its mouth; the Pegans were in Dudley (now Webster), on a reservation of two hundred acres of land; the Pawtuckets were on the Merrimac river where Chelmsford now is; the Quaboags were located in Brookfield; the Wamesits were for a time on the Merrimac river, at Lowell; the Pennakooks were on the Merrimac river near Concord." — Drake's Indian History.

---

* Records of the U. Col. Hazard, 11, 92.

In 1668 Roger Williams says, "that all the Neipmucks were unquestionably subject to Narrhigonset Sachems, and in a special manner, to Mejksah, the son of Canonicus, and late husband, to the old Squaw Sachem, now only surviving." Hubbard states the Nipmucks were tributary to Massasoit and to Philip, Sachem of Mount Hope.

"This Squaw Sachem, as is believed, was chief of those inland Indians since denominated the Nipnets, or Nipmucks, and lived in 1621 near Wachusett Mountain." — Drake's North American Indians.

The Indians in exchange for their land with the English demanded certain articles in return. The following deed was given to Capt. Miles Standish for the ancient town of Bridgewater, a part of Duxbury. An extract of the considerations, viz.: "Ousamequin, Sachem of the Contrie of Pocannuket." Ousamequin, which name Massasoit adopted during the latter part of his life, gave a deed of land to the English, usually called Saughtuckett. It was dated 1649.

The consideration for which the Sachem granted the deed was as follows:

A Treaty with the Nipmucks.

In 1643 Governor Winthrop relates that "At this court Cutshamekin and Squaw Sachem, Mascononoco, Nashacowam and Wassamagon, two Sachems, near the great hill of the west, called (Warchasset, Wachusett,) came into the court and according to their former tender to the governor desired to be received under our protection and government, &c upon the same term that Pumham and Sacononoco were; so we causing them to understand the articles, and all the ten commandments of God, and they freely assenting to all, they were solemnly received, and then presented by the Court with 20 fathoms more of Wampum and the Court gave each of them a coat of two yards of cloth and their dinner; and to them and their men every one of them a cup of sack at their departure, so they took their leave and went away very joyful."— Governor Winthrop's Journal, 2, 156.

In 1643 Massasoit resided with Nashoonon, chief of the Nipmucks.

In Winthrop's Journal Nashoonon is Nashacowam.

A more extended account of this early treaty is to be found in the records of the Massachusetts Bay.

" Wossamegon, Nashowanon, Cutshamache, Mascanomet & Squa Sachim did voluntarily submit themselves to us, as appeareth by their covenant subscribed wth their own hands, hear following & oth^r articles to wch they consented. Wee have and by these presents do voluntarily & wthout any constraint or psuasions, but of o^r owne free motion, put o'selves, o^r sub-

---

7 coats, a yd and half in a coat — 9 hatchets, — 8 Howes, — 20 Knives, — 4 Moose Skins — 10 yds and a half of Cotton.

" The land conveyed in the deed extending in length and the breadth thereof as followeth, that is to say; from ye weare at Saughtuckett seven myles due east, and from said weare seven (miles) due west, and from said weare seven myles due north and from said weare seven (miles) due south," etc.

jects, lands & estates under the government & jurisdiction of the Massachusetts, to be governed & ptected by them, according to their just lawes & orders, so farr as wee shal bee made capable of understanding them ; & wee do pmise for o^{r}selves all o^r subjects and all o^r posterity, to be true and faithfull to the said government & ayding to the maintainance thereof, to o^r best ability. & fro^m time to time to give speedy notice of any conspiracy, attempt or evill intention of any which wee shall (or) heare of against the same : and we pmise to be willing fro^m time to time to be instructed in the knowledg & worship of God, in witness whereof wee have hereunto put o^r hands the 8th of the first m^o. a 1643–1644."

CUT SHAM A CHE
NASH OWA NON
WOS SAM E GON
MASK A NOM ETT
SQUA SACHIM

CERTAIN QUESTIONS PPOUNDED TO THE INDIANS & ANSWERS.

1. To worship ye onely true God, wch made heaven & earth & not to blaspheme him.

An: We do desire to rev'ence ye God of ye English, & to speake well of him, because wee see hee doth better to ye English than othe^r Gods do to others.

2. " Not so swear falcely,

An ; They say they know not w^t swering is among y^e.

3. Not to do any nnnecessary worke on ye Sabbath day, especially wthin ye gates of christian towns.

An: It is easy to y ^{m}: they have not much to do on any day, & they can well take their ease on y^t day.

4. To hono^r their parents & all their supio's.

An. It is their custome to do so, for the inferio's to hono^r their supio's

5. To kill no man wthout just cause and just authority

An: This is good and they desire to do so.
6. To comit no unclean lust, &c......
An: Though sometime some of y^m do it, yet they count that naught, and do not alow it.
7. Not to steale
An; They say to y^t as to ye 6th quere
To suffer their children to learn to reade God's word y^t they may learn to know God aright & worship in his owne way .
They say as opportunity will serve, and English live among y^m they desire so to do.
That they should not be idle
To these they consented, acknowledging y^m to bee good
Being received by us they psented 26 fathoms of wampum, & the Court directed the Treasurer to give them five coats, two yards in a coate, of red cloth & a potfull of wine.— Mass. Col. Records, Vol. II, p. 55.

Rev. John Eliot, a clergyman of Roxbury, N. E., educated at Cambridge, England, became interested in the benevolent project of introducing Christianity into the Nipmuck country and in educating the natives, Mr. Eliot having acquired the rudiments of the Indian dialect, it is said, from native servants in his own family.*

He was accompanied in his "journeys" by his friend Major-General Daniel Gookin, an English gentleman, born in the county of Kent, who had at first made a settlement in Virginia, but came to Cambridge, N. E., in 1644. Maj. Gookin was the superintendent of all the Indians that had subjected themselves to the provincial government, and in Mr. Eliot's missionary visits to the Indians, he himself, at the same time, administered civil affairs among the natives.

---

*Mr. Eliot says that "an Indian taken in the Pequot wars, and who lived in Dorchester, was the first native who taught him words and was his interpreter."

"He took the most unwearied pains in his strange lessons from this

In 1646 the General Court of Massachusetts "ordered and decreed that two ministers should be chosen by the elders of the churches every year, at the Court of Elections, and so to be sent, with the consent of their churches with whomsoever would freely offer themselves to accompany them in that service to make known the heavenly counsel of God among the Indians in a most familiar manner, by the help of some able interpreter, as might be most available to bring them to the knowledge of the truth, and their conversion to Jesus Christ, and for this end something might be allowed them by the General Court to give away freely to those Indians whom they should perceive most willing and ready to be instructed by them."—Palfrey's History of New England.

A week before it had passed this order Rev. John Eliot had made his first essay in preaching to the Indians. A young man who had been a servant in an English house, and understood his own language, and had a clear pronunciation, Mr. Eliot took into his family; and having, with his assistance, translated the Lord's Prayer and the Decalogue, he soon acquired a knowledge of the Indian language.

Ten pounds were voted to Mr. Eliot as a gratuity from the Court in respect of his great pains and charge in instructing the Indians in the knowledge of God.

Rev. John Eliot obtained for the Indians a grant of land, to which he gave the Indian name Noonanetum [Rejoicing].

Daniel Gookin, who accompanied Mr. Eliot in his journeys, says: "The first place he began to preach at was Nonantum, near Watertown, upon the south side of Charles River,

---

uncouth teacher, finding progress very slow and baffling, receiving no aid from other tongues which he had learned in England, and which were so differently constituted, inflected and augmented."

Mr. Eliot also secured natives to reside with him in his family and to accompany him on his visits, to interchange with him words and ideas.—Memorial History of Boston, pages 260-261.

about four or five miles from Roxbury, where lived at that time Waban, one of their principal men, and some Indians with him."

Mr. Eliot set out upon his mission in October, 1646, and sent out forerunners to apprise the Indians of his intentions.*

Waban, a grave and wise man of the same age of the missionary (forty-two), a person of influence, met him at a small distance from their settlement, and welcomed him to a large wigwam on the hill Nonantum.

A number of Indians assembled here to hear the new doctrine.

After a short service of prayer in English, Mr. Eliot delivered a sermon from Ezekiel 37 : 9, 10 : " Then said He unto me, Prophesy unto the wind (to which the Indian term " Waban " is said to answer), Prophesy son of man, and say to the wind (say to Waban) thus saith the Lord God, Come from the four winds, O breath, and breathe upon those slain, that they may live. So I prophesied, as He commanded me, and the breath came into them, and they lived and stood upon their feet an exceeding great army." Having closed his sermon, he was desirous of knowing whether he had conveyed his sentiments intelligibly in a language so new to himself, he therefore inquired whether they comprehended his meaning, to which they replied : " We understood all."

Waban particularly received those happy impressions, which remained through life, and qualified him effectually to aid in the design of (Christianizing) his countrymen.

" Having given the children some apples, and the men some tobacco, and what else they then had at hand, . . . they departed with welcomes."

---

* For speedily transmitting intelligence "the Indian messengers ran swiftly, and at every settlement fresh messengers are speeded away to reach the chief's wigwam. When within about a mile of the place the messenger commences hallooing, and all who hear begin to halloo, whereby a great concourse is soon gathered to hear the news."

Before the end of the year three other visits were made. "As soon as ever the winter was passed," Mr. Eliot's labors were resumed.

John Wampus, a native, brought his son and several Indian children to the English to be instructed.

A school was soon established among them, and the General Court having given the neighboring Indians a tract of highland, called Nonantum, and furnished them with various implements of husbandry. The Indians many of them professed christianity, and the whole in the vicinity became settled, and the Indians conducted their affairs with prudence and industry, and they adopted the customs of the English, made laws, and had their magistrate.*

Mr. Eliot's efforts were put forth for the civilization as well as the Christianization of the people. He encouraged the building of farm-houses, and the making of homes for separate families, the planting of gardens and orchards, the raising and utilizing of flax and hemp.—Palfrey, II, 336, 337.

Mr. Eliot in writing to the corporation of London, in 1649, says "that a Nipnet Sachem hath submitted himself to the Lord, and much desires one of our chief ones to live with him and those that are with him."

---

*John Wampus was a Sagamore of the Hassanamesit tribe. He is mentioned as being some time of Hassanamesit.

"In January, 1666, Robert Wayard, of Hartford, Ct., conveyed by deed, a tract of land situate in Boston, to John Wampus, an Indian of Boston, bounded on the common, etc., being 300 feet by 30, with a dwelling house thereon. This tract is now partly covered by St. Paul's church.

"The records of Suffolk county give further evidence of his concern in the sale and purchase of real estate.

"Tradition states John Wampus crossed the Atlantic and was in London, that he returned to New England in the same ship with a Dr. Sutton, that his health failed on his return, and that he received particular attention from him on this voyage."

Mr. Eliot writes again to the same society in the year 1651: "There is a great country called Nipnet, where there be many Indians dispersed, many of whom have sent to our Indians desiring that some may be sent unto them to teach them to pray to God."

It would appear that in England there was a lively sentiment in favor of Christianizing the heathen Nipmuck " in these ends of the earth," as well as other natives in the new world, and that the occupancy of New England by the English adventurers should result not only in the accumulation of gold, but that Christianity should be promulgated " in this hideous and howling wilderness," and throughout their possessions in America.

In writing of New England, Captain Weymouth, an historian of the time, asserts, that " the result hoped for in planting settlements on these shores was to Christianize these dark regions of America," which were designated by the English as the West Indies.*

CHAPTER II.

RECORDS FROM THE ROYAL HISTORICAL SOCIETY, LONDON.

The Christian education of the Nipmuck Indians through the correspondence of Rev. John Eliot, and the publication in London of a series of the " Eliot Tracts."

---

*"The first royal charter for establishing the colony of New England had declared that to win and incite the natives of that country to the knowledge and obedience of the only true God and Saviour of mankind and the Christian faith is our royal intention and the adventurers' free profession, is the principal end of the plantation."

In July, 1649, such was the effect of the report from New England on Cromwell, Calamy and others, as well as on the Long Parliament, that an act or ordinance was found with this title:

"A Corporation for the promoting and propagating the Gospel of Jesus Christ in New England."

Thus the New England Company was established by the Long Parliament.

"All honor then to Cromwell and the Commons of England in Parliament assembled as the founders of the first Protestant mission to Pagans."

This society continued until the "Restoration of the Monarchy," 1660.

A general collection or subscription was to be made through all counties, cities, towns and parishes of England and Wales, for the purposes of the corporation.

Nearly $12,000 were forthwith collected by voluntary subscription throughout England and Wales, and several manors, lands and houses were purchased. An amount of at least £11,430 was expended in the purchase of landed property at Eriswell, in Suffolk, and a farm at Plumstead, in Kent, as well as several houses in London.

All these purchases were conveyed to this parliamentary corporation, or to some of the sixteen members as its trustees.

The corporation appointed commissioners and a treasurer in New England, who received the income transmitted to them by the corporation of England for the maintenance of missionaries and school teachers among the natives till the restoration of Charles II.

It is said Mr. Eliot's first effort to form an Indian town at Nonantum in Newtown proved a failure in his instruction to the natives on account of its being so near Boston and other English settlements. The surroundings of a so-called Christian community were unfavorable to influencing the natives from heathenism to Christianity, and he desired a position more remote, and petitioned for a grant at Natick, and in 1651 the General Court set apart two thousand acres of land for an Indian plantation.

In 1651 Rev. John Eliot removed to Natick. In 1660 a native church was formed in this settlement, and though Mr. Eliot was a clergyman, having the care of a church in Roxbury for twenty-five years, he preached and taught the natives, establishing schools and native churches with Christian teachers.*

"These commissioners received from the London Society authority to establish a school for the natives at Cambridge. Young men among the Indians were received as pupils to be educated for teachers. The society distributed bounties to encourage education; they printed catechisms in the native language and furnished books for teachers."—Palfrey, I, 333.

"In 1658 Eliot's native teachers received two pounds each for their services, while Eliot received two pounds for Bibles, spectacles, and primers for the natives."—Palfrey, I, 333.

"The expenses of the London Society in this, the eighth year of its establishment, was five hundred and twenty pounds in salaries to teachers and the expenses of pupils in the Cambridge schools."—Palfrey, I, 333.

RECORDS RECEIVED FROM THE ROYAL HISTORICAL SOCIETY, LONDON.

"(May 29, 1660.) Then this Corporation, created by the Long Parliament, ceased.

"There was, therefore, a short cessation of the income, for the Royalist vendor of the property at Eriswell in Suffolk, re-

---

*Tradition states there is still to be seen at Natick the oak tree under which Mr. Eliot instructed the natives.

The Nipmuck Indians had a constant and friendly intercourse with the Natick Indians, and became interested with them in the preacher of the "new Faith."

entered and obtained from the tenants a good deal of the rents until the Company was revived or created anew by the Order in Council, when he was obliged by the decree in a Chancery suit to fulfil the contract he had entered into with the former Corporation.

"The Ordinance could no longer be recognized, but by the exertions of 'the excellent Robert Boyle, so notable for his beneficence,' and others, an Order of Charles II, in Council was obtained April, 1661, for a new Charter of Incorporation vesting in the Company then created (and now subsisting) the property which had been given or bought for the purposes of the late reported Corporation."

"ORDER IN COUNCIL, FOR THE NEW ENGLAND COMPANY'S CHARTER.

At the Court at Whitehall the 10th day of April 1661.

PRESENT:

The King's Most Excellent Majesty.

His Royal Highness the Duke of York.
Lord Chancellor.
Duke of Albemarle.
Marquis of Dorchester.
Lord Great Chamberlain.
Lord Chamberlain.
Earl of Northumberland.
Earl of Berks.
Earl of Norwich.
Earl of Sandwich.
Earl of Lauderdale.
Lord Viscount Valentia.
Lord Roberts.
Lord Seamore.
Mr. Comptroller.
Mr. Vice Chamberlain.
Mr. Secretary Nicholas.
Mr. Secretary Morris.

Sir Anthony Ashley Cooper.

"Upon reading of Mr. Attorney General his report to this Board upon a Petition of divers for propagating the Gospel in America to him referred by Order of the 14th of November 1660, and a draft prepared for renewing the Charter of the

Corporation therein specified and full debate thereof had; It is ordered that the said Corporation may by the said Charter have power to purchase £2000 per annum and may have liberty to transport yearly £1000 in Bullion or foreign money making entry from time to time of what shall be so transported in the Port of London in the Custom House there. And the Lord Viscount Valentia is to consider of and examine the list of names of the members whereof the said Corporation is to consist and to offer the same to the Board and according to this direction Mr. Attorney is to fill up the blanks and perfect the said draft of a Charter. And also to add thereunto a clause that all lands tenements and hereditaments heretofore given or bought to the use or uses in this Charter mentioned shall from henceforth be vested in the said Corporation and their successors with power to sue for and recover the same and any arrears thereof due.

"JOHN NICHOLAS."

The charter was completed February 7, 1661-2.

"The members of the Company were forty-five in number, and included Churchmen and Dissenters.

"Lord Chancellor Clarendon and other noblemen head the list, and Boyle, the first Governor, with several surviving members of the late reputed Corporation, and many Aldermen and Citizens of London, are included in it. The yearly REVENUE of the Company's lands, money, and stock was to be applied for the promoting and propagating the Gospel of Christ unto and amongst the heathen natives in or near New England and parts adjacent in America, and also for civilizing, teaching, and instructing the said heathen natives in or near New England, and their children, not only in the principles and knowledge of the true religion, and in morality and the knowledge of the English tongue, and in other liberal arts and sciences, but for the educating and placing of them or their children in some trade, mystery, or lawful calling."

RECORDS OF THE ROYAL HISTORICAL SOCIETY OF LONDON PRESENTED FOR THE "RECORDS OF OXFORD."

Extracts from a letter dated Lincoln's Inn, London, November, 1878. From Henry W. Busk, Esq., a member of the New England Company, to Rev. Brooke Herford of Chicago, U. S. A.:

"The labours of the Company and the Commissioners* and others in America were carried on unremittingly till the American War of Independence interrupted the usual remittances. When the 13 provinces were acknowledged as independent States, the Company could not safely exercise its charter trusts out of the King's dominions, and at first transferred these operations to New Brunswick, and appointed Commissioners there so far as concerned the income of the Charter Fund. But the efforts there were not successful, and a new plan, recommended by one of the New Brunswick Commissioners, was, after consulting the Governor of the Province and other in-

---

*"Increase and Cotton Mather were among the Commissioners, and were frequent correspondents of the Company after 1671." — London Records.

From the funds of this corporation an allowance of £50 per annum was paid to Mr. Eliot as a stipend in supplement of his moderate salary of £60 as a minister of Roxbury. Fifty pounds was also allowed to Governor Mayhew for his interest in the education and Christianizing the Indians of Martha's Vineyard. Governor Mayhew was a co-worker with Eliot.

The income of the English Society amounted to the then large sum of about seven hundred pounds.

September 5, 1661.

Mr. Eliot published the New Testament and other books for the instruction of the natives. In 1663 the Old Testament was printed at Cambridge, Mass., in the Natick or Nipmuck dialect and was the first Bible printed in America.

In 1890 a single copy of the Eliot Bible of the edition of 1663 was sold in London for £250.

habitants, adopted in 1807, and acted on till 1822, when this plan also was found to have failed. The Company then transferred its operations to other parts of British America, principally near the Grand River north of Lake Erie, and near Lake Ontario, at the Bay of Quinté, and near the Rice and Chemong Lakes.

"During the suspension of remittances to America the Company accumulated and invested the income of all the three funds. By decrees of the Court of Chancery in 1792, 1808, and 1836, all the three funds have been regulated. Boyle's rent-charge is applicable by the Company for the advancement of the Christian religion among infidels in British America; so also the income of the accumulations of that fund. The income of Dr. Williams' fund and accumulations is applicable by the Company towards the advancement of the Christian religion among Indians, Blacks and Pagans in British Plantations and Colonies, and for their education, etc. The income of the Charter Fund and of its accumulations is applicable in Upper Canada."

SKETCH OF NEW ENGLAND COMPANY BY HENRY W. BUSK.

"Those stations which have been most permanently mentioned are the following :

"1. Among the Mohawks and other Six Nations Indians settled on the banks of the Grand River, between Brantford and Lake Erie.

"2. On the shores of the smaller Lakes, Rice Lake twelve miles south of Peterborough and (Mud or) Chemong Lake ten miles north of Peterborough.

'3. On the banks of the Garden River, near Sault Ste. Marie (the rapids between Lake Superior and Lake Huron).

"4. On Ruper Island, in British Columbia.

"The Indians of the Six Nations include the Mohawks, Oneidas, Onondagas, Cayugas, Senecas, and Tuscaroras. Up to the time of the American War of Independence the first five named inhabited the valleys on the rivers and lakes of Central New York.

"There are two schools near the Mohawk village close to Brantford, as well as a parsonage for the church there. This church possesses the communion plate and a large English Bible, presented by 'Good Queen Anne' to the Indian church in the Mohawk valley, which the Indians had been obliged to abandon. The old Mission Church was built by the Mohawks about 1782, about one mile south-east of the city of Brantford on the north-east of Grand River. In this church they placed the bell they received from London.

The Rev. John Eliot, in his last illness, observed: 'There is a cloud, a dark cloud, upon the Work of the Gospel among the poor Indians. The Lord revive and prosper that Work and grant that it may live when I am dead.'

"We have throughout tried to do our very best for our red brethren. What success we have had in doing so you might best learn by a visit to our Mohawk Institution close to Brantford, where the superintendent will be glad to show you what is being done for the education, etc., of some ninety or more of the native boys and girls. In the Mohawk Parsonage is our aged missionary Canon Nelles,* and not many miles off are several thousand Indians, with nine day-schools on the Tuscarora Reserve, and the Rev. Isaac Barr at the Kanyenga Parsonage, and a native curate, the Rev. Albert Anthony, and several interpreters and school-teachers, as well as Methodist and Baptist ministers on this Reserve, and at Chemong Lake and at the Bay of Quinté. The members of the Company have always been a mixture of Churchmen and Dissenters working harmoniously together.

"In many parts of America the natives seem to be dying out. We have the satisfaction of feeling that with us they

* Now Archdeacon Nelles.

are increasing and improving in spite of the bad example and influence of unprincipled Whites.

"Mr. Robert Ashton, our present superintendent of the Mohawk Institution, has filled that post for six years, and is always much pleased with the visits of enlightened friends of the Red men. When you call there you will perhaps be a little surprised at the civilization and attainments, physical, intellectual, moral, and religious, of the eighty or ninety young people there training. At a few miles distance you will find the Six Nations Reserve, some ten miles long by six broad, with 3,000 Red men (five-sixths of them professing Christianity), aided by a considerable staff of native as well as white clergy and other officers, in making progress and gradually overcoming obstacles and resisting temptations and bad examples."

In 1874 Lord Dufferin accompanied by Lady Dufferin visited the Mohawk Church as Governor-General of Canada, and received addresses from the Indians, and added his signature in the Bible that already bore those of R. R. H., the Prince of Wales, and R. R. H., the Duke of Connaught.

Hon. Robert Boyle, of Stalbridge Manor, was the fast friend of the distinguished Rev. John Eliot, and identified with him for many years in his efforts to educate and Christianize the Nipmuck Indians — " the poor souls of the West Indies," as then styled. Mr. Eliot recognized Hon. Robert Boyle, the governor of the corporation for propagating the gospel in New England, as the source of the life and efficiency of the society.

Rev. Mr. Eliot, in his correspondence with Hon. Robert Boyle relative to the Nipmuck country and the native Indians, very quaintly addresses him as " Right honorable, deep learned, charitable, indefatigable and nursing father" of the natives of the Nipmuck country.

Robert Boyle was celebrated for his unrivaled learning, and for his great excellencies of Christian character.

NOTE. — Rev. Mr. Mayhew forwarded the following sketch to the London Society, etc. :

"Laban Panu, who died at Gayhead, November 6th, 1715, when he was ten Years and about nine Months old, was the son of a Christian Indian teacher.

"He was till he was near nine Years old rude and disorderly, was apt to profane the Sabbath Day, and could scarcely be restrained from playing at Meeting: nor did the many good Instructions and Exhortations given him by his Parents appear to have any good Effect upon him.

"His Parents, grieved with his Miscarriage, at length began to deal more sharply with him, taking therein that Advice of the wise Man, Correct thy Son, and he shall give thee rest; and as they found the Counsel good, so they found the Promise true; for due Corrections thus added to good Instructions, did, by God's Blessing, soon produce a remarkable Change in the Carriage and Behaviour of their Child."

"He about this time told his Mother, that formerly he had not believed there was a God, but now he was persuaded that there was one, who had placed him here in the World."

"And for what End, said his Mother, do you think God has placed you here as he has done? That I might seek and serve him, said the Child; and as God has placed us here upon Earth, so he will shortly remove us again from it. His Mother then proposing the Doctrine of the final Judgment to him, he readily asserted his firm Persuasion of the Truth and Certainty of that Doctrine; and he then carried himself as one, that must be brought into Judgment for all he said and did, or ought to do. He applied himself with Diligence to the reading of his Books, which he had before too much neglected; and he now also studied his Catechism, and would often of his own accord repeat by Heart the Questions and Answers, which he had before learned; and he and some of the other Children of the Family, and some also of another Christian Family that lived near by, used by turns to catechise one another; by which Means the Knowledge of this Child, as well as some of the rest, was considerably increased."

"His Mother sometimes hearing of him at these Exercises, would ask him, whether he really believed the Truth of the Answers in his Catechism which he repeated; making this Demand more especially when he came to Answers of the greatest Importance; and he would still, in Answer to her, declare his firm Belief of the Truths which he so learned.

"His Mother observing that he was alone, saying something which she could not so hear as to understand, she once asked him what, and to whom he used to speak in his Retirement?

"To which he answered, that he used to speak to God, and pray to him, to pardon all his Sins, and to make him good. His Father also sometimes found him alone in the Forest, calling on the name of the Lord; and sometimes heard him in the Depths of the Night, when he was upon his Bed, praying to God for his Mercy and Salvation.

"He talked often of his own frailty and Mortality.

"He was sick but about a Month before he died; in which time he behaved himself as became a Youth that remembered his Creator.

"Soon after he was taken ill, his Mother asking him, whether he were willing to die and leave this World, and all his Enjoyments in it, he after a little Pause said, that he found in himself an Unwillingness at present so to do. But why so said his Mother to him, this is a very troublesome World, here are many Afflictions to be undergone; whereas Heaven is a most excellent Place, wherein there is no Trouble or Sorrow to be indured."

"I am concerned, said the child weeping, for my Little Brother, (one younger than himself). I now keep with him and look after him; but if I die, I can take no more care of him.

"Don't, said his Mother, let that trouble you; if you die before your Brother, it will not be long before he will follow after you; and if you go to heaven, he will, if he loves and serves God, come thither to you, and there live with you forever; the which that he may do, I will endeavour to teach him to know and serve the Lord.

"Do you therefore seek to God to prepare you for your End; and be willing to die, and go to your God, when he sees meet to call you."

"Yes said Laban smiling, I will be so; I will now set my Heart no longer upon my Brother, nor be unwilling to leave him; Come hither Joseph, said he to him; who then coming to him, he took him by the Hand and said, Farewel my Brother, you shall not offend (or hinder) me any longer, be thou diligent in seeking after God!

"After this he never discovered the least unwillingness to die, but set himself to seek the Lord with his whole Heart, and called daily upon him for his Mercy to be extended to him for the sake of Jesus Christ his only Saviour."

"He underwent much Pain in the time of his Sickness, yet he said it was God that laid the same upon him, and he did bear with much Patience the mighty Hand of God which he was then under, constantly trusting in and crying to him only for Deliverence.

"When he perceived that he was nigh to Death, he said but little to any that were about him, but kept almost continually praying to God, often saying, Oh! my Heavenly Father, have Mercy on me.

"When his Friends asked him whether he were willing to die, and whether he had Hopes that God would save him, he still answered affirmatively to these Questions. After his Voice so failed him that he could not pronounce perfect Sentences, he still kept praying to God and saying, Woi—Woi—Woi; which may be rendered in English, I pray— I pray—I pray, which were the last Words he ever was heard to speak."

CHAPTER III.

Hassanamisset.

The territory of Hassanamisset (now Grafton) has an historic record of great interest.

It was one of the Indian reservations for the Christianized Indians set off by the provincial government upon the petition of Rev. John Eliot.

The grant was made May 15, 1654, viz.: "Liberty is granted to the Indians of Hassanamiset, being about 16 miles west of Sudbury, to make a town there, provided it does not prejudice any former grant, nor that they shall dispose of it without leave first had and obtained from this court."* (The Indians were allowed to build towns of their own wigwams.)

In 1654 the General Court, on Mr. Eliot's petition, set apart this tract of land (Hassanamiset) for the use of the Indians to prevent any conflicting claims between the English and the natives.

"No Indian town gave stronger assurances of success than Hassanamiset; at that time it had become the central

*Archives of Mass., Vol. 30.

point of civilization and Christianity to the whole Nipmuck country."

A school was here established, where the Bible was read and studied in the Indian language. Young men were here educated and sent into the neighboring towns to preach the gospel (as Christian teachers). A regular government was created, and the forms of law strictly observed. The population of the town was small, yet, by reason of their constant intercourse with their neighbors, a large number of natives enjoyed the benefits of this school, and before the year 1674, within which Manchaug, now Oxford, was included, seven new towns of praying Indians, as they were termed, were formed in the neighborhood, most of which were furnished with teachers from this place. A church was here established.

The following is from an old record:

"Hassunnimesnt it lieth upon Nichmuke River; The people were well known to the English so long as Connecticot Road lay that way, and their Religion was judged to be real by all that travelled that journey and had occasion to lodge, especially to keep a Sabbath among them."

In 1674 Rev. John Eliot and Maj. Gookin visited all the "Christianized Indians" of the Nipmuck country. Gookin, in his description, says:

"Hassamanesit signifieth a place of small stones it lieth about thirty eight miles from Boston west southerly, and is about two miles eastward of Nipmuck river (Blackstone) and near unto the old road way to Connecticut."

Hubbard describes it as a place up into the woods beyond Medfield and Mendon.

It was called Hassanamisco by the Indians, and went by that name until 1735, when it was incorporated and named Grafton.

James the printer, one of the Indians of Hassanamessit, was distinguished for his assistance in printing the Indian Bible, being employed in setting up the type.

In 1709 the English and Indian Psalter was published by a son of Samuel Green and James the printer, within his Majesty's Province of the Massachusetts Bay, in New England.

James had been apprenticed to Samuel Green to learn the printing trade in Boston.

Hubbard's account of James the printer:

" When he was put to an apprenticeship (after leaving the 'Charity School' at Cambridge) for sixteen years, He had obtained some skill in printing, and might have obtained more had he not like a false villain ran away from his master before his time was out!"

" Printer" became the surname of the family, and his reputed descendants have lived in Grafton.

The magistrates were directed to take care to have a court held once every quarter at such place or places where the Indians did ordinarily assemble to hear the word of God, with permission of the Indian chiefs "to bring any of their own people to the said courts, and to keep a court of themselves once every month."

Pennahannit, called Captain Josiah, was "Marshal General" over all the Christianized Indian towns, and used to attend the courts.

The following is said to be a copy of a warrant which was issued by the ruler Waban for this court :

" You, you big constable, quick you catch um Jeremiah Offscow, strong you hold um, safe you bring um, afore me, Waban, Justice of the peace."

" A young justice asked him what he should do when Indians got drunk and quarreled. He replied, ' tie um all up, and whip um plaintiff, whip um 'fendant, and whip um witness.' "*

"*May* 14, 1704.

" The township of Sutton was purchased by the English of

---

*Allen Biog. Dictionary.

John Wampus, and some other Indians of the Nipmuck country.

"Sutton is situate in the Nipmug country between the towns of Mendon, Worcester, New Oxford, Sherburne and Marlborough, of eight miles square; within its limits is included a tract of land four miles square called Hassanamisco, an Indian reservation.

"Sutton Yielding, Rendering and Paying therefore unto our Sovereign Lady Queen Anne, her Kings and Successors, one-fifth part of all the Gold and Silver Oar and Precious stones, which from time to time, and at all times forever hereafter, shall happen to be found, gotten, had, or obtained in any of the said lands and Premises, or within any part or parcel thereof. In lieu and stead of all Rents, Services, Dues, Dutys, and demands whatsoever from the said lands and premises, and for every part and parcel thereof."

As the Indians were diminished in Hassanamisco [Grafton] the white people became proprietors, in 1728, of the soil, by purchase, for the consideration of £2,500, and the grant was made on condition "that they should provide preaching and schooling and seats in the meetinghouse for the remaining Indians."

The General Court, from the first, appointed a committee of three to superintend and take care of the Indian property, both personal and real. In 1765 there were fourteen Indians in town; their numbers gradually diminished; but it was not until about the year 1825 that the last of the Nipmucks ceased to exist. They received their yearly income in the month of May from their funds, at which time they usually had a joyous holiday. Blankets, psalters and psalm-books were distributed among them as well as money.

Sept. 17, 1674, Rev. John Eliot, with Major Gookin, visited Pakachoag, now in Worcester. Maj. Gookin writes:

"We took leave of the Christian Indians at Chabanakongkomun, (now Webster), and took our journey, 17th of the seventh month, by Manchage (Oxford) to Pakachoag, a part of Worcester, which lieth from Manchage, north-west, about twelve miles. We arrived there about noon. We repaired to the Sagamore's house, called John ...., who kindly entertained us. There is another Sagamore belonging to this place, of kindred to the former, whose name is Solomon, *alias* Woo-anakochu. This man was also present, who courteously welcomed us. As soon as the people could be got together, Mr. Eliot preached unto them, and they attended reverently. Their teacher, named James Speen, being present, read and set the tune of a psalm that was sung affectionately. Then the whole duty concluded with prayer.

"After some short respite, a Court was kept among them. My chief assistant was Wattasacompanum, ruler of the Nipmuck Indians, a grave and pious man of the chief Sachems blood of the Nipmuck country. He resides at Hassanamisset, but by former appointment calleth here, together with some others. The principal matter done at this Court was, first, to constitute John and Solomon to be rulers of this people and co-ordinate in power, clothed with the authority of the English government, which they accepted; also, to allow and approve James Speen for their minister. This man is of good parts and is pious. He hath preached to this people almost two years, but he yet resides at Hassanamisset, about seven miles distant. Also, they chose and the Court confirmed a new constable, a grave and sober Indian called Matoonas. Then I gave both the rulers, teacher, constable and people their respective charges, to be diligent and faithful for God, zealous against sin, and careful in sanctifying the Sabbath.

"Having sent a grave and pious Indian to be a teacher in Nashaway, near Lancaster, with a letter of advice and exhortation, written and dated at Pakachoag, and nominated one of that tribe, who was present, as constable, with power to apprehend drunkards, take away their strong drink, and bring the offenders before himself for punishment, an office which the candidate refused to accept until he could consult his friends, the exercises were concluded with singing a psalm and offering prayer and they retired to rest. The next morning early, they passed to Marlborough and thence returned to their homes.— Mass. Hist. Coll. 1, 192 ; Hubbard's Narrative, 101.

Maj. Gookin sent Jethro of Natick, one of the most noticeable of the Christianized Indians, though it is said "these Indians, in general, made but sorry Christians" to Nashaway to preach to the natives of that place, Mr. Eliot having never visited them.

Maj. Gookin gave to Jethro a letter written by himself to the Indians, desiring them to keep the Sabbath, and to abstain from drunkenness to which they were much prone.

Jethro was made a constable that he might exercise authority and when placed in office had with the power given to him a black staff as his insignia of office.

The chiefs and Sagamores were tributary and subordinate. Wattasacompanum was chief ruler, his efforts were to preserve friendly relations when the planters first arrived, with the Indians.

The principal settlement of the Indians in Worcester was on the hill rising in the south part of the town and extending into Ward, called by them, Pakachoag. It is described by Gookin : *

"This village lyeth about three miles south from the new road way that leadeth from Boston to Connecticut ; it consists of about twenty families, and hath about one hundred souls therein.

"This town is situated upon a fertile hill, and is denominated from a delicate spring of water that is there."

In 1674 the township of Oxford was known as a tract of land lying in the Nipmuck country, by its Indian name of Mauchage, Manchage or Manchaug.

---

* On this range of highland is the site of "Holy Cross College."

The first record of Manchang, now Oxford, was made by Rev. John Eliot and Major-General Gookin, Sept. 17, 1674, O. S. on their " journey " to Pakachoag a part of Quinsigamond now Worcester.

"In 1674 Rev. John Eliot and General Gookin visited the new Christianized towns in the Nipmuck country. The first of these, says Gookin is, ' Manchage [Oxford] which lieth to the westward of Nipmuck river [Blackstone] about eight miles, and is from Hassanamesitt west by south, about ten miles, and it is from Boston about fifty miles. To it belongeth about twelve families and about sixty souls. For this place we appointed Waberktamin, a hopeful young man, for their minister. There is no land yet granted by the general Court to this place, nor to any other of the praying towns. But the court intended shortly upon the application and professed subjection of those Indians unto the yoke of Christ, to do for them as they have done for other praying Indians.' " *

The church was formed in Manchage [Oxford] it is said in 1672.

JULIA JAHA.

"Lo, the poor Indian, whose untutored mind
Sees God in clouds or hears Him in the wind."
POPE.

Julia Jaha was the last of the Nipmuck Indians in Oxford, her mother was of the Pegan tribe of Nipmuck Indians living on a reservation in Webster, Mass., and the father of Julia was a Mohegan. The parents of Julia, with their

---

* Gookin's Historical Collections of the Indians in New England, printed in Coll. Mass. Hist. Society in 1792.

"The tract of land from Marlborough to Manchaug [Oxford,] was with few exceptions of a cleared space on which the Indians reared their corn an unbroken wilderness interspersed with a few meadows or marshes as they were styled at that time."

children, lived in a sorry little cottage. When Julia was a child, one lovely sunny morning in the spring of the year, she being seated on a mossy little bank, as she gazed upon the river and sky, admiring their beauty, and the woods just appearing in their foliage, with the gay songs of the birds which arrested her attention, she exclaimed to herself, "God must have made all so beautiful," and hastening to her mother with questions about God, inquiring if all good people would at death live with Him, and to confirm her belief she inquired of her mother, "Will priest Williams be there too." Julia had seen Rev. Mr. Williams, the clergyman of Dudley,[*] at the Indian funerals, and may be she had attended church service and sat in one of the high corner pews. Julia was taught to read while young. From her childhood she thought much of God, and was instructed in her catechism and received many good counsels from her mother, nor were these lessons without good effect.[†]

When Julia was some twelve years of age her mother died. She was surprised to witness with what willingness her mother left her family, without distrust or anxiety, in God's care. She was persuaded the Christian faith of her mother gave her this happiness in the hour of death. Julia was then removed from her home and placed at service in the family of the late Major John Brown of Dudley, where she was taught all the nice arts of housekeeping. She ever recalled the family with great respect. The young ladies were so elegant and the sons were all her young masters never to grow old, and Julia, after living a long and Christian life, in her departure from earth was heard by the clergyman who attended her to whisper in broken accents, "Blessed are the dead which die in the Lord."[‡]

---

[*] Mr. Williams was the clergymen in Dudley from June 12, 1799, to March 16, 1831.

[†] Julia Jaha, known by marriage Julia Daille.

[‡] On a Memorial Day in memory of the Huguenots of Oxford, June 29, 1881, Julia was invited to be present, as the sole remnant of

Julia ever testified that her tribe were conscious of great injustice done to them in all their transactions with the English, and then added with much feeling of grief, "They would destroy the graves of our dead as of no account and make a field of grain of our Indian sepulchre."

On Joshua Pegan's old field the first church in the town of Dudley was erected on the summit of a hill. The Pegan tribe of Indians gave four acres of land for its site in 1734, "on condition that all of their tribe, who should ever inhabit the town, should have the right to convenient seats in the meeting-house on days of public worship." As late as 1790, there were about a dozen of this tribe left who owned some two hundred acres of good land near the center of the town. They were cared for by a committee by the order of the General Court.*

About five miles distant from Manchaug, now Oxford, a second town, called Chabanakongkomun, now Webster,† Major Gookin narrates:

"It hath its denomination from a very great pond, that borders upon the southward of it. This village is fifty-five miles south-west of Boston. There are about nine families and forty-five souls. The people are of sober deportment, and better instructed in the worship of God than any of the new praying towns. Their teacher's name is Joseph, who is one of the church of Hassanamessit; a sober, pious and ingenious person, and speaks English well, and is well read in the Scriptures.

---

the Nipmuck Indians of Oxford. On receiving a gift of money from Hon. Zachariah Allen of Providence, R. I., and other gentlemen present, she was much gratified with their attentions and the kindness extended to her. She exclaimed to a friend, "They have to-day made me a queen and crowned me with silver."

*The Indian seats in the church were two large corner pews in the gallery, over the door of the church, the places which in other churches were devoted to slaves or the poor.

†Sometimes named Chaubunagungamaug and Chargoggagoggmanchoggagogg.

He was the first that settled this town, and got the people to him about two years since. It is a new plantation, and is well accommodated with uplands and meadows. At this place dwells an Indian called Black James, who, about a year since, was constituted constable of all the praying towns. He is a person that hath approved himself diligent and courageous, faithful and zealous to suppress sin; and so he was confirmed in his office another year. In 1674 Mr. Eliot preached unto this people, and we prayed and sang psalms with them, and exhorted them to stand fast in the faith.

" A part of one night we spent in discoursing with them, and resolving a variety of questions propounded by them, touching matters of religion and civil order.

" The teacher Joseph and the constable James went with us into the next town, which is called Maanexit."

In a letter from Rev. John Eliot to Hon. Robert Boyle, of London, dated April 22, 1684, are the following extracts:

"This last gift of £400 for the impression of the Indian Bible doth set a diadem of beauty upon all your former acts of pious charity, and commandeth us to return unto your honour's all thankful acknowledgments according to our abilities."

Nov., 1683, £460 had also been advanced by the society.

" The places where the Indians meet to worship God and sanctify the Sabbath are many; the most are stated places, in the Massachusetts; since the wars, are contracted into four — Natick, Ponkipoy (Stoughton), Wamesut (Lowell) and Chachaubunkkakowok (Webster).

" The occasional meetings are at places of fishing, hunting, gathering chesnuts in their season.

" In Plymouth Pattent there are about ten places where they meet to worship God.

" An intelligent person of (Marthas) Vineyard reckoned up unto me ten places where God is worshiped every Lord's day in that Island. In Nantucket there be about five places of prayer and keeping Sabbaths.

"The seven old Christianized towns (praying towns) were Natick, Pakemitt or Punkapoag (Stoughton),— Ockoocangansett (Marlborough), — Wamesitt (Lowell), — Hassanamesit (Grafton),—Nashobah (Littleton),— Magunkook (Hopkinton). These Indian communities extended from Hassanamesit eastward to English settlements on the eastern coast."

Maj. Gookin, in his journal containing a sketch of a visit with Rev. John Eliot to the Nipmuck country in 1674, mentions the new Christianized towns, Manchaug (Oxford), twelve families,—Chabanakongkomun (Webster), five miles southerly, nine families,—Maanexit on Quinebaug river, four or five miles further south,— Quantisset (Thompson Hill), and Wabquasset, (Woodstock).

The territory of the jurisdiction of this tribe is not (definitely) defined by early historians. Gookin, high authority, includes within the Nipmuck country, as it was called, ten villages of Christianized Indians. Hassanamisset (Grafton), Manchang (Oxford), Chabanakongkomun (Webster), Maanexit, Quantisset (Thompson Hill), Wabquasset (Woodstock), Quinsigamond (Worcester and Ward), Waentug (Uxbridge), Weshakin (Sterling and Nashua), near unto an English town called Lancaster and Quaboag or Quabaug (Brookfield).

CHAPTER IV.

SKETCH OF JOHN ELIOT.

Mr. Caverly, in his Sketche of the life of the distinguished Rev. John Eliot, relates (in the year 1631) when Mr. Eliot and his two brothers, Philip and Jacob, had resolved to leave England for a home in the Colonies, they made a visit to the tower of London to take leave of their uncle, Sir John Eliot, who was there imprisoned, being accused of uttering seditious speeches. " Hearing their approaching foot steps Sir John rising up turns himself as from a deep sleep, or from an absorbing reverie." After an exchange of friendly greetings, he pauses, listening to a brief delail of their designs for the future in leaving England for the New World.

" An extended hand, a half suppressed adieu, and the brothers leave. 'The Knight sinks back on his couch, thoughtful, silent, at rest.' "*

Rev. John Eliot of England, sailed in November, 1631, in

---

* Sir John Eliot, born in 1590, was a member of Parliament from Newport, and afterwards representing Cornwall, was a leader in the House in the latter part of the reign of James I, and in the first part of Charles I. In May 29, 1628, Sir John was charged with having declared in the House, that the Council and Judges conspired to trample under their feet, the liberties of the subject and the privileges of Parliament.

" He, with others, was summoned before the King's Bench, which led to his imprisonment. Sir John died in the Tower Nov. 27, 1632. This event was announced throughout the realm as the death of a martyr.

" The ancestor remote of the Rev. John Eliot, was Sir William d'Aliot, who came with William the Conqueror in 1066, when he landed in England with a fleet of seven hundred ships.

"Among the descendants was Augustus Eliot, honored as Lord Heathfield, and Sir Gilbert Eliot, Earl of Minto."—Life of Eliot by Caverly.

"the Lyon," with Governor Winthrop's family and others, bound for Boston, in New England. The Governor, himself, was already there. Arrived at Boston, Elliot, afterward had charge of a church in Roxbury. Soon following, Eliot's own affianced bride and other English emigrants, left England for New England, and made a settlement at Roxbury.—London Records of the New England Company.

Rev. John Eliot was born in 1604, at Nasing, in Essex, and educated at Cambridge. Eliot resigned his charge of the church in Roxbury in 1688, and died at the age of 86 in 1690, leaving his Indian work at Natick to be continued by one of the native Christian teachers.

When Mr. Eliot could no longer from declining years visit and instruct the Indians, he persuaded several families in Roxbury to send their negro servants to him, that he might instruct them in the Christian faith.

A PICTURE OF THE HOME LIFE IN THE NEW WORLD OF REV. JOHN ELIOT.

"In 1650 Mr. Eliot received at his quiet humble cottage at Roxbury, Father Druillettes, a Jesuit Missionary among the Indians in Canada, who had been sent by Governor d'Aillebout to the Governor of Plymouth and Massachusetts Colony to engage the English in commercial relations with a view to secure them in an alliance against the Mohawk Indians, the enemies of the French. Father Druillettes has left a charming letter in French, describing his visit though not successful in his mission. Governor Endicot of Salem, treated him in a friendly way, and talked French with him. Governor Bradford of Plymouth invited him to dinner, and, 'it being on Friday entertained him with fish!'"

The Father describes his visit to "Mr. Heliot at Roxbury, who, it being November, invited him to stay and thus defer his journey back to Canada through the wintry wilderness;

but the priest could not remain."—Extract from Boston Memorial History.

One loves to think of Eliot's humble cottage as thus graced. His Indian interpreters might have been crouching by the cheerful chimney; and one or more Indian youths, whom Eliot always had near him, might have looked on in wonder as the cassocked priest and the Puritan discussed the difficulties of the Indian tongue, in which both of them attained great skill, and accomplished their ministry as translators and preachers.

Besides a wife and daughter, Mr. Eliot had five sons, all of whom he trained for Harvard College; one of those died in his course, the other four became preachers.

Mr. Eliot in his visits to the Natick Indians was not unmindful of even the children, for " he always supplied himself with apples, nuts, sweetmeats, and other little gifts for the papooses.

"His own comfort and needs dropping out of thought in his care for others."

He often carried on his Indian visits heavy and miscellaneous burdens.

The cast-off clothing, and even much that had not come to that indignity, of his own parishioners and friends and the widest compass of neighbors, was solicited and generally was borne on his horse's shoulders or crupper to eke out the civilized array of his red pupils."

MR. ELIOT'S "JOURNEYS" TO THE INDIAN VILLAGE OF NATICK.

Mr. Eliot's rule was "to visit Natick once a fortnight, visiting in the alternate week Cutshamakin, in Dorchester, in all weathers, riding on his horse eighteen miles, by a way through woods, over hills, and swamps and streams, which his many journeys ultimately opened into a road from Boston to Natick."

A LETTER FROM JOHN DUNTON TO REV. DR. SAMUEL ANNESLY, IN LONDON.

"In this Letter I design to give you an account of my Ramble to Natick. A town of converted Indians, it is (as I am informed) about forty years since that the Great and Good Mr. Eliot, Pastor of the church in Roxbury (about a mile from Boston), set himself to learn the Indian Tongue, so that he might more easily and successfully open to them the Mystery of the Gospel. 'This Reverend Person, not without very great Labour and Pains translated the Bible into the Indian language (Twelve of which he has presented me withal, charging me to let you have one of them); he has also Translated several English Treatises, of Practical Divinity and Catechisms, into the Indian Tounguc. Twenty-six years ago he gathered a church of converted Indians in a Town called Natick, being about twenty miles distant from Boston....In this Town of Natick being the first formed town of the converted (or as they are called, Praying) Indians, there was appointed a General Lecture to be annually kept, and the Lecture to be preached half in the Indian, and half in the English Tongue for the Benefit of all that did repair to it:*

"To this Lecture (being kept in the Summer time) it is very usual for severall of the Bostonians (or inhabitants of Boston) to go; and I being acquainted with some that intended to go thither, and being (you know Sir) of a Rambling Fancy, and still for making New Discoveries, as also I had a great desire to be among the Indians, resolved to take that opportuity, and go along with them....

"The Day of the Natick Lecture being come, and all things being ready for our Journey, I mounted on my steed with Madam Brick (Breck) (the Flower of Boston) behind me ac-

---
*John Dunton's Letters from New England, page 207. In the Publications of the Prince Library.

companied with Mr. Green and his Wife, Mrs. Toy, the Damsel, Mr. Mallinson, Mr. King, and Mr. Cook and Mrs. Middleton; with thirty or forty Persons more unknown, who went on the same Errand as we did, *vide licet*, to hear the Natick Sermon preached to the converted Indians, as is the usuall Custom every year.

"Being thus equipp'd Sir, and my Companions such as I have mentioned.... we set forward for Natick the Indian Town, we set forward through many Woods whose well spread Branches made a pleasing shade, and kept us from the Sun's too scorching heat; which made me say to my fair Fellow Traveller behind me, That we were much beholding to those woods for their refreshing Shade which they afforded us; (of which we were then the more sensible, because we had but lately rid over some open Commons).

"Madame Brick told me, what I said was very true; But, added she, if these poor Woods afford us such a delightful shade, O what a blessed shade is Jesus Christ, who screens us from the Scorching Beams of Divine Wrath; and whom the Scripture represents, with respect to his People, as the Shadow of a great Rock in a weary Land; To signifie that Comfort and Refreshing that true Believers find in him; 'Madam,' said I, you have spoke true in what you've said; and yet Christ is represented as a Sun, as well as a Shade; To this Mrs. Toy who rid by us reply'd, He is indeed represented both as a Sun and as a Shade, and yet no contradiction; He is a Sun, shining with the Warm Beams of Love and Grace, to cherish and revive the Drooping Soul, and as a Shade for the Refreshment of the Weary and heavy laden, ' You are right,' said Mr. Green, who over-heard us; Christ is set forth in Scripture, under several Denominations to represent to us that fulness that is in him, and to shew us that there is nothing we can want, but 'tis to be found in him : And such a Saviour (said his Wife) it is we stand in need of, that is an All sufficient Good, and adequate to all our wants. And surely, said I, such a Saviour is only Jesus Christ; He is the great Panpharmacon, who cures all our Diseases, and supplies all our Wants;

"If we want Riches, he exhorts us to buy of him gold try'd in the Fire; if we want cloathing, he has the only garment of Salvation; if we are sick, he is the great Physician; if we are wounded, he is the Balm of Gilead; if we are hungry, he is the Bread of Life; and if we are thirsty, he can give us Living Waters; And when the Royal Psalmist would sum up all, in a few words, he tells us, He is both a Sun and Shield and will Grace and Glory, and no good thing will he withhold from them that walk uprightly."

"I had scarce done speaking, when Mr. Cook rides up to me, and says, I thought we had been going to Natick to hear a Sermon there; 'Why so we are,' said I, 'Why then,' said he, do you forestall the Market, and make a Sermon on the Road? I told him 'twas no Sermon, but only a discourse that happen to be rais'd among us. . . .

"Mr. Cook so rid on before to Water-Town, whither we all came presently after, and when we presently alighted and refresh't our Luggage, and while others were engaged in Frothy Discourses, the Widow Brick and I took a view of the Town.

"Having well refresh'd ourselves at Water-Town, we mounted again, and from thence we Rambled through severall Tall Woods between the Mountains, over many rich and pregnant Valleys, as ever eye beheld, beset on each side with variety of goodly Trees. So, had the most Skilful Gardner design'd a Shady Walk in a fine Valley, it wou'd have fallen short of that which Nature here had done without him; which is a clear Demonstration that Nature Exceeds Art, and that Art is but a weak and imperfect Imitation of Nature; which has far more beauty in her Works, than Art can e'er pretend to; Art may (for instance) delineate the Beauty of a Rose, and make it very lovely to the Eye, but Nature only gives it Life and Fragrancy.....

"As we rid along that lovely valley I have mentioned Sir, we saw many lovely Lakes or Ponds well stored with Fish and Beavers.... (We had about Twenty Miles to Natick, where the best Accommodations we cou'd meet, were very course. We ty'd up our Horses in two old Barns that were almost laid in Ruines But there was no place where we con'd bestow ourselves unless, upon the Green-sward, till the Lecture began.

"The Wigwams or Indian Houses are no more than so many Tents, and their way of Building 'em is this: They first take long Poles, and make 'em fast in the ground, and then cover them with Mats on the outside, which they tye to the Poles. Their Fire place is made in the Middle, and they leave a little opening upon the Top uncover'd with the Mats, which serves for a chimney. Their Doors are usually two, and made opposite to each other, which they open or shut according as the Wind sits, and these are either made of Mats or the Barks of Trees."—John Dunton's Letters from New England.

"The men being most abominably slothful, and making their poor Squaws (for so they call their wives) do all their Drudgery, and Labour in the Field as well as at Home, planting and dressing their Corn and building also their Wigwams (or houses for them).... They continue in a place until they have burnt up all the Wood there-a-bouts and then remove their Wigwams and follow that therefore Wood which they cann't fetch home to themselves; And therefore thinking all others like themselves; They say English come hither because they wanted firing.

"Their coats are made of divers sorts of Skins, whence they have their Deer-Skin Coats; their Beaver-Coats; their Otter-Coats, their Rakoon-Skin Coats and their Squirrel Skin Coats. They have also a Coat or Mantle curiously made of the finest and fairest feathers of their Turkies, which their old Men make, and is with them as velvet is with us in Esteem. Within this Coat or Skin they creep very contentedly, by day or night, in the House or in the Woods; and sleep soundly too counting it a great happiness that every man is content with his skin.... They have also the skin of a great Beast called Moose, as big as an Ox, which some call a red Deer, which they commonly paint for their Summer Wearing, with variety of Forms and colours.

" We went to visit their Indian Sachim and Queen; I stepped up and kiss'd the Indian Queen, making her two very low Bows, which she returned very civilly. The Sachim was very tall and well limb'd, but had no Beard, and a sort of Horse Face. The Queen was well shap'd, and her Features might pass pretty well; she had Eyes as black as Jet, and Teeth as white as Ivory; her Hair was very black and long, and she was considerably up in years; her Dress peculiar, she had Sleeves of Moose Skin, very finely dress'd and drawn with Lines of various Colours in its Asiatick Work, and her Buskins were of the same sort; her mantle was of fine blew cloath, but very short, and ty'd about her Shoulders and at the Middle with a Zone, curiously wrought with White and Blew Beads into pretty Figures; her Bracelets and her Necklace were of the same sort of Beads, and she had a little Tablet upon her Breast very finely deck'd with Jewels and Precious Stones; her Hair was comb'd back and ty'd up with a Border, which was neatly work'd both with Gold and Silver....

"After we had been entertained by the (Indian) King and Queen, and left them, We were told that the meeting was near beginning, upon which Notice we went to the Meeting, where Mr. Gookins preached upon this Text:

"'It is appointed unto Men once to dye, and after that, the Judgment.' The poor Indians appear'd to me to sit under the Word with great Seriousness and Attention, and many of them seem'd very much affected under it...."

"It was about Four in the Afternoon when the Lecture was ended, And we, having 20 long miles back to Boston, were making the best of our way, and therefore Mr. Mallinson, one of our Company, presently cry'd to Horse, to Horse, which we did accordingly in the same Order as we came.... After three hours hard Riding we got safe home to Boston."

Sketch of Robert Boyle.

In 1644 Robert Boyle returned from his travels on the continent to England, and only after waiting four months, such was the confusion consequent upon the battle of Marston Moor, reached Stalbridge Manor, which he had inherited from his father's estate; he subsequently removed to Oxford and then to London, where he passed the remainder of his life.

The political condition of England during Boyle's life was unfavorable to the repose of scholarship, as he was born during the reign of Charles I, lived during the Commonwealth and the turmoil of the Restoration, through the reigns of Charles II and James II, and died soon after the accession of William of Orange.*

---

*Robert Boyle actively promoted the interests of the East India Company, being one of the directors of the company.

He gave a handsome douceur for the translation of Grotius' Truth of the Christian Religion into Arabic, paid the expense of printing it at Oxford in 1660, and disseminated it widely amongst Arabic-speaking people.

He paid £700 towards printing and circulating the Bible in the Irish dialect by Dr. Wm. Bedell, Bishop of Kilmore, in Ireland, and contributed largely towards another edition to be circulated among the Welsh and in the Highlands of Scotland.

He contributed largely towards publishing Bishop Burnet's History of the Reformation.

Extract from a letter from the London Propagation Society:

"*Sept.* 14, 1677.

"To the Honorable Robert Boyle, Esq., one of the directors of the

Extract from the will of Hon. Robert Boyle is dated the 18th day of July, 1691, in the third year of the reign of our sovereign lord and lady William and Mary, by the grace of God King and Queen of England, Scotland, France and Ireland, defenders of the faith. The will was signed 25 July, 1691.

"First and chiefly, I commend my soul to Almighty God, my Creator, with full confidence of the pardon of all my sins in and through the mediation of my alone Saviour Jesus Christ; and my body I commit to the earth, to be decently buried within the cities of London or Westminster, in case I die in England, without escutcheons or unnecessary pomp, and without any superfluous ceremonies, and without the expense of above two hundred and fifty pounds.

"Being likewise desirous when I come to die to have nothing to do but to die Christianly, without being hindered, by any avoidable distraction, from employing the last hours of my life in sending up my desires and meditations before me to heaven."

One of the items as found in the will of Hon. Robert Boyle:

"Whereas I had set apart, among other things, the sum of £400 for certain pious uses, and whereas his late Majesty King Charles the Second having, by his special grace and favour without my seeking or knowledge, been pleased to constitute me governor of the corporation for propagating the Gospel amongst the heathen natives of New England and other parts of America,

---

East India Company for trade, and governor of the Corporation of the Gospel and the conversion of the American natives in New England.

"Your charity is not limited only to the East Indies, for the poor souls of the West Indies are also bound to bless you, you being the head of that corporation which is established by his Majesty at London for the receiving and disposing of the benefactions of well-minded Christians (to which the said corporation do usually add of their own no small mites), to be transmitted to the commissioners of the united colonies in New England, and there to be employed for the propagation of the Gospel."— Life of Robert Boyle, London edition.

hath thereby given me opportunity to discern that work to be unquestionably pious and charitable; and whereas I have given and paid the sum of three hundred pounds towards that piety, I do hereby give and devise the sum of one hundred pounds more to the said corporation (though, by reason of sickness and infirmity, I have resigned the office of governor), to be set aside and employed as a stock for the relief of the poor Indian converts, which I hope will prove of good effect for the advancement of the pious work for which they are constituted, and which I heartily pray him, whose glory the work itself tends unto (and I hope the persons intrusted with it aim at), to give them a prosperous success."

"From a fund arising under the 'will' of the Hon. Robert Boyle, the first governor of the Company."

"As re-established after the restoration. By virtue of his 'will' the Company in 1695 acquired a perpetual rent-charge of £90 a year for Missionaries to the natives of New England."

"The income of the funds subject to the Hon. Robert Boyle's Trust, is applicable to the following purpose: For the advancement of the Christian religion among infidels in divers parts of America under the Crown of the United Kingdom."

In person the Hon. Robert Boyle was tall and slight in figure, of quiet manners, but of great elegance and dignity.

He was unostentatious in all affairs of public or private life.

Charles II, James II and William III were so charmed with his conversation that they often sought his society, admitted him to the palace with the slightest possible formality and discoursed with him with familiarity.

These three sovereigns successively offered him a peerage, but all these honors he declined in his devotion to learning.

He died December 31, 1691, aged 65 years; his remains were laid in the chancel of St. Martin's in the Field, Westminster. The audience at his funeral included nearly all the people of station, influence or learning in the Kingdom. Bishop Burnet preached his remarkable sermon from the words: "For God giveth to a man that is good in his sight, wisdom, and knowledge and joy."

Bishop Burnet sums up his brilliant eulogium of his character in the following strain:

"I will not amuse you with a list of his astonishing knowledge, or of his great performances in this way. They are highly valued all the world over, and his name is everywhere mentioned with particular characters of respect."*

---

*The family position of Hon. Robert Boyle may be of interest to the antiquary: He was the son of the Right Hon. Richard Boyle, the first Earl of Cork, in Ireland. "The Earl of Cork," who being born a private gentleman, and the younger brother of a younger brother, to no other inheritance than is expressed in the motto, which his humble gratitude inscribed upon all the palaces which he built, and indeed ordered to be placed upon his tomb.

"God's Providence, mine Inheritance." By which Providence, and God's blessing upon his own prudent industry, he raised himself to such an honor and estate, and left such a family as never any subject in these three Kingdoms did, and (which is more) with so unspotted a reputation of integrity, that the narrowest scrutiny could find nothing to except against, in all the methods of his rising, though they were searched into most severely.

"This noble Lord was blessed with an ample progeny, having five sons, whereof he lived to see four of them Lords, and Peers of the Kingdom of Ireland, and the fifth (Robert) though not equal in titles, yet as truly famous, and honorable for his piety, parts and learning. He had also eight daughters, whereof the eldest, the Lady Alice, was married to the Lord Baramore; the second, the Lady Sarah, was married to the Lord Digby, of Ireland; the third, the Lady Letitia, to the eldest son of the Lord Goring, who dyed Earl of Norwich; the fourth, the Lady Joan, to the Earl of Kildare, Primier Earl of Ireland, and of the Antientest House in Christendom, of that degree, the present Earl being the sixth, or seventh and twentieth of lineal descent from the same."

"(A great Antiquary hath observed, that the three Antientest Families in Europe for Nobility, are the Veres in England, Earls of Oxford, and

CHAPTER V.

Philip's War.

"Philip's War, 1675-76, was very disastrous to the labors of Mr. Eliot, and almost entirely suspended them. The irritation against the Indians was very great, and jealousy and distrust of his converts were everywhere rife, and the rage of the people was violent and alarming.

"Mr. Gookin and Mr. Eliot incurred much abuse."— Morton's N. E. Mem. 391.

---

the Fitz-Geralds in Ireland, Earls of Kildare, and the Momorancies in France.)

"The fifth, the Lady Katherine, was married to the Lord viscount Ranelaugh; the sixth, was the Lady Dorothy Loftus; the seventh, the Lady Mary, which shut up and Crowned this Noble Train, was Married to Charles (Rich), Earl of Warwick, of whom it may be truly sayd: 'Many Daughters, all his Daughters, did virtuously, but she surmounted them all.'

"The eighth, the Lady Margaret died unmarried.

The Earl of Cork states that "Being the second son of a younger brother, and it pleased the Almighty by his divine providence to take me, as it were, by the hand, and lead me into Ireland; when I happily arrived at Dublin, on the Midsummer-eve, the 23d of June, 1588.

"When I first arrived at Dublin in Ireland, all my wealth then, was twenty-seven pounds, three shillings in money, and two tokens which my mother had given me, viz.: a diamond ring, which I have ever since and still do wear, and a bracelet of gold worth about ten pounds; a taffety doublet, cut with and upon taffety; a pair of black velvet breeches laced; a new Milan fustian suit laced and cut upon taffety; two cloaks; competent linen and necessaries with my rapier, and dagger."

The Earl of Cork married Catherine, the daughter of Sir Geoffrey Fenton.

EXTRACT FROM A LETTER FROM REV. JOHN ELIOT TO HON. ROBERT BOYLE, AFTER PHILIP'S WAR.

"ROXBURY, *October* 23, 1677.

"Right honourable nursing father:

"The poor praying Indians do thankfully acknowledge that (under God our heavenly father, and under Jesus Christ our redeemer, who redeemeth us out of all our troubles) you have been the means and instrument in his hand, to save and deliver us. God moved your heart to own us, in that black day when all were against us, and we were almost ready to be swallowed up in destruction; which dark time we ought not to forget, nor your owning kindness unto us in that dark day. And since that, your charity hath greatly revived and refreshed us. Many of our aged, decrepid, fatherless, and widows, still wear the garments, not yet worn out, which your charity did the last winter, clothe us withal. And although we yet know not what our honoured commissioners will do for us, whose favour we doubt not of.

"Nothwithstanding Philip had renewed a treaty of peace with the English in 1671, he appears to have been in a conspiracy with the Indians against the English that there should be a general uprising of the Indians to destroy all the English plantations in the country. The Narragansett Indians having promised Philip to furnish him with four thousand fighting men in the spring of 1676, to aid in exterminating the English.*

---

* One of the articles of Philip's Treaty with the English, 1671:

"I am willing and do promise to pay unto the government of Plimouth, one hundred pounds in such things as I have; But I would intreat the favor that I might have three years to pay it in, for as much as I cannot do it at present.

"I do promise to send unto the Governor, or whom he shall appoint, five wolves heads, if I can get them ; or, as many as I can procure, until they come to five wolves yearly."

"In 1671 Philip had been compelled by the English to deliver up all the English arms in his tribe. The compulsion rankled sorely; to the Indians it appeared an aggression as they had become acquainted with the use of English fire-arms, and being convinced of their superiority over bows and arrows, would give almost any amount in wampum, beaver skins, or even in land, in exchange for them."

Though not an unprejudiced historian, Hubbard states:

"It is apparent upon what terms the English stood with the Narragansetts, ever since the cutting off Miantonomo, their chief sachem's head by Uncas, it being done with the advice and consent of the English. Anno 1643."

"A taste for havoc was established between heathen Wampanoag and half converted Nipmuck. Without provocation, and without warning, they gave full sway to the inhuman passions of their savage nature, and broke into a wild riot of pilage, arson and massacre."— Palfrey, III, 159.

In the summer of 1675, and in the autumn and winter following, the Nipmuck Indians burned the towns of Brookfield, Lancaster, Mendon, and Worcester, which were the only English settlements in the present Worcester county.

Brookfield, the Indian name of which was Quaboag or Quabaug, originally included North and West Brookfield. This place was, for a long time, an isolated settlement between the towns on the Connecticut river, viz., Agawam (Springfield), Hartford, Windsor and Weathersfield and the sea-board. It suffered severely by the assaults of the Indians. Brookfield was granted for a township in 1665. It was the nearest settlement to Marlborough.

"At what is West Brookfield, near to the south-west end of Wekabaug* Pond, on a knoll below the junction of the waters of the pond with the Quaboag river, stood Mark's garrison."

---

*" In the Indian language meaning Sweet Water."

Mrs. Mark, being left alone, one day, discovered hostile Indians near the garrison, waiting for an opportunity of attack; she immediately put on her husband's wig, hat and great coat, and taking his gun went to the top of the fortification ; " marching backwards and forwards, and vociferating, like a vigilant sentinel, All's well! All's well!" This ruse led the Indians to believe they could not take the place by surprise and they retired.*

MEMINIMISSET, NOW NEW BRAINTREE.

On the westerly side of the town of Brookfield there is a large brook called Meminimisset brook, the name given to it by the Indians. On this brook there is a luxuriant meadow of several hundred acres called Meminimisset. When a hideous swamp, this was the headquarters of the Indians at the time when Brookfield was burnt by the Indians. The General Court of Massachusetts having granted six thousand acres of land to certain persons of the ancient town of Braintree, in the county of Suffolk, for services by them done to the public. It was called and known by the style of Braintree Farms. This tract of land, with a part of Brookfield and a part of Hardwick, was incorporated 1751 with the name of New Braintree.†

The town of Lancaster goes far back into the history of Massachusetts ; it had been known to the English in 1643 as

---

*The Indian proprietors of Quaboag, now Brookfield, had given to the Rev. John Eliot, late of Roxbury, clerk, deceased, "a tract of land at a place known as 'Alum Ponds,' lying in the wilderness west of Brookfield, of one thousand acres, as a tribute of their affection for him." Date of the grant September 27, 1655. This grant was confirmed by the Legislature in 1715 to John Eliot, his grandson.

†Meminimisset was known, in 1675, as the "chief Indian town of the Nipmuck Indians;" and also as the place where Capt. Edward Hutchinson, of Boston, was shot by the Indians in an effort to make a treaty with them and the English. Mrs. Rowlandson, of Lancaster, was taken by the Indians to this place while a captive.

the Indian town of Nashaway. It was incorporated as a town in 1653.

Sterling was for many years the second parish in Lancaster; in 1781 it became incorporated and received its present name.

Gov. Winthrop's History of New England dates the settlement of the Indian town of Nashaway, May, 1644, by the English, and refers to events preceding that time.

The whole of the territory was in subjection to Sholan, or Shaumaw, Sachem of the Nashuays, and whose residence was at Waushacum,* now Sterling, then a part of Lancaster.† Sholan occasionally visited Watertown for the purpose of trading with Mr. Thomas King who resided there.

"He recommended Nashawogg to King as a place well suited for a plantation, and desired the English would come and set down by him."

Stipulating not to molest the Indians in their hunting, fishing or planting places.

MENDON.

"At a General Court holden in Boston, October 16, 1660, they judge meete and proper to grant a plantation."

The deed from the Indians to the English is dated April 22, 1662, witnessed by John Eliot, Sr. and John Eliot, Jr.

Jan. 1, 1669, O. S. "The town men chose the Colonell to be returned to the Courte to gain power to take the verdict of ye jury upon ye death of John Lovett — to marry — and to give the present constable his oath."

These powers were conferred upon Colonel Crowne at a General Court at Boston, May, 1669, O. S.

The English who made a settlement in Mendon were from Braintree and Weymouth.

With the distinguished names of Atherton and Crowne, are

---

* Sometimes spelled Weshakim.   † History of Lancaster.

found Abraham Staples (gentleman), Ferdinando Thayer, Daniel Lovett and others.

The Indian name of the town of Mendon was Nipmug.

In the first settlement of the town by the English, there were four gentlemen elected by the Court, called the committee for Nipmug, Major Humphrey Atherton and three others and "only three of them shall be and are hereby impowered to make a valid act there."

May 15, 1667, the plantation of Nipmug which was now called Quinshepange was incorporated by the name of Mendon, Suffolk county.

EXPEDITION OF THE ENGLISH INTO THE NARRAGANSETT COUNTRY.

In the autumn of 1675 it appeared to the English that the Indians had withdrawn themselves into their winter quarters; some to the Dutch river (Hudson); others to the Narragansett fort.*

The English were persuaded that there should be an immediate attack where so many of the Narragansett Indians were

---

Settlement of Worcester.— A tract of land eight miles square was purchased of the Indians for twelve pounds lawful money. The deed bears date July 13, 1674.

Dec. 2, 1675, Increase Mather writes:

"This day all the houses in Quonsukamuck (Worcester) were burnt by the Indians."

The buildings had been previously deserted by the inhabitants through fear of an Indian attack.

A second attempt to make an English settlement at Quinsigamond (Worcester) was undertaken in 1683, and the name of Worcester given to the settlement in 1684, from a petition of Major Daniel Gookin and others.

In 1694 the settlement was abandoned.

In 1713 a permanent settlement was made in Worcester by the English.

* The fort of the Narragansetts was in South Kingston, R. I.

gathered together, for if not attacked they would join Philip in the spring, in exterminating the English throughout the country.

When the soldiers were mustered into service on Dedham Plain against the Narragansett Indians, in what was called the "Narragansett fight," they were told by authority of government,

"That if they 'played the man,' took the fort, and drove the enemy from the Narragansett country, they should have a gratuity of land, besides their wages."

The ancestors of the following families of Oxford were engaged in the taking of the Narragansett Fort, viz.:

Peter Shumway of Topsfield, Mass. ; Lieut. Isaac Learned, Framingham, Mass. ; Stephen Butler of Boston, Mass., and the descendants of Major Bradford of Plymouth, Mass.

DESCRIPTION OF THE NARRAGANSETT FORT, AS GIVEN BY HUBBARD.

"The fort was raised upon a kind of island of five or six acres of rising land in the midst of a swamp ; the sides of it were made of pallisadoes, set upright, which was compassed about with an hedge of almost a rod thickness, through which there was no passing, unless they would have fired a way through, which then they had no time to do. The place where the Indians used ordinarily to enter themselves, was upon a long tree over a place of water, where but one man could enter at a time, and which was so waylaid that they would have been cut off that had ventured there ; but at one corner there was a cap made up only with a long tree, about four or five feet from the ground, over which men might easily pass, but they had placed a kind of a block-house right over against the said tree, from thence they sorely galled our men that first entered, some being shot dead upon the tree, and some as soon as they entered."

The Narragansetts having been driven out of their country,

fled through the Nipnet plantations toward Wachuset hills, meeting with all the Indians that had harbored during the winter in those woods about Nashua; they all combined against the English to exterminate them.

Philip was not discovered when the fort was taken by the English, and yet soon afterward he was at Lancaster when the attack was made upon that place by the Indians. It is supposed he was concealed in the Narragansett country.

At the outbreak of the Narragansett war in 1675, the Nipmuck Indians joined King Philip, and after his defeat in his own country, the lands about the Wachusetts became one of the head-quarters of his followers, where he was frequently present.

Although some of them had received the Christian instruction of Eliot and Gookin, they made the disastrous attack upon Lancaster.

It was on February 10, 1675, O. S., that the Indians made a descent upon Lancaster with 1,500 warriors, and massacred or carried into captivity the inhabitants. Early in the morning the Wampanoags under Philip, accompanied by the Narragansetts, his allies, and the Nipmucks whom Philip had persuaded to join with him, made this attack upon Lancaster, joined by the Nashaways under Sagamore Sam. The Indians directed their course to the home of Master Joseph Rowlandson, the minister of Lancaster; the house was defended as a garrison, it was filled with soldiers and inhabitants to the number of from forty to fifty. Mr. Rowlandson himself was absent from home, being in Boston to request Governor Leverett and Council to give the town of Lancaster military aid.

"The enemy after several unsuccessful attempts to set fire to the building, filled a cart with combustible matter and approached in the rear."

Hubbard relates, "The fortification was on the back side of the house, being closed up with fire-wood. The Indians reached so near as to fire a leanter (leanto), and in this way soon the whole house was enveloped in flames, and the inhabitants finding further resistance useless were compelled to surrender to avoid perishing in the ruins."

The story of Mrs. Rowlandson's captivity must be read in her "Inimitable Removes," as the narrative presents scenery and pictures of Indian life that cannot elsewhere be found.

Mrs. Rowlandson narrates: "At length they came and beset our own house, and quickly it was the dolefullest day that ever my eyes saw. The house stood upon the edge of a hill; some of the Indians got behind the hill, others in the barn, and others behind any thing that could shelter them; from all of which places they shot against the house, so that the bullets seemed to fly like hail, and quickly they wounded one man among us, then another, and then a third. About two hours (according to my observation in that amazing time) they had been about the house before they prevailed to fire it (which they did with flax and hemp, which they brought out of the barn, and there being no defence about the house, only two flankers at two opposite corners, and one of them not finished) they fired it once and one ventured out and quenched it, but they quickly fired it again, and that took. Now is that dreadful hour come, that I have often heard of (in the time of the war, as it was the case of others), but now mine eyes see it. Some in our house were fighting for their lives, others wallowing in their blood, the house on fire over our heads, and the bloody heathen ready to knock us on the head if we stirred out. Now might we hear mothers and children crying out for themselves and one another, Lord what shall we do!

"Then I took my children to go forth and leave the house, but as soon as we came to the door and appeared, the Indians shot so thick that the bullets rattled against the house as if one had taken a handful of stones and threw them, so that we were forced to give back. We had six stout dogs belonging to our garrison, but none of them would stir, though another time, if an Indian had come to the door they were ready to fly upon him and tear him down.

Mrs. Rowlandson was shot through the side and the same bullet wounded her child of six years old.

"The Indians laid hold of us pulling me one way, and the children another, and said come go along with us, I told them they would kill me; they answered if I were willing to go along with them they would not hurt me.....

"Now we must go with those barbarous creatures with our bodies wounded and bleeding, and our hearts no less than our bodies; about a mile we went that night, up upon a hill within sight of the town, where they intended to lodge.

"There was hard by a vacant house deserted by the English before, for fear of the Indians, I asked them whether I might not lodge in that house that night? To which they answered, what will you love Englishmen still?

"This was the dolefullest night that ever my eyes saw."

Mrs. Rowlandson is now a captive of the Indians, is treading her way through the thickets of trackless forest in the midst of winter, with no comforts to supply her necessities and nothing but the unmingled fear of a hopeless captivity in the future.

"The next morning one of the Indians carried my poor wounded (child) upon a horse; it went moaning all along, I shall die, I shall die; I went on foot after it, with sorrow that cannot be expressed.

"At length I took it off the horse, and carried it in my arms, till my strength failed and I fell down with it. They then set me upon a horse with my wounded child . . . . , and there being no furniture upon the horse's back, as we were going down a steep hill, we both fell over the horse's head, at which they like inhuman creatures laughed and rejoiced to see it, though I thought we should there have ended our days as overcome with so many difficulties.... After this it quickly began to snow, and when night came on, they stopped; and now down I must sit in the snow, by a little fire, and a few boughs behind me with my sick child ...., and (she)'calling much for water, being through the wound fallen into a violent fever.

"The morning being come they proposed to go on their way; one of the Indians got up upon a horse, and they set me up behind him, with my poor sick child .... A very wearisome tedious day I had of it; what with my own wound, and my child being so exceeding sick, and in a lamentable condition with her wound, it might easily be judged what a poor feeble condition we were in, there being not the least crumb of refreshing that came within either of our mouths from Wednesday night to Saturday night, except only a little cold water.

"This day in the afternoon, about an hour by sun, they came to the place where they intended, viz.: an Indian town called Menimimisset (New Braintree), northward of Quaboag (Brookfield).

"The next day was the Sabbath. I sat much alone with my poor wounded child, which moaned night and day, having nothing to revive the body or cheer the spirits of her; but instead of that, one Indian would come and tell me one hour, and your master will knock your child on the head, and then a second, and then a third, your master will quickly knock your child on the head. This was the comfort I had from them; miserable comforters were they all.

"Thus nine days I sat. My child being ready to depart this sorrowful world, they bid me carry it out to another wigwam. (I suppose because they would not be troubled with such spectacles.)

"About two hours in the night, my sweet (child), like a lamb, departed this life on February 18, 1675. It being about six years and five months old .... In the morning, when they understood that my child was dead, they sent for me to my master's wigwam. (By my master in this writing must be understood Qunnaopin, who was a Sagamore, and married K. Philip's wife's sister; not that he first took me, but I was sold to him by a Narraganset Indian, who took me when I first came out of the garrison.) I went to take up my dead child in my arms to carry it with me, but they bid me let it alone. There was no resisting, but go I must and leave it. When I had been awhile at my master's wigwam, I took the first opportunity I could get to go look after my dear child.

"When I came, I asked them what they had done with it? They told me it was upon the hill; then they went and showed me where it was where I saw the ground was newly digged and where they told me they had buried it. There I left that child in the wilderness. . . .

"I went to see my daughter Mary, who was at this same Indian town, at a wigwam not very far off, though we had but little liberty or opportunity to see one another. She was about ten years old, and taken from the door at first by a praying Indian, and afterward sold for a gun. When I came in sight, she would fall a weeping, at which they were provoked and would not let me come near her, but bid me begone, which was a heart-cutting word to me. I had one child dead, another in the wilderness, I knew not where; the third they would not let me come near to. . . .*

"For as I was going up and down mourning and lamenting my condition, my son came to me, and asked me how I did. I had not seen him before since the destruction of the town, and I knew not where he was till I was informed by himself that he was amongst a smaller parcel of Indians, whose place was about six miles off. With tears in his eyes, he asked me whether his sister Sarah was dead, and told me he had seen his sister Mary, and prayed me I would not be troubled in reference to himself. . . .

"In time of his master's absence to burn and assault Medfield, his dame brought him to see me.

---

* She parted with Mary; saw her no more until she was restored to her in Dorchester after her captivity.

"The next day the Indians returned from Medfield (all the company), for those that belonged to the smaller company came through the town that now we were at; but before they came to us, oh the outrageous roaring and hooping that there was! They began their din about a mile before they came to us; by their noise they signified how many they had destroyed (which was at that time twenty-three); those that were with us at home were gathered together as soon as they heard the whooping, and every time the other went over their number those at home gave a shout that the very earth rang again, and thus they continued until those that had been upon the expedition were come to the Saggamore's wigwam. And then, oh the hideous, insulting and triumphing there was over some Englishmen's scalps that they had taken and brought with them as their manner is.

"The Indians now began to talk of removing from this place, some one way and some another."

Hubbard states that ten days after the attack upon Lancaster "the Indians were so flushed with this success, that two or three hundred of them came wheeling down to Medfield, and they burnt near one-half of the town, killing about twenty persons."—Hubbard's "Indian Wars," p. 168.

Mr. Hubbard states with great credulity, "The week before this disaster was heard a very hideous cry of a kennel of wolves round the town, which raised some of the inhabitants, and was looked upon by divers persons as an ominous presaging of the following calamity."

"In 1676, this 26th day of March, being the first day of the week, as the first of the year after our Julian account, seemed ominous at the first, on sundry accounts, threatening a gloomy time, yet proved in the issue, but as a lowering morning before a lightsome day."*

---

*February 21, 1676. In the attack upon Medfield, "Philip had been seen by the inhabitants riding upon a black horse, leaping over fences, exulting in the havoc he was making.

Mrs. Rowlandson while in captivity, continuing her narrative "upon the Sabbath days I could look upon the scene, and think how people were going to the house of God to have their souls refreshed, and their homes and their bodies also. I remember how, on the night before and after the Sabbath, when my family were about me, and relations and neighbors with us, we could pray and sing, and refresh ourselves with the good creatures of God."

Some of the Indians, with the master and mistress of Mrs. Rowlandson pursued their way through the forest toward Northampton. Mrs. Rowlandson narrates "I carried only my knitting work, and two quarts of parched corn. Being very faint I asked my mistress to give me one spoonful of meal, but she would not give me a taste; I was at this time knitting a pair of white cotton stockings for my mistress.

"On the morrow we must go over Connecticut river to meet with King Philip. In this travel up the river, as I sat among them musing on things past, my son Joseph unexpectedly came to me; we asked of each other's welfare, bemoaning our doleful condition.

"We travelled all night, and in the morning we must go over the river to Philip's crew. I fell a weeping; then one of them asked me why I wept; I could hardly tell what to say, yet I answered, they would kill me. No, said he, none will hurt you. Then came one of them, and gave me two spoonfuls of meal (to comfort me), and another gave me half a pint of pease.

"Then I went to see King Philip, he bid me come in and sit down, and asked me whether I would smoke it.

"Now the Indians gather their Forces to go against Northampton; over night one went about yelling and hooting to give notice of the design. Whereupon they went to boiling of ground nuts and parching of corn (as many as had it) for their provision, and in the morning away they went.

"During my abode in this place Philip spake to me to make a shirt for his boy, which I did, for which he gave me a shilling. I offered the money to my master, but he bid me keep it, and with it I bought a piece of horse flesh. Afterward he asked me to make a cap for his boy for which he invited me to dinner. I went and he gave me a pan cake about as big as two fingers; it was made of parched wheat, beaten and fryed in bear's grease, but I thought I never tasted pleasanter meat in my life.

"There was a squaw who spoke to me to make a shirt for her sannup for which she gave me a piece of bear another asked me to knit her a pair of stockings for which she gave me a quart of pease. I boiled my pease and bear together, and invited my master and mistress to dinner; but the proud gossip, because I served them both in one dish would eat nothing, except one bit he gave her upon the point of his knife.

"The Indians returning from Northampton brought with them horses and sheep. I desired them that they would carry me to Albany upon one of those horses and sell me for powder, for so they had sometimes discoursed, but instead of going to Albany or homeward we must go five miles up the river and then go over it.

"When we were at this place my master's maid came home, she had been gone three weeks into the Narragansett country to fetch corn where they had stored up some in the ground.

"She brought home about a peck and a half of corn — this was about the time that their great Captain Naananto was killed in the Narragansett country.*

"My son being about a mile from me I asked liberty to go and see him; they bid me go and away I went.

---

* An attack was made on Northampton, March 14.— Hubbard's "Indian Wars."

Naananto (Nanunttenoo) *alias* Canonchet.

The chief Sachems usually changing their names at every great dance. — Hubbard, page 82.

"And going among the wigwams I went into one and there found a squaw — showed herself very kind to me, and gave me a piece of bear.... In the morning I went again to the same squaw, who had a kettle of ground nuts boiling; I asked her to let me boil my piece of bear in her kettle, which she did and gave me some ground nuts to eat with it. Sometimes I met with favor and sometimes with nothing but frowns.

"I asked my master if he would sell me to my husband, he answered nux, which did rejoice my spirit. Instead of going toward the bay (which was what I desired) I must go with them five or six miles down the river. Here one asked me to make a shirt for her papoos, for which she gave me a mess of broth, which was thickened with meal made of the bark of a tree, and to make it better she had put into it about a handful of pease and a few roasted ground nuts.

"About this time they came yelping from Hadley and brought a captive with them, viz. Thomas Read, I asked him about the welfare of my husband, he told me he saw him such a time in the bay and he was well but very melancholy.

"My son came and told me; he had a new master; he was carried away and I never saw him afterward till I saw him at Piscataqua in Portsmouth.

"My mistress' papoos was sick and died, I went to a wigwam, they gave me a skin to lye upon, and a mess of venison and ground nuts, which was a choice dish among them.

"On the morrow they buried the papoos, and afterward, both morning and evening, there came a company to mourn and howl with her.

"Many sorrowful eyes I had in this place; now must we pack up and begone from this thicket, bending our course toward the bay towns.

"We began this remove by wading over a river. Then I sat down to put on my stockings and shoes, with the tears running down my eyes and many sorrowful thoughts in my heart. But I got up to go along with them. Quickly there came up to us an Indian, who informed them that I must go to Wachuset to my master, for there was a letter come from the council to the Sagamores about redeeming the captives.

"At last after many weary steps, I saw Wachuset hills, but many miles off. Philip (who was in the company) came up and took me by the hand and said two weeks more and you shall be mistress again, I asked him if he spoke true? He answered yes, and quickly you shall come to your master again, who had been gone from us three weeks. After many weary steps we came to Wachuset where he was, and glad was I to see him. He asked me when I washed me, I told him not this month; then he fetched some water himself and bid me wash, and gave me the glass to see how I looked and bid his squaw give me something to eat. So she gave me a mess of beans and meat, and a little ground nut cake. I was wonderfully revived with this favor showed me.

"My master had three squaws, living sometimes with one and sometimes with another; one, this old squaw, at whose wigwam I was and with whom my master had been these three weeks; another was Wettimore, with whom I had lived and served all this while. A severe and proud dame she was, bestowing every day in dressing herself, near as much time as any of the gentry of the land. Powdering her hair and painting her face, going with her necklaces, with jewels in her ears and bracelets upon her hands. When she had dressed herself, her work was to make girdles of wampum and beads.

"The third squaw was a younger one, by whom he had two papooses.

"By that time I was refreshed by the old squaw, Wettimore's maid came to call me home, at which I fell a weeping. Then the old squaw told me, to encourage me, that when I wanted victuals that I should come to her and lye in her wigwam.

Then I went with the maid, and quickly I came back and lodged there....

"The squaw laid a mat under me and a good rug over me, the first time I had any such kindness showed me. I understood that Wettimore thought that if she should let me go and serve with the old squaw she should be in danger not only to lose my service, but the redemption pay also. There came an Indian and asked me to knit him three pairs of stockings for which I had a hat and a silk handkerchief.

"Then came Tom and Peter with the second letter from the Counsel about the captives, though they were Indians I got them by the hand and burst out into tears. When the letter was come, the Sagamores met to consult about the captives and called me to them to enquire how much my husband would give to redeem me. When I came I sat down among them as I was wont to do, as their manner is; then they bid me stand up, and said they were the General Court.... At a venture I said twenty pounds, yet desired them to take less, but they would not hear of that, but sent that message to Boston, that for twenty pounds I should be redeemed."

"An attack was made by the Indians upon the town of Marlborough, the most part of which was destroyed March 26. The Indians burnt the deserted houses at Marlborough, April 17–March 21, the next day they set upon Sadbury."—Hubbard's Indian Wars.*

---

*It is said, "Mrs. Rowlandson was at Wachusett when the Indians returned from Marlborough, and witnessed their grand pow wow, preparatory to attacking Sudbury, as well as their rejoicing on returning from that slaughter of the English."

It is said that "Wachusett" was at this time the "headquarters" of the hostile Indians as not only appears from Mrs. Rowlandson's narrative, but from those of Hubbard and Mather. The letters of Capt. Henchman, in command of the colony forces, and official communications from the General Court, May 3, 1676. It sent Seth Perry as its

"And so they ended their business and went to Sudbury fight. When my master came home he came to me and bid me make a shirt for his papoos of a holland laced pillow beer. A squaw gave me a piece of fresh pork and a little salt with it, and lent me her frying pan to fry it, and I cannot but remember what a sweet pleasant and delightful relish that bit had to me to this day.

"It was their usual way to remove when they had done any mischief. We went about three or four miles and then built a great wigwam big enough to hold an hundred Indians which they did in preparation for a great day of dancing. They would now say among themselves that the governor would be so angry for his loss at Sudbury that he would send no more about the captives, and not stir.

"Then they catched up their guns and away they ran as if an enemy had been at hand and the guns went off apace.

"I manifested some great trouble and they asked me what was the matter. I told them I thought they had killed the Englishman (for they had in the meantime told me an Englishman was come). They said no; they shot over his horse and under and before his horse, and they pushed him this way and that way at their pleasure, showing what they could do. Then they let them come to their wigwams. I begged of them to let me see the Englishman, but they would not, but then when they had talked their full with him they suffered me to go to him. We asked each other of our welfare and how my husband did and all my friends; he told me they were all well and

---

"messenger to the Sachems of Wachuset, with a letter addressed to the Sagamores about Watchusetts, Philip, John, Sam, Waskaken, Old Queen and Pomham," all leading sachems.

"A praying Indian was at Sudbury fight, though, as he deserved, he was afterward hanged for it, his squaw with him with her papoos on her back. There was another praying Indian so wicked and cruel as to wear a string about his neck strung with Christians' fingers."

would be glad to see me. Among other things which my husband sent me, there came a pound of tobacco which I sold for nine shillings in money. For many of them for want of tobacco smoked hemlock and ground ivy."

EXTRACTS FROM MRS. ROWLANDSON'S REMOVES.

After Mrs. Rowlandson's capture she was taken to Wachusett mountain and by successive "Removes" through the wilderness to Northfield on the Connecticut, above Deerfield.* "After many weary steps," returning from her wilderness — winter wanderings, Mrs. Rowlandson states, "we came to Wachusett," as they approached it through a great swamp, up to their knees in mud and water, she says, "going along, having, indeed, my life, but little spirit, Philip (who was in the company) came up and took me by the hand and said 'two weeks more and you shall be mistress again.' I asked him if he spoke true; he answered 'yes, and quickly you shall come to your master again.'"

Mrs. Rowlandson remained at Wachusett, until released.

Not only was King Philip with her captors, but several others of the leading Sagamores, and among them, Quannapin, the master of Mrs. Rowlandson, and his wife, the celebrated "Swaw Sachem," "Metamoo," "Queen of Pocasset."†

"On a Sabbath day the sun being about an hour high in the afternoon, came Mr. John Hoar (the council permitting him, and his own forward spirit inclining him) with the two forementioned Indians, Tom and Peter, with the third letter from the council. When they came near I was abroad; they presently calling me in, and bid me sit down and not stir." He at

---

* One account states "Mrs. Rowlandson was taken as far as Brattleborough, or beyond in the forest."

†"Metamoo was next unto Philip in respect to the mischief that hath been done and the blood that hath been shed in this warr."— Cotton Mather.

once opened negotiations for Mrs. Rowlandson's release, the narrative continues :

"In the morning Mr. Hoar invited the Saggamores to dinner, but when we went to get it ready he found they had stolen the greatest part of the provisions Mr. Hoar had brought.

"Mr. Hoar called them betime to dinner, but they ate but little, they being so busy in dressing themselves and getting ready for their dance which was carried on by eight of them, four men and four squaws ; my master and mistress being two. He was dressed in his holland shirt, with great laces sewed at the end of it ; he had six silver buttons; his white stockings, his garters hung round with shillings, and had girdles with wampum upon his head and shoulders. She had a Kersey coat covered with girdles of wampum from the loins upward. Her arms from her elbows to her hands were covered with bracelets ; there were handfuls of necklaces about her neck and several sorts of jewels in her ears. She had fine red stockings, and white shoes; her hair powdered, and her face painted red, that was always before black. And all of the dancers were after the same manner. There were two others singing and knocking on a kettle for their music.

"On Tuesday morning they called their General Court (as they stiled it), to consult and determine whether I should go home or no. And they all seemingly consented that I should go, except Philip, who would not come among them.

"Philip called me to him and asked me what I would give him to tell me some good news and to speak a good word for me that I might go home to-morrow. I told him I could not tell what to give him ; I would any thing I had, and asked him what he would have. He said, two coats and twenty shillings in money, and half a bushel of seed corn and some tobacco. I thanked him for his love, but I knew that good news as well as that crafty fox."

Philip's War.

On the 30th of April, O. S., Mrs. Rowlandson was released to Mr. Hoar.

Mrs. Rowlandson's house at Lancaster, was pleasantly situated on the brow or (eminence) of a small hill commanding a fine landscape view of a lovely valley with a gentle river, and the amphitheatre of the hills to the west, north and east; it was about one-third of a mile south-west of the church.

The cellar on the side of the house was filled up about the commencement of the present century, at this time also " where the garden once was," a number of very aged trees, more or less decayed, dating far back in the past to the home of Mrs. Rowlandson.

Hubbard states:—" Mrs. Rowlandson being brought to Boston on the election day, May 3d, it was generally looked upon as a smile of Providence, and doubtless was a return of prayer and answer of faith, with which Mr. Rowlandson had been upheld and supported from the day of her captivity; his two children, a son and a daughter, were returned to them from their captivity. It is said Mrs. Rowlandson was redeemed for £20.

" Mr. and Mrs. Rowlandson now resided in Charleston and Boston, till May, 1677. They removed to Weathersfield, Ct. Mr. Rowlandson died before Lancaster was resettled.

" He had commenced preaching in Lancaster in 1654, became established as the clergyman in 1658–1660, and was the minister of the town until it was destroyed in Philip's war, 10th of February, 1676.

" Mr. Rowlandson, it is said, was celebrated for his powers of entertainment, 'so merry and facete,' that he was the life of company and the great wit of his day."

Mrs. Rowlandson narrates that the South church in Boston, hired a house for (us,) and that we received gifts from friends and from England, ' that in a little time we might see the house furnished with love.' "

CHAPTER VI.

EXTRACTS FROM THE NARRATIVE OF COL. CHURCH OF "PHILIP'S WAR."

"I was beginning a plantation at a place called by the Indians Sogkonate, and since by the English Little Compton, I was the first Englishman that built upon that neck, which was full of Indians. My head and hands were full about settling a new plantation where nothing was brought; to no preparation of dwelling-house, or out-houses, or farming made, horses and cattle were to be provided, ground to be cleared and broken up; and the utmost caution to be used, to keep myself free from offending my Indian neighbours all around about me."*

In 1675 Philip's war commenced, and Philip the great sachem of Mount Hope was sending his messengers to all the neighbouring sachems, to engage them in a confederacy with him in a war against the English.

Among others, Philip sent six men to Aswonhoks, Squaw Sachem of the Sogkonate Indians, to engage her in his interest. "Aswonhoks so far listened unto them, as to call her subjects together; to make a great dance, which is the custom of that nation when they advise about momentous affairs. But what does Aswonhoks do, but sends away two of her men that well understood the English language (Sassaman and George by name) to invite Mr. Church to the dance, Mr. Church upon the invitation, immediately takes with him Charles Hazelton, his tenant's son, who well understood the Indian language and went to the place appointed, where they found an hundred of Indians gathered together from all parts of her dominions."

---

*In 1674 Mr. Church had purchased of the company some of the court grant rights, and made a settlement in that portion of Plymouth colony next to Rhode Island.

Aswonhoks herself, was leading the dance, but she was no sooner sensible of Mr. Church's arrival than she orders him to be invited into her presence; "she told him King Philip had sent six men of his with two of her people, who had been over at Mount Hope to draw her into a confederacy with him in a war with the English, desiring him to give her his advice in the case, and to tell her the truth, whether the Umpame men (as Philip had told her) were gathering a great army to invade Philip's country." He assured her he would tell her the truth, and give her his best advice; then he told her it was but a few days since he came from Plymouth, and the English were then making no preparation for war, that he was in company with the principal gentlemen of the government, who had no discourse at all about war and he believed no thought about it. He asked her whether she thought he would have brought up his goods to settle in that place, if he apprehended entering into war with so near a neighbor; she seemed to be somewhat convinced by his talk, and she said she believed he spoke the truth.

Then she called for the Mount Hope men, who made a formidable appearance, with their faces painted and their hair turned up in comb fashion, with their powder horns and shot bags at their backs; which among that nation is the posture and figure of preparedness for war, and then told them what Mr. Church had said in answer to it. They were furious against the advice of Mr. Church, being joined by Little Eyes, one of the queen's council. Mr. Church told her he was sorry to see so threatening an aspect of affairs, and stepping to the Mount Hopes, he felt of their bags, and finding them filled with bullets, asked them what those bullets were for; they scoffingly replied, "to shoot pigeons with."

Then he told Aswonhoks he thought it most advisable for her to send to the governor of Plymouth, and shelter herself and people under his jurisdiction. She liked this advice and desired him to go in her behalf to the Plymouth government, which he consented to, and at parting advised her, whatever she did, not to desert the English interest, to join with her neighbors in a rebellion which would certainly prove fatal to her. She thanked him for his advice, and sent two of her men to guard him to his house, which when they came there, urged him to take care to secure his goods, which he refused, as he had decided to move none of his goods from his house, that there might not be the least offense given to the Indians by such a course of action, but desired them if what they feared should happen, they would take care of what he left, and directed them to a place in the woods where they should dispose of them, which they faithfully observed.

Mr. Church then hastened to Pocasset,* where he met with Peter Nunnuit, the husband of the queen of Pocasset, who was just then come over in a canoe from Mount Hope. Peter told him that there would certainly be war; for Philip had held a dance of several weeks' continuance and had entertained the young men from all parts of the country; and added that Philip expected to be sent for to Plymouth to be examined about Saussaman's death, who was murdered at Assawomset Pond (Middleborough) knowing himself guilty of contriving that murder. Peter desired Mr. Church to see his squaw. Mr. Church advised her to go to the island and secure herself and those with her, and send to the governor of Plymouth. The same Peter told him that he saw Mr. James Brown of Swansey (one of the magistrates of Plymouth jurisdiction) and his interpreter and two other men who brought a letter from the governor of Plymouth to Philip.

He observed to him further that the young men were very eager to begin the war and would have fain killed Mr. Brown of Swansey, but Philip prevented it, " telling them his father

---

* The mainland over against the easterly end of Rhode Island, where now is Tiverton.—Hubbard.

had charged him to show kindness to Mr. Brown."—Philip's War, page 9.

Mr. Church proceeded at once to Plymouth to wait on the governor, where he arrived in the morning, though he had en-route called on some of the magistrates who were of the council of war to meet him at the governor's house. He gave them a statement of what had been communicated to him, which caused them to hasten preparations of defence.

During the month of June, 1676, Captain Church, in passing over with a canoe from Pocasset to Rhode Island, which he was often accustomed to do, several Indians made signals to him as if to communicate with him; having only one Englishman with him and two Indians, he directed them to keep off the canoe while he went on shore to speak with them.

The Indians informed him they were weary of fighting for Philip, and were resolved to fight for him no longer.

All they desired of Capt. Church was to acquaint the Governor of their decision, and that they would live quietly with the English as they had formerly done, and that they would deliver up their arms, or would go out with the English if he pleased to accept of them and fight for him. They desired further conversation with Captain Church and wished him to appoint a time and place. He made an appointment with Aswonhoks, being three miles off, he told George to inform her, her son Peter, their chief captain, and one Nompash, an Indian that Capt. Church had formerly much respected to meet him two days after, at 12 o'clock, at Seaconet, at a rock at the lower end of Captain Richmond's farm, which was a very noted place at Sogkanate point, and if that day should prove stormy or windy they were to expect him the next moderate day.

In keeping his appointment Capt. Church was accompanied with only his own man and two Indians, and as soon as he had landed found Aswonhoks and those he had named to meet him. They successively gave him their hands, and expressed themselves glad to see him, and gave him thanks for exposing himself to visit them. They walked together about a gun shot from the water, to a convenient place to sit down, when at once rose up a great body of Indians, who had been concealed in the tall grass and gathered around them till they had closed them in, being all armed with guns, spears, hatchets, &c., with their hair trimmed and faces painted in their warlike appearance.

It was doubtless somewhat surprising to a gentleman at first, but without any visible discovery of it Mr. Church spoke to Aswonhoks and told her that a messenger had informed him she had a desire to see him and discourse about making peace with the English. She assured him she wished to unite with the English if the government of Plymouth would firmly engage to them that they, and all of them and their wives and children should have their lives spared and none of them transported out of the country they would subject themselves to them and serve them in what they were able.

Capt. Church answered them he was well satisfied the government of Plymouth would readily concur with what they proposed and would sign their articles.

Capt. Church expressed his pleasure of their return and of the former friendship that had been between them. The chief captain rose up and expressed the great value and respect he had for Mr. Church, and bowing to him said: "Sir, if you'll please to accept of me and my men, and will lead us, we'll fight for you and will help you to Philip's head before the Indian corn be ripe." And when he had ended, they all expressed their consent to what he said, and told Church they loved him, and were willing to go with him and fight for him as long as the English had one enemy left in the country.

"Their friendship ever continued to Mr. Church." Then Mr. Church proposed unto them that they should select five men to go with him to Plymouth; they told him they would not choose, but he should take which five he pleased; finally it was agreed they should choose three men and he two.

They objected that he should travel through the woods, as it was unsafe for him and they might lose their friend.

After Aswonhoks consulted Capt. Church of what course she should pursue nothing is related of her until about the close of the month of June. A squaw Sachem of Seaconet, one of Philip's allies, sent three messengers to the Governor of Plymouth, promising submission to the English, on condition of life and liberty being granted to her subjects.

She and her people, some ninety in number, surrendered themselves to Major Bradford.

Capt. Church wrote an account of his interview with the Indians, and drew the articles of peace and dispatched Peter with them to Plymouth for the governor if approved to sign. By midnight Capt. Church was aroused by an express from Major Bradford, who was arrived with the army at Pocasset to whom Church repaired, he returned to go to Aswonhoks and inform her the army was arrived. The next morning the whole army marched toward Sogkonate. Capt. Church with a few men went to inform Aswonhoks and her people to come to the English camp. He informed her he was come for her and her people to Punkatese, where Major Bradford now is with the army, expecting her and her subjects to receive orders until further notice could be had from the government.

The next day at twelve o'clock she with her people appeared before the English camp at Punkatese. Mr. Church tendered to the major to serve under his command, provided the Indians might be accepted with him to fight the enemy.

The major told him his orders were to improve him, but as for the Indians he would not be concerned with them. And soon ordered Aswonhoks and her subjects to repair to Sandwich to remain so six days. Mr. Church told them he would meet them, and that he was confident the governor would commission him to improve them. The major hastened to send them away with an Indian in front with a flag of truce in his hand.

Mr. Church soon repaired to the governor, who informed him he had confirmed all he had promised Aswonhoks, and had sent the Indian back who had brought the letter. Capt. Church informed the governor of what had passed with Aswonhoks and her subjects.

Church requested the governor to give him a commission to command the Sagkonate Indians to fight Philip. The governor assured him a commission if he would accept it, and get good Englishmen enough to make up a good army.

Mr. Church, on his return to confer with Aswonhoks, after crossing Sippecan river (Rochester) he with his party proceeded and crossed another river and opened a great bay, where they might see many miles along the shore, where were flats and sands; and hearing a great noise below them toward the sea, they dismounted their horses and came near the bank and saw a vast company of Indians of both sexes and of all ages, some on horseback running races, some at foot ball, some catching eels and flat fish in the water, some clamming, etc. Mr. Church was soon informed that the Indians belonged to Aswonhoks and her company. Soon a party of Indians all mounted on horseback and well armed came riding up to Mr. Church, but treated him with all due respect. Mr. Church dispatched a messenger to Aswonhoks to tell her he was come to meet her and that he designed to sup with her in the evening and to lodge in her camp that night. Upon their arrival they were conducted to a shelter open on one side, Aswonhoks and her chiefs received them, and the multitude gave shouts as made the heavens to ring.

It being now about sun setting or near the dusk of the evening, the Netops came running from all quarters laden with the tops of dry pines and the like combustible matter, making a huge pile thereof near Mr. Church's shelter, on the open side thereof; but by this time supper was brought in, in three dishes, viz.: a curious young bass in one dish, eels and flat fish in a second, and shell fish in a third, but neither bread nor salt to be seen at table; but by that time supper was over, the mighty pile of pine knots and tops, etc., was fired, and all the Indians, great and small, gathered in a ring around it. Aswonhoks and the oldest of the people, men and women mixed, kneeling down made the first ring next the fire, and all the lusty, stout men standing up made the next, and then all the rabble in a confused crew surrounded on the outside.

Then the chief captain stepped in between the rings and the fire with a spear in one hand and a hatchet in the other danced around the fire and began to fight with it, making mention of all the several nations and companies of Indians in the country that were enemies to the English, and at naming of every particular tribe of Indians, he would draw out and fight a new fire-brand, and at finishing his fight with each particular firebrand would bow to him and thank him, and when he had named all the several nations and tribes, and fought them all, he stuck down his spear and hatchet and came out and another stepped in and acted over the same dance with more fury if possible than the first, and when about a half a dozen of their chiefs had thus acted their parts the captain of the guard stepped up to Mr. Church and told him they were making soldiers for him, and what they had been doing was all one swearing them, and having in that manner engaged all the stout, lusty men. Aswonhoks and her chiefs came to Mr. Church and told him that now they were all engaged to fight for the English, and he might call forth all, or any of them at any time as he saw occasion to fight the enemy, and presented him with a very fine firelock. Mr. Church accepts their offer drew out a number of them and set out next morning before day for Plymouth, where they arrived the same day.*

It is to be mentioned that these Indians did not belong to Philip, but were under the Seaconet squaw, who was nearly related to Philip, and her subjects had fought for Philip till they despaired of any success or good to themselves. But these Seaconet Indians ever remained firm in their friendship for Col. Church and faithful in the service of the English.

Hubbard states, "that Capt. Church with the English, and with these Seaconet Indians under his command, from June to the last of October following, had subdued by killing or making prisoners, seven hundred Indians, and also three hundred Indians were induced to submit voluntarily to the English government."

Hubbard states, "that this act of these Indians broke Philip's heart as soon as ever he understood it, so as he never rejoiced after or had any success in any of his designs, but lost his men one after another till himself at last fell into hands of those under Capt. Church's command."

Many tribes deserting Philip he had returned to Mount Hope, his son and his wife were soon after captured, he said, "Now my heart breaks; I am ready to die."

For through the vigilance and bravery of Capt. Church with the Seaconet Indians under his command, Philip was found to have returned to his old home at Mount Hope, though deserted by most of his followers, still bitter against the English. Here he was killed August 12, 1676, by being shot through the heart, in the marshes of that place by a Seaconet Indian. Thus fell the last chief of the Wampanoags and with his death the power of the Indians was destroyed.†

---

* Mr. Church received a captain's commission July 24, 1676.

† The sword of Col. Church is still preserved in the Historical Society at Boston as a relic of Philip's war.

On the 28th of August occurred the death of Annawon, Philip's great captain and one of his chief counsellors, and his death with that of Philip ended this disastrous war.*

It is said that Philip at the commencement of his rebellion had about three hundred fighting men under him, besides those that belonged to his kinswoman, Wetamore, drowned about Taunton, that had almost as many under her, and one Quenoquin, a Narragansett Sachem, that lived near him and joined with him in his hatred to the English.

Mather has this record of James Printer:

July 8, 1676; "Whereas, the council at Boston had lately emitted a declaration, signifying that such Indians as did within fourteen days, come into the English, might hope for mercy, divers of them did this day return from among the Nipmucks. Among others James, an Indian, who could not only read and write, but had learned the art of printing, notwithstanding his apostacy, did venture himself upon the mercy

---

*Annawon, when made a prisoner by Captain Church, fell upon his knees before him and speaking in English said: "Great Captain, you have killed Philip and conquered his country, for I believe that I and my company are the last that was against the English, so suppose the war is ended by your means, and therefore these things belong to you." Then opening his pack he pulled out Philip's belt, curiously wrought with wampum, being nine inches broad, wrought with white and black wampum in various figures and flowers, and pictures of many birds and beasts. This when hung upon Capt. Church's shoulders reached his ankles.

And another belt of wampum he presented him, wrought in the same manner, which Philip was accustomed to place on his head; it had two flags on the back part which hung down on his back, and another small belt with a star upon the end of it which he used to hang on his breast, and they were all edged with red hair which Annawon said he got in the Mohogs country. Then he pulled out two horns of glazed powder and a red cloth blanket. He told Capt. Church these were Philip's royalties which he was wont to adorn himself with when he sat in state.

Annawon added he thought himself happy to present them to Capt. Church.

and truth of the English declaration, which he had seen and read, promising for the future to venture his life against the common enemy."

A letter written by a Christian Indian, "supplicating mercy," is preserved in one of a series of tracts, first printed in London 1676.

This letter was signed by John and other Nipmuck Sagamores, and sent by a party with a white flag, July 6, 1676, from Nashaway.

John subscribed this paper:

"Mr. John Leveret (Gov. Leveret).—My Lord, Mr. Waban and all the chief men our brethren, praying to God.

" We beseech you all to help us; my wife she is but one, but there be more prisoners, which we pray you keep well.

" Mattamuck his wife, we entreat you for her; and not only that man, but it is the request of two Sachems.

" Sam Sachem of Weshakin
and Pakashoag Sachem."

"And that further you will, consider about the making peace. We have spoken to the people of Nashobah (viz.: Tom Dubler and Peter) that we would agree with you and make a covenant of peace with you.

" We have been destroyed by your soldiers; but still we remember it now, to sit still; do you consider it again; we do earnestly entreat you that it may be so.

" By Jesus Christ.

"O let it be so! Amen, Amen."

Mattamuck, his mark *N*.
Sam Sachem, his mark *F*.
Simon Pottoquam, scribe ‡
Uppanippaquim, his mark *C*.
Pakaskoag, his mark *F*.

Mather's History, 43.
Hubbard's Narrative, 101.

The result of Philip's war was, the whole territory eventually became the plantation of the English.

And yet the country continued to be exposed to the Indian raids, instigated by the French, until the close of the French war.

CHAPTER VII.

Governor Mayhew's Sketch of Philip's War.

"During the late distressing war between the English and the Indians in New England, in the years 1675 and 1676, wherein almost all the Indian Nations on the Main were united against us, a censorious Spirit possessed too many of the English, whereby they suffered themselves to be unreasonably exasperated against all the Indians, without distinction.

"Of such there were some on these Islands, who could hardly be so moderated by Governor Mayhew and others in Government with him, as to be restrained from rising to assay the disarming even these Island Indians; they being then twenty to one of the English, and having Arms.

"For the Satisfaction of these jealous English, Capt. Richard Sarson, Esq; being ordered with a small Party to treat with the Natives on the West End of the Vineyard, who were most to be doubted, as being nearest the Continent, about three Leagues off, having the greatest Acquaintance and Correspondence there, and being the latest that had embraced Christianity, he returns with this wise and amiable Answer,

"That the delivering their Arms would expose them to the Will of the Indians engaged in the present War, who were not less their own than Enemies to the English; that they had never given occasion for the Distrust intimated; that if in any thing not hazarding their Safety they could give any Satisfaction or Proof of their Friendship and Fidelity, they would readily do what should reasonably be demanded of them; But in this Particular, they were unwilling to deliver their Arms, unless the English would propose some likely Means for their necessary Safety and Preservation.

"With this Reply, they drew a Writing in their own Language, wherein they declared, That as they had submitted freely to the Crown of England, so they resolved to assist the English on these Islands against their Enemies, which they accounted equally their own, as Subjects to the same King.

"And this was subscribed by Persons of the greatest Note and Power among them.

"Having this Return the Governor resolved, and accordingly imployed them as a Guard in this time of eminent Danger; furnishing them with suitable Ammunition, and giving them Instructions how to manage for the common Safety. And so faithful were they, that they not only resolutely rejected the strong and repeated Sollicitations of the Natives on the neighboring Main, but in observance of the general Orders given them, when any landed from thence to sollicit them, tho' some were nearly related by Marriage, and others by Blood, yet the Island Indians would immediately bring them before the Governor to attend his Pleasure;

"Yea, so entire and firm did their Friendship appear, that tho' the War, on account of the Multitudes of Indians then on the Main, had a very dismal Aspect; yet the English on these Islands took no care of their own Defence, but left it wholly to these Christian Indians to watch for and guard them; not doubting to be advertised by them of any approaching Danger from the Enemy. And thus while the War was raging in a most dreadful manner thro'out the Neighboring Countries, these Islands enjoyed a perfect Calm of Peace; and the People wrought, and dwelt secure and quiet.

This was the genuine and happy Effect of Mr. Mayhew the Governor's excellent Conduct, and of the introduction of the Christian Religion among them."

Governor Mahew perfected himself in the Indian language, and ordinarily preached in some of the assemblies of the natives one day every week, sometimes traveling the distance of twenty miles through the forest with no English house for lodging.

Rev. James Keith of Bridgewater.

His influence and advice with the civil authorities of the colony were considerable.

In the subject of the capture of Philip's squaw and child, as to the question of what should be the disposal of the son was in consideration, and the opinion of grave divines sought. Mr. Keith's opinion, stated in a letter to Rev. Mr. Cotton, in favor of mercy and dissenting from most others, had great weight indeed if it were not decisive. The life of Philip's son was spared.*

During this war Philip's women and children were made prisoners; most of them, it would appear, were brought into Boston, as well as the prisoners of war. At first they were assigned to such English families as would receive them as servants, but before the war ended they were sent to the West Indies to be sold as slaves. Philip's wife and child became also the slaves of a West Indian planter. Rev. Mr. Eliot made his protest at the time but without avail against this additional

---

*A letter of Rev. James Keith, dated October 30, 1676, showing his interest upon the subject, is found in the History of Bridgewater.

Rev. James Keith was from Scotland (one of the Border Clans). The name anciently de Keith. He was educated at Aberdeen; he came to Boston in 1662, and was introduced to the church of Bridgewater by Dr. Increase Mather, whom he ever considered his best friend and patron.

barbarity of the English, "that an Indian princess and her child must be banished from the cool breezes of Mount Hope and from the wild freedom of a New England forest and consigned to hopeless slavery."

Fearing, in 1636, that the Narragansett Indians would join the Pequots in hostilities against the English, and to perpetuate a peace between the colonies and the Narragansetts, the governor sent a messenger to Miantonomo, their chief sachem (a nephew of Canonicus), to invite him to Boston.*

"Miantonomo, the Sachem of the Narrhagansets, came to Boston (being sent for by the Governor), with two of Canonicus's sons and another Sachem, and near twenty of their men. The Governor, having notice by Cushamakin, the Massachusetts Sachem, sent twenty musketeers to Roxbury to meet them. They came to Boston about noon, where the Governor had called together all the Magistrates and Ministers to give countenance to their proceedings, and to advise about the terms of peace. After dinner, Miantonomo declared what he had to say to them in several propositions, which were to this effect, that they had always loved the English, and now desired a firm peace with them, and that they would continue war with the Pequots and their confederates, till they were subdued, and desired the English would do so too; Promising to deliver their enemies to them or kill them, and two months after to send them a present. The Governor told them they should have an answer the next morning, which was done, upon articles subscribed by him, and they also subscribed with him, wherein a firm peace was concluded.—Hubbard's Indian Wars, p. 25.†

---
*The Pequot war in the colony of Connecticut in 1637.

† Corn court leads off from Faneuil Hall square on the south of the hall. Here in early times was a public corn market, situated at the water's edge. In this court, now shut in by high business blocks, stands an inn which makes the boast of being the oldest in Boston. Samuel Cole kept tavern here in 1634, and under many succeeding land-

A Letter to Sir Henry Vane.

Faithful in his misfortunes, Rev. Roger Williams sent a letter to Sir Henry Vane, governor of the Massachusetts and warned him of the impending danger from the Pequots, and volunteered his services to defeat the conspiracy if possible. In the governor's reply Mr. Williams was urged to use his utmost endeavors to prevent the threatened alliance of the Pequots with the Narragansetts.

Mr. Williams plead with Canonicus the chief of the Narragansetts, and with Miantonomo, his nephew and heir, to stand fast in their allegiance with the English, for the Pequots made an effort to have the Narragansetts and Mohegan Indians join them and exterminate the English.

Previously to the Pequot war the Naragansetts, the most numerous of the Indian nations, were wavering in their allegiance to the English and hesitated in joining them against the Pequots. They, however, decided in favor of the English.

Roger Williams in a letter to Major Mason, gave an account of his services to the colonies of Massachusetts and Plymouth, in regard to the Indians, as follows: "In accordance with letters received from the Governor and Council of Boston, requesting me to use my utmost and speediest endeavors to break and hinder the league labored for by the Pequots and the Mohegans against the English, the Lord helped me immediately to take my life in my hand, and scarcely acquainting my wife, to ship myself all alone in a poor canoe, and cut through a stormy wind, great seas, every minute in hazard of my life, to the Sachem's home. Three days and nights my mission forced me to lodge

---

lords the house has afforded shelter and entertainment to many distinguished people.

When Miantonomo, the Narragansett chief, was entertained by Governor Vane in 1636, he, and twenty of his followers, were banquetted in the tavern. Landlord Cole was a substantial citizen, a selectman of the town and a charter member of the Ancient and Honorable Artillery Company.

and mix with the bloody Pequot, ambassadors; whose hands methought, reeked with the blood of countrymen massacred on Connecticut river. I could not but nightly look for their bloody knives at my own throat likewise." "God wondrously preserved me, and helped me to defeat the Pequot negotiations and designs, and to promote and finish, by many travels and charges the English league with the Narragansetts and Mohegans against the Pequots."

"When the English forces marched through the Narragansett country, against the Pequots, I gladly entertained at my home in Providence, General Stoughton and his officers."*

In 1642 letters from the Connecticut court and from two of their magistrates came to Boston, stating that it was feared the Narragansett Indians were conspiring against the English colonies, "being influenced by Miantonomo, who was of a haughty spirit and aspiring mind, the heir apparent of all the Narragansett nations after the death of the old Sachem, Canonicus, who was his uncle." Mr. Hubbard describes Miantonomo "as a very goodly personage, of tall stature, as well as haughty in his designs."

"The governor and the magistrates, as many as could convene together before the court, ordered that all the Indians within their jurisdiction should be disarmed, which they willingly yielded unto." Miantonomo was sent unto, and by his readiness to appear satisfied the English that he was innocent of a conspiracy.

But Miantonomo returned to his home dissatisfied at the treatment he received from the English, who regarded him as a culprit, and refusing to him a seat. Notwithstanding the treaty signed at Hartford, Miantonomo in 1643, engaged in war with the Mohegans and was made a prisoner by Uncas and taken to Hartford.

---
*Z. Allen, LL. D.

The magistrates of Hartford having no cause of complaint against the Narragansett chief, advised that the whole affair should be referred to the commissioners of the United colonies, who assembled in Boston, September, 1643.

"Was Miantonomo to be punished because he had disregarded the treaty by neglecting to notify the English that he proposed to make war upon Uncas?" But this was not true according to Winthrop's own testimony; in his journal Winthrop had recorded, "Miantonomo sent to Mr. Haynes at Hartford to complain of 'Onkus;'" and Governor Haynes had replied "that the English had no hand in it, nor would encourage them."

"Miantonomo gave notice hereof also to our governor," Winthrop himself continues the journal, and the chief was told to take his own course. Miantonomo took his own course. "In this difficulty," says Winthrop, after giving the decision of the commissioners, "we called in five of the most judicious elders (it being the time of the general assembly of the elders), and propounded the case to them. They all agreed that he ought to be put to death."

Winthrop's statement of the commissioners is that they "taking into consideration what was safest and best to be done, were all of opinion that it would not be safe to set him (Miantonomo) at liberty. Neither had we sufficient ground for us to put him to death."

"There were found no criminal allegations against Miantonomo and nothing worthy of death had been done by him, and yet it was decided to take his life without committing a crime worthy of death. There was word sent to Hartford to deliver over Miantonomo to Uncas to be massacred."

The death of the brave Miantonomo in 1643 by Uncas the Mohegan, with the consent of the English, had resulted in an implacable malice between the rival Indians and a deeper enmity toward the English, as his life was sacrificed through their influence.

Philip's War.

Rev. Roger Williams states the Narragansett Indians had been restrained until their treatment had become too offensive to endure as is testified to in an official message sent to Governor Winthrop in Connecticut, by the Legislature of Rhode Island, dated October 26, 1696, and certified at Newport by the Secretary of State, as follows:

"We believe that if matters come to a just enquiry concerning the cause of the Indian War, that our Narragansett Sachems were subjects to his Majesty, and by his Commissioners were taken under his protection, and put under our government. They manifested to us their submission by appearing whenever sent for."

"Neither was there any manifestation of war against us from them; but always the contrary, until the United Colonies forced them to war, or to such submissions as it seems they could not submit to. The United Colonies (Plymouth, Massachusetts and Connecticut), thus involved us in these hazards, charges and losses, to our outer Plantations."

"The Narragansetts and Mohawks are the two greatest nations of Indians in this country. They have been confederates, and are both, as yet, firmly and peaceably disposed to the English. I do humbly conceive, in case of unavoidable war with either of them, to make sure of the one as a friend."

"The Narragansetts have ever continued friendly from the first, and they have been true to you in the Pequot War, and induced the Mohegans to come in. Then ensued the downfall of the Pequots."

During the Pequot war in 1637, Rhode Island was protected by the friendly Narragansetts.*

---

* In 1643 was formed the union of New England; Providence and Rhode Island both pleaded for admission.

Rev. Roger Williams was sent to London. He was welcomed by his

The English colony of Plymouth were hospitably received by the natives on their arrival to this country. The first native Indian who visited them greeted them kindly in a few English words which he had learned from fisherman and other voyagers on the coast of Maine. Some accounts state that this native Indian had been kidnapped by Capt. Hunt in 1614, and had been taken to England and sold into slavery, but had found his way back to his native land.

Soon after the first settlement of the English colony at Plymouth, Massasoit, "the chief Sachem of all that side of the country," came to the English at Plymouth, March 16, 1621, and entered into a treaty with them.

"In the autumn, nine of the neighboring Sachems came in and made a treaty of peace, and agreed to become subjects of the King of Great Britain."

This compact entitled them to be treated as fellow-subjects.

Massasoit, though a native Indian, possessed the elements of a great and noble mind and a generous heart. His character is without reproach as it regards his treatment of the English from the time he arrived at Plymouth to extend to them his friendship, till the time of his death in 1661; in all this period

steadfast friend Sir Henry Vane (who) was now an influential member of parliament. He obtained a charter. He visited London a second time and was successful in his efforts to prevent a separation of Rhode Island from the common government. The people wished him to be commissioned by the English Council as governor of the province. He declined to accept the tempting commission.

Roger Williams was a native of Wales, born in 1606, educated at Cambridge, England; the pupil of Sir Edward Coke, in after years the personal friend of Milton.

The lands which he received from Canonicus and Miantonomo were freely distributed among the colonists, only two small fields to be tilled and planted by his own hands, and kept by the founder for his own plantation.

in not a single instance did he depart from the agreements of the treaty which he made with the English.*

Mr. Edward Winslow stated in a letter to a friend in England:

"We have found the Indians very faithful in their covenants of peace with us, very loving and ready to pleasure us. We go with them in some cases, fifty miles into the country; and walk as safely and peaceably in the woods, as in the highways in England. We entertain them familiarly in our houses; and they are friendly in bestowing their venison upon us.

"They are a people without religion yet very trusty, quick of apprehension, humorous and just."—Z. Allen's Address, p. 15.

In 1622, Mr. Weston, a merchant of London, having procured for himself a patent for a tract of land in Massachusetts Bay of the London Stock Company, he sent two ships with fifty men or more, at his own expense, to form a settlement at Weymouth.

Morton states: "The Indians complained of them for stealing their corn, and that they care not for the rule of right."

Governor Bradford wrote to the manager of the Weston Colony, warning him against such doings. "Early in the spring Gov. Bradford received information that the Massachusetts Indians had entered into a conspiracy to drive away the

---

* Old records of the times state that Massasoit, when he came to make the treaty with the English at Plymouth, was distinguished from the other natives with him only by "a string of white bone beads about his neck; his face was painted of a sod red, and both face and head were profusely oiled."

Massasoit, also called Osemequin, Sachem of the Wampanoags, at his death was succeeded by his son, Wamsutta, called by the English name of Alexander, who had no affection toward the English, neither to their persons nor their religion, but had endeavored to influence the Narragansetts to rise against the English. At his death his brother Philip, known as Metacomet, succeeded him, and was called generally for his haughty and ambitious spirit King Philip.

English of the Weston Colony including the Plymouth settlement. Massasoit, grateful for the kindness he had received from the English, advised them as the only means of safety to take the lives of the conspirators, which Capt. Miles Standish effected.

When the news of this affair reached Holland, Mr. Robinson, the pastor, wrote: "Concerning the killing of these poor Indians, of which we heard at first by reporte, and since by more certaine relation. 'Oh, how happy a thing had it been if you had converted some before you had killed any; besides where bloud is one begune to be shed, it is seldome stanched for a long time after.'"

In the same letter to Captain Standish, "Let me be bould," he adds, "to exhorte you seriously to consider of the disposition of your Captaine, whom I love, and am persuaded the Lord in great mercie and for much good hath sent you him, if you use him aright.

"Ther is cause to fear that by occasions espectially of provocation, ther may be wanting that tenderness of the life of man made after God's image which is meete."

It is said, the Indians have ever been distinguished for friendship, justice, magnanimity and a high sense of honor, but their revenge for real or supposed injury was implacable; any act of kindness received by them was never to be forgotten, but returned, however distant the opportunity.

The same noble traits of character are now to be found in the native red men of this country as in the time of Governor Mayhew, Rev. Roger Williams and Rev. John Eliot.

The late Hon. Zachariah Allen, LL.D., of Providence, R. I.,* in response to an address before the Historical Society of Rhode Island, April 10, 1876, in which he delineated the Indian character so truthfully, recognizing their love of justice

---

* Hon. Zachariah Allen was president of the Historical Society of Rhode Island.

and appreciation of kindness, he invoked sympathy for their sufferings.

Mr. Allen had the satisfaction of receiving the official congratulations of two distinct tribes of Indians in the Dominion of Canada. The Ojibways and the Pattawatomies, who in their distant lodges sent him their thanks and congratulations.

The Ojibways returned their thanks and congratulations to Mr. Allen as their friend.

"At a council of Indians (Pattawatomies), the chiefs, councillors and principal men and warriors wish to thank Mr. Allen for his kindness, and express our pleasure at finding the Red men have such a good and faithful friend as Mr. Allen. We all, both men, women and children, shake hands in our hearts with Mr. Allen.

"May 24, 1877.

"'Their names and totems are affixed to the official letters."
— Life of Hon. Z. Allen.

A POEM.

"Ye say they all have passed away,
That ancient race and brave;
That their light canoes have vanished
From off the crested wave;
That 'mid the forests, where they roamed,
There rings no hunter's shout.
But their names are on your waters,
Ye may not wash them out.

"Their memory lingers on your hills,
Their baptism on your shore;
Your everlasting rivers speak
Their dialect of yore.
Old Massachusetts wears it,
Within her lordly crown,
And broad Ohio bears it,
'Mid all her young renown.

"Connecticut hath wreathed it
Where her quiet foliage waves,
And bold Kentucky breathed it,
Through all her ancient caves,
Monadnoc, on his forehead hoar,
Upholds the sacred trust;
The mountains are their monuments,
Though ye destroy their dust.

"Think ye the Eternal's ear is dull,
His sleepless vision dim?
Think ye He'll fail in justice full,
To the wronged who call on Him?"

L. H. SIGOURNEY.

CHAPTER VIII.

CHAPTERS OF "HUGUENOT HISTORY."

1515-1547.

Francis de Valois, Count of Angoulême, ascended the throne of France as the successor of Louis XII, in 1515.

The reign of Francis I, commences the era of modern France, in the development of the arts, especially architecture and sculpture, of which Francis was the lavish patron.

French literature in the sixteenth century was revived in France. Francis had a sympathy with learned men; they received special marks of his favor.

In 1493 Jacques Lefévre, a professor in the University at Paris, who had taken his degree as doctor in theology, gave great attention to the study of the Bible and evangelical knowledge. Thus a new life and a new doctrine had penetrated the University.

During the reign of Francis I, the doctrines of Martin Luther, the great German Reformer, had gained an entrance into France, but the Reformation had for nearly half a century been established in England.

NOTE.—These remarkable men, called the "Reformers," commenced with John de Wycliffe, an English Reformer, born in 1324, and died December 31, 1384, at the rectory of Lutterworth. Wycliffe was educated at the university of Oxford. During the reign of Edward III and Richard II, he preached the doctrines of the Reformation. Richard withdrew his influence, which had been in favor of Wycliffe, when God (says the annalist) withdrew his hand from him. Richard, after being deposed, was confined at Pontefract castle where he soon terminated his life.

At the commencement of the fifteenth century, a few miles from Rochester, stood Cowling Castle in the midst of lovely meadows watered by the Medway.

"The fair Medwaya that with wanton pride,
Forms silver mazes with her crooked tide."

In this quiet retreat resided Sir John Old Castle, Lord Cobham, a gentlemen in great favor with Henry IV. Lord Cobham defended the doctrines of Wycliffe with his sword, saying he would not submit to decrees as dishonor to the everlasting Testament. Thus died a Christian, illustrious after the fashion of his time.

During the reign of Henry VIII, Oxford and London did homage to the learned Erasmus, but he was dethroned by Luther, the monk of Wittemberg. "Luther and Calvin do not appear in England, but ships from the harbors of the Low Countries brought Luther's books to London. In Henry VIII reign, 1525, or later, the universities, the rectories, and the palaces, as well the cottages and the shops of the tradesmen, desired to possess the scriptures."

Subsequently to Luther, John Calvin, the French Reformer's writings, were still more widely disseminated in France.

Francis I endeavored to oppose them by prohibiting all books of Luther and Calvin from his kingdom, and by penal laws and capital punishment to suppress the reformed religion.

Francis I died in 1547, at the age of fifty-three.

In 1529, during the war between France and Germany, two ladies were permitted to restore peace to Europe. Margaret of Austria, aunt to Emperor Charles V, of Germany, and Louisa, mother to Francis I, of France, met at Cambrai and settled the terms of pacification between the French king and the emperor. The peace of Cambrai was called "The ladies' peace."

In 1544, Francis and Charles, tired of harassing each other, concluded at Cressy a treaty of peace.

NOTE.— Martin Luther, in speaking of his own delighted use of the Lord's Prayer, wrote that his custom in private was to take its separate petitions, one by one, and to enlarge upon them; and he says: "And so I have often learned more in one prayer, than I could have from much reading and composing."

During this period from the peace of Cambrai, 1529, to that of Cressy in 1544, the Reformation had gained much ground in Germany.

The Emperor Charles V, appointed a diet of the empire to be held at Spire. The diet issued a decree confirming the edict published against Luther at Worms.

Against this decree as unjust, the Elector of Saxony, the Landgrave of Hesse, the Duke of Lunenburg, the Prince Anhalt, together with the deputies of fourteen imperial or free cities of Germany, entered into a protest.

On that account they were called Protestants, a name that has since become common to all who have receded from the church of Rome.

At the diet of Augsburg the Protestants of Germany presented their system of opinions as composed by Philip Melancthon, a gentleman of most finished education and extremely graceful as a public orator, and withal a lenient Reformer.

This system known as the Confession of Augsburg, from the place where it was presented, was publicly read in the diet.

A decree was issued against the Protestant tenets, which caused the Protestant princes to assemble at Smalkalde and there concluded a league of mutual defense.

The companion of Francis I was his sister Marguerite of Valois, Queen of Navarre. A princess narrates, Brantôme (the courtly historian), of "vigourous understanding and great endowments, both natural and acquired."

The most learned men in the Kingdom acknowledged Marguerite their patroness. When ambassadors from foreign countries had presented themselves at the French court, they were accustomed to wait on Marguerite. They were greatly pleased with her — and on leaving France the fame of her extended to other countries, so states Brantôme, and he adds: "The king would often submit to her matters of importance, leaving them to her decision."

Marguerite de Valois, sister to Francis I, was educated "with strictness by a most excellent and most venerable dame, in whom all the virtues at rivalry, one with another, existed together." [Madame de Châutillon, whose deceased husband had been governor to King Charles VIII.] Marguerite was provided with every kind of preceptors, who made her proficient in profane letters, as they were then called. She learned Latin, Greek, philosophy, and especially theology. "She had a heart," says Brantôme, "devoted to God, and she loved mightily to compose spiritual songs."—History of France, M. Guizot.

Marguerite, seeking for some natural emblem which might express the wants and affections of her soul, took, says Brantôme, that of the flower of the marigold, "which, by its corolla and leaves, has the greatest affinity with the sun, and follows it wherever it goes." She added the following device: "I follow not the things below."

"To testify," adds the courtly writer, "that she directed all her actions, thoughts, wishes and affections to this great Sun, which was God."

She is one of the most remarkable characters of history. Neither Germany nor England presents such a picture as Marguerite of Valois.

Marguerite, while residing at the court of her brother, obtained the books and small treatises called, in the fashion of the time, "Tracts of Luther," and became a Protestant. Thus, amid the brilliancy of the court of Francis I, was one of those conversions of the heart which in every age are produced by the word of God. The opinions and influence of Marguerite had no small share in extending the doctrines of the Reformation in the kingdom of France.

Marguerite, at one time, had so much influence on Francis I, her brother, as to engage him to hear the great Reformer, Melancthon, preach the Reform doctrines, but through the persuasion of Cardinal de Tournon, Francis declined.

Marguerite extended to Calvin her protection; she invited him to her court receiving him with distinguished kindness.

Marguerite, in deep sadness at the course of Francis, wrote a book, entitled "*Mirroir de l'âme péchereuse*" ("The Mirror of a sinful soul"), which was supposed to reflect a likeness of her brother.

Marguerite had visited Spain to attend her brother, Francis I, when at Madrid, sick and a prisoner of Charles V, having been taken in the battle of Pavia, February, 1525.

It was through her influence that the Emperor had treated her brother according to his rank, and finally restored him to his kingdom.

Attending the court, in its progress through the provinces, she employed herself in describing the manners of the time, and especially those of the priests and monks. "On these occasions," continues Brantôme, "I often used to hear her recount stories to my grandmother, who constantly accompanied her in her litter, as dame d'honneur, and had charge of her writing desk."

According to some we have here the origin of the Heptaméron; but more recent and esteemed critics have satisfied themselves that Marguerite had no hand in forming that collection, in some parts chargeable with worse than levity, but that it was the work of Desperiers.

In the Revue des Deux Mondes M. Ch. Nodier, LXX, p. 350.

"Desperiers is in reality and almost exclusively author of the Heptaméron. I scruple not to say I have no doubt of this, and entirely coincide in the opinion of Bonistuan, who, solely on this account, omitted and withheld the name of the Queen of Navarre."

"If as I think, Marguerite did compose some tales, doubtless the most harmless of those in the Heptaméron, it must have been in her youth — just after her marriage with the Duke of Alençon (1509)." — D'Aubigny.

"Every one loved her," narrates Brantôme. For "she was very kind, gentle, condescending, charitable, very easy of access, giving away much in alms, overlooking no one but winning all hearts by her gracious deportment."

In 1534, Clément Marot, accused of heresy, sought the protection of Renée in Ferrara. He met Calvin in Ferrara, who was engaged on a translation of the Psalms in verse.

Marot translated thirty of the Psalms and dedicated them to Francis 1, who not only accepted the dedication, but recommended the work and the author to Charles V, "who accepted the translation graciously, commended it both by words and by a present of two hundred doubloons, which he made to Marot, thus giving him courage to translate the rest of the Psalms, and praying him to send him as soon as possible the Psalm (Trust in the Lord, for He is good), so fond was he of it."

Singular sympathy between Charles V, and his great adversary, Luther, who said of that same Psalm, "It is my friend."

Marot published in 1541 the first thirty Psalms; in 1543, he added twenty others, and dedicated the collection "to the ladies of France."

NOTE.—"The Psalms, translated into French metre by Clément Marot, were set to music by Goudimel, and became extremely popular in the salons of Paris, and at the palace of the Louvre. It is said, that they greatly aided the Protestant cause, and induced people to read the Scriptures, from which the beautiful poetry was drawn which so much charmed their imaginations."

L. of C.

CHAPTER IX.

1547-1559.

Henry II, succeeded his father Francis I, as King of France. He married Catherine, the daughter of Lorenzo de Medici, Duke of Urbino.

Catherine assumed an important part in the government of France. She fascinated all strangers by her elegant manners and great personal beauty, but was noted for her powers of dissimulation of character and her cruelty of disposition.

The preamble to the edict of Châteaubriand, issued in 1551, declares that all efforts to suppress heresy had failed, and that it required the severest measures "to conquer the willfulness and obstinacy of that wretched sect, and to clear the kingdom of them." Edict after edict was issued against them.

In June, 1559, Henry II issued a decree by which the judges were bound to sentence all Lutherans to death, and this decree was published and confirmed by all the parliaments.

Henry II was succeeded by his son Francis II, a youth of sixteen years, who was married to Mary, Queen of Scotland, who had been sent to France in her childhood to be educated. Francis assured his mother she should administer the government in his name. But the house of Lorraine and Bourbon were not disposed to favor that a woman from a foreign country should control the government of France.

In 1560, the balance of power between the two parties at the French court was so equally divided it was now doubtful

---

NOTE.—In the reign of Henry II, the term Huguenot was applied to all opponents of the Catholic Church of France and Holland. They were so designated during the sixteenth and seventeenth centuries. The name of Huguenot was one of reproach. This term, as applied to the Protestants of France, is of uncertain origin.

In public documents they were styled of the "new religion," or "Reformed" (or of the Reformed church).

if the Huguenots would not control the government of France, as the strife between the parties had divided the kingdom.

The Reformation had great leaders, men who had power and were experienced in the affairs of the world. The Protestants had now become formidable by their numbers, leaders and influence.

"In 1558, the Venetian ambassador stated the number of the Reformers at four hundred thousand. In 1559, at the death of Henry II, Claude Haton, a contemporary chronicler, on the Catholic side, stated that the Reformers composed a fourth of the population of France."—French History, Guizot.

In 1559, the Queen of Navarre, Jeanne d'Albret, the daughter of Queen Marguerite, became passionately devoted to the faith and cause of the Reformation. Brantôme says, in her early youth "she was as fond of a ball as of a sermon." Her husband, Anthony de Bourbon, and his brother Louis de Bourbon, Prince of Condé, became devoted to the cause of the Reformation. Admiral de Coligni openly identified himself in the cause.

On the death of Francis II (1561), Catherine de Medici, the Queen mother, was appointed guardian to her son Charles IX, only ten years of age at his accession, and invested with the administration of the kingdom, though not with the title of regent.

Catherine attempts to govern France by balancing the Catholics against the Protestants, in consequence of her maxim, "divide and govern."

When, in 1562, the edict of January was given, there was an effort made to induce the Queen to evade the edict; in declining, the Queen made reply, "that the Calvinists were a powerful party."

The edict of January gave to the Huguenots a formal approval under the authority of the royal seal. The Catholic church denounced the government. A Franciscan monk reading the royal ordinance in his church of Saint Croix, in Provins, remarked, "Well, now gentlemen of Provins, what must I and the other preachers of France do? Must we obey this order? What shall we tell you? What shall we preach? 'The gospel,' Sir Huguenot will say," adding, stating to his own view the errors of Martin Luther, and Calvin, and other preachers of erroneous doctrines, "Is not this preaching the Gospel?"

The "Edict of January" was soon followed by the massacre of Vassy, under the Duke of Guise, this was the first aggressive step which caused the first civil war in France. These civil wars desolated the kingdom for over thirty years, only interrupted by occasional truces, almost to the close of the sixteenth century.

The Prince of Condé, Louis de Bourbon, was the leader of the Huguenots, and he demanded the punishment of the Duke of Guise as the author of the massacre of Vassy, and sent to the Admiral Coligni to solicit his support. Coligni was at his pleasant castle of Châtillon-sur-Loing, surrounded by his young family. The admiral continued to hesitate before joining him, it was the fear of initiating a "Civil War."

"Peace was far distant,"— peace, which Coligni preferred to his own life, but would not purchase it dishonorably by the sacrifice of civil liberty or his Protestant faith. Many persons of the highest rank in France, at this time came forward and declared themselves to be Protestants, those of large influence and of extensive landed possessions.

The Huguenots had now rendered themselves masters of cities in almost every French province. Many of the nobility were included in their number, among whom was the Count de la Rochefoucauld, the Earl of Montgomery, and others of

---

NOTE.— "Mem. — de Claude Haton," 211, 213.
"The Rise of the Huguenots of France."— Prof. Baird.

high station. One of the Châtillon, Francois d'Andelot, a younger brother of the Admiral Coligni, Colonel-General of the French infantry, whom the army had surnamed " La Chevalier sans peur," (the knight without fear.)

"The Cardinal Odet de Châtillon, elder brother of Admiral Coligni, under the suspicion that he was a Protestant, he is cited by the Pope's *new nuncio* to appear at Rome, he demanded the red cap taken from the Cardinal. The Constable de Montmorency at his palace of Chantilly, espoused his defense, I am myself a papist; my nephew shall leave neither cap nor dignity, seeing the King's edict gives him that liberty, if otherwise, 'my sword shall be a Huguenot.'"

In 1563 the two Montmorencys, the Constable and his son, the Marshal, espoused Coligni's cause as their own, publicly declaring that any blow aimed at the Châtillons, save by legal process, they would regard and avenge as aimed at themselves.

The edict of Amboise was a half way measure, neither was the accord acceptable to Catholic or Protestant.

The peace of Amboise terminated the first civil war. The royal edict of Pacification was signed March, 1563.

"The prince (Condé) and the Admyrall," wrote the special envoy Middlemore to Queen Elizabeth, "have been twice with the quene mother since my commynge hyther, where the admirall hath bene very earnest for a further and larger lybertye in the course of religion, and so hath obtayned that there shall be preachings within the townes in every valliage, whereas before yt was accordyd but in the suburbs of townes only, and that the gentyl men of the visconte and provoste of Parys shall have in theyr houses the same lybertye of religion as ys accordyd elzwhere. So as the sayd Admyrall doth now seame to lyke well inoughe that he shewyd by the waye to mislyke so muche, which was the harde articles of religion concludyd upon by the prince in his absence."

Letter from Orleans, March 30, 1563.

MSS. State Papers Office.
Duc d'Aumale, Vol. I, 411.
"Rise of the Huguenots," Vol. II, 117.

Elizabeth of England was greatly interested in the state of affairs in France.

And new troops would have entered France from the German borders "This day" writes Cecil To Sir Thomas Smith, ambassador at Paris, Feb. 27, 1562-3,

"Commission passeth hence to the comte of Oldenburg to levy eight thousand footemen and four thousand horse, who will, I truste passe into France with spede and corradg. He is a notable, grave and puissant captayn, and fully bent to hazard his life in the cause of religion."

TH. WRIGHT
Queen Elizabeth and her Time.

But Elizabeth's troops, like Elizabeth's money, came too late.

Of the latter Admiral Coligni plainly told Smith a few weeks later: "If we could have had the money at Newhaver (Havre) but one XIII daies sooner, we would have talked with them after another sorte, and would not have been contented with this accord."

Duc d'Aumale, I, 439.

In 1569 the Prince of Condé was killed at the battle of Jarnac. Coligni now placed the young Henry of Navarre, only sixteen years of age, and the young Prince of Condé, at the head of the Protestant party.

Admiral Coligni was assassinated previous to the massacre of Paris.

"Thus says Davila, died the Admiral Gaspard de Coligni, who had filled the Kingdom of France with the glory and terror of his name for the space of twelve years."

Fleury 24, 45, states the heirs of Coligni were permitted to enter into their estates.

The Massacre of Paris on St. Bartholomew's Day occurred August 24, 1572, a striking picture of which is drawn by Fenelon, the French ambassador at the court of England, in his account of his first audience after that barbarous transaction. " A gloomy sorrow," says he, " sat on every face; silence, as in the dead of night reigned through all the chambers of the royal apartment; the ladies and courtiers clad in deep mourning were ranged on each side; and as I passed by them, in my approach to the queen, not one bestowed on me a favorable look, or made the least return to my salutations." — From Fenelon's Despatches.

"La Rochelle the stronghold of the Huguenots, before which in a manner was assembled the whole force of France, became now the theatre of a civil war, she shut her gates and sustained a siege of eight months.

" During the siege the citizens repelled nine general and twenty particular assaults, and obliged the Duke of Anjou who conducted the attack, and lost twenty-four thousand men, to grant them an advantageous treaty of Pacification in 1573.* Thus ended the fourth civil war."

Charles IX died at the youthful age of twenty-five years; he was succeeded by his brother, the Duke of Anjou, as Henry III, who was also in extreme youth.

The south of France was at this time filled with Protestants, and many were found in the northern provinces.

Henry III and Catherine his mother, failed in establishing peace with their government for fifteen years.

During this time different parties were aspiring to the crown of France.

Henry III of Valois, was at the head of the royal authority; Henry of Guise was the leader of the zealous Catholics and the League; Henry of Navarre was the leader of the Huguenots.

The Duke d'Aumale in his Histoire des Princes de Condé,

---
*Davila, lib. 5.

narrates of the battle of Coutras, in 1587. " The Bearnesé was on horse-back whilst his adversary was banqueting."

Joyeuse when near to Coutras, found the town occupied by the Protestant advance-guard.

The battle began on October 20, 1587, shortly after sunrise.

Before mid-day the battle was won, and the royalist army routed, and the Duke de Joyeuse in command, was fatally wounded.

The following is a description of the battle of Coutras :

" His body was taken to the king's quarters ; there it lay, in the evening, upon a table, in the very room where the conqueror's supper had been prepared ; but the king ordered all who were in the chamber to go out, had his supper things removed else whither, and with every mark of respect, committed the remains of the vanquished to the care of Viscount de Turenne, his near relative.

"On the one side, there was gilded armour, gloriously damasked, glittering in the sun ; painted lances covered with ribbons, with their banderolles dancing in the air ; rich coats of velvet, with broad lace, and galoons of gold and silver ; .... large and beautifully colored plumes waving on their crests ; .... scarfs magnificently embroidered and edged with long gold fringe, and all the young cavaliers carrying the ciphers and colors of their mistresses, as if they were marching to a carousal, and not on the point of giving battle."

" On the Huguenot side, they arranged themselves in a line, and in a deep and solemn voice, sung the hundred and eighteenth Psalm ; then knelt while the minister d'Amour, made a short but fervent prayer.

" It is said this attitude was mistaken by the young cavaliers, who exclaimed : ' S'death ! they tremble ; the cowards are at confession.' The venerable minister drew his sword at the conclusion of his prayer, and mingled with the combatants."

" The army led by Navarre, consisted of old soldiers inured

to toil and labor, whose mien was fierce and menacing; uncombed, ill clothed, with their long buff coats all bespattered; over their coarse threadbare clothes, having no other ornament than their trusty bilbo by their sides, and sound armour on their breasts, mounted on traveling horses, without housings," &c.

"After the battle, Navarre repaired to the castle of Coutras. Henry III, to restore the royal authority, endeavored to moderate the difference between his Catholic and Protestant subjects, reducing both to a dependence upon himself.

"Henry granted peace to the Protestants on the most advantageous conditions. They obtained the public exercise of their religion, except within two leagues of the court; party chambers, consisting of an equal number of Protestants and Catholics, were elected in all the parliaments of the kingdom for the more equitable administration of justice."—DAVILA.

There was for Henry III but one possible ally who might do him effectual service, and that was Henry of Navarre, and the Protestants. Henry III was a Catholic, and the prospect of an excommunication troubled him greatly if he had recourse to this party, and Catholicism was in a large majority in France. Henry of Navarre enlisted Swiss infantry and German cavalry, and being still supported by his nobility, and by the princes of the blood, he assembled an army of forty-two thousand men. With these two forces the two kings advanced to the gates of Paris, July, 1589, and were ready to crush the League.

August 2, 1589, Henry III, the last king of the House of Valois, was assassinated.

CHAPTER X.

1589-1685.

The death of Henry III left the succession open to the king of Navarre, who as next heir to the crown assumed the government under the title of Henry IV. The desertion of his troops obliged him to abandon the siege of Paris, and retire into Normandy. There he was followed by the forces of the League, and by the Duke of Mayenne. In this extremity Henry IV applied to the Queen of England. Elizabeth sent him a present of twenty-two thousand pounds, to prevent the desertion of the German and Swiss soldiers, and a reinforcement of four thousand men. He again marched towards Paris, and had almost taken the city by storm; but the Duke of Mayenne entering it with his army, Henry thought it more prudent to retire.

In 1590, soon after, Henry IV attacked the Duke of Mayenne at Ivri, and gained a complete victory. Henry's bearing on this occasion was truly heroic. "My lads," said he to his soldiers, "if you should lose sight of your colors, rally towards this," pointing to a large white plume which he wore in his hat; "you will always find it in the road to honor. God is with us!" added he emphatically, drawing his sword, and rushing into the thickest of the enemy; but when he perceived their ranks broken, and great havoc committed in the pursuit, his natural humanity and attachment to his countrymen returned, and led him to cry, "Spare my French subjects!" forgetting that they were his enemies.--- Davila, lib. xi.

The Duke of Mayenne was urged to call an assembly of the states, in order to deliberate on the election of a king. The Catholic friends of Henry IV demanded of him now to de-

---

NOTE.— Sully tells us wherever the battle raged there towered the white plume.

clare the sentiments of his religion, and their jealousy appeared to increase as he approached nearer to the full possession of his throne.

Henry IV, soon after the taking of Dreux, solemnly made his abjuration at St. Dennis, and received absolution from the archbishop of Bourges.—Davila, lib. xiii.

This course of Henry was highly agreeable to the French nation, though the more zealous Catholics suspected his sincerity. His Protestant allies, particularly the Queen of England, expressed much indignation at this interested change in his religion, though he was influenced by the celebrated Marquis de Rosni, afterward Duke of Sully, and prime minister to Henry IV.

Henry was crowned with much solemnity at Chârtres, and all promised a speedy pacification. The Duke of Mayenne retired from Paris. The Duke of Guise made peace, and Henry returned to Paris in triumph where he was received with every possible mark of loyalty! Henry now saw himself established in his kingdom.

In 1594, while these events were taking place in France, war was still carried on with the Protestants in the Low Countries. Queen Elizabeth aided Prince Maurice with her power against Spain.

The war against the Spanish forces in the Low Countries was still continued; besides several bodies of Germans and Swiss, the states took into their service two thousand French veterans, disbanded by Henry IV, on the conclusion of the peace of Vervins; and that prince generously supplied the republic with money.

In 1600 the two armies came to a general engagement at Nieuport, near Ostend. "The conflict was terrible. The field was obstinately disputed for three hours. The Spaniards were defeated with a loss of five thousand men by the valor of the English forces under Lord Vere, who led the van of the confederates. A share of the honor was due under the military skill of Prince Maurice to a body of Swiss immediately under his command, who supported the English troops.

"This victory was of the utmost importance to the United Provinces, as the defeat of their army must have been followed by the loss of their liberties and their final ruin as independent states."—Russell, History of Modern Europe, vol. I.

NOTE.— "Lord Vere a man whose Coat of Armour made more Renowned than his coat of Arms."

"And whose personal Achievements in the field, especially at the Battle of Nieuport ennobled more than the high blood derived from his Ancestors, but his unstained piety gave him the highest character of all."

Sir Horace [Horatio] Vere, an English nobleman; he was the defender of the Protestants in the Netherlands.

"This noble Lord was one, that could as well wrestle with God, as fight with men, and may be thought to have gotten his victories upon his knees in the closet, before he drew his sword in the field.

"And when he had overcome his enemies he could overcome himself also, being one of the humblest souls, in whom so much true worth lodged, that we have heard of."— Life of Lady Vere. Distinguished Christians of the Church Nobility and Gentry. London edition. 1683.

The victories of Lord Vere were long remembered and honored by the English nation and by the Protestants of France and Netherlands.

An epitaph upon the Right Honorable and Religious, the Lady Vere, wife to the most Noble, and Valiant Lord Horatio Vere, Baron Tilbury, who died at the advanced age of ninety years.

Anno Christi, 1671.

"Noble her self; more Noble, 'cause so neer
To the thrice Noble, and Victorious Vere.
That Belgick Lion, whose loud fame did roar,
Heard from the German to the British shoar.
His Trophies she was Joyntur'd in (so say
The Lawyers) Wives shine by their Husbands Ray.
See therefore now, how by his side she stands,
Tryumphing 'midst the Graves, those *Netherlands*.
Rather in Heaven, those only we confess,
Are truly called Th' *United Provinces*."

CHARLES DERBY.

April 13, 1598, Henry IV secured to the Protestants their civil rights by the "Edict of Nantes, called the Edict of Peace," which confirmed to them the free exercise of their religion, and gave them equal claims with the Catholics to all offices and dignities.

They were also left in possession of their fortresses, which were ceded to them for their security. This edict afforded to the Protestants a means of forming a kind of republic within the kingdom.

In maintaining the Edict of Nantes Henry IV assured his Parliament that established laws should be respected.

"You see me here in my cabinet, not as the kings, my predecessors, nor as a prince who gives audience to ambassadors — but dressed in my ordinary garb as a father of a family, who would converse with his children. I know there have been parties in the Parliament, and that seditious preachers have been ejected. I will put good order into these people. I will shorten by the head all such as venture to foment faction.

"I have leaped over the walls of cities, and I shall not be terrified by barricades.

"I have made an edict, let it be observed.

"My will must be executed, not interpreted."

With all his errors, Henry IV was a great king, and did more for the prosperity of France than any monarch who had preceded him.

Sully, his chief minister, thus describes him :

"He was candid, sincere, grateful, compassioned, generous, wise, penetrating, and loved by his subjects as a father."

NOTE.— "Nantes, the capital of ancient Brittany, is described as a quaint tumble-down old city, where the houses, with their upper stories projecting over the narrow streets, seemed to be tipsy and the streets crazy. In the old round-towered castle, which they now use as a barrack the good Henry of Navarre signed the famous Edict of Nantes."

In 1610 Henry assisted in the coronation of his queen, Mary de Medicis, and is assassinated the following day by Ravaillac.

Jane d'Albret was the daughter of Henry II, King of Navarre, and Marguerite, sister of Francis I, King of France, and was carefully educated in the Protestant faith from her childhood. She married Anthony of Bourbon, son to Charles, Duke of Vendome, and was the mother of Henry IV, King of France.

"Jane of Navarre inherited the genius and elegance of Marguerite, with acquirements far beyond that period. She possessed the amiable and graceful attractions of domestic life in her character, having great simplicity and purity of manners; she wrote with ease, and spoke Latin and Spanish with fluency. Men of talent and learning thronged her court."

When Anthony of Bourbon, King of Navarre and Béarn, had openly left the Protestants and joined the Princes of Guise, the Queen in disappointment retired to her own dominions on the northern slope of the Pyrenees. There with her son Henry, the Prince of Béarn, and her daughter, the Lady Catharine, in the midst of her own subjects, she was studying, more than any other of her age, the true welfare of her people, and in

---

NOTE.— In 1604 Henry IV when he was informed of the death of his sister, Catharine de Bourbon (Duchess de Bar), exclaimed, "All! all! mother and sister!"

The Duchess de Bar was carried to Vendome, and buried in the tomb of her ancestors, by the side of her mother, Queen Jane of Navarre.— Sully's "Memoirs."

NOTE.— The cradle Henry IV was rocked in, a great tortoise shell, is still kept at Pau in Béarn.

NOTE.— Navarre a small kingdom in the south of France.

NOTE.— The Queen of Navarre had the New Testament printed at her own expense, the Catechism and the prayers used in the Church of Geneva. The same were also translated into the Gascoin and printed at La Rochelle for the province of Contabria under the jurisdiction of Navarre.

educating her son soon to appear in history as the leader of the Huguenot party, and on the expiration of the Valois line, to succeed to the throne of France as Henry the Fourth. She had already established the principles of the Reformation in her kingdom, upon which she hoped to see her son lay a foundation of a great and glorious career.

The first preliminary devised by Catharine de Medici for confirming a pretended peace, which was only a ruse to more surely destroy the Protestants, was to send an envoy to Rochelle, in the King's name, to treat with the Queen of Navarre about the marriage between her son Henry and the King's sister, the Lady Marguerita, for which purpose he extended to them an invitation to come to court, where the proposed marriage could be more fully concluded.

Upon the earnest solicitation of the King the Queen of Navarre went the March following (1572) from La Rochelle to the court, which was then at Blois, accompanied by a great retinue.

The articles of marriage were concluded between the King's sister and the Prince of Navarre; the King was to give his sister for her dowry three hundred thousand crowns, each crown being valued at four and fifty shillings.— Life of Jane of Navarre.

"Accordingly on May 6 she took her journey from Blois, and arrived on the 15th at Paris, to make suitable preparations for the marriage and the arrival of her son. She went from place to place in the city into several houses and shops in order to furnish herself with such things as were suitable to adorn the approaching marriage.

"An Italian it is said sold to the Queen of Navarre poisoned perfumes (also perfumed gloves that were poisoned) and was afterward heard to boast of what he had done.

She preserved her own chaste and simple style of dress, which might have been termed almost a censure on the costumes of the court.

"Soon after her arrival she fell sick of a continued fever and died June 9, Anno Christi, 1572."— Life of Jane of Navarre. London edition. 1683.

While in Paris the Queen had written to Prince Henry.

"My son," she concluded, "you have rightly judged from my letters, that their great object here is to separate you from me and from God..... Pray earnestly to God, whose assistance you need at all times, but especially at the present; and I too, will add my fervent prayer, that he will grant you in all your just desires."

"As her strength was decaying, the Queen requested that a clergyman might be present in her sickness, to give her counsel from the Scriptures. She listened to the reading of the fourteenth to the completion of the seventeenth chapter of St. John's Gospel, and in conclusion to the thirty-first Psalm, in which the prophet, among other things, commends his spirit into the hands of God, because, said he, 'Thou hast redeemed me, O Lord God of truth!' If Jane of Navarre were a perfect pattern, nothing was ever suggested to lessen her, but that which was her true glory, her receiving the Reformation."

"She both received it and brought her subjects to it. She not only reformed her court, but her whole principality, to such a degree that the golden age seemed to have returned

NOTE.—Catharine de Bourbon, the sister of Henry IV, was alone in the court circle by her simplicity of manners and unostentatious plainness in dress. The dresses, though of the richest material (for she encouraged the silk looms of France), were neither "flounced nor furbelowed;" she wore her hair cut as prescribed, even when other court ladies of rank in the reformed church refused.

The simplicity of her life discovered itself in her pure, transparent complexion, the delicacy of which was heightened by the lawn kerchief that shaded her neck in spite of Marguerite de Valois' ridicule.

The Lady Catherine married Charles, Duke de Bar. "He was the son of Lorraine, her former suitor. It would seem that the admiration which animated the father had been entailed with his fortunes upon the son."

under her; or rather, Christianity appeared again with the purity and lustre of its first beginnings."—Bishop Burnet, Essay on the Memory of Queen Mary, p. 29.

The Queen of Navarre, Jeanned' Albret, who had gone to Paris in preparation for the marriage, had died there June 8, 1572.

"It was in deep mourning that her son the King of Navarre, arrived at court, attended by eight hundred gentlemen, all likewise in mourning. 'But,' says Marguerite de Valois herself, 'the marriage took place a few days afterwards with such triumph and magnificence as none others of my quality; the King of Navarre and his troop having changed their mourning for very rich and fine clothes, and I being dressed royally, with crown and corset of tufted ermine, all blazing with crown-jewels, and the grand blue mantle with a train four ells long borne by three princesses, the people choking one another down below to see us pass.' The marriage was celebrated August 18, by the Cardinal of Bourbon, in front of the principal entrance of Notre-Dame."

NOTE.—It may be of interest to some to observe the changes in the style of dress for the last three centuries. It is said "Marguerite of Valois, both before and after her marriage with the King of Navarre, though she required no aid of art, being singularly beautiful, and yet she often wore false hair and paint. One of the Queen of Navarre's gowns was black satin, covered with embroidery, the expense of which was from four to five hundred crowns, and many other costly gowns. The mourning at this period was black, white and gray, with violet or blue stockings."

Marguerite being seized with a sudden devotion she presented to the church one of these gowns, adorned with gems of great value.

Henry of Navarre wore at his marriage with Marguerite of Valois a uniform of pale, yellow satin, covered with the richest embroidery, wrought in relief, and decorated with pearls.

King Henry at his second marriage with Mary de Medici was dressed in white satin, embroidered with gold and pearls. Mary of Medici, niece to the Great Duke of Tuscany, was extremely elegant in all her style of dress.

Henry IV was succeeded by his son Louis XIII, during whose minority Mary de Medici, his mother, was appointed regent. Cardinal de Richelieu was the minister of state, and a great favorite of Louis XIII. At this time the Huguenots were able to offer a powerful resistance, as they had become very numerous in the provinces. They still retained La Rochelle, which enabled them to continue a communication with England.

Cardinal Richelieu, though a Catholic prelate, was not a bigot or a persecutor, but a statesman. He was as ready to enter into alliances with Protestant powers as with Catholic powers, for political purposes. Richelieu with his army and navy laid siege to La Rochelle in 1627, to increase the royal government. The siege continued fifteen months, as the city was supported by the English fleet, and by German recruits. La Rochelle from 30,000 inhabitants was reduced to 5,000, from famine. The possession of the city was given to the royal troops October 30, 1628.

Mazarine, prime minister of France, was the successor of Richelieu. At the Mazarine palace he died in 1661, at the age of fifty-one years. "A few days before his death he was carried, in his chair, to the promenade, exquisitely dressed and rouged; the courtiers ironically complimented him on his appearance, telling him he never looked 'so fresh and vermilion.' Mazarine had completed his political career; he had married his nieces to the first nobles in Europe, and amassed immense wealth. His love of fine paintings became a passion. His health was daily failing, and he consulted his physicians upon the nature of his malady, who frankly told him he could not live longer than two months. The cardinal, in his dressing-gown and nightcap, tottered to his gallery of pictures. Brienne, his friend, followed him; 'he stood gazing upon them with hands clasped.' 'Look,' he exclaimed, 'look at that Correggio! this Venus of Titian! that Deluge of Carracci! Oh, my friend, I must quit all these. Adieu, dear pictures, that I loved so truly, that have cost me so much!' 'I shall never see them more where I am going.'"—The History of France, by M. Guizot and Madame Guizot de Witt.

Madame de Maintenon, the Last Years of Louis XIV.
By the Author of Mirabeau.
A translation from the French (Madame de Maintenon.)

Françoise d'Aubigné was descended from an honorable and ancient family of France; her grandfather, Theodore Agrippa d'Aubigné, was a Huguenot, and the devoted friend and companion of Henry IV. Her father, Constant d'Aubigné, had acquired consideration at court and wealth for his treachery to the Huguenots; his father disinherited him; he was then detected in a treasonable correspondence with the English, and imprisoned by the government.

Françoise was born in the prison of the Conciergerie of Niort, 1635. Her godfather was the celebrated Duke de la Rochefoucauld, her godmother was the daughter of the Baron du Neuillant, the governor of Niort.

In great destitution were the parents of Françoise. Madame de Villette, a sister of her father, and a Huguenot, brought them relief, removing the little Françoise to her home. But when Constant d'Aubigné was transferred to a prison at Bordeaux the mother took Françoise to share with her a prison life with her father. In 1639, after unwearied solicitations, Madame d'Aubigné obtained her husband's enlargement, after which they embarked for Martinique, to make their fortunes in a new world of surroundings.

During the voyage little Françoise fell dangerously ill, and was at last laid out as dead. The body was just about to be committed to the sea when the mother, as she held it in a last passionate, parting embrace, felt a slight movement. "My child is not dead!" she shrieked. "Her heart beats!" The little girl was put back into bed, and in few days was restored to health.

By what trifles are the destinies of men and of nations decided! Had not the mother's heart craved for yet another embrace, or had the sailor who was to have been the gravedigger of the sea been but a moment quicker, the edict of Nantes might never have been revoked, and the latter years of Louis the Fourteenth might have been wholly different. What wonderful events hang upon moments! — upon some apparently insignificant life!

The mother of Françoise, who had herself been so schooled in adversity, desired to instil into the child's mind something of her own courage and fortitude.

"One day while in Martinique the house took fire. Seeing little Françoise weep bitterly, Madame said reprovingly, 'I thought you had more courage. Why should you weep thus for the loss of a house?' 'It is not for the house I am weeping,' answered the child, quickly, 'but for my doll!'"

The child is the father of the man — the mother of the woman.

In those words are the germ of the future intensely selfish nature of Madame de Maintenon.

In Martinique Constant d'Aubigné again acquired wealth, owning large plantations, but gambled them away and died. Madame d'Aubigné returned to France. Françoise was again committed to the protection of Madame de Villette, who readily undertook the charge, and at once proceeded to train her little niece in the doctrines of the Reformed faith.

"Years of poverty, of successive misfortune, of silent endurance, of living in the shadow of life, had hardened and chilled Madame d'Aubigné's character into coldness and severity, beneath which her virtues and affections were concealed. Madame de Villette, who had lived in the sunshine of life, was on the contrary, smiling, tender, loving, and so child-like, the little Françoise soon began to prefer this cheerful lady to the troubled, saddened mother, and to embrace all her teachings with the utmost docility.

"One day Françoise refused to accompany her mother to mass. Madame d'Aubigné with her usual energy at once appealed to Anne of Austria, to issue an order for the girl's restoration to her own custody. The order was granted, and the young Huguenot was handed over to her god-mother, the Countess de Neuillant, to be brought back to the Catholic faith. But Françoise was not yet to be converted, so as a punishment for her contumacy she was set to perform the most menial offices, among others, to measure out the corn for the horses, and to look after a flock of turkeys. 'It was there, in the farm yard,' she used to say, 'I first began to reign.'"

As not even these degradations could bend her firm spirit, she was consigned to a convent. Mademoiselle d'Aubigné, after a time, renounced her Protestant faith.

Leaving her convent life, and her mother having died, "Mademoiselle d'Aubigné, after a training to wither the heart and to fill the soul full of bitterness, the flavor of which abides with us evermore. A childhood of privation is a poor preparation for a noble life; little that is truly generous, tender and merciful ever comes from it, but much that is hard, cold, selfish and hypocritical."

"Mademoiselle d'Aubigné was beautiful, graceful, accomplished, clever, spirituelle," and when sixteen years of age, she was married to the Abbé Scarron.

After his death, Madame Scarron was reduced once more to a state of destitution, being deprived of her pension by the death of Anne of Austria.

In 1669 the Maintenon estate was for sale; the King purchased it, and bestowed it upon Madame Scarron, it being a most convenient residence for the royal children, and for herself, their guardian, the estate being in the near vicinity of Versailles.

"Madame de Maintenon erased from her carriage the arms of Scarron, substituting her own in their place — she had now assumed that title. Although she had been mixed up with the society of the Fronde, of which throughout his life Louis entertained the greatest horror, Louis, ill-educated himself, hated learned women." It would appear that Madame de Maintenon aspired to govern the mind of Louis XIV. Even as early as 1676, writing of Madame de Maintenon, Madame de Sévigné says, "Every thing is subject first to her empire."

Louis XIII was succeeded by his son, Louis XIV, whose mother, Anne of Austria, was declared regent of the kingdom.

The reign of Louis XIV was the greatest in French history, great in the grandeur of its King, the splendor of its court, the commanding talent of its generals and its ministers, the success in its arms, the nobleness of its literature.

Marmontel narrates that throughout his life Louis XIV was always governed, either by his ministers or the ladies of his court. It would appear that no important act of that long reign emanated from the unprejudiced judgment of the monarch — the most absolute that ever reigned over France. Perhaps there is no more extraordinary history upon record than that of Madame de Maintenon at the court of Louis XIV, who governed by her influence one of the proudest sovereigns and through him the entire kingdom of France.

In 1683 the Queen of Louis XIV, who was extremely fond of Madame de Maintenon, died in that lady's arms. From that hour Madame de Maintenon appeared to propose for herself but one object in life — to become the wife of Louis XIV.

Duke St. Simon's Testimony.

"She brought to pass what our eyes have seen, but which posterity will refuse to believe. But what is very certain and very true is, that in the middle of the winter which followed the Queen's death, Louis XIV was privately married to Madame de Maintenon.

"She had great remains of beauty, bright and sprightly eyes, an incomparable grace," says St. Simon, who detested her, "an air of ease and yet of restraint and respect, and a great deal of cleverness, with a speech that was sweet, correct, and in good terms, and naturally eloquent and brief."

The marriage of Louis XIV to Madame de Maintenon was known only to a few persons at the French court, for Louis never publicly acknowledged her as his queen.

He regarded her with great respect, and her opinion was sought by him on all occasions.

Madame with her needlework now sat by him in all his consultations with his ministers of state, and he would very gallantly inquire of her at the end of these interviews:

"What does your solidity think?"

And yet this brilliant long reign of seventy years of Louis XIV became sad and mournful to the French court. For the King kept up all his old state with all his untameable pride, for it was glory only he had sought, and yet with the weight of years his strength and spirit were gone.

And Madame de Maintenon, though she had attained the summit of her earthly hopes in her marriage with Louis, would say: "No one could guess what a dreadful thing it was to have to amuse an unamuseable king."—The last record of Madame de Maintenon.

October 22, 1685, the King struck a blow against her greatness and prosperity, from which, even at the present day, France has never wholly recovered. It was on that day that, yielding at last to the solicitations of Madame de Maintenon and Father La Chaise, his confessor, he revoked the Edict of Nantes, and blotted out all the previous glory of his reign.

NOTE — Père la Chaise, a French Jesuit, confessor of Louis XIV, born August, 1624; died January, 1709. He promoted the Revocation of the Edict of Nantes. The King built for him a country-seat called "Mount Louis." Its gardens are now the cemetery Pere la Chaise, in Paris.

Duke St. Simon, a courtier of Louis XIV, writes of the revocation of the Edict of Nantes, though himself a Catholic, that it was ruinous to the interests of France.

EXTRACT FROM BISHOP BURNET'S HISTORY OF HIS OWN TIME.

He writes: "While I was in Paris I took a little house, and lived by myself as privately as I could until the beginning of August, when I went to Italy.

"I found the Earl of Montague at Paris, with whom I conversed much, and from him I had knowledge of the affairs of the court that the king had been for many years weakening the interests of the Protestants."

Rouvigny, who was the deputy-general of the churches, (known at the English Court as Earl of Galway still remained firm to the Huguenots;) he told me that he was long deceived in his opinion of the king.

CHAPTER XI.

COLONIAL HISTORY.

Hon. William Stoughton, of Dorchester, Hon. Joseph Dudley, of Roxbury, contemplating a settlement, petitioned the General Court in respect to the ownership of lands in the Nipmuck country, and the rights of the Indians in them.

The Court replied to this petition May 11, 1681, as follows:

"The Court judgeth it meete to grant this motion, and doe further desire & impower the wor'pfll Wm. Stoughton & Joseph Dudley Esqrs. to take particular care & inspection into the matters of the land in the Nipmug Country, what titles are pretended to by Indeans or others, and the validity of them, and make returne of what they find therein to this Court as soone as may be.— Mass. Col. Rec., V, 315.

They further reported, October 16, 1681:

"Since which time, in September last, perceiving a better vnderstanding amongst them, wee warned seuerall of the principall claymers to attend vs into the country & travajle the same in company with us as farr & as much as one weeke would allow us & find that the southerne part, clajmed by Black James and company is capable of good setlement, if not too scant of meadow, though vncerteine what will fall w'thin bounds if our lyne be to be quaestioned."
— Mass. Col. Rec., V, 328.

The boundary between the Massachusetts and Connecticut colonies was at this time unsettled.

The same commissioners, Stoughton and Dudley, were authorized by the General Court to treat with the Indians for that purpose, and "to agree with them upon the easiest terms that may be obtejned." — Ibid, 329.

The action of the Court appears limited to the Nipmuck lands. On February 18, 1681-2, another report was made by the commissioners to the Court, stating that they had agreed for all the land belonging to the Hassanamesit and Natick Indians.

"lying fower miles northward of the present Springfield road, & southward to that, haue agreed betweene Blacke James & them, of which wee adnised in our late returne, wee haue purchased at thirty pounds money & a coate.

"The southern halfe of sajd country we haue purchased of Blacke James & Company, for twenty pounds."— 1 Mass. Col. Rec., V, 342.

Stoughton and Dudley being approved by the Court, one thousand acres of land were voted to each for their "great care & pajnes."

These grants were surveyed by John Gore, at Manchaug, in one plat, and confirmed to Stoughton and Dudley June 4, 1685.

In act of the General Court in confirming this grant it is described, viz.: " Conteyning 1800 acres with allowance of additions of two hundred more next adjoyning to compleat the same to 2000 acres....in the Nipmug Country, at a place called Marichouge [Manchaug] the line being marked with rainging markes in the corners with S. D." [the initials of grantees]. — 2 Ibid, 343. 3 Ibid, 488.

"According to the earliest plan in the Oxford Reckords, 'Manchaug Farm' measured 674 rods on its east and west lines, and 434 rods on its north and south lines. This included both Stoughton and Dudley's shares. A later plan, made after the incorporation of the town of Dudley, in 1731, gives 'Manchaug Farm' as 1100 acres, the property of the 'heirs of Mr. Dudley,' and 'belonging' to Oxford. A still later plan made in 1756 shows 1020 acres as in Oxford, and belonging to Thomas Dudley —and adjoining it on the east; in Sutton, is shown the balance of the plat as 'now Richard Waters,' and others."

At Natick, May 19, 1682, these deeds, dated Feb. 10, 1681-2, were delivered. The commissioners reported to the

---

NOTE.— On the back of the original deed is the following: viz. "That on the twentieth day of May 1685 full and peassable possession and seizure, of the Lands within mentioned to be granted with the appurtenances was given by Benjamin the brother of Black James and Simon Wolomp son of the sayd Black James by delivery of a turffe of the Land called Mayanexet upon a small twigg, in the name of the whole, unto the within named William Stoughton and Joseph Dudley, which was so done under a tree growing on the sayd Mayanexet land, and then marked S. D. in the presence of us."

Whose names are underwritten.

JOHN BLACKWITH,
ROBT. PURDOUR.

NOTE.— The Huguenots in the Nipmuck country.

court on May 27, 1682, that they had purchased "from the principall men of Naticke . . . of a parcell of remote & wast land, belonging to said Indians, lying at the vtmost westerly bounds of Naticke, and, as wee are informed, is for quantity about —— acres, more or lesse, being mean land." These deeds received the confirmation of the Court.—Ibid, 361.

The first deed was executed for the consideration of thirty pounds, and its first signature was that of Waban, who was chief at Natick. Attached to the same deed were twenty-two added signatures. In the second deed, executed for twenty pounds, was the signature of Black James of Chaubunagungamaug, followed by twenty-nine other signatures, "all that part of the Nipmug country, . . . lying and being beyond the great ryuer called Kuttatuck, or Nipmug [Blackstone] Ryver, and betweene a rainge of marked trees, beginning at sajd riuer and running south east till it fall vpon the south lyne of the sajd Massachusets colony on the south, and a certaine imaginary lyne fowre miles on the north side of the road, as it now ljeth, to Springfeild on the north, the sajd great riuer Kuttatuck or Nipmuck on the eastward, and the sajd patent lyne on the westward."—Mass. Col. Rec., V, 361.

First Deed.

"To all Christian People to whom this present Deed shall come;

"Know ye, that we Waban, Pyambobo, John Awassawog, Thomas Awassawog, Samuel Awassawog, John Awassawog, Jr., Anthony Tray, John Tray, Peter Ephraim, Nehemiah James, Rumeny Marsh, Zackery Abraham, Samuel Neaucit, Simon Sacomit, Andrew Pittyme, Ebenezer Pegin, John Magnaw, James Printer, Samuel Acompanit, Joseph Milion, and Samuel Cocksquamion, Indian natives, and natural descendants of the ancient proprietors and inhabitants of the Nipmuck country (so called) and lands adjacent within the

Colony of Massachusetts, in New England, for and in consideration of the sum of thirty pounds, current money of New England, to us in hand, at and before the ensealing and delivery of these presents, well and truly paid by William Stoughton, of the town of Dorchester, Esq., and Joseph Dudley, of the town of Roxbury, Esq., both within the Colony of Massachusetts, the receipt of which valuable sum we do hereby acknowledge ourselves therewith fully satisfied, have granted, bargained, and sold unto said William Stoughton and Joseph Dudley, their heirs and assigns, forever, all the lands lying within the said limits or bounds, be they more or less. In witness whereof, we have hereunto put our hands and seals this 10th day of February, Anno Domini, one thousand six hundred and eighty-one, and in the four-and-thirtieth year of the reign of our Sovereign Lord, King Charles the Second, over England," &c.

"Signed, sealed, and delivered in presence of us,
    Samuel Ruggles, Sen.,
    Daniel Morse,
    Samuel Gookin,
    John Allen,
    Obadiah Morse."

"Waban, *X*   his mark and seal.
Pyambobo, *O*   " "
John Awassawog, *O*   " "
Samuel Awassawog, *m*   " "
Samuel Bowman, *h*   " "
John Awassawog, Jr., *V*   " "
Anthony Tray, *A*   " "
Thomas Tray,   " "
Benjamin Tray, *P*   " "
Jethro, *B*   " "
Joseph Ammon, *Jo*   " "
Peter Ephraim, *be*   " "

Andrew Pittyme, *An* his mark and seal.
Nehemiah, " "
Zackery Abraham, *Π* " "
Samuel Neaucit, *M* " "
Thomas Waban, *m* " "
George Moonisco, *G* " "
Eleazer T. Pegin, " "
Simon Sacomit, " "
Great Jacob Jacob, " "
Elisha Milion, *O*, " "

In the second deed is the following : "All that part of the sajd Nipmug country . . . lying & being on the south part of the sajd colony of the Mattachusets, beyond the great riuer, . . . bounded with the Mattachusets patent line . . . on the south, and certeine marked trees, beginning at the sajd riuer and runing south east, till it strike vpon the bounds the of sajd patent line; on the north, the said great riuer; on the east, and coming to a point on the west."—1 Mass. Col. Rec., V, 362-365.

Feb., 1681-2. The commissioners reported to the Court, " The whole tract in both deeds conteyned is in a forme of a trjangle & reduced to a square, conteyneth a tract about fifty miles long and twenty miles wide."— Ibid, 342.

In the second deed there was a reservation of five miles square, to the native Indians, which might be chosen in two separate tracts of land. The first was on the Quinebaug river at Maanexit, three or four miles southerly of Chaubunagungamaug. The other tract of land, four or five miles south-easterly of Maanexit, in the present town of Thompson.—1 Mass. Col. Rec., V, 488.

Most of the first reservation was subsequently conveyed to Dudley or his heirs, and a part of the land was incorporated in the town which received his name.

The second deed was of the same date, the same territory

included, with the consideration of twenty pounds lawful money of New England, making fifty pounds as the full payment for the relinquishment of the Indian title to the tract of country thus conveyed, but had a reservation, viz.: "Reserving always unto ourselves, our heirs and assigns, out of the above said grant, a certain tract of land five miles square, at such two places as we shall choose, to be wholly at our own use and dispose." This reservation was at "Chaubunagungamaug, surveyed in October, 1684, to Black James and others. It extended west from Chaubunagungamaug pond (from which the Indian town here took its name), over Maanexit river (French river). Nearly all this tract, with other lands between the towns of Oxford and Woodstock, became the property of Joseph Dudley, and afterwards fell to his sons, the Hon. Paul and William Dudley. Part of this Indian land is now within the limits of Thompson, Ct., and part in Dudley."

Second deed, signed sealed and delivered in presence of,
    William Parker,
    Isaac Newell,
    John Gove,
    Samuel Ruggles, Jr.,
    Peter (his X mark) Gardiner,
    Ralph Brodhurst.

Black James, *U*	and seal.
Sam Jaco, *E*	"
Benjamin, *O*	"
Simon Wolamp, *Lo*	"
Wolowa Nonck, *F*	"
Pe Pey Pegans,	"
Poponi Shant, *Ts*	"
Cotoosowk, son of Wolompaw, by his order,	
Wabequola, *Wab*	
Siebquat, his mark, *S*	

A grant of land was made to Robert Thompson in the Nipmug country, as follows:

"This Court, being informed by our agents, now in England, of the good will & friendship of Maj Robert Thompson, of London, & his readiness vpon all occasions to be assistants to them in the service of this colony, wherein they are, according doe, by way of gratuity, give vnto the said Major Thompson & his heires, fiue hundred acres of land in the Nipmug country, to be lajd out, to him w'th all reasonable conuenience. Dated May 16th, 1683." — 1 Mass. Col. Rec., V, 409.

Major Robert Thompson, who is mentioned in this grant, had been for a length of time a resident of Boston, New England.

He was a member of the first corporation established in England, by an act of Parliament July 19, 1649, for the Propagation of the Gospel among the Indians of New England, and when the Hon. Robert Boyle resigned the office of president of the society, he was succeeded by Major Thompson.

He received a special grant of five hundred acres of land from Massachusetts, besides his share of the grant for Oxford, in 1683, in acknowledgment of his good will and friendship for the colony. This grant was afterward laid out in the territory EAST of Woodstock, which became the north part of Killingly. In 1731 the General Assembly of Connecticut granted to Joseph Thompson, Esq., of the Inner Temple, London, grandson and heir of the said Robert Thompson, Esq., of the parish of Stoke, Newington, deceased, two thousand acres,

NOTE.—Governor Gurdan Saltonstall, in behalf of his great grandfather, Sir Richard Saltonstall, owned one thousand acres here.

Josiah Wolcott, of Salem, had two thousand acres here, formerly the property of Thomas Freake. The first sale of land in this tract was by this Mr. Wolcott and his wife Mary (Freake) Wolcott, of Salem, to Josiah Sabin, April 10, 1716.

near the grant before to his grandfather, which, with the five hundred as aforesaid, making two thousand five hundred acres, was given in remembrance of the valuable services of Major Thompson. In 1730, "The North Parish of Killingly" was, in honor to Major Thompson, changed to Thompson's Parish. In 1785 it was again changed to Thompson.

The grant for Oxford, Mass'tts, was made May 16 — 1683.

"This court haueing information that some gentlemen in England are desirous to remove themselves into this colony, & (if it may be) to setle themselues vnder the Massachusetts; for the incouragement of such persons, and that they may haue some from among themselues, according to their motion, to assist & direct them in such a designe, this Court doth grant to Major Robert Thompson William Stoughton and Joseph Dudley, Esq., and such others as they shall associate to them, a tract of land in any free place, conteyning eight miles square, for a towneship, they settling in the sayd place w'thin fower yeares, thirty familjes & an able orthodox minister, and doe allow to the sayd towneship freedom from conntry rates for fower years from the time aboue ljmitted "— May 16, 1683." — Mass. Col. Rec., vol. V, p. 408.

"The plan, a copy of which is now in the town clerk's office, comprehended forty-one thousand two hundred and fifty acres, or a little less than sixty-five square miles, and was two thousand one hundred and fourteen rods, or six and two-thirds miles on the easterly side; three thousand three hundred and forty rods, or about ten and a half miles on the southerly; one thousand nine hundred and sixty-eight rods, or about six miles on the westerly; and three thousand two hundred and sixteen rods, or about ten miles on the northerly. The description in the deed of division — hereafter described — begins at the south-west corner of Worcester, which was near the present village of Auburn, and from thence the line ran nearly south, to the north-west corner of Mr. Dudley's grant of one thou-

sand acres before alluded to,* and thence south fifteen degrees
east, by the west line of said farm to a point about one and a
quarter miles south-westerly of the village of West Sutton,
and a mile and a half west of Manchaug pond, known as
'Manchaug Corner' — thence west fifteen degrees south, to a
point a little north of Peter pond in the easterly part of
Dudley, and thence continuing westerly, crossing the Quinebaug river to a point in the vicinity of Sandersdale, in the
easterly part of Southbridge, thence northerly to a point about
two miles westerly of Charlton city, on the Sturbridge line,
thence easterly, bearing northerly, to the south-west corner of
Worcester.

"These lines enclosed, besides the present town of Oxford,
nearly the whole of Charlton, about one-fourth of Auburn,
one-fifth of Dudley, and three or four square miles of the
north-eastern portion of Southbridge.

"Through this tract there ran, due north and south a 'way,'
twenty rods in width, called 'the common way.' The design
of this unusual provision can only be conjectured, but as it is
called on an old plan the 'proprietors' common way,' it
was a reserve for the purpose of access to the several allot-
ments of the lands west of the village. We find no subsequent allusion to it in the records, and later it is believed,
it became a part of the village territory, and its western lines
the boundary. This dividing line cut off from the main grant
eleven thousand two hundred and fifty acres of the eastern
portion, a tract six and two-thirds miles long, and two and
one-half miles wide, which was given to the (planters) for a
'Village,' or a general Plantation.

"The remaining thirty thousand acres was divided into five
equal parts, the division lines running easterly and westerly.
These parts were allotted as follows: The northernmost to

---

*The Huguenots in the Nipmuck country.

Robert Thompson, the second to Daniel Cox, the third to William Stoughton, the fourth to John Blackwell, and the southernmost to Joseph Dudley. Mr. Cox's portion is subdivided on the plan between Blackwell, Freak and Cox. All the bounds mentioned in this deed were of a transient nature — marked trees, a heap of stones, or a stake, constituting them all except one, which is permanent, and this was at the northeast corner of the natural pond at the present Hodges' village. This bound marked 'the village line,' as it was called Mr. Blackwell's north line joined the village line at this point, so that the pond was in the north-eastern angle of his portion, and is called on the plan referred to, 'Blackwell's pond.' On another plan of early date his share is designated as now 'Papillon's,' and on another later as 'Wolent's and Williams'.'"

The following letter from Dr. Cox, of England, to Governor Bradstreet, dated "London, October 10, 1684.

NOTE.— Josiah Wolcott, Esq., a gentleman in his time distinguished in the history of the town — as was Mr. Williams, both were grandsons of Peter Papillon of Boston.

NOTE.— The deed of division gives the Indian name to the pond which was "Augutteback."

NOTE.— The deed of division is a document of historical interest, and is now in possession of the New York Historical Society. It was presented by Charles Welford, Esq., of London, in the year 1872. This deed is on parchment, and elegantly executed, and is in good preservation, the prominent words and phrases in old English German text. In size its length is two feet three inches, and two feet five inches in width; it is closely written in a legible hand.

Attached to the instrument are five loops of parchment, bearing only the remains of seals in wax at the bottom of the parchment like pendants.

The left hand seal bears the name of Joseph Dudley, and the second William Stoughton, and the fifth has the name of John Blackwell.

On the back of the document are the signatures of witnesses, viz.: Samuel Witty, Edward Thomas, Daniel Bondet, J. B. Tuffean and William Blackwell.

"Divers persons in England and Ireland, gentlemen, citizens, and others, being inclined to remove themselves into foreign parts, where they may enjoy, without interruption, the public exercise of the Christian religion, according to what they apprehend to be of Divine institution, have prevailed with Mr. Blackwell to make your country a visit, and inquire whether they may be there welcome, and which they may reasonably expect — that liberty they promise themselves and others, who will attend their motion."

Among the associates of these three gentlemen whose names appear in the grant for Oxford, were Doctor Daniel Cox, Captain John Blackwell, of London, and Thomas Freake, of Hannington, in the county of Wilts, England.

It would appear that these gentlemen were Puritan Dissenters, who designed to remove and settle permanently in this country, but they were deterred by a favorable change in England in political and church affairs by the death of Charles II, and the short reign of James II, and William III succeeding to the throne of England, giving to England a constitution protecting the rights of the people.

On the petition of these grantees, in 1685, the General Court extended the time for settling upon this grant the thirty families, as follows:

"In answer to the motion and request of William Stoughton and Joseph Dudley, Esq., on behalf of Major Thompson and themselves, desiring this Court's favor to enlarge the time of their grant of their plantation, this Court do enlarge the time for settling that plantation therein mentioned, the space of three years from this day. January, 1685." — See Records of General Court, vol. V, p. 594.

CHAPTER XII.

"The Huguenot's Farewell."

"And I obey—I leave their towers
    Unto the stranger's tread;
Unto the creeping grass and flowers,
    Unto the fading pictures of the dead.

"I leave their shields to slow decay,
    Their banners to the dust;
I go, and only bear away
    Their old majestic name — a solemn trust.

"I go up to the ancient hills
    Where chains may never be;
Where leap in joy the torrent rills,
    Where man may worship God, alone and free.

"There shall an altar and a camp,
    Impregnably arise;
There shall be lit a quenchless lamp,
    To shine unwavering through the open skies.

"And song shall 'midst the rocks be heard,
    And fearless prayer ascend;
While thrilling to God's most Holy Word,
    The mountain pines in adoration bend.

"And there the burning heart no more,
    Its deep thought shall suppress;
But the long buried truths shall pour
    Free currents thence amidst the wilderness.

"Then fare thee well, my mother's bower,
    Farewell, my father's hearth!
Perish my home! whence lawless power
    Hath rent the tie of love to native earth.

"Perish! let death-like silence fall,
    Upon the lone abode;
Spread fast, dark ivy — spread thy pall!
    I go up to the mountains, with my God."

                          Mrs. Hemans.

The Edict of Nantes.

At the revocation of the Edict of Nantes 1685, many of the French exiles from Normandy, Languedoc, and other parts of France, repaired to England and Ireland. In London they were received with great kindness. Here the French artisans commenced trades in silk, tapestries, fine linens and the building of ships, and reached great success in other commercial departments.

"The Episcopal church is not without its own traditions of amity with the Huguenots. In the closing years of the sixteenth century the silk looms of the French and Flemish refugees filled the crypt of Canterbury Cathedral, and to this day the descendants of the persecuted people maintain their worship beneath the roof of that ancient and accredited home of Anglican religion."—Wm. R. Huntington, D. D.

The Protestant countries of Europe, England, Holland, Germany and Switzerland, extended their sympathy and hospitality to the Huguenots.

"The cordial understanding that existed between the Reformed Churches of France and the Church of England, dated from the time of Calvin."

On their part the English Reformers showed no less cordiality toward Calvin and other Continental divines, freely acknowledging the validity of their orders, and inviting their counsel and concurrence in the most important measures.

The Church of England extended to them a generous welcome. Bristol next to London presented great attractions to the French refugees, for here they enjoyed the favor and patronage of the Bishop, Sir Jonathan Trelawney, and a church offered them for French service.—Dr. Baird.

Many refugees escaped to England without being able to secure any portion of their estates. For these provision was already secured. There was a balance that remained of a fund raised some few years before by contributions throughout England for the relief of French Protestants. Additional benefactions were added in April, 1686. The fund thus contributed amounted to the sum of a quarter of a million pounds sterling, known as the Royal Bounty. A royal letter or brief enjoining these collections was necessary in order to their legality, but as neither Charles II nor James II had any sympathy in the movement, it was done reluctantly. Refugees were assisted by the committee that dispensed the Royal Bounty, or by the consistory of the French church in London.

"A brief for a collection on behalf of the Protestant refugees, was issued by King William III, in the year 1699. The proceeds amounting to nearly twelve thousand pounds, were intrusted as usual to the Chamber of the city of London, for safe keeping. From this fund disbursements were made by the Chamberlain, upon the order of the Archbishop of Canterbury, Sir William Ashurst, and others composing the Committee."

In the early part of the seventeenth century it would appear from the history of the Church of England of that time that the French divines were held greatly in favor by the English church, as extracts from an ancient "Treatise," by Bishop Hall will establish their relations of church sympathy. Bishop Hall refers to Dr. Prideaux, of Oxford, and Dr. Primrose of the French church, in London.

While many of the French exiles were leaving the Old World and abandoning their homes, they sought protection and new homes on the shores of New England. "America was regarded by the wandering Huguenot as a blissful home," and no inconsiderable number came to this country.

Mrs. Lee states with great truthfulness:

"In viewing the refugees, we are not to lose sight of the peculiar circumstances under which they fled to this country; — whole families together, women tenderly educated, and unaccustomed to hardship. 'men of refined and cultivated minds.' 'Some few were able to secure a portion of their wealth, others escaped with only their lives.' But they all brought with them those accomplishments and mental acquisitions which they had gained in polished society. Wherever the Huguenots made a settlement they were among the most estimable citizens."

Dr. Snow, in his history of Boston, states that "during the summer of 1686 a number of vessels arrived at that port, having on board French refugees.

"Many of whom were of the company who came to New Oxford, and had left England in reference to a settlement on that grant for a township."

Thursday, July 5th. On this day Foy arrives. Several gentlemen came over with Foy, some of them with estates.— Diary of Samuel Sewell, vol. 1, p. 219.

Gabriel Bernon arrived in Boston July 5, 1688, in the ship Dolphin, John Foy, master, with a company of forty persons.

Bernon certifies he paid the passage of over forty persons to America. Bernon ship'd himself with his family, servants, and associates, with Capt. Foye and also with Capt. Ware.

Foy did not sail from Gravesend before April 26, 1688, when Bernon signed a contract with Pierre Cornilly.— Bernon Papers.

Bernon arrived in London from Amsterdam early in the year 1687.

Here he was introduced to Mr. Robert Thompson by a French refugee.

Mr. Thompson was the president of the Society for Promoting and Propagating the Gospel in New England.

The General Court of Massachusetts had granted to a company, organized with Robert Thompson at its head, a large tract of land, eight miles square, for the site of a settlement in New Oxford, in the Nipmuck country. No settlement had as yet been made. Bernon was made a member of this society for propagating the gospel among the Indians, and was offered a share in the company's Massachusetts lands, and became the founder of Oxford. Isaac Bertrand du Tuffeau, a refugee from Poitou, hearing of Bernon's plans, offered to proceed to New England, obtain a grant, and commence a plantation. Bernon advanced money for the settlement.

There was a French congregation in Boston established in 1685; a French church was erected in 1715 on School street. Rev. Laurent Van den Bosch was the first minister of the French congregation in Boston, having removed from Holland to England; he conformed to the English church, and received a license from the Bishop of London. Mr. Van den Bosch was not received favorably in Boston. He was succeeded by Rev. David de Bourepos, who came from the island of St. Christopher to Boston in 1686, but subsequently in 1687 removed to New Rochelle, Staten Island, and New Paltz, in the New York province. Rev. Pierre Daillé came to Boston in 1696, from New York, where he had been the French minister. Mr. Daillé was possessed of great learning; he wrote Latin fluently.

The English sometimes attended the French church, as Rev. Pierre Daillé was a favorite in society, but some of the English Puritans could not be pleased when a liturgy formed a part of the church service, or with any observance of Christmas or Easter.

In the famous diary of Samuel Sewall there is the following item:

"This day I spake with Mr. Newman about his partaking with the French Church on the 25th of December on account of its being Christmas day, as they abusively call it."

Yet the excellent Cotton Mather said:

"'Tis my hope that the English Churches will not fail in Respect to any that have endured hard things for their faithfulness to the Son of God."

NOTE.— Diary of Samuel Sewall, vol. 1, p. 491.
NOTE.— A large folio French Bible was presented to the French Protestant Church of Boston by Queen Anne.

In the French church after the benediction the congregation was dismissed with an injunction to remember the poor as they passed the alms chest at the church door.

The will of Peter Daillé, of Boston, clerk, is on record in the Probate Office of Suffolk County, Boston.

In respect to his funeral, there is a "restriction that there be no wine at my funeral, and that none of my wife's relations have mourning clothes furnished them except gloves, and a request that 'all ministers of the Gospel within the sd Town of Boston and to the Rev. Mr. Walter of Roxbury shall have scarves and gloves, as well as my bearers.'"

The following bequests:

"I give all my French (and Latin) Books to the French Church in Boston (where I have been a Teacher) as a Library to be kept for the use and benefit of the Ministers." — Vol. II, p. 238.

"Item: I give and bequeath to my loving wife Martha Daillé, the sum of Three hundred and fifty pounds in Province bills or silver equivalent thereto, and my negro man serv^t named Kuffy, and also all my plate, cloaths, household goods and furniture, to hold the same, to her the s^d Martha Daillé, her heirs executors admin^{rs} and assigns forever.

"Item: I give devise and bequeath unto my loving Brother Paul Daillé (in Amsfort) in Holland and to his heirs and assigns forever all the residue of my estate both real and personal wheresoever the same is lying, or may be found.

"I give five pounds to old Mr. John Rawlins, French Schoolmaster.

"Ult^o: I do hereby nominate and appoint my (good friend Mr James Boudoin the sole) executor of this my last Will and Testament.

NOTE.— Mr. Daillé was married three times. His first wife Esther Latonice, died Dec. 1696.

"In Witness whereof I have hereunto put my hand and seal the day and year first within written.

"DAILLÉ." (SEAL).
"Witnesses:
"BENJAMIN WADSWORTH,
"PHEBE MANLEY,
"MARTHA WILLIS."

Offered for probate, May 31, 1715.

The date given of the notice of his death in the Boston News Letter of May 23, 1715:

"On Friday morning last, the 20th current, Dyed here the Reverend Mr. Peter Daillé, Pastor of the French Congregation, aged about 56 years. He was a person of great Piety, Charity, affable and courteous Behaviour, and of exemplary life and Conversation, much Lamented, especially by his Flock, and was Decently Interred on the Lord's Day Evening, the 22d Instant."

Rev. André Le Mercier, a graduate from the Academy of Geneva, while in London, was invited to come to Boston by the French church, and one hundred pounds per year promised him. Le Mercier was a native of Caen, Normandy.

Soon after the arrival of the French minister Le Mercier a small brick church was erected on School street upon the land which had been purchased with King William's gift. Mr. Le Mercier was the minister of the French church for thirty-four years until 1748.

In 1730, O. S.
Mr. Daniel Johonnot,
   Le Mercier,
   Andrew Sigourney,

NOTE—In 1715 Andrew Faneuil, James Bowdoin, Daniel Johonnot and Andrew Sigourney were influential members in the church, and each at his death left a generous bequest to the minister of the French church.

Mr. Martin Brimmer,
    John Petel,
    Adam Duckeran,
petitioned the General Court of Mass. Bay, praying the Court to confer on them the rights and privileges of denizens or Free born subjects of the King of Great Britain or otherwise as the Court shall see meet for reasons mentioned.

The prayer was so far granted as that the petitioners shall within this Province hold and enjoy all the privileges and immunities of his Majesty's natural born subjects.

Jour. House Rep.
    Mass. Bay
        in New England.

FRENCH SETTLEMENT OF OXFORD, 1687.

There are no records of the Oxford French settlement until November, 1687.

A letter of a French Protestant refugee in Boston, dated November, 1687, published by the French Protestant Historical Society:

[TRANSLATION.]

"The Nicmok country belongs to the President, himself (Gabriel Bernon), and the land costs nothing. I do not know as yet the precise quantity that is given to each family; some have told me it is from fifty to a hundred acres, according to the size of a family. . . . It lies with those who wish to take up lands whether to take them in the one or the other plantations (Boston or New Oxford) — on the sea board or in the interior. The Nicmok plantation is inland, at a distance of twenty leagues from Boston, and equally distant from the sea; so that when the settlers wish to send any thing to Boston, or to obtain any thing from thence, they are obliged to transport it in wagons. In the neighborhood of this settlement

---

NOTE.—Bulletin, xvi, 73.

there are small rivers and ponds abounding in fish, and woods full of game. M. Boudet is their minister. The inhabitants as yet number only fifty-two persons."—Bulletin, xvi, 73.

At this time the number of French in Boston was very small.

"Here in Boston," says the French refugee, writing in November, 1687, "there are not more than twenty French families, and they are every day diminishing on account of departing for the country to hire or buy land,* and to strive to make some settlement. They are expected this spring from all quarters. Two young men have lately arrived from Carolina, who give some news from that colony."—Report of a French Protestant refugee in Boston, 1687. Translated from the French by E. T. Fisher, Brooklyn, N. Y.

May 24, 1688, is the date of the deed of Dudley and other proprietors, to Gabriel Bernon. The deed of division was executed July 3, 1688.

These documents would prove that the thirty families were occupying their French plantations in the spring of 1688, the stipulated time having expired in the January previous.

In the deed of division dated July 3, 1688, there is a description of Mr. Dudley's portion of land, where it names his northeastern bound as "a white oak, square driven in the meadow, by the river which runs by and from the French houses. This bound was about one-third of a mile down the river from where the road to Webster now crosses it, and of course due south from the north-east corner of the Augutteback pond."†

This is the only record we have relating to the existence of the houses of the French habitans at that time, and is a confirmation of their location from tradition.

* The French plantation of New Oxford.

† The Augutteback pond is the original lake in Howarth's, not the present reservoir.

The deed to Bernon required that he should build a corn or grist mill within twelve months from the date of his deed; 1689 is the next record of the French settlement.

In March, 1689, is the contract of Mr. Church for the mill for New Oxford.

Mr. Bernon states that he had built in New Oxford "a corn miln [mill], a wash leathern miln, and a saw miln." The corn mill was the upper site near what is known as Rich's mill. The saw mill near the south village street on the highway leading to the French fort. The wash leather mill on the same river, situated between the corn and saw mills.

These mills were located upon the river east of the village street. In the village records in 1714, the one near the south end is called the "Old Mill Place," and was the saw mill. At a later date the corn mill was built, at the upper site.

THE OLD FRENCH MILL OF NEW OXFORD.

["*contract De Mr Cherch pour Le Moulin de New-oxford.*"]

"Articles of Agreement had made concluded and agreed upon by and Between Caleb Church of Watertown Millright and Gabriel Bernon of Boston Merc^t this   Day of March Anno Domini One Thousand six hundred Eight Eight Nine.

"Imp^s The said Caleb Church doth Covenant and Agree with the s^d Gabriel Bernon that he shall and vill att his own Proper Costs and Charges Erect Build and finish a Corn or Grist mill in all poynts workmanlike in Such Place in the Village of Oxford as shall by the s^d Bernon be Directed the s^d Mill House to be Twenty two foot Long and Eighteen foot Broad and Eleven foot stud Substantially and Sufficiently covered with a jett to Cover the Wheele and a Chamber fitt for the Laying and Disposing Corn Bags or other Utensills Necessary for the s^d Mill and the s^d Church doth Covenant to find att his Own Proper Costs all the Iron Worke Necessary for the s^d Mill and all other Things Except what is hereafter Expressed

"Item, the said Gabriel Bernon doth Covenant and Agree with the said Caleb Church that hee will bee att the Charge of searhing Preparing and Bringing to Place the Mill Stones for the s^d mill and that he will by the Oversight and Direction of the s^d Church Make Erect and finish the Earth of the Dame that shall bee by the s^d Church adjudged necessary for the s^d Mill and also will dig and Prepare the Place where the Mill shall be Erected and also will allow to the s^d Church five hundred foot of Boards and   Persons to help for the Cutting Down of the Timber and will bee att the Charge of Bringing the Timber to Place and further doth Covenant to pay to the s^d Church for his Labor and Pains herein the Sume of forty Pounds two thirds thereof in money the Other Third in goods att money price in Three Equall Payments One Third att the ffalling the Timber One Third att the Raising and the Last att the finishing the s^d mill

"Lastly the s^d Church doth Covenant and Promies to finish the s^d Mill all sufficient and workemanlike and Sett her to Worke by the Last day of Augt next after the Day of the Date hereof In Wittness whereof they have hereunto sett their hands and seals the day and Year first above written

"CALEB CHURCH.   [Seal.]

"Sealed and Delivered
 "in Presence of

"I. BERTRAND DUTUFFEAU
"THO DUDLEY."

On the back of the original paper is the following:

" Within named Caleb Church do ingage and promis to find the stones and laye them on to make mele at my one costs and charge for the which m^r Bernon doth ingage and promis to paye for the same one and twenty pounds in corent mony for the same to be concluded when the mill grinds

"Boston May: y⁰ 20: 1689
"Richard Wilkins   Caleb Church
"Edmond Browne   Gabriel Bernon."
                                        [Seal.]

	L	s:	d
"ffor the mill in first the sum of forty pounds	40	00:	
secondly for the stones of the said one and twenty pounds	21	00:	
forthely for an addition to the house six pounds (sic)	6	00:	
	67	00:	

Two receipts from Mr. Church:

"Received one third Part of the within mentioned sume of forty wch is Thirteen Pounds six shillings and Eight Pence two thirds in money and one third in Goods by me

"Caleb Church."

"More I have received fifty three pounds tirteen shillings wich the above said sum are in all the sum of sixty and seven pounds in full following our s^d bargain Boston: 4 february 1689-90 received by my

"Caleb Church."

"Peter Basset   in witness
"Gabriel Depont   present."

— Bernon Papers.— Dr. Baird.

CHAPTER XIII.

INTERCOLONIAL WARS.

1. *King William's War*, 1689.

The French settlement is established at Oxford. The inhabitants are located on their plantations. Rev. Daniel Bondet is their minister; he so states in a letter to Lord Cornbury, and accompanied these French Protestants to New Oxford.

The mills are being erected for the convenience of the inhabitants.

When in 1689 King William's war was declared in the colonies it continued nearly eight years, and was the cause of the French inhabitants abandoning the settlement of New Oxford, it being unsafe to remain from the hostility of the Indians.

M^r. Danl. Bondet's Representations referring to N. Oxford, July 6th, 1691.

He mentions it as upon "an occasion which fills my heart with sorrow and my life of trouble, but my humble request will be at least before God, and before you a solemn protestation against the guilt of those incorrigible persons who dwell in our place.

"The rome [rum] is always sold to the Indians without order and measure,....insomuch that according the complaint sent to me by Master Dickestean with advice to present it to your honor.

"The 26 of the last month there was about twenti indians so furious by drunkness that they fought like bears and fell upon one called remes...., who is appointed for preaching the gospel amongst them he had been so much disfigured by his wonds that there is no hope of his recovery. If it was your pleasure to signifie to the instrumens of that evil the jalosie of your athoreti and of the publique tranquility, you would do great good maintaining the honor of God, in a Christian habitation, comforting some honest souls which being incompatible with such abominations feel every day the burden of afflixion of their honorable perigrination aggravated. Hear us pray and so God be with you and prosper all your just undertakins and applications tis the sincere wish of your most respectuous servant.

"D. Bondet,
"minister of the gospell in a
"French Congregation at New Oxford."

1693 is the date of the following record:

"André Sigourney aged of about fifty years doe affirme that the 28 day of nonemb^r last past he was with all of the village in the mill for to take the rum in the hands of Peter Canton and when they asked him way (why) hee doe abuse so the Indiens in seleing them liquor to the great shame and dangers of all the company, hee s^d Canton answered that itt was his will and that he hath right soe to doe and asking him further if itt was noe him how (who) make soe many Indieans drunk he did answer that hee had sell to one Indian and one squa the valew of four gills and that itt is all upon w^{ch} (which) one of the company named Ellias Dupeux told him that hee have meet an Indian drunk w^{ch} (which) have get a bott (le) fooll (full) and said that itt was to the mill how sell itt he answered that itt may bee truth.

"André Sigournay."

"Boston, Dec. 5, 1693."

The original document is in the possession of the Hon. Peter Butler. Quincy, Mass. — Huguenot Emigration to America, vol. 2, p. 273.

In 1693 Daniel Allen was chosen representative from New Oxford to the General Court at Boston. Mr. Allen's name is found in the list for 1693, as from this place.

In this county Lancaster, Mendon and Oxford were represented.

Oxford having been granted by the Provincial government the privilege of representation was made liable to taxation.

In 1694 a moderate assessment was made and sent with an order for its collection, to the "Constable of the French Plantations."

The following was sent in reply to this order:

[*Andrew Sigourney to Sir William Phipps, etc.*]

"To His Excellency Sir William Phipps, Kn't Capt. General and Governor in Chief of their Majesties' Province of the Massachusetts Bay in New England, and to the Honorable Council":

"*The humble petition of Andrew Sigourney, Constable of the French Plantation,*

"Humbly Sheweth unto Your Excellency and to Your Honors, that your petitioner received an order from Mr. James Taylor Treasurer for collecting eight pounds six shillings in our plantation for Poll money, now whereas the Indians have appeared several times this Summer, we were forced to garrison ourselves for three months together and several families fled, so that all our Summer harvest of hay and corn hath gone to ruin by the beasts and cattle which hath brought us so low that we have not enough to supply our own necessities many other families abandoning likewise, so that we have none left but Mr. Boudet our minister and the poorest of our plantation so that we are incapable of paying said Poll unless we dispose of what little we have and quit our plantations. Wherefore humbly entreat this Honorable Council to consider our miseries and incapacity of paying this poll, and as in duty bound we shall ever pray."*

---

* Mass. Archives, C, 502.—Payment was not enforced. We find an act later, "abating, remitting and forgiving" taxes from this place to the amount of thirty-three pounds and six shillings.—Province Laws, 698, p. 341.

This paper without date is endorsed, Read Oct. 16, 1694. —Mass. Archives, C, 502.

Mr. Sigourney's declaration "The Indians have appeared several times this summer, we were forced to garrison ourselves for three months together, and several families fled." This statement reveals the cause of the decline and final extinction of the settlement.

Not long after the date of this petition, Rev. Mr. Bondet retired from the New Oxford settlement, and became a resident of Boston. He left his plantation of two hundred acres of land, which he and his heirs never claimed.

The Society for Propagating the Gospel Among the Indians of New England was incorporated by Parliament in 1649. It was this society that appointed the Rev. Daniel Bondet to preach to the remaining Nipmuck Indians in the Indian town of Manchaug (Oxford village), where he commenced his labors with both the French and these natives in 1687.

At this time Major Robert Thompson, the first named in the grant for Oxford, was President of the Society.

"During this summer of 1694, a daughter of Mr. Alard, one of the refugees in the settlement of Oxford, on leaving her home, near the lower mills, accompanied by two younger children of the family, was murdered by some roving Indians, and the younger children were made prisoners, and taken to Quebec. Several months must have elapsed before the parents knew the fate of their children who were captured."—Note, Bernon Papers.

The following sketch is a transcript from an interesting and valuable paper, entitled :

NOTE.—Andrew Sigourney, Constable (Connétable), an ancient officer only second to the crown of France, formerly the first military officer of the crown.—See Constable Montmorency.

"A MEMOIR OF THE FRENCH PROTESTANTS WHO SETTLED AT OXFORD, MASSACHUSETTS, 1687, BY REV. ABIEL HOLMES, D. D., OF CAMBRIDGE, MASS., COR. SEC'Y MASS. HIST. SOCIETY."

"Every thing concerning this interesting colony of exiles has hitherto been learnt from tradition, with the illustrations derived from scanty records, and original manuscripts. Many of these manuscripts, which are generally written in the French language, are in the possession of Mr. Andrew Sigourney,* of Oxford, and the rest were principally procured by Mr. Sigourney for the compilation of this memoir."

"Mr. Andrew Sigourney is a descendant from the first of that name who was among the original French settlers of Oxford. To his kindness I am entitled for nearly all my materials for this part of the memoir. After giving me every facility at Oxford, in aid of my inquiries and researches, he made a journey to Providence for the sole purpose of procuring for me the Bernon papers, which he brought to me at Cambridge. These papers were in the possession of Philip Allen, Esq. (Governor Allen, of Providence, a descendant of the Bernon family), and who has indulged me with the MSS. to the extent of my wishes."

Rev. Abiel Holmes, D. D., visited Oxford, Mass., in April, 1817. He writes:

"I waited upon Mrs. Butler†, who obligingly told me all she could recollect concerning the French emigrants."

"Mrs. Butler was the wife of Mr. James Butler, who lives

---

*Andrew Sigourney (Captain), son of Anthony Sigourney, of Boston, was born in Boston, Nov. 30, 1752.

NOTE.—Capt. Sigourney made his journey to Providence in a one-horse chaise, and subsequently to Cambridge, in the same manner of traveling.

†Mrs. Butler was the daughter of Anthony Sigourney of Boston, and was b. in Boston, March 23, 1741-2.

near the First Church in Oxford;* and when I saw her, was in the seventy-fifth year of her age. Her original name was Mary Sigourney. She was a granddaughter of Mr. Andrew Sigourney, who came over when young with his father (Andrew Sigourney, 1st, from France).

Mrs. Butler's Reminiscences.

Her grandmother's mother (the wife of Captain Germaine), died on the voyage, leaving an infant of only six months (who was the grandmother of Mrs. Butler) and another daughter, Marguerite, who was then six years of age.†

"The information which Mrs. Butler gave me, she received from her grandmother, Mrs. Mary (Germaine) Sigourney, who lived to the age of eighty-three years, and from her grandmother's sister, Marguerite (Germaine), married to Captain de paix Cazeneau, who lived to the age of ninety-five or ninety-six years, both of whom resided and died in Boston.

Reminiscences of Mrs. Mary (Germaine) Sigourney of Boston, as Given to Mrs. Butler.

"The refugees left France in 1684, or in 1685, with the utmost trepidation and precipitancy. The great grandfather of Mrs. Butler (Captain Germaine), gave the family notice that

---

*The church on the north common.

NOTE. — Mrs. Butler in her interview with Rev. Abiel Holmes, D. D., narrates facts relative to the Germaine ancestry in leaving France, and not of the Sigourney family.

†In an ancient French prayer-book of the Sigourney family, published 1641, there is the record of Marguerite (Germaine) Cazeneau's birth, viz.: Aunt Casno, born ye 12 Decemb. 1671. Mother Sigourney (Mary Germaine), ye 2 March, 1680.

In 1686, at the time of Mrs. Germaine's death, leaving an infant, Mary Germaine, the grandmother of Mrs. Butler, was six years of age, and her sister, Mrs. de Paix Cazeneau, was fifteen years of age.

they must go. They came off with secrecy, with whatever clothes they could put upon the children," and left without waiting to partake of the dinner which was being prepared for them. When they arrived at Boston they went directly to Fort Hill, where they were provided for, and there continued until they went to Oxford.

Mrs. Butler's account was entirely verbal, according to her recollection.

Mrs. Butler stated the " French built a fort on a hill at Oxford, on the east side of French river." She also stated another fort and a church were built by the French in Oxford.

Dr. Holmes writes :

"Mrs. Butler lived in Boston until the American Revolution, and soon afterward removed to Oxford. Her residence in both places rendered her more familiar with the history of the emigrants than she would have been, had she resided exclusively in either. She says they prospered in Boston after they were broken up at Oxford. Of the memorials of the primitive plantation of her ancestors she had been very observant, and still cherished a reverence for them."

In 1817, very soon after my visit to Mrs. Butler, I received a letter from her husband, expressing his regret that she had not mentioned to me Mrs. Wheeler, a widow lady, the mother of Mr. Joseph Cooledge, an eminent merchant in Boston. Her maiden name was Oliver (Olivier). She was a branch of the Germaine family, and related to " Old Mr. Andrew Sigourney,"

NOTE.—*French Families.*—Mrs. Butler named as of the first emigrants from France, the following families: Bowdoin and Boudinot came to Boston; could not say whether or not they came to Oxford. Bouyer, who married a Sigourney. Charles Germaine, removed to New York. Olivier did not know whether this family came to Oxford, or not; but the ancestor, by the mother's side, was a Sigourney.

NOTE. — Bouyer married Marie Anne, daughter of Daniel Johonnot, and Susanne Sigourney Jansen, who was daughter of Andrew Sigourney, Sr.

in whose family she was brought up, and at whose house she was married.* Mrs. Butler supposed she must be between eighty and ninety years of age, and that being so much older than herself, she had heard more particulars from their ancestors. But on inquiry for Mrs. Wheeler, in Boston, I found that she died a short time before the reception of the letters.

How much do we lose by neglecting the advice of the son of Sirach? "Miss not the discourse of the elders; for they also learned of their fathers, and of them thou shalt learn understanding, and to give answer as need requireth."

DR. HOLMES CONTINUES MRS. BUTLER'S REMINISCENCES.

"Mrs. Johnson (Jansen) the wife of Mr. Johnson (Jansen), who was killed by the Indians in 1696, was a sister of the first Andrew Sigourney.†

"The husband, returning home from Woodstock while the Indians were massacreing his family, was shot down at his own door.

---

*Mrs. Marguerite Wheeler was the daughter of Antoine and Mary Sigourney Olivier (French refugees). She was born at Annapolis, Nova Scotia, November 6, 1726. She was married three times; in her first marriage to Joseph Cooledge of Boston; in her second marriage to Capt. Israel Jennison of Worcester, a son of Peter Jennison and a nephew of Hon. William Jennison; after Mr. Jennison's death she was married to the Rev. Joseph Wheeler, who was a member of the Provincial Congress in 1774; removed to Worcester in 1781, where he was register of the Probate Court till his death in 1793. Mrs. Wheeler died in Boston, at her son's house, Mr. Joseph Cooledge, 1816, aged 90 years.

NOTE.— Captain Israel Jennison died in Worcester, September 19, 1782. Mr. Joseph Wheeler died in Worcester, 1793.

† Mrs. Susanne Johnson (Jansen) was the daughter of the first Andrew Sigourney and sister to Andrew Sigourney, Jr., who rescued her from the Indians. It was early evening when the massacre of the Jansen family occurred; Mrs. Jansen was anxiously awaiting the return of Mr. Jansen from Woodstock.

The names of the three unfortunate children of Jean Jansen who were massacred by the Indians were: Audré (Andrew), Pierre (Peter), Marie (Mary). Jean Jansen was a native of Holland, but of French extraction.

"Mr. Sigourney, hearing the report of the guns, ran to the house and seizing his sister carried her out of a back door and took her over French river, which they waded through, and fled towards Woodstock, where there was a garrison. The Indians killed the children, dashing them against the jambs of the fire-place."

FROM WOODSTOCK RECORDS.

"The inhabitants were aroused at the break of day by the arrival of the fugitives with their heavy tidings. The news of the massacre spread through the different settlements, filling them with alarm and terror. The savages might at any moment burst upon them. Their defenses were slight, ammunition scanty, their own Indians doubtful; the whole population, men, women and children, hastened within their fortifications. Posts were at once dispatched to Lieutenant-General Stoughton, commander of the Massachusetts forces, and to Major James Fitch at Norwich. The day and night were spent in watching and terror, but before morning the arrival

---

NOTE.—The chimney base of the Jansen house is still preserved in Oxford at the Memorial Hall, as a relic of the massacre of the Jansen family. The name of Jansen is, in the Boston Records, Jeanson.

A memorial stone has been erected on or near the site of the dwelling on the old Dudley road, on land belonging to the late Charles A. Sigourny, Esq., of Oxford. Tradition states Captain Andrew Sigourney visited yearly the site of the Jansen house to mark the ruins.

NOTE.—"Mrs. Shumway, living near the Jansen house, showed Mrs. Butler the spot where the house stood, and some of its remains.

"Col. Jeremiah Kingsbury, fifty-five years of age (1817), had seen the chimney and other remains of that house.

"His mother, aged eighty-four years, told Mrs. Butler that there was a burying place called 'the French Burying Ground,' not far from the fort at Mayo's Hill. She herself remembered to have seen many graves there."

Mrs. Shumway was the wife of Peter Shumway whose ancestor was a Huguenot from France.

of Major Fitch, with his brother Daniel, a few English soldiers, and a band of Pequots and Mohegans, somewhat allayed apprehensions. No enemy had been seen, but it was rumored they had divided into small companies, and were lurking about the woods.

"It was proposed to leave a sufficient number of men for the defense of Woodstock, and send others to range for the marauders. The Wabquassets eagerly welcomed Major Fitch as their friend and master, and offered to join the Mohegans in their congenial service. The Woodstock authorities would gladly have employed them, but could not supply them with ammunition according to the laws of Massachusetts. To refuse their offer at this critical juncture, or to send them forth without ammunition, might enrage and forever alienate them, while conciliation and indulgence might make them the firm friends and allies of Woodstock. Under these circumstances, Major Fitch took the responsibility of employing and equipping these Indians; calling them all together he took their names, and found twenty-nine fighting men, twenty-five native Wabquassets, and four Shetuckets, married to Wabquassets.

"Eighteen Wabquassets and twenty-three Mohegans then sallied out together, under Captain Daniel Fitch, to range through Massachusetts, with a commission from Major Fitch, as magistrate and military officer, asking all plantations to which they might come for supplies and accommodations. Scarcely had they gone forth when four strange Indians were discovered at the west end of the town, but whether enemies or not they could not tell. At evening a scout from Providence arrived, being the captain with fourteen men, who had been out two days northward of Mendon and Oxford, but made no discovery. Captain Fitch and his men were equally unsuccessful, and the invading Mohawks effected their escape uninjured."

NOTE.—Miss Larned's History of Windham County.

"It is stated on the intelligence of those outrages, and the appearance of hostile parties near Woodstock, Major James Fitch marched to that town. On the 27th a party was sent out of thirty-eight Norwich, Mohegan and Nipmuck Indians, and twelve soldiers, to range the woods toward Lancaster, under Captain Daniel Fitch; on their march they passed through Worcester, and discovered traces of the enemy in its vicinity."

A LETTER FROM CAPTAIN DANIEL FITCH TO THE RT. HON. WILLIAM STOUGHTON, ESQ., LIEUTENANT-GOVERNOR AND COMMANDER-IN-CHIEF, ETC.

"Whereas we are informed of several persons killed at Oxford on Tuesday night last past, and not knowing what danger might be near to Woodstock and several other frontiers toward the western parts of the Massachusetts province, several persons offering volunteers, both English and Indians, to the number of about fifty (concerning which the bearer, Mr. James Corbin, may more fully inform your honor), all of which were willing to follow the Indian enemy, hoping to find those that had done the late mischief: In prosecution whereof, we have ranged the woods to the westward of Oxford, and so to Worcester, and then to Lancaster, and were freely willing to spend some considerable time in endeavoring to find any of the enemy that may be upon Merrimac or Penicook rivers, or any where in the western woods; to which and we humbly request your Honor would be pleased to encourage said design, by granting us some supply of provisions and ammunition; and, also, by strengthening us to any thing wherein we may be short in any respect, that so we may be under no disadvantage or discouragement." They may further inform your Honor that on the Sabbath day coming at a place called Half Way River, betwixt Oxford and Worcester, we came upon the fresh tracks of several Indians, which were gone towards Worcester, which we apprehend were the Indians that did the late damage at Oxford, and being very desirous to do some service that may be to the benefit of his Majesty's subjects, we humbly crave your Honor's favorable assistance.

"Herein I remain your Honor's most humble servant, according to my ability.   DANIEL FITCH."

"LANCASTER, 31st August, 1696.

"Not far from Oxford, in the village of the Wabquassets, a clan of the Nipmuck tribe, near New Roxbury, or Woodstock, lived an Indian known to the English as 'Toby,' who was distinguished among his more sluggish and pacific people for a restless, scheming disposition. Toby is now the 'great man or captain' among these Nipmuck Indians."

"On Tuesday, the twenty-fifth of August, 1696, Toby, with a party of Indians, toward evening approached the 'French houses' at New Oxford. The habitation of Jean Jansen was situated on what has ever since been known to the English as Johnson's plain."

"Toby leaving his residence, is sometimes privately among his relatives at Woodstock, and at hunting houses in the wilderness."

"But his activity in the service of the Canadian enemy is greater than ever. At one time, he appears at a meeting of the Canada Mohawks with their brethren among the Five Nations, and tells them if they will 'but draw off the friend Indians from the English,' they can 'easily destroy' the New England settlements."

NOTE 1.—Huguenot Emigration to America. Dr. C. W. Baird, vol. II.

NOTE.—"January 29, 1700, Governor Winthrop, of Connecticut, in correspondence with Governor Bellemont of New York, referred to it as an occurrence to be remembered, and the friendly Mohegans who met in council at New London, spoke of Toby as the Indian 'that had a hand in killing one Jansen. One Toby....the principal instigator....who had a particular hand in killing one Jansen.'"

Documents relative to the Colonial History of the State of New York. Vol. IV., pp. 612-620.

"At another time he is in Norwich, Connecticut, bearing a belt of wampum to the loyal tribes, inviting them to join in a general uprising."*

REMINISCENCES OF MRS. MARY GERMAINE SIGOURNEY, AS GIVEN TO MRS. MARY SIGOURNEY BUTLER.

Immediately following the massacre, the Huguenots decided to abandon the settlement in New Oxford. Early on the morning of their departure, the different families bade adieu to their homes and plantations; the doors of their dwellings were closed, and the narrow diamond casements were darkened by the heavy inside shutters, and their homes with their gardens, orchards and vineyards were again to be deserted for new homes, leaving their harvests and vintage unharvested.

---

*"The Information of Black James, taken from his own mouth on Feb. the 1st, 1699-1700:

"That he being in the woods a hunting, came to a place near Massomuck to a great Wigwam of five fire places and eleven hunting Indians; he went into the Wigwam towards one end of it, and saw an Indian w[ch] seemed to hide himself, he turned himself towards the other end of the Wigwam, and met there a man called Cawgatwo, a Wabquasset Indian, and he asked if he saw any strange Indians there; he said I saw one I did not know; then Toby came to him, and another stranger and Cawgatwo told him that was Toby; he said he would go away to-morrow, they bid him not go away, for to-morrow they should discourse; the next morning they went out and called this James and bid him come and see the Wampom they had gathered; he asked what that Wampom was for, they said it was Mohawk's Wampom; the Dutchman had told them that the English had ordered to cut off all Indians, and they had the same news from the French, and therefore we are gathering and sending Wampom to all Indians, that we may agree to cut off the English; and Cawgatwo told this James that Toby brought that Wampom and that news from the Mohawks; then he went home and told his own company, and desired them to send Word to the Mohawks and Nihanticks of this news."

(Information respecting a rumored rising of the Indians. Documents, etc., Vol. IV, pp. 613–616.)

The refugees repaired to their chapel for a matin service; they then retired to the little churchyard in front of the chapel to take leave of the graves of their friends. In imagination one can picture the little groups as they departed in a silent procession and moved onward over the forest paths toward Boston.

Nothing can be added to this simple narrative of Mrs. Mary Germaine Sigourney who was herself one of the refugees and whose reminiscences have been treasured so sacredly by her descendants.

Mary Germaine, born in France in 1680, must have been at this time sixteen years of age, and her sister, Mrs. Marguerite (Sigourney) Cazeneau, twenty-five years of age.

THE DESERTED HOUSE.

Life and thought have gone away
    Side by side,
Leaving door and windows wide:
Careless tenants they!

All within is dark as night:
In the windows is no light;
And no murmur at the door,
So frequent on the hinge before.

Close the door, the shutters close
    Or thro' the windows we shall see
    The nakedness and vacancy
Of the dark deserted house.

Come away; no more of mirth
    Is here or merry-making sound.
The house was builded of the earth,
    And shall fall again to ground.

Come away; for life and thought
    Here no longer dwell;
    But in a city glorious—

A great and distant city have bought
    A mansion incorruptible.
    Would they could have stayed with us!
                    TENNYSON.

A French document signed in Boston, September 4, 1696, by the principal French planters of "new oxford," shows that Mrs. Jeanson and her brother, Mr. Sigourney, had returned from Woodstock, to which place they had fled on the night of the massacre, August 25th, and, also, the abandonment of the French plantations in New Oxford, and the return of the French inhabitants to Boston.

The first record we find of the French refugees after leaving New Oxford is the following certificate, signed in Boston, September 4, 1696, O. S.

Nous sousignes certiffions et ateston que Monsr. Gabriel Bernon non a fait une despence [depense] considerable a new oxford pour faire valoir la Ville et encourager et ayder les habitans. et quil [qu'il] a tenu sa maison en etat jusques a ce que en fin les Sauvages soient venus masacrer et tuer John Johnson et ses trois enfens [enfans] Jet que netant [n'etant] pas soutenu il a été obligé et forse d'abandoner son Bien. en foy de quoy lui avons signe le present Billet, a Baston le 4ᵉ Septembre 1696 :*

JERMONS   BAUDOUIN   BENJA FANEUIL
JAQUES MONTIER   Nous attestons ce qui est desus et
† marque   [est] veritable.
X marque de PAIS CAZANEAU
     MOUSSET Entien [Ancien]
V marque de ABRAHAM SAUUAGE
     JEAN RAWLINGS Ancien
* marque de la vefue de JEAN JEANSON
     P. CHARDON
CHARLE GERMON   Entien

---

*NOTE.—We subscribe, certify and attest that Mr. Gabriel Bernon has been at a considerable expense at New Oxford for to make valuable the village, and to encourage, aid the inhabitants, and that he held his house and estate until the time the Savages came and massacred and killed John Johnson and his three children, and not being protected he was obliged and forced to abandon his goods.

In faith of which we have signed the present bond.

BASTAN,* the 4th September, 1696.
     *The French orthography of Boston.

Nous certiffions que ce sont les marques de personnes susdites.

  DAILLÉ Ministre BAUDOUIN
  JACQUES MONTIER BARBUT
  ELIE DUPEUX ANDRÉ SIGOURNAY
  JEAN MAILLET JEAN MILLET Ant.

Nous declarons ce que dessus fort veritable ce que John Johnson et ces trois enfans ont été tué le 25ᵉ Auost [Aout] 1696 : en foy de quoy avons signé.

  MONTEL DUPEUX I. B. MARQUE DE JEAN BAUDOUIN
  JACQUES DEPONT PHILIP [obscure]
  JERMON RENÉ GRIGNON

Je connais et le soy d'experiance que Mr. Gabriel Bernon a fait ses efforts pour soutenir notre plantation, et y a depancé pour cet effet un bien considerable.

  BUREAU L'AINÉ [the elder or senior]
  PETER CANTON

We underwritters doe certifie and attest that Mr. Gabriel Bernon hath made considerable expences at New oxford for to promote the place and incourage the Inhabitants and hath kept his house until the s^d 25th August that the Indians came upon s^d Plantation & most barbarously murthtred John Evans John Johnson and his three childrens. Daeed Bastan 20th Septemb. 1696.

    JOHN USHER
    WM STOUGHTON
  JOHN BUTCHER INCREASE MATHER
  LAUR HAMMOND CHARLES MORTON
    JER. DUMMER
    NEHEMIAH WALTER min^r
    WM. FOX.

    TRANSLATION.

"By original manuscripts, dated 1696, and at subsequent periods, it appears that Gabriel Bernon, merchant, of an ancient and noble family in La Rochelle, was the president of the French plantation in Oxford, and expended large sums of money for its improvement. An original paper in French, signed at Boston, Sept. 4, 1696," by the principal French planters, certifies this fact in behalf of Mr. Bernon; and subjoins a declaration that the massacre of Mr. Johnson [Jansen] and of his three children by the Indians was the unhappy cause of his losses, and of the abandonment of the place.

FROM AN ANCIENT RECORD OF 1697.

All the places are named between New York and Boston "where travelers could find entertainment for man and beast."

And over this forest path all the French refugees traveled from Oxford via Boston, to New York, and New Rochelle, N. Y.

"From New York to Boston it is accounted 274 miles, thus, viz.: From the post-office in New York to Jo. Clapp's in the Bowery, is 2 mile [which generally is the baiting place, where gentlemen take leave of their friends going so long a journey], and where a parting glass or two of generous wine

"If well applied, make their dull horses feel
One spurr i' the head is worth two in the heel."

From said Clapp's (his tavern was near the corner of Bayard street), to half-way house, 7 miles; thence to King's bridge, 9; to old Shute's at East Chester, 6; to New Rochel Meeting-House, 4; to Joseph Norton's, 4; to Denham's, at Rye, 4; to Knap's, at Horseneck, 7; to Belben's, at Norwalk, 10; to Burr's, at Fairfield, 10; to T. Knowles' at Stratford, 9; to Andrew Sanford's, at Milford, 4; to Capt. John Mills', at New Haven, 10; to the widow Frisbie's at Branford, 10; to John Hudson's, at Guilford, ——; to John Grissil's, at Killinsworth, 10; to John Clarke's, at Seabrook, 10; to Mr. Plum's, at New London, 18; to Mr. Sexton's, 15; to Mr. Pemberson's, in the Narragansette country, 15; to the Frenchtown, 24; to Mr. Turnip's, 20; to

Mr. Woodcock's, 15; to Mr. Billings' farm, 11; to Mr. White's, 6, to Mr. Fisher's, 6; and from thence to the great town of Boston, 10, where many good lodgings and accommodations may be had for love and money."

CHAPTER XIV.

RESETTLEMEMT OF THE FRENCH IN OXFORD — INTERCOLONIAL WARS.

II. *Queen Anne's War.*

At the close of King William's War, the peace of Ryswick, in 1697, was of short continuation. In 1702, England was engaged in war with France and Spain, and the American colonies were interested in what was called Queen Anne's War.

In 1699 there was a resettlement of French Protestants at New Oxford, with the Rev. James Laborie for their minister. Queen Anne's War soon commenced. This war between England and France greatly exposed the New England colonies to increased Indian irruptions and barbarities. And this war caused the dispersion of the second French settlement in New Oxford. An ancient record of this settlement is the petition of the "Inhabitants of the town of New Oxford," by James Laborie, their minister, dated October 1, 1699."

[*James Laborie* "*Tou His Excellencie and tou the Honorable Council.*"]

"MY LORD AND MOST HONORABLE COUNCIL:

"Mr. Bondet, formerly minister of this town, not only satisfied to leave us almost two years before the Indians did commit any act of hostility in this place, but carried away all the books which had been given for the use of the plantation, with the acts and papers of the village, we most humbly supplicate your Excellency and the most Honorable Council to oblige Mr. Boudet to send back again said books, acts, and papers belonging to said plantation.*

"The inhabitants, knowing that all disturbance that hath been before in this plantation, have happened only in that some people of this plantation did give the Indians drink without measure, and that at present there is some continuing to do the same, we most humbly supplicate your Excellency, and the Honorable Council to give Mr. James Laborie, our minister, full orders to hinder those disturbances which put us in great danger of our lives. The said inhabitants complain also against John Ingall, that not only he gives to said Indians drink without measure, but buy all the meat they bring, and goes and sell it in other villages, and so hinders the inhabitants of putting up any provisions against the Winter. We most humbly supplicate your Excellency and most Honorable Council to forbid said John Ingall to sell any rhoom, and to transport any meat out of the plantation that he hath bought of the Indians, before the said inhabitants be provided."

ROYAL HISTORICAL SOCIETY, 11 CHANDOS STREET,
CAVENDISH SQUARE, W., 28, 6, '84.

DEAR MADAM — At last I am able to send you all the information that is probably now to be had here about M. Boudet.

The "Society for the Propagation of the Gospel," to which you refer, is now known as the "New England Company,

---

* NOTE.— Mr. Boudet was the minister of the church and public clerk, and the custodian of the records.

The records of the French settlement in Oxford, are not to be found with French records in Boston. They were doubtlessly sent to England by Mr. Boudet.

London," whose history I have the pleasure to send you by book post. The secretary of the company (Dr. Venning) has been kind enough to make a most careful search through the papers of the company, but only, I regret to say, with small result, as all the papers of the company between the years 1685 and 1696 inclusive, were destroyed by fire many years ago. The only notice he has found is in the minutes of a meeting held 17th Feb., 1698:

"A letter from Richard, Lord Bellemont, to the governor, being read, relating to a proposal of providing five itinerant ministers to preach the Gospel to the Five Nations of the Indians,

"Ordered, That Monsieur Bondet (recommended by Mr. John Ruick) be one of the said five ministers, and that the other four be sent from Harvard College in Cambridge, to be chosen by the Commissioners there. And that the said five ministers dwelling in and preaching to the inhabitants of those Five Nations have £60 per annum allowed them out of the stock of the Company in New England."

With many regrets that I am able to add so little to your knowledge of M. Bondet,

I remain, dear madam,
Very faithfully, yours,
P. EDWARD DOVE.

Mrs. MARY DE W. FREELAND.

LAMBETH PALACE, S. E.,
13 *March*, 1884.

MADAM — I am directed by the Archbishop of Canterbury to acknowledge the receipt of your letter of 20 Feb.

His Grace desires me to inform you that he believes the Society for the Propagation of the Gospel have no records prior to the establishment of the Society.

For information as to records, prior to that date, it might be advisable for you to apply to Professor Baird of New York, or to S. W. Kershaw, Esq., M. A., Librarian Lambeth Palace.

I am, madam,
    Yours faithfully,
      MONTAGUE FOWLER,
        Chaplain.

MRS. MARY DE W. FREELAND.

A LETTER FROM THE LORD BISHOP OF LONDON.

    LONDON HOUSE,
   ST. JAMES' SQUARE, S. W.,
     March 22, 1884.

MADAM — I have much pleasure in forwarding to you the enclosed extract from Bishop Compton's Registry.

You will observe that Daniel Bondet was ordained Deacon & Priest on the same day.

No less than 27 Frenchmen were ordained by the Bishop of London between Feb. 28, 1685, & August 26, 1686, and all of them were made Deacons and Priests at the same time.

This is not the case with the English Clergymen ordained at the same period. They remained for some time in the Diaconate. I infer therefore that the French Clergy were ordained for service abroad where they would not have an opportunity of obtaining Priest's Orders; and it is probable that they did not officiate in England.

NOTE:—   LAMBETH PALACE, S. E.,
            11 *June*, 1884.

DEAR MADAM — I am directed by the Archbishop of Canterbury to thank you for your letter of the 10th inst., and to send you the enclosed autograph.

   I am, dear madam,
     Yours faithfully,
      MANDEVILLE B. PHILLIPS,
         Asso. Secretary.

MRS. M. DE W. FREELAND.

You have I understand received from the Secretary of the Society for the Propagation of the Gospel all the information they have in their office respecting Mr. Boudet and I fear that there are no further records of him in England

      I am Madam
        Yr obedient Servant
         J. LONDON.

Mrs. MARY DE W. FREELAND.

DOCUMENTS RECEIVED FROM THE LORD BISHOP OF LONDON.

Extract from Bishop Compton's Register of the Names of Persons ordained by him; preserved in the registry of the See of London.

A Latin copy of the ordination of Rev. Daniel Boudet was enclosed in the Lord Bishop of London's letter and the copy certified by the Sub-Dean of St. Paul's Cathedral.

A translation.

  13 day of April 1686

On this day Daniel Boudet of France was admitted to holy orders as Deacon and Priest by the above written Lord Bishop.

The Lord Bishop above written is the Reverend in Christ, Father Henry, Bishop of London by divine authority.

        FULHAM PALACE,
         June 30, 1884.

Mrs. M. DE W. FREELAND:

The Bishop of London is very sorry that he cannot give Mrs. Freeland any information about records of the "Lords of Trade" or as to the office in which they are likely to be found. He has no doubt that the Sec. of the Soc. for Propagation of the Gospel, will give Mrs. Freeland any information he can if he be applied to but he has of course very little spare time.

"James Laborie in this particular most humbly supplicate your Excellency and the most Honorable Council to give him a peculiar order for to oblige the Indians to observe the Sabbath Day, many of the said Indians to whom the said Laborie hath often exhorted to piety, having declared to submit themselves to said Laborie's exhortations if he should bring an order with him from your Excelléncy, or from your honorable Lieutenant Governor, Mr. Stanton, or the most Honorable Council.

"Expecting these favors, we shall continue to pray God for the preservation of your Excellency, and the most Honorable Council, etc.

JAMES LABORISH."

This petition is indorsed "L re, written 1st Xbr 99 with a proclamacon for the observance of the Lord's Day inclosed."

MONSIEUR LABORIE TO THE EARL OF BELLEMONT.

"At NEW OXFORD, this 17th June, 1700.
"MY LORD :

"When I had the honor to write to your Excellency, I did not send you the certificate of our inhabitants with reference to Monsieur Bondet, for the reason that they were not all here. I have at length procured it, and send it to your Excellency. As to our Indians, I feel myself constrained to inform your Excellency that the four who came back, notwithstanding all the protestations which they made to me upon arriving, had

---

NOTE.— Same year " His Excellency also acquainted the board that by express from New Oxford that he had received a letter from Lieutenant Sabin of Woodstock," " concerning the Indians who had gone eastward."—Council Rec., 94.

Advised and consented that his Excellency issue forth his warrant to Mr. Treasurer, to pay forty shillings unto John Ingall, sent with an express from Oxford bringing the news."
February 7th, 1699.—Council Rec., 95.

no other object in returning than to induce those who had been faithful to depart with them. They have gained over the greater number, and to-day they leave for Penikook — twenty-five in all — men, women and children. I preached to them yesterday in their own tongue. From all they say, I infer that the priests are vigorously at work, and that they are hatching some scheme which they will bring to light so soon as they shall find a favorable occasion."

EARL OF BELLEMONT TO THE LORDS OF TRADE, LONDON (July 9, 1700).

"Mons. Labourie is a French minister placed at New Oxford by Mr. Stoughton, the Lieutenant-Governor, and myself, at a yearly stipend of £30, out of the corporation money; there are eight or ten French families there that have farms, and he preaches to them. * * *

"The Indians about the town of Woodstock and New Oxford, consisting of about forty families, have lately deserted their houses, and corn, and are gone to live with the Penicook Indians, which has much alarmed the English thereabouts, and some of the English have forsaken their houses and farms and removed to towns for better security. That the Jesuits have seduced these forty families is plain. * * * Mr. Sabin is so terrified at the Indians of Woodstock and New Oxford quitting their houses and corn, that he has thought fit to forsake his dwelling and is gone to live in a town. All the thinking people here believe the Eastern Indians will break out against the English in a little time."

THE COMMERCE OF OXFORD NEARLY TWO HUNDRED YEARS AGO.

In 1700, during the time of the return of the French refugees to the settlement of Oxford, "from time to time wagon

NOTE.— Pennacook was the name of an Indian settlement at the present site of Concord, N. H.

loads of dressed skins were sent down to Providence, to be shipped to Bernon (who was residing in Newport) for the supply of the French hatters and glovers in Boston and Newport," quite a contrast to transportation by railroad of the present time. "Several of the French Protestants in Boston were engaged in the manufacturing of hats. They were supplied with peltries for this purpose by Bernon, who received the dressed skins from his 'Chamoiserie' at Oxford, and forwarded them to Peter Signac, John Baudouin and others in Boston, as well as to John Julien, who pursued the same business in Newport.

"A cargo shipped in August, 1703, to his agent Samuel Baker, comprised otter, beaver, raccoon, deer and other skins, valued at forty-four pounds."

The dressing of chamois skins, and the making of gloves, were among the arts in which the Huguenots excelled.

"Hat making was among the most important manufactories taken into England by the refugees. In France, it had been almost entirely in the hands of the Protestants. They alone possessed the secret of the liquid composition which served to prepare rabbit, hare and beaver-skins; and they alone supplied the trade with fine Caudebec hats, in such demand in England and Holland. After the Revocation, most of them went to London, taking with them the secret of their art, which was lost to France for more than forty years.

"It was not until the middle of the eighteenth century, that a French hatter, after having long worked in London, stole the secret the refugees had carried away, took it back to his country, communicated to the Paris hatters and founded a large manufactory."*

A record from the French church in Boston, dated June 29,

---

* History of the French Protestant Refugees, from the Revocation of the Edict of Nantes to Our Own Days. Charles Weiss. Vol. I, book III, Chapter III.

1702, signed by Peter Chardon and René Grignon. The French Protestants of Boston, in a petition to Governor Bellemont, to the Council and Assembly of Representatives, then in session in Boston, for aid in support of the Gospel ministry among them.

(We) "have borne great charges in paying taxes for the poor of the country, and in maintaining their own poor of this town and those of New Oxford, who by occasion of the war withdrew themselves, and since that they have assisted many who returned to Oxford in order for their re-settlement." (They) "have recourse to this honorable Assembly, which God has established for the succour of the afflicted, especially the faithful that are strangers."

Gov. Dudley to (Boston, July 7th, 1702) Mr. Gabriel Bernon, in reply to his petition for aid in the protection of his property against the Indians. "Herewith you have a commission for captain of New Oxford. I desire you forthwith to repair thither and show your said commission, and take care that the people be armed, and take them in your own house, with a palisade, for the security of the inhabitants; and if they are at such a distance in your village that there should be need of another place to draw them together in case of danger, consider of another proper house, and write me, and you shall have orders therein.   "I am, your humble servant,

"J. DUDLEY."

The resettlement of French Protestants in Oxford, is named in the Council records. In the summer of 1703, soldiers were stationed here for the protection of the inhabitants from the Indians.

"An accompt of wages and subsistence of thirteen soldiers, whereof one a sergeant, posted at Oxford and Hassanamisco in

---

NOTE.—In 1702, the Indians were conspiring to attack the settlement. Lieut. Tobin of Woodstock reported to the Massachusetts Council, April 9, 1702: "That the Indians were plotting mischief, and that he had ordered a garrison to put in repair and a military watch kept."

the summer past, was laid before the board and there examined and stated the whole sum, with other incidental charges amounting to forty pounds, fifteen shillings, three and a half pence.
"Ordered paid Dec. 24th, 1703."
— Council Rec., 509.

In 1704 Bernon had transactions in business with people in New Oxford.

CHAPTER XV.

J. DUDLEY TO G. BERNON.

"BOSTON, 20*th May*, 1707.

"Sr: I am very unhappy in my affayres at Oxford, both with your Cooper & the negro Tom. I must desire you to take other care of your affayres than to improve such ill men that disquiet the place, that I have more trouble with them than with seven other towns. If you do not remove them yourself, I shall be obliged to send for the Negro & turn him out of the place, & I understand Cooper is so criminal that the law will dispose of him. I pray you to use your own there not to Destroy or Disturb the Governour or your best friend, who is, Sr., your humble servt.,   "J. DUDLEY.

"Send an honest man and he shall be welcome. I pray you to show what I write to Mr. Grignon."

"To Mr. GABRIEL BERNON, Newport, Road Iland."

Mr. Bernon soon makes an engagement with new tenants.

NOTE 1.—In 1704, James Laborie left Oxford, and was in October established over the French church in New York. A final abandonment of the settlement ensued, and no further record of its history is to be traced.

NOTE 2.—The accounts of the Chamoiserie show that Oxford continued to be occupied by the French until 1704.

AGREEMENT BETWEEN GABRIEL BERNON AND OLIVER AND NATHANAEL COLLER.

"Know all men by these presents that I Gabril Bernon hath bargind with and let vnto Oluer Coller and Nathanel Coller my howse and farme at new oxford Called the olde mill; with four Cowes and Calfes the which said farm and Cowes I have let for five years upon the conditions as foloweth —— that they brake up and monnure and plant with orchod two Acers and half of land with in the s^d Term of Fiue and also to spend the remain-part of their time to work upon the other lands; and all that is soed dow now to ly to English grass and at the end of fiue years for s^d oluer Coller and Nathanel Coller for them to resine up peceble posestion of the s^d hous farm and four Cowes and Calves and half the increes to the s^d Gabril Bernon or his heirs or asigns the s^d two Acers and half of land ly a boue the spring on the side of the hill; and for thare in Conrigment I haue let them one pare of oxen for one year, the which s^d oxen they must Deliuer to me at s^d term; and in case the oxen be lost they must make them good; Exsept by the enemy.

"to the performence of this our bargin we have heer unto set our hands in the presents of us ——
memerandom they have
ingaged to brak up half
one Acer of land evere
year and to pay the three
first yers six shilling p year
and two last years to
pay tweny shilling p   "The mark of X OLUER COLLER
year and we have   "The mark of — NATHANAEL COLLER
ualled the s^d four
Cows at tw pounds
    "JOSEPH TWICHELS
    "THOMAS ALLERTON"

G. BERNON TO GOV. DUDLEY.

PROVIDENCE, 1st *March*, 1710.

Translation.

"Mr. Dudley your son told me the last time I had the honour to see him, that it was your Excellency's design to re-establish New Oxford: as it also appears through the public news.

"I hope your Excellency will be so good as to take into consideration the fact that Mr. Hoogborn has done his utmost to ruin my interest in the said Oxford.

"He has caused Couper to abandon the old mill, and Thomas Allerton [to leave] my other house, threatening that he would hinder them from haying, and [declaring] that I had no power to settle them. When I made complant of this to him he told me that he would drive me from the place, myself.

"Samuel Hagburn was one of the thirty English settlers, and was the first named in the deed of Dudley, etc., to them. In 1726 an entry was made of an extract from his will, on the records of the Congregational Church, by which, although not a member of it, he bequeathed to it the sum of fifty pounds." For that I have been treated, after spending at the said Oxford more than fifteen hundred pistoles [and] the better part of my time during more than twenty years possession.

"Should it please your Excellency to examine the case you will find that I have chief had at heart the furtherance of your Excellencies wishes. I have been found singularly attached to your person, more than to all else that I have had in the world.

"It is notorious that the said Mr. Hoogborn, your brother, has caused the planks of my granary to be torn up; that he has conveyed them elsewhere, and that by his orders the oxen that I was reserving to be fattened have been put to work."

By this record, notwithstanding Dudley's censure of Cooper, he remained in occupancy of the farm called the "Old Mill," and that he and the Collers had been dispossessed by Hagburn.

Bernon thus relying upon his possession to ownership of the lands which were occupied by his tenants without conveyance by deed.

G. BERNON TO THE SON OF GOV. DUDLEY.

"SIR: "*October*, 1720.

"I would entreat you to assist me in petitioning his Excellency and the General Assembly, inasmuch as the inhabitants of New Oxford oppose my rights to lands.

"The Court and Government can confirm my title, and then I can dispose of what I have there, and pay my debts, and have wherewithal to help myself; and thereby ease my mind and body, which is now more than the Pope can do.

"The above said inhabitants oppress me as I can make it appear by Maj. Buor, who would have bought my plantation. The inhabitants told him not to do it;—that my title was nothing worth, that they also pretended that they would dispute my title with Mr. Dudley and Mr. Thompson. They also abused me in a very outrageous manner in Maj. Buor's presence; as he states in his certificate, which I make bold to send to you enclosed in this.

"Ephraim Town, John Elliott, and John Chamberlin, for whom I have advanced considerably to uphold my said plantation, will not pay me what they owe me. Besides, the loss of my servant, who was drowned, was fifty pounds loss to me. These men, and one Josiah Owen, my last tenant, hugger-mugger together to cheat me of a hundred pounds in cattle and movables that I had upon the place, so that I am not able to advance any more.

"I see myself about ruined by this oppression and malice. Sir—you are perfectly acquainted with the affairs at New Oxford, and I do not understand things as well as I would. Therefore I intreat of you, Sir, to help me. Your charity and generosity are (so to speak) interested in it.

"I am so hard driven by my dunning creditors — the masons and carpenters and others that I employed to build my house in Providence, that I know not what to do: and, besides my wife now lying in, six or seven children implore my compassion, which makes me implore that of Government, and yours, Sir, that my title may be confirmed, after a possession of 36 years, so that I may sell it. Within 30 years I have laid out on it £200, for which reason my family did slight me, as well as my best friends. I have always been protected by Mr. Dudley, your honored father, who always thought as I did, that I might sell it, and not be in any wise molested. But I don't know whether it won't be a mistake. Indeed, one cannot always forsee the events of things, often hid from the wisest. But this I see, — the Evil one still reigns, and God suffers it, to try his children.

"My great desire is to keep myself in the fear of God, and to love my neighbor, and to seek lawful means to maintain my family. My great age of nearly eighty years does not dispense me of this duty. I address myself to you with all humility to assist me, that I may be assisted by the Governor. Such a testimony of your love and favor will rescue me, to terminate my days in America, or to return once again to Europe. Surely my staying or going depends upon the action of the Assembly. But be it as it will, Sir, as an honest, well-minded man ought, I pray for the government, and all the faithful in Christ.   "GABRIEL BERNON.
"From my chambers at Mr. Harper's,
   "adjoining unto Judge Sewalls, Oct. 1720."

"In Sept., 1714, it was voted that 'the committy shall take care to notify Mr. Gabriel Bernon to come and join us in settling division lines between us and him.'* Again in Oct., 1718, a similar vote was taken." †

---

* Prop. Rec. 3.   † Ibid. 27.

"But there was a good reason why this matter was not attended to by Bernon. The complicated nature of the case is shown in his deed from Dudley and company. Du Tuffeau, at the beginning of the settlement had 'elected' seven hundred and fifty acres, which were deeded to him and Bernon jointly. Afterward, to Bernon, seventeen hundred and fifty acres were granted, which were deeded to him in his own right, and also to Bondet were deeded two hundred acres.* These grants were all embraced in one plat and conveyed as a whole. We have no intimation of a mutual division, and without this, no power but a court could give to either of the grantees an indisputable right to a single acre which should be set off and located.

"Another point which is shown in the deed, added to the complications, namely; that a very valuable portion of the land taken up and occupied by Du Tuffeau and Bernon, jointly, was not included in the conveyance. This was a long triangular tract of nearly five hundred acres, lying between Bernon's land, as deeded, and the land of the village proprietors. Its westerly line ran over the high land between the site of the fort and Bondet hill, and continuing in a course north, thirteen degrees east, crossed the present Sutton road at the fork, about three-fourths of a mile easterly of Main street. This line is called in the town records, 'Bernon's line,' and has been marked on the western boundary of the estate now known as the Ebenezer Rich farm, by permanent division fences to the present day.

"On this tract were the fort and the grounds around it, where Bernon had expended considerable money, and the upper mill site. It also enclosed some of the best farming lands within the limits of the town. Of course Bernon was anxious to retain it, but he could plead possession only, as ground of owner-

---
* There is no proof that Bondet ever had possession of this grant or received any benefit from it.

ship. In conveying his property he followed the deed he had received from Dudley and company, and did not include the disputed tract.

"Du Tuffeau having died before the autumn of 1720, Bernon applied to the probate court of Suffolk county for a letter of administration on his estate, as chief creditor. This was granted Dec. 5th, and he was enabled in due course of law thereby to take possession of the twenty-five hundred acres as sole owner. Negotiations with Thomas Mayo, Samuel Davis and William Weld, all of Roxbury, soon followed, and a sale of the tract was made to them early in the spring of 1721, for twelve hundred pounds, current money of New England.*

"On March 27th, 1721, at a meeting of the village proprietors to hear what the 'Gentlemen which signifie that they have bought Mr. Bernon's farm, have to be communicated to the inhabitants and proprietors of Oxford village,' and to 'act as shall be thought best to come at their own rights:'—

"'Voted and chose Dea. John Town, Benoni Twichel, and

---

* The quantity of land sold was twenty-five hundred acres, and the description in the deed is as follows: "Beginning at a walnut tree marked S. D., standing at the southwest corner of Manchaug, and thence running west, fifteen degrees south, three hundred and fifty-two perches, from thence to be set off by a line to be drawn parallel to the utmost easterly line bounds of the said Oxford village and township, as far as will complete the full quantity of twenty-eight hundred and seventy-two acres."

Of this were reserved one hundred and seventy-two acres of meadow in one piece which Dudley gave to the village. But the two hundred acres for Bondet's farm are not mentioned. A provision in it required the annual payment of forty shillings quit-rent to Dudley, etc. This deed was dated March 16th, 1720-1, and is recorded in Suf. Co. Rec., xxxv, 119.

It is said that Weld, coming to see the premises in the spring after the snow had gone, was dissatisfied, and soon after sold his share to Davis.

"Thomas Mayo never came to Oxford, but his son John did, and Samuel Davis came in 1728 or 9, probably the latter."

Isaac Learned' to act as a committee to establish the line between the said farm and the village, and instructed them to 'improve' John Chandler, Esq., as surveyor.

"The report of this committee, dated April 11th, 1721, was accepted at a meeting of the proprietors, Sept. 21st, 1721. In accordance with its terms, a portion of land at the north end of the Bernon tract was released to the village, and the triangular plat which had been in dispute was yielded to the purchasers.

"John Mayo, son of Thomas, made a home on the height near the fort, and died there, and his descendants continued to occupy the premises for many years. Davis chose for his dwelling, a spot nearly half a mile northerly from the fort, on the farm now known as the Nathaniel Davis place, where he died.*

"The facts in connection with the delivery of the deed to Bernon are remarkable. It will be remembered that it was drawn May 24th, 1688, probably upon the completion of the contract to settle the thirty families. There was in it, however, a consideration which had not been rendered, namely, the building of a grist mill, for which reason it was not at once delivered. A little less than two years passed, the mill was built, and Bernon had Church's receipt for the same. Two days after the date of this receipt, we find two of the grantors acknowledging the deed before a magistrate — but still it was not delivered. Years passed; the first colony flourished a while and became extinct—the second colony began and continued five years and was abandoned—for nine years afterward the plantation lay waste. Then the thirty English families came in and laid the foundations of a permanent settlement. Bernon gave up his right in the mills, and gave the valuable stones and irons for the benefit of the new colony. At last, after his hopes and

---

* Persons living in Oxford well recollected the leaden sash and the small diamond panes of glass of the old windows of this ancient house of Samuel Davis, which many years ago gave place to more modern ones.

expectations had been again and again disappointed, and he had grown old, and become unable for lack of means to assist the settlement further, on Feb. 5th, 1716, nearly twenty-eight years after the deed was written, it was acknowledged by Dudley, and passed over to him."

"Six days afterward, Feb. 11th, 1716, he conveyed the property for a thousand pounds to James Bowdoin,* who held it until March 16th, 1720-1, when he re-conveyed it to Bernon,† who the same day executed the deed to Mayo, Davis and Weld."
* Suf. Rec. xxxi, 79.
† "This conveyance was made by returning the deed he had received, with an indorsement upon it in legal form, signed, sealed, and witnessed by John Mayo, Samuel Tyler, Jr., and acknowledged before John Chandler, Justice of Peace." — Ibid.

DEED, DUDLEY, ETC., TO BERNON.

"This indenture made the 24th day of May A. D. 1688 * * * between Joseph Dudley of Roxbury, William Stoughton of Dorchester * * * Esqs. Robert Thompson of London * * * Merchant, Daniel Cox of London aforesaid, Doctor in Physick, and John Blackwell of Boston * * * Esq. on the one part and Gabriel Bernon of Boston aforesaid, Merchant on the other part — Witnesseth

"Whereas Isaac Barton, [Bertrand,] Gentleman, hath heretofore had the allowance [of said parties of the first part] to elect and make choice of 500 acres of land * * * within * * * the southeast angle of [a tract of land called New Oxford village] to and for the use of him the said Barton and the said Gabriel Bernon, * * * and whereas since the electing of the said 500 acres, he [Betrand] hath proposed that he may have 250 acres more of said land * * * to the use aforesaid; and he the said Gabriel Bernon that he may have 1750 acres more of the said lands, * * * adjoining to the said 500 acres to and for the the use of said Gabriel Bernon, his heirs and assigns—

"Now these presents witness that [the above named parties of the first part] as well for and in consideration that the said Gabriel Bernon hath undertaken and by these presents doth undertake and engage within twelve months after the day of the date of these presents at his own proper cost and charges to erect build and maintain a Corn or Grist Mill in some convenient and fitting place within the said

Deed of Gov. Dudley to Bernon.

By another paper in the MS. Collection, it appears that Mr. Bernon petitioned the King in council for certain privileges, which indicate the objects to which the enterprise of this adventurer was directed. It is entitled, "the humble Petition of Gabriel Bernon of Boston in New England." It states:

town of Oxford for the use of the inhabitants of said town and village [unto which mill * * * said inhabitants shall be obliged] at all times forever hereafter to make their suit as also for and in consideration of the sum of 5 shillings * * * paid by said Bernon * * * and the rents and convenants hereafter mentioned * * * [the parties of the first part] do grant bargain sell and confirm to the said Isaac Barton and Gabriel Bernon * * * all that tract * * * of 500 acres * * * elected as aforesaid by said Isaac Barton, to hold to them the said Isaac Barton and Gabriel Bernon * * * and all that and those 250 acres more desired by said * * * Barton as aforesaid, and 1750 acres more desired by the said Gabriel Bernon adjoining to the said 500 acres * * * within the southeast angle of Oxford village * * * as followeth * * *

"Beginning at a walnut tree marked (S. D.) standing at the west angle of Manchaug — and thence running W. 15° S. 352 perches, and from thence to be set off by a line to be drawn parallel to the utmost easterly line and bounds of the said Oxford village * * * as far as will complete the full quantity of 2872 acres * * * so that if the said line shall *not* extend unto and include and take in the utmost westerly part of the said 500 arces * * * said Barton elected for himself and the said Gabriel Bernon * * * the said 500 acres shall nevertheless be included * * * within the * * * 2872 acres aforementioned * * * the whole quantity of 2872 acres shall be set out accordingly whereof the forementioned 500 acres and 250 acres more desired by the said Isaac Barton to be jointly held and enjoyed by them the said Isaac Barton and Gabriel Beruon * * * also 1750 acres more thereof to be held and enjoyed by him the said Gabriel Bernon [his heirs and assigns for their use and behoof] and 200 acres more thereof to the use of Daniel Bondet, his heirs and assigns forever.

"Excepting and reserving to [said parties or the first part] 172 acres of meadow land * * * in one entire parcel and adjoining unto the lands of Manchaug aforesaid [in such place as they may choose.]

"And providing [the parties of the first part or any two or more of

"That being informed of your majesty's pleasure, particularly in encouraging the manufactory of Rosin, Pitch, Tarr, Turpentine, etc., in New England, in which manufactory your Petitioner has spent seven years time and labor and considerable sums of money and has attained to such knowledge and perfection, as that the said comodities made and sent over by him have beene here approved of and bought for your Majesty's stores; your Petitioner's seal and affection to your Majesty encouraged him to leave his habitation and affairs (being a merchant) and also his family to make a voyage to England on purpose humbly to propose to your Majesty in how great a measure and cheap price the said Navall stores may be made

---

them resident in New England may lay out over such lands] such common paths or ways * * * as they shall judge necessary or commodious for the said [township or village.] Yielding and paying therefor yearly and every year on the 24th of March at or in the Town house of Boston aforesaid, unto [said parties of the first part] or to their certain attorney deputy or agent by them * * * appointed to receive the same, the annual rent of 40 shillings current money of New England. * * * And the said Gabriel Bernon for himself his heirs and assigns * * * doth convenant, grant and agree with [the parties of the first part] that he [or his heirs or assigns] will well and truly pay or cause to be paid to the said [parties of the first part] the said yearly rent [as aforesaid] and that in case of non-payment thereof or any part thereof [it shall be lawful for the parties of the first part to] enter said premises and distrain and the distresses there found from time to time to lead carry away sell or dispose at such rates as they can get for the same * * * and with the proceeds imburse and satisfy themselves [for all arrearages and charges] rendering the overplus (if any be) to him the said Gabriel Bernon * * *

"And that in case of his the said Isaac Barton and Gabriel Bernon deserting or relinquishing the said lands [or there shall not be found on said premises sufficient goods] for satisfying within any twelve months after the same shall grow due, this present grant and all the matters and things therein contained shall thenceforth cease, determine, and be utterly null and void, and the lands * * * shall revert * * * unto [the said parties of the first part] and shall and may lawfully be by

and brought into any of your Majesty's kingdomes to the great promotion and advantage of the Trade and Commerce of your Majesty's subjects of New England, all which is most evident by the annexed paper."

He prays his Majesty to take the premises into consideration, and to grant him his royal patent or order for providing and furnishing his Majesty's fleet with the said stores under the conditions his Majesty in his royal wisdom should think fit, or otherwise to except him out of any patent to be granted for the said manufactory, that he, may have liberty to go on and continue in the said manufactory in any part of New England."

This paper is indorsed: "Peticon of Gabriel Bernon."

them entered upon, possessed and enjoyed as in their former estate * * *

"[The parties of the first part] convenant and agree with said Isaac Bartron and Gabriel Bernon their heirs and assigns [that they the said Bartron and Bernon performing the afore named acts faithfully as specified, may] have hold and enjoy the premises hereby granted against [said parties of the first part] or any other person or persons lawfully claiming or to claim the same or any part thereof * * * by, from or under them or any of them.

"In witness whereof the said Joseph Dudley, William Stoughton, Robert Thompson, Daniel Cox and John Blackwell have hereunto set their hands and seals the day and year first above written. JOSEPH DUDLEY and a seal, WILLIAM STOUGHTON and a seal, JOHN BLACKWELL and a seal. Feb 6th 1690 William Stoughton Esq. and John Blackwell, Esq. acknowledge this instrument to be their voluntary act and deed.

"Before SAM^l. SEWALL *Ass'it*

"Signed sealed and delivered in presence of us by Joseph Dudley, William Stoughton and John Blackwell, Daniel Allen, Richard Wilkins, Jno. Herbert Howard, Suffolk etc., Boston 5th of February 1716.

"The Hon. Joseph Dudley Esq., personally appeared before me the Subscriber one of his Majesty's justices of the Peace in Said County, and did acknowledge this Instrument to be his free act and deed.

"SAMUEL LYNDE—*February* 5th 1716.

"Received and accordingly entered and examined.

"John Ballantyne Regr."
Suffolk Co. Rec. XXX, 268.

"Papiers qui regarde deux voyages de Londre pour les affaires a fabriquer des Resme.
Examne le premier Octobre 1719."

By a statement of G. Bernon, intended to prove his claim upon the plantation, it appears that he considered "the Plantation of New Oxford" indebted to him for 2,500 acres of land, besides the amount of expenses laid out by him upon the place. This claim appears to have been made about the year 1717, or 1720; for on his account there is a charge of interest "for above 30 years." The statement alleges that 500 acres of the plantation were "granted by their excellencys Mr. Dudley and Mr. Stoughton to Isaac Bertrand Du Tuffeau and Gabriel Bernon in the year 1687," and that 250 acres were "granted since, making in all 750 aikers;" and that "their excellencys Mr. Dudley and Mr. Stoughton did grant to the said Mr. Bernon for his own use alone 1750 aikers more, which makes in all 2500 aikers, which Mr. Bernon justly claims, upon which he hath built a corn miln, a wash leathern miln and a saw miln, and laid out some other considerable expenses to improve the town of New Oxford, as he has made appear by the testimonys of several worthy gentlemen whose names he has hitherto subjoined."

By a plan of Mr. Gabriel Bernon's land in Oxford, taken in 1717, it appears, that it measured 2,672 acres, "exclusive of Mr. Daniel Bondet's of 200 acres, and out of said 2672 acres must come out 172 acres of meadow in one entire piece, which Mr. Dudley and Compa. give to the village." The tract of land "within this Plan" was estimated by the selectmen of Oxford "to be worth one thousand pound;" and this valuation was certified by them on the plan, 11 January 1716–17. Signed Richard Moore, Benoni Twitchel, Isaac Larned. Another certificate was given on the same paper by the selectmen of Mendon, concerning the justness of the above valuation, adding, "that we know nothing but the said Bernon hath been in the quiet possession of said land for or nere thirty years." Signed Thomas Sanford, Robert Evans, Jacob Aldrich.

November, 1720, Bernon made application for reimbursement of money expended upon the French settlement.

"THE HONORABLE PETITION OF GABRIEL BERNON OF NEW OXFORD, IN NEW ENGLAND.

"To his excellency Samuel Shute, and to his Majesty's council, and house of representatives in General Court assembled, Gabriel Bernon, one of the most ancient families in Rochelle, in France, begs of your excellency and honor graciously to assist him in his great necessity, and that your excellency and honors would be pleased to take into your wise consideration; that your petitioner, upon the breach of the edit of Nantes, and the persecution of France, fled to London; upon his arrival ——— Tefferau, Esq., treasurer of the Protestant Churches of France presented your petitioner to the honorable, the Society for the propogating of the Gospel among the Indians in New England; of which Mr. Thompson, the Governor, offered to instal him in the said Society, and offered him land in the government of the Massachusetts Bay, whereupon one Isaac Bertrand du Tuffeau desired your excellency's and honors petition 'to assist him, the said Bertrand du Tuffeau, to come over to New England, to settle a plantation for their refuge;' which he did, by advancing unto the said Tuffeau the sum of two hundred pounds sterling; and since three hundred pounds eight shillings and ten pence; which with the exchange and interest from that time would amount to above one thousand pounds. The said Isaac du Tuffeau being arrived at Boston, with letters of credit from Major Thompson and your humble petitioner, delivered them to his late excellency Joseph Dudley, Esq., and the honorable William Stoughton, Esq., deceased, who did grant to the said Du Tuffeau seven hundred and fifty acres of land for the said petitioner at New Oxford, when he laid out or spent the above said money. Further more, the said Du Tuffeau did allure your excellency's and honor's petitioner, by exciting of him by letters to come to Boston, as he can show. The said Du Tuffeau's 'being (through poverty) forced to abandon the said plantation, sold his cattle and other moveables for his own particular use, and went to London, and there died in a hospital.' Your excellency's and honor's petitioner being excited by letters of the said Tuffeau's shipped himself, his family, and servants, with some other

To prove his claims on the plantation of New Oxford Bernon gives the testimonies of several worthy gentlemen whose names he has hitherto subjoined:

The four elders of the French Church Mousset ⎫ Rawling ⎬ Daillie minis- Charden ⎪ tre of the Babut ⎭ French Church.	William Fox Benj. Faneuil P. Jermon Jacques Montier Paix Cazaneau Abraham Sauvages Jacques Depan Jean Beaudoin René Grignon Phellipe Emgerland	Governor Usher William Stoughton Increase Mather mtre Charles Morton mtre Jer. Dummer Nehemiah Walter minr. John Butcher Laurence Hammond

By the Inhabitants of New Oxford

Montel	Ober Jermon
J. Dupen	Jean Maillet
Capt. Jermon	Andre Segourne
Peter Cante	Jean Milleton
Bercau Caćini	Peter Canton
Elie Dupen	&c,

" The Widow Leveufe Jean Johnson of which her husband and three children was kil and murder by the Ingen."

families, as can be made to appear; and paid to Captain Fayle, and Captain Ware, passage for above forty persons. Your excellency's and honor's petitioner being arrived at Boston, presented letters from Major Thompson, afore mentioned to the above said Dudley and Stoughton, Esqrs. who were pleased (besides the seven hundred and fifty acres that were granted to Bertrand du Tuffeau and your humble petitioner,) to grant to your petitioner one thousand seven hundred and fifty acres of land more; and for a more authentick security, his late Excellency and Honor was pleased to accompany me to New Oxford, to put me into possession of the said two thousand five hundred acres of land, which I have peacefully enjoyed far better than these thirty years last past, having spent above two thousand pounds to defend the same from the Indians, who at divers times have ruined the said Plantations,˙ and have murdered men, women, and children.

" Your excellency's and honor's petitioner does now most humbly represent, that the inhabitants of New Oxford, do now dispute my right and title in order to hinder me from the sale of the said plantations, which would put me to the utmost extremity, being now near eighty years of age, and having several children by my first wife, and so seeing children

"Records from the English Settlement May 13th 1713.

"Surveyed for Joseph Chamberlin sen^r Round the great house 40 acres being a home lott in Oxford; and four acres and one Rood in it being allowed for a highway going through * * * surveyed by John Chandler Jun. approved and established by order of the original proprietors provided he pay for the bettering of his lott by former Improvement and building.

"By John Chandler who made such an agreement at the beginning." — *Village Rec.* 13.

Joseph Chamberlin's house lot in the English settlement of Oxford, was on the French Plantation of Rev. Daniel Bondet and subsequently in the English settlement it came into the possession of the descendants of Thomas Mayo.

Joseph Chamberlin's choice of a house lot is the first on record, being by estimation the most valuable.*

"Oxford the 4 of february 1714 Joseph Chambbarline siner

---

of my children—I have since married an English women, by whom also I have several children, all which have dependance (under God) for a subsistence on me, after I have spent more than ten thousand pounds towards the benefit of the country; in building ships, making nails, and promoting the making of stuffs, hats, and rosin etc.

"Your petitioner, therefore, doth most humbly beg your excellency and honor's compassion and that you would graciously be pleased to grant me such titles as may confirm to me and mine the said two thousand five hundred acres of land without any misunderstanding, clear and free from any molestation either from the inhabitants of the said New Oxford, or any pretensions of the above said Bertrand du Tuffeau, so that I and mine may either dispose of, or peaceably and quietly live upon, the said plantation of New Oxford; and your petitioner shall ever pray for, and devote himself to your government, beging leave to assure you, that he is, may it please your Excellency's and Honor's your most Dutiful and Obedient Servant. "GABRIEL BERNON."

*The Oxford records state that in 1713, when the English settlement was commenced, there were French orchards and a house once belonging to the Huguenots, which were regarded by the English as improvements

House loute bein uponn boundet hel* so caled, bounded on the nourest with a stake and a hape of stons rouncing a hundred and twenty rodes soourly on burnnnn line† to a black oke running westerly sixty rods to a stack and a hepe of stones then ronning nurarly on hundred rods to a stack an Hepe stones foust named * * * provided he pays as tow men shal judge is beater than other lots in sd village." Ibid.†.

"The highway which passed through this plantation was Woodstock 'great trail' which passed from Johnson [Jansen] plain north easterly over Bondet hill near the 'great house' which stood on its eastern slope."

A large hollow in the earth now marks the site of the "great house" which was once the home of Rev. Daniel Bondet.

Mr. John Mayo who was a native of Oxford, and lived near the place said it was used as a tavern in the second French settlement or early in the English town history.

In by-gone time the old Boston road or old Connecticut road was the thoroughfare in a quiet way from Boston to the Connecticut towns.

It entered the town from what was afterward the Sutton road, passing near the mills of Ebenezer D. Rich, and from this point entering the road which afterward passed the farm house of Samuel Davis, and continued on until the foot of the French

---

to the plantations, for which those who came into possession of them were required to make a suitable compensation to the village corporation.

"Jan. 25th 1714 Voted that Ebbenezar Humphry should have the orchard joining to the South west corner of his home lot making allowance to the Town in money to full of what tow men shall judge it to be worth."—*Oxford Records*, p. 69.

There are vestiges of this Huguenot orchard still remaining; some very ancient trees with hollow trunks are said to have been standing in the English settlement.

* Rev. Daniel Bondet's Hill (plantation.)
† Gabriel Bernon's boundary line.

fort hill was reached, and then, when near the house of late John Mayo in the first English settlement, designated as near the site of a French house, about one-half mile distant from the French church and churchyard, here the road entered a broad Indian path known as the "Woodstock trail," passing near the residence of the late John Hurd and entering the highway near the late Peter Shumway's residence, and continued to Woodstock. The present highway from these points is nearly on the paths of the old Connecticut road and Woodstock trail.

"It was voted * * * in Nov. 30, 1714 that the committy shall begin to lay out meddow att East End of the great meddow, from thence to the meddow on Elliat's mill brook, from thence to the croth of the Reveir so down strame the Reveir; to the line from thence to bundits meddow." [Bondet's meadow.]

REMAINS OF THE FRENCH FORT.

Dr. Holmes writes: "My first visit to Fort Hill in Oxford was 20th April, 1819.

"Mr. Mayo, who owns the farm on which the fort stands, believes that his grandfather purchased it of one of the French families; and Mr. Sigourny, of Oxford, writes it was bought of his ancestor, Andrew Sigourny.*

"I measured the fort by paces, and found it 25 paces by 35 within the fort; on the outside I discovered signs of a well, and, on inquiry, was informed that a well had recently been filled up there.

"On a second visit to the fort, in September of the same year, 1819, I was accompanied, and aided in my researches,

---

*The ancestor of Mr. Mayo purchased the estate of Gabriel Bernon, the president of the French settlement.

The ancestor of Capt. Sigourny had taken this plantation as his estate and resided at the fort while in the settlement, as the keeper of the French garrison—Bernon—could not give a deed to Sigourny, as he had not received a conveyance of the land by a deed at that time.

by the Rev. Mr. Brazer, then a professor in our University, who went over from Worcester, and met me by agreement in Oxford. We traced the lines of the bastions of the fort.

"We next went in search of the Johnson place, memorable for the Indian massacre in 1696. Mr. Peter Shumway, a very aged man, of French descent, who lives about thirty rods distant from it, showed us the spot. It is at a considerable distance from the village, on the north side of the road to Dudley,* and is now overgrown with trees. We carefully explored it, but found no relics.

"The last year (1825) I called at Mr. Shumway's. He told me that he was in his ninety-first year; that his great grandfather was from France; and that the plain on which he lives is called 'Johnson's Plain.'

FRENCH CHURCH-YARD.

"While Mr. Brazer was prosecuting our inquiries concerning a second fort and a church that had been mentioned to me by Mrs. Butler, he received a letter (1819) from Mr. Andrew Sigourny, informing that Captain Humphrey, of Oxford, says his parents told him there was a fort on the land upon which he now lives, and also a French meeting-house, and a burying-ground, with a number of graves; that he had seen the stones that were laid on the top of them, as they lay turf, and that one of the graves was much larger than any of the others; that they were east and west, but this, north and south; and that the Frenchman who lived in this place, named Bourdine, had been dead but a few years."†

"In May, 1825, I visited Captain Ebenezer Humphrey, and

---

* The north side of the "old road" to Dudley, which passed Mr. Shumway's residence.

† The flat stones were placed on the ground to preserve them from the molestations of wild beasts. The small fort and orchard were north of the church.

obtained from him satisfactory information concerning the plan of this second fort, and the meeting-house, and the burying-ground.

"Captain Humphrey was in his eighty-fourth year. He told me that his grandfather was from England, and that his father was from Woodstock, and came to Oxford to keep garrison (in the second French settlement). He himself now lives where his father lived, about half a mile south-east from Oxford village. His house is near a mill, standing upon a small stream that runs on the left near the great road leading to Norwich.

"About fifty or sixty rods from his house he showed me the spot where the fort stood, *and near it the lot* upon which were the meeting-house and burying-ground. No remains of either were visible. He pointed to an excavation of the earth, where, he said, was a well, which had been filled up. It was at the place of the fort, and had been, probably, within it.

"In the lot there were apple trees, which, he told me, he heard his father say, 'The French set out.'*

"The field was under fine cultivation, but I could not forbear to express my regret that the memorial of the dead had not been preserved.

"He said an older brother of his had ploughed up the field, and it was in this state when it came into his possession. He told me that one of his oldest sisters said she remembered the old horseblock that stood near the French meeting-house.

"He said he had seen the blood on the stones of the Johnson (Jansen) house; and that Mrs. Johnson on the night of the massacre went to Woodstock.

"Bourdille †(so he pronounced it) lived near the brook which

---

* The remains of the apple trees were visible in 1854 on the fort lot.

His father must have been a competent witness, for he was seventy years old when he told him this, and he himself was then twenty years of age.

† The same as Bourdillon.

runs by his house. The land of Captain Humphrey, upon which were a French fort, church and burying-ground, lies near the foot of Mayo's hill, on the summit of which stood the great fort, whose remains are still to be seen."*

It was stated by the late Capt. Andrew Sigourny that Mrs. Andrew Sigourny, Sr., who came from France, was buried in this church-yard, as was Mr. Jansen and his three children. Capt. Humphrey stated that he recollected twenty graves in the French burying-ground.

Mr. Ebenezer Humphrey of Oxford, a grandson of late Captain Humphrey, and a resident proprietor of the landed estate of Captain Humphrey, in 1890 states that his grandfather informed his father " that the French church was on the north side of the extremely small church-yard," and to enter the church the narrow avenue of access passed through the church-yard as in European countries.

The locality of the church-yard is still pointed out by Ebenezer Humphrey. Mrs. Adaline D. E. Moffat, a lineal descendant of Captain Humphrey (a grand-daughter), is the only person now living to whom Captain Humphrey pointed out the grave of Jean Jansen as the one placed north and south in the French burying place. In the English settlement it was designated as the "giant's grave," his three children being placed at the foot of his grave, and is so designated at the present time.

A few years since there was an old road that passed nearer to the French church-yard than the present road as it now

---

*Dr. Holmes writes of this interesting place: " We feel reluctant to take leave without some token of remembrance, beside the mere recital of facts, some of which are dry in detail, while many others are but remotely associated with it.

" Were any monumental stone to be found here, other memorials were less necessary. Were the cypress, or the weeping willow, growing here, nothing might seem wanting to perpetuate the memory of the dead."

passes to the fort. This old road entered the land of Ebenezer Humphrey in the lowlands, not far from a large oak tree, now standing (1890). It can be easily pointed out by the proprietor. This road was closed several years since as not required for travel. The old road is thus described : " A way'laid out from the four rod way to beniemanne lands home lot, begining att a wihite oake tree on the lowlands on ye Southwardly Side of the frinch burying place, from thence marked on the North sid to nelands home lot ; said way is tow rods wide february the sixt on 1713-4."— *Village Record.*

There is no authentic description of the French church and church-yard in "new oxford " excepting the one given by Captain Humphrey to Rev. Abiel Holmes, D. D., and also the locality of the church with its church-yard as pointed out by Captain Humphrey to his descendants. "The large stones said to have been a part of the foundation of the building as seen within the memory of persons now living is erroneous, the stones having been excavated by the Humphrey family." The church and church-yard lot of land can still be traced by the division wall or stone foundation of a fence separating it from the small fort lot containing an orchard and well as placed by Arthur Humphrey for cultivation, which fact Dr. Holmes so much regretted in his interview with Captain Humphrey.

The landed estate belonging to the late Captain Humphrey has remained in the family since the English settlement of the town in 1713, his father being the original proprietor and is now owned and occupied by Ebenezer Humphrey, the fourth in descent from the first of the name.*

In confirmation of Benjamin Kneeland's first lot of land

---

* Ebenezer Humphrey, a lineal descendant of Captain Humphrey, and the present owner of this estate, which has been in the possession of his ancestors since 1713, induced by an antiquarian interest, opened one of the graves, as plainly indicated by the dimensions, but found only the earth, which gave indications of what had been once a grave.

taken in Oxford, and the old road leading to his homestead, a deed given by Marvin Moore to Ebenezer Humphrey, in 1796, contains the following item :

"One tract of land in Oxford containing by estimation four acres be it more or less laid out southward from the house lot Benjamin Nealand (Kneeland) first took up in Oxford at a place called the stony runs it being in low of meadow in said lot bounding southwardly on a four rod high-way going estward from Ebenezer Humphreys house to Thomas Hunkins* bounded part on said Humphrey land west and Northwardly and estwardly on said Hunkins land however else bounded."†

At the French fort in Oxford there was a bridle-path winding down through the French orchard to the church and mills, and entering on to the Woodstock trail and the trading-house, or, as they were then styled, "the trucking-house," and to the dwellings of other refugees in the valley within view of the fort. There are still to be seen traces of bridle-paths and cart-ways which have long since gone into disuse.

Many old paths abandoned, of which only the faintest tradition and slightest trace remain of those silent highways.

The natives had no roads; they had trails or paths to suit their convenience; they were quite well defined when the English colony came to this section of country. There were tracks through the forest from one Indian settlement to another, from the seacoast to the Connecticut valley. In 1630 the Wabquasset Indians had visited Boston, passing over the Woodstock trail.

The roads in those days were only bridle-paths, or, as they were called, " bridle-roads, " through the forest, unfenced and ungraded, and were indicated by marked or hewn trees and stones. The land-holders whose land bounded on these highways

---

* The Stony run remains with its boundary wall the same as anciently at the present time.

† Known as once the Harwood farm.

or through whose land these rude highways passed, were allowed to maintain bars or huge gates across them to prevent their cattle from straying, as there was a great scarcity of fences.

There were formerly gates to pass through leading to the residence of the late John Mayo at the French fort.

THE NAMES OF HUGUENOT FAMILIES WHO MADE A SETTLEMENT AT NEW OXFORD.

Benjamin Faneuil.
Jean Boudoin.
—— Montel.
I. Dupeux.
Capt. Jermon [Germain].
{ Charles [Germain].
{ Ober Germon [Germain].
{ Pierre Jermon [Germain].
Francois Bureau, l'ainé.
Elie Dupeux.
Jean Martin.
André Sigournais, Sr.
André Sigournais, Jr.
{ Jean Mallet, anc.
{ [amien] [Elder] in the French church.
Peter Canton.

M. Alard.
M. Bourdille [Bourdillon].
René Grignon.
Jean Jansen.
Capt. de Paix Cazeneau.
Isaac Bertrand Du Tuffeau.
Rev. Jaques [James] Laboric.*
Rev. Daniel Bondet.
Jean Machet.
Elie Boudinot.
Daniel Johonnot.
Jean Papineaux.
Daniel Allen.
Gabriel Du Pont.
Jacques Du Pont.

---

*Jacques Laboric of Cardaillac, Province of Guyenne, completed the study of theology in the Academy of Geneva March 12, 1688 (Livre du Rectuer).

He was ordained in Zurich Oct. 30, 1688, and went to England; he arrived at the time of King William's coronation; he obtained a license from the Bishop of London, for teaching grammar and catechising in the parish of Stepney. He officiated in several of the French churches of London for nine or ten years, and then, in 1698, came to America.

After a residence for some time in the French settlement in New Oxford as a clergyman over the French church, and engaged as a missionary among the savages in the vicinity, he went to New York, and was the minister of the French Reformed church in that city for two years, Oct. 15, 1704, to August 25, 1706. After this he engaged in the practice of

Elie Boudinot was a wealthy French merchant of Marans, in France, known in his own country as Seigneur de Cressy. His name and title are found written on the fly leaf of a book in the possession of one of his descendants.

Gabriel Bernon, President of the settlement; Isaac Bertrand Du Tuffeau was the Magistrate of the French settlement of New Oxford, being appointed by the General Court on the twenty-first day of June, 1689, to be " Commissioner for the Towne of New Oxford to have Authority for Tryall of small Causes not exceeding forty shillings, and to act in all other matters as any other Assistant may doe, as the Lawes of this Colony direct."

Du Tuffeau was from Poitiers, the principal town in the province of Poitou.

When in Oxford he was married to Demoiselle Rochefoucauld, a lady descended from one of the most noble families in France.

CHAPTER XVI.

FRENCH GARDENS.

There are French gardens, vineyards and orchards of which we have descriptions that carry us far back to those days of the Huguenots leaving France.

"The Huguenots were acknowledged to be the best agriculturists, wine growers, merchants and manufacturers in France.

---

medicine and surgery, and about the year 1716 settled in Fairfield county, Connecticut, as a physician, occasionally assisting the Church of England missionary; he married Jeanne de Ressignier, in a second marriage Abigail Blacklach, August 29, 1716, and died about 1731, leaving two sons, James and John, both of whom became physicians.

NOTE.— Bernon resided in Boston.

French Gardens.

No heavier crops were grown in France than on the Huguenot farms in Bearn, and the south-western provinces. The slopes of the Aigoul and the Epernon were covered with their flocks and herds. The valley of the Vaunage was celebrated for its richness of vegetation, and was called by its inhabitants the 'Little Canaan.' * * * The diligence, skill and labor with which they subdued the stubborn soil and made it yield its increase of flowers and fruits, and corn and wine, bore witness in all quarters to the toil and energy of the men of the religion." — *Smiles' History of the Huguenots*.

Disosway in his "Huguenots in America," states: "The different parts of the country to which they came were greatly benefited by the introduction of their superior modes of cultivation of the soil, and of different valuable fruits which they brought from France. * * * When Charles II, in 1680, sent the first band of French Protestants to South Carolina his principal object was to introduce into that colony the excellent modes of cultivation which they had followed in their own country."

In 1709 Lawson in his "Journal" gives us pictures of the Huguenots in their scattered settlements in South Carolina, and states "their lands presented the aspects of the most cultivated portions of France and England."

Tradition states that the plantations of the French *habitans* of New Oxford were cultivated with such care and taste that the whole settlement presented to view one beautiful garden. There is found at the ruins of the French fort in Oxford, which was once the plantation of André Sigournais, in the French settlement of 1687, remains of a vineyard, orchard and garden.*

---

* The following fact was communicated to the writer of the Memoir of the French Protestants, Rev. Dr. Holmes, by the late Capt. Andrew Sigourney, of Oxford, Mass., who was born in Boston 1752:

"A bill of lading, dated London, March 5, 1687, of a variety of Merchandise, etc., shipped on board the ships *John* and *Elizabeth*, mentions

On a second visit to the fort, in September of the same year (1819), we " were regaled with the perfumes of the shrubbery, and the grapes there hanging in clusters on the vines, planted by the Huguenots above a century before."

" Grape vines, in 1819, were growing luxuriantly along the line of the fort; and these, together with currant bushes, roses, and other shrubbery nearly formed a hedge around it. There were some remains of an apple orchard. The currant and asparagus were still growing there. These, with the peach, were of spontaneous growth from the French plantation; the last of the peach trees was destroyed by the memorable gale of 1815," as stated by Mr. Mayo, the landed proprietor.

Mrs. Lee, the author of the " Huguenots in France and America " writes of the French garden of Andrew Sigourney :

" 'The narrative of Mr. John Mayo (given to her in 1828, when he was eighty-one years of age) is perhaps the most graphic. He says the fort of the French was near my house; it inclosed about a quarter of an acre and was about square. There was a very considerable house, with a cellar, well, etc., within the fort. There was a garden outside the fort, on the west, containing asparagus, grapes, plums, cherries, and a bed of gooseberries. There were probably more than ten acres cultivated around the fort ; some of the apple trees and pear trees are still standing, also the currant bushes and cinnamon rose bushes, asparagus, etc."

---

among the rest, ' two chests of vine plants, marked X 5 X,' and were to be delivered to Mr. Daniel Stading, or Petre à Sailes " (of Boston for the French settlement of New Oxford).

The bill of ship lading was on a half sheet of paper, large size, of a thick course quality of paper and much discolored by time. It was folded in a small square form.

Some years since, on the decease of Capt. Andrew Sigourney, of Oxford, his executor, Capt. William Sigourney, found the ship lading bill of these same vines and fruit trees. The bill was afterward destroyed, with other French papers, by fire.

A portion of the garden was devoted to herbs, roots, medicinal sweet mint, and remnants still remained of blood root, Solman's seal and some others.

Very little remains at the present time of this once lovely French flower garden, vineyard and orchard (having passed into the hands of the restorer)—a remnant of the cherry trees which had replanted themselves, the fruit retaining its rich flavor, but in size resembling the wild cherry. These cherry trees formed a lovely trellis for the grape vines, but unfortunately they were destroyed; with these vines clusters of asparagus, stray hop vines and rose trees, had formed a French garden and vineyard for two centuries.

Mr. Mayo stated to Dr. Holmes: "Every thing here is left as I found it."

The descendants of Mr. Mayo shared in his refinement of taste.

"The flower thereof falleth and the grace of the fashion of it perisheth."

A LETTER FROM THE LATE MRS. L. H. SIGOURNEY.

HARTFORD, *Sept. 30th*, 1856.

MY DEAR MISS DE WITT:

On returning from a little visit to my daughter I found your box of delightful Huguenot grapes awaiting me. Their fragrance betrayed them ere the casket was fully opened. This sentiment of remembrance on your part was indeed very kind, and I earnestly thank you. Does it require much stretch of the imagination to depict that saintly group who, for "righteousness sake," left the vine-clad hills of la belle France, and sought among these shaded valleys, "a faith's pure shrine?"

Your own ruined fort is peculiarly rich and graphic in its delineations, especially so to us, who regard the ancestral name of Sigourney with respect and affection.

I hope this Huguenot vine may long flourish; I have pressed some of its clusters into a little wine, thinking that the most enduring form in which they could be treasured. Should it succeed well, I shall hope you will taste it with me, when it attains its maturity, the next year.

I trust your loved mother and sister are well. I often think of you as a peculiarly happy family not to have been severed and tossed about, as so often happens "amid the chances and changes of this mortal life." Please remember me affectionately to them, and believe me,

Very sincerely your friend,
L. H. SIGOURNEY.

AN EXTRACT FROM A LETTER OF DR. OLIVER WENDELL HOLMES TO MRS. FREELAND, DATED BEVERLY FARM, JUNE, 1881.

"I remember my father's visit to Oxford, and the enthusiasm with which he explored the traces of the French Pilgrims. I have not forgotten, either, my own visit many years ago to the fort and the scenes of the massacre by the Indians, and how I looked for the rose bushes and the grape vines which my father had seen, and of which Mrs. Sigourney had sung. There is no town in New England which can show more interesting localities than Oxford. The French exiles rested there, as a flight of tropical birds might alight on one of our New England pines, and one can hardly visit the places that knew them without looking for some relics of their sojourn as he would hunt for an empty nest or a painted feather after the bird has flown."

Rev. Dr. Abel Holmes states:

"In the year 1822 a letter was also received from a lady, well known in our literary community, enclosing a poetical tribute to the memory of the Huguenots of Oxford, which is not less worthy of her pen, than of her connexion.* Her marriage with a worthy descendant of one of the first French fami-

---
* L. Huntly Sigourney.

lies that settled in Oxford fairly entitled her to the subject which her pen will perpetuate, should the Memoir be forgotten. A leaf of the grape vine was enclosed in the letter which has this conclusion: 'We received great pleasure from our visit to Oxford, and as we traced the ruins of the first rude fortress erected by our ancestors, the present seemed almost to yield in reality to the past. I send you a leaf from the vine, which still flourishes in luxuriance, which, I am sorry to say, resembles our own natives of the woods a little too strongly. Something beside, I also send you, which savours as little of the Muse's inspiration, as the vine in question does of foreign extraction; but if poetical license can find affinities for the latter, I trust your goodness will extend its mantle over the infirmity of the former.'"

AN EXTRACT FROM THE POEM OF L. H. SIGOURNEY, RECEIVED BY REV. DR. HOLMES.

"'The savage arrow scath'd them, and dark clouds
Involved their infant Zion, yet they bore
Toil and affliction with unwavering eye
Fix'd on the heavens, and firm in hope sublime
Sank to their last repose. Full many a son
Among the noblest of our land, looks back
Through Time's long vista, and exulting claims,
These as his Sires."—L. H. S.

Mrs. Lee writes: "The Huguenots, after their return to Boston (from Oxford), gratified their taste in the cultivation of rare and beautiful fruits and flowers. Vestiges long remained of their cultivated and refined tastes." And adds, "A friend of mine, now no more, the honored and regretted Daniel Sargent, Esq., told me, he perfectly recollected 'fine gardens pointed out to him when a boy, as having belonged to the Huguenots.'"—*Mrs. Lee*, ii, 68.

There were the rich and luxurious French gardens of Daniel Johonnot of Boston, and of his son Zachariah Johonnot, rivaling gardens of India in splendor, which were cultivated through their wealth to remind them in sweet memories of the lovely homes of their ancestors in sunny France.

The beautiful garden of Daniel Johonnot was by his "will" bequeathed to his son Andrew as a choice inheritance, and again by him bequeathed to his son Andrew.

These gardens were ornamented with flowers and shrubs of exquisite varieties and choice fruit trees, and were for many years remembered by the inhabitants of Boston.

And the gardens of Zachariah Johonnet were afterward inherited by his son Peter. These gardens are said to have been filled with rare fruit trees, beautiful flowers and shrubs from the "dear fatherland." Tradition states that every tree, shrub and flower came from France, and that these gardens extended in length entire streets.

There was also the spacious garden appurtenant to the rich mansion of Andrew Faneuil* in Boston; he had acquired a taste for flowers which he gratified in one immense French garden, containing seven acres of land, interspersed with choice fruit trees. The garden was of such loveliness that it was styled an "Eden of beauty." Choice tropical fruits were cultivated in hot-houses, the first of their kind in New England.

"The deep court-yard," says Miss Quincy, in her memoir of her mother, "ornamented by flowers and shrubs, was divided into an upper and lower platform by a high glacis, surrounded by a richly wrought railing, decorated with gilt balls." †

The terraces, which rose from the paved court behind the house, were supported by massive walls of hewn granite, and were ascended by flights of steps of the same material.

---
*The residence of Andrew Faneuil was on Treamount St. (Tremont St.), opposite the King's chapel and its church-yard. On the death of Andrew Faneuil, it became the home of his nephew, Peter Faneuil where he lived and died.

†Memoir of the Life of Eliza S. M. Quincy, p. 88.

One of the ornaments of this tasteful garden was a summerhouse which resembled an eastern pagoda, and from the little spire which surmounted it, there glittered and whirled about in olden times a gilded grasshopper, for a vane in imitation of the one upon the Royal Exchange in London. This summerhouse from its elevated situation commanded a lovely view, and for many successive decades of years the Johonnet and Faneuil gardens were remembered for their choice fruits and flowers as things of æsthetic beauty.

At the commencement of the sixteenth century, there lived in a small castle near Gap, in Dauphiny, the noble family of Farel.—*History of France, M. Guizot.*

Among the French gardens, vineyards and orchards there is a description of an orchard at the ancient home of William Farel in France, which d'Aubigné has so quaintly and beautifully described:

"In these Alpine solitudes, three leagues from the town of Gap, in the direction of Grenoble, not far from the flowery turf that clothes the tableland of Bayard's mountain, on the extended plain, stood a house of the class to which in France the appellation of 'gentilhommière'* is attached (a country gentleman's habitation). It was surrounded by an orchard which formed an avenue to the village — there lived a family bearing the name of Farel, a family of long-established reputation, and as it would appear, of noble descent. In the year 1489, at a time when Dauphiny was suffering from oppression, a son was born in this modest mansion, who received the name of William Farel." †

---

* Some of the Huguenots were termed "gentilhomme" (gentlemen). In old France "gentilhomme" meant much more than "noble;" a man's ancestors must have been noble for at least three generations, else he dared not assume that envied designation of which the King himself was proud, considering it amongst his highest honors to be called "premier gentilhomme de France (the first gentleman of France).

† John Calvin, in writing of William Farel, dwells upon the disinterestedness of his character, and speaks of him as a man of such noble birth.

"Grenoble to Gap, distant a quarter of an hour's journey from the last post-house, and a stone's throw to the right from the high road, is the site of the house which belonged to the father of the Farel still pointed out. Though it is now occupied by a cottage only, its dimensions are sufficient to prove that the original structure must have been a dwelling of a superior order. The present inhabitant of the cottage bears the name of Farel."

A description of the modern French garden of the late Charles Sigourney, Esq., of Hartford, Ct., who was a lineal descendant of Andrew Sigourney, who came from France, and was in the French settlement of Oxford, and afterward became a resident of Boston.

Mrs. Sigourney describes her beautiful home with its lovely rose gardens:

"The mansion was environed by an extensive lawn, whose curving gravel walks were adorned with shrubbery, and spacious gardens, one of which stretched downward to the fair river that girdled the domain, from which it was protected by a mural parapet. One of the most unique features of scenery was a grove sloping rather precipitously to the borders of the same graceful stream, traversed by winding paths, and shaded by lofty trees. On its margin, and partially sustained by the trunk of a strong oak that bent over the water, a rustic recess with two or three seats, called the Hermitage, had been constructed. It was approached by a kind of wilderness path through the lawn grounds (where every thing grew as it pleased, yet pleased to grow gracefully). * * * An adjoining eminence was crowned by a summer-house, on whose vane, which was in the form of an arm and hand with a pointing finger, was the classic inscription, 'Ut ventus vita,'—our life is as the wind, our domain was beloved by the flowers.

"Roses of every hue and variety cast their perfume upon the air; the clematis threw over the piazzas its rich masses of cerulean blue; brilliant woodbines and trumpet honeysuckles spanned the arching gate-ways, or clung to the trellises of the summer-house; the alternate white and purple lilacs bowed their heads over the avenue alloted to them, as if in close consultation; the neighboring lilacs bent back their listening petals; on the border of the gravel walks the gorgeous coxcomb flaunted, the peony and lupine advanced their pretensions; the pansy lifted its deep eye of intelligence, and the arbor-judea waved its pendulous banner when the slightest zephyr claimed homage.

"(Birds, fearing no shaft of the fowler, peopled the boughs, and made a paradise of song.) (A line of foot-bridges with their passing groups, rendered picturesque its adjacent lowlands, where were groups of little ones, who amassed daisies and king-cups, or gadded after the bright-winged butterfly.) Garden seats were placed in different positions, so as admirably to reveal the charms of nature and art which were here combined, the velvet lawn, the stream that at one point exhibited a slight cascade, and at another seemed to have a lake-like termination. The trees which were scattered here and there seemed instinct with the spirit of grace; and methought I had never beheld such enchanting moonlights as fell through their chequering branches."

> Fain would I bear away,
> And keep the changeless picture in my heart
> Of those fair woods and waters,—summer dress'd
> And angel-voiced, until I lay me down
> On the low pillow of my last repose.—*L. H. Sigourney.*

On leaving the village street in Oxford in a southerly direction to visit the site of the ancient French gardens and ruins of the fortification, you will take the first road on your left hand; it is now known by a guide-board as "Huguenot avenue."

"A high way laid out Feb. 6th 1714* by the Select men beginning att the Eight rod way on the southwardly sid of an orchard neer the old mill† running over the old mill brook to a rock on the East of said Brooke, from thence marked on the northwardly side with mark trees tel it coms to barnon's‡ land neer the North East corner of Joseph Chamberlin seneor's home lot (In the French settlement the home lot of Rev. Daniel Bondet) said way being four rods wide."

Soon a view is presented of the site of the French fort, situ-

---
* Village Rec., p. 132.
† French Mill of Gabriel Bernon.
‡ Gabriel Bernon's land.

There was once a large orchard planted by the Huguenots on the north-west corner of the way four rods wide as it entered the Eight rod way, and within the present century the remains of another orchard of apple trees was to be seen, and it is said vestiges of these old trees are now to be found on the late Capt. Humphrey estate. The rock over the brook remains the same partly concealed under the bridge, and a modern mill is now seen on the site of one of the old French mills of Gabriel Bernon. The ancient site of the Humphrey house is passed on your left hand, shaded by its ancient elms and a memorable oak. The descendants of Capt. Humphrey continue still in the possession of this ancient estate. There was the old path or road leading to the French church-yard entering at the oak tree in the lowlands, and now, if the traveler should inquire his way, he is told by some obliging countryman " to rise a holler, keep straight along until you reach the top of a hill," and he pursues the winding highway.

He soon passes on the left hand an eminence, the site of the ancient French church and church-yard. The valley below the church, shaded by dark plumy pines, and the site of the lower fort (as it was called), built to protect the French refugees during church service and the burial of their dead, and then is passed on the left the opening of the old Boston road, as it was called two hundred years ago the "Kenecticut road," and then on the Woodstock trail he passes on his right hand the site of the Rev. Daniel Bondet's plantation and its high round top hill, known at the present day as "Bondet's hill," and soon on his left hand he pursues his way on a slope of the French orchard of some five acres of land, once belonging to Andrew Sigourney as a part of his plantation.

ated pleasantly in a close of ten acres of cultivated land crowning the height of the plantation. There was once a vineyard on the south side of the fortification, the grape-vines of which caressed the rude palisade, and supplied wine to the refugees (it is said the French have wonderful proclivities for the grape vine). The hop vine and the rose tree had their share of culture in the garden on the west side of the fort, and thus the fort appeared to rise from this garden of roses and vines.

Within the site of the French fortifications there is still to be discovered the outline of the small cellar of the garrison-house. On the south side of the palisade was the vineyard; outside of the fort, on the north side of the garrison-house, there was a stone chimney, and its uncouth wide fire-place, a part of which is still standing, and the ancient well is still preserved. There are now to be seen the ancient stone steps ascending a terrace from the garden, leading to the house on its north-westerly limits, just as they were in position when the settlement was abandoned, not having the misfortune to have passed into the hands of the restorer. At the base of the terrace, west of the fort, was the garden, and the orchard lying westerly of the garden.

"The main block house was thirty feet long and eighteen feet wide, with a doubled wall cellar twenty-four feet long by twelve feet wide and about six feet deep. The inner wall supported the floor beams; the outer wall, three feet from this, was made of heavy boulders on a foundation about three feet deep, and supported the logs forming the walls of the house."

A covered stone drain seventy feet in length, constructed when the fort was built, is still to be seen in good preservation.

"At the south-west corner of the cellar a flight of stone steps have been unearthed, which led to the cellar of this blockhouse. On clearing out the debris and rubbish at this point, three or four of the original benches, or offsets, cut in the hard earth, for laying the steps when the cellar was built, were found as distinct as if just made."

The fireplace was in the middle of the north side of the house. It was nearly ten feet wide at the opening of the jambs, and admitting logs eight feet long at the back.

The broad foundations (one hundred square feet) supporting it and its chimney, almost wholly outside of the house, gave ample room for those huge logs and for an outside oven.

There was but this one fireplace to this old garrison-house. There was no annex attached to this block-house *of any description*. Mr. John Mayo remembered the garrison-house, as his ancestors had purchased this estate of M. Gabriel Bernon.

Mr. John Mayo, in his description of the French garrison-house (as he well remembered it in good preservation when his father resided on the French plantation), informed Mrs. J. P. Davis, his granddaughter, that the port-holes were only on the south side of the house, as there was lying southerly of the garrison-house at some little distance a line of forest running easterly and westerly, forming as it were a boundary, and from this point the French must have feared an invasion of the Indians.

THE OXFORD FORT.

Notes on its construction, etc.

The French plantations of Rev. Daniel Boudet and André Sigournay were not included in the large tract of land purchased by Gabriel Bernon of Dudley and others. The French made a first settlement in (New) Oxford in 1687. A garrison-house was erected on the plantation of Sigournay, and he was the Commandant of the fort. He planted a vineyard, orchard, and cultivated a garden of much beauty, composed of shrubs and rose trees which he obtained from France. This garrison-house remained until after the English settlement in 1713. The site of its ancient cellar is still to be seen, with its immense stone chimney foundations and fireplace, with the remains of that once lovely vineyard, orchard and garden, and these were the only relics to be seen on the site of the French fort in 1884. This fortified garrison-house was surrounded only by a palisade of logs and earthworks. It is conjectured by some that "the fort was built of stone, the walls some four feet high, banked with earth and topped with logs, and having a ditch surrounding it, with perhaps a stockade beyond," and that certain outlines of the fort are indicated "by the solid stone foundations, three feet in thickness and just covered by the sod enclosing the whole area." There is no record or reliable tradition to support these theories.

The only explanation that can be given of this view of these fortifications is the following: The large area of land now surrounding the site of the French fort was in ancient times composed of several small lots of land. One of these parcels, lying south of the ruins of the fort, was separated by a wall of stone running east and west near the vineyard, which was outside of the fort. This was rebuilt several times by the Mayo family during the 130 years of their residence on the farm, and every time removed three or more feet south of the old wall; and besides, this wall intersected another wall at right angles, running south and north, which extended from the highway boundary wall. What is now thought to be the site of an old ditch surrounding the fort is only the appearance of the ground from whence was removed one of these former walls. The last of these old walls was removed some 50 years since.

All the debris of these old walls was deposited in the French vineyard, under the vines and among the shrubs and rose trees of the French garden. This accounts for the supposed fortification wall of "some three feet in thickness and just covered by the sod." When this supposed discovery was made there was no vestige of a wall standing. The wall now placed is a modern wall just erected in imitation of what was in imagination supposed to be the original wall of defense.

It also appears that there were no stone walls three feet in thickness around the "French garrison-house" as a defense against the natives, the first French settlement having been abandoned in August, 1696, and a second French settlement made in Oxford in about 1699, and continued until 1704, only 17 years after the first fort was erected.

Gabriel Bernon, the President of the "French habitants," petitioned Governor Dudley for protection against the natives. Governor Dudley, in reply to his petition, dated July 7, 1702, writes:—

"Herewith you have a commission for Captain of New Oxford. I desire you forthwith to repair thither and show your said commission, and take care that the people be armed, and take them in your own house with a palisade, for the security of the inhabitants; and if they are at such a distance in your village that there should be need of another place to draw them together in case of danger, consider of another proper house, and write me, and you shall have order therein.

"I am your humble servant,
"J. Dudley."

In Lincoln's "History of Worcester" is found the description of a garrison-house of this period, 1675–1713, in Worcester:—

"On this road (Marlborough to Brookfield) south of the fording place, was erected at a very early period, one of those edifices called block or garrison-houses, and denominated on the records 'the old Indian fort.'

"The structure for defense against the tribes prowling in the forests, so far as specimens have survived the waste of time, or description been preserved by tradition, had great uniformity in construction. They were built of timbers, hewn on the sides in contact with each other, firmly interlocked at the ends, and fastened together with strong pins. They were generally square and two stories in height. The basement was furnished with a single thick door of plank. The walls were perforated with narrow loop-holes for the use of

French Fort.

musketry against an approaching foe. A ladder, easily drawn up if the lower floor was forced, ascended to the next room, which projected two or three feet over on each side, having slits for infantry, and wider port-holes for cannon. The gentle slope of the roof afforded an elevated position to overlook the surrounding country, and was sometimes crowned with a little turret for an observatory. These watch-towers, impervious to ball or arrow, were of abundant strength to resist an enemy unprovided with artillery, and might defy any attack except that by fire on the combustible materials. To these wooden castles, in the infancy of the country, the inhabitants repaired on the alarm of danger, and found ample protection within the rude fortresses, seldom reduced by the savage, of too fierce temperament to await the lingering progress of a siege. Lincoln mentions " another of these fortresses of logs " for the protection of Quinsigomond (Worcester), and then " The third of these wooden castles was on the new Connecticut road north of Lincoln Square, affording shelter to the traveller and defending the mills on the stream."

In the " Memorial History of Boston " is a description of the fortification of Charlestown, " which was begun as early as 1630, when a fort was built on the top of Town Hill, with palisadoes and flankers made out, which was performed at the direction of Mr. Graves by all hands, men, women and children, who wrought at digging and building till the house was done. The fort was maintained at great expense, and was fostered by the colony because of its importance." The works were abandoned just previous to 1700.

The fortifications are described in New York city as existing in 1700 or about that time. " The city lies crowded below Wall Street with only a path stretched out along Chatham Street and the east side. A line of crumbling palisades and earthworks extending originally from river to river, still fenced Wall Street from the open beyond."

Dr. Holmes visited Oxford in 1817 and had an interview with Mrs. Mary Sigourney Butler, who lived in Boston until the American Revolution and soon after removed to Oxford. Dr. Holmes states "of the memorials of the primitive plantation of her ancestors she had been very observant, and still cherished a reverence for them." Mr. John Mayo, who resided at this time on the plantation of her ancestor, Andrew Sigourney, Captain Humphrey, Mr. Peter Shumway, who was of French extraction, Mrs. Kingsbury* and her son, Col. Jeremiah Kingsbury, had rendered Mrs. Butler every assistance in her researches. They were all persons of great intelligence and respectability, and were living on the landed estates of their ancestors adjacent to the French fort, and all lived to be more than 90 years of age, with the exception of Col. Kingsbury, who was more than 80 years of age. These persons had never seen any stone fortifications around the French fort, in the English settlement of 1713.

In 1720 Thomas Mayo of Roxbury purchased the plantation on which was the French fort. This estate continued in the Mayo family for some 130 years. If there had been stone fortifications or walls four feet in height and three feet in thickness around the fort, would there not have been some remains? In 1819 Mr. Mayo informed Dr. Holmes: "Every thing here is left as I found it."

NOTES.

A new modern cellar wall has been laid in imitation of the ancient cellar wall,† which quite destroys its interest as a relic

---

* The widow of Capt. Jeremiah Kingsbury.

† Mrs. J. P. Davis of Worcester, a lineal descendant of Mr. John Mayo, recollects the old walls which stood on the southerly side of the ruins of the French fort. In 1884 the remains of the two walls were to be seen, which formed a salient angle. These walls had been built in the English settlement in making divisions of land.

of the past. Its ancient outline was all that was desirable to preserve, with its foundation of an ancient stone chimney and fire-place.

The safety of the garrison-house would not have permitted an ell attached to the house. The house may have extended beyond the cellar wall.

There was but one chimney attached to this garrison-house, and that was built outside of the house on its north side. There was but one chimney to houses of that period, and to some modern houses of only 100 years ago one chimney of huge dimensions was deemed sufficient. There were no ovens; all was done in kettles or in the ashes, excepting a stone oven, in the chimney outside of the house.

Some few relics have been found, of which there is no proof of their ever belonging to the French, as the cellar was used by the Mayo family for the place of all refuse for more than 100 years.

There could not have been any old pottery belonging to the French. They confined themselves to utensils made of pewter and wooden ware, excepting some few who had brought from France small articles of silver plate. André Sigournay is said to have brought from France a small silver pitcher concealed with other valuables on his person, which was of great service to his family in their flight. The pitcher is now in the possession of Charles Sigourney Burnham of New York, a grandson of the late Charles Sigourney of Hartford, Conn.

Then still descending into the valley a tiny river is seen disappearing altogether from view, then reappearing, yet flowing ceaselessly, with trees skirting its bank, in all their varied shades of color. The river, fringed with tall grass and meadow flowers of blue gentian and the clematis with its fluffy blossoms, with graceful bends loses itself in the rich river meadow lands, and flows into the French river. This river had strength sufficient to turn the wheels of the French mills, and could be heard as it tumbled into the mill-race.

On its banks were the mills and rustic French dwellings, with casement windows aglow with brilliant blossoms, encircled with orchards, vineyards and parterres of flowers dotting the whole valley, which must altogether have presented a most romantic landscape of loveliness, stretching far into the valley, through which passed the rude bridle-paths and foot-trail which led the refugees to the mills, church, church-yard, and other French plantations in the valley.

The remains of the ancient bridle-path can be traced on the Harwood farm, so called, to the fort, and extending to the site of the French church and church-yard.

On the right hand of the Sutton road, one mile distant from the village street, is the site of one of the French mills of Gabriel Bernon.

"In the midst of a small meadow which is skirted by wooded uplands, and in midsummer is so overhung and shut in by trees and wild undergrowth as to be hidden from the casual observer. Here the substantial dam, some sixty feet in length, both wall and embankment, stands almost entire — a deep trench to convey the water from the pond to the mill-wheel, a distance of seventy-five feet, is distinctly to be seen — the position of the mill can be fixed — and the waste-way, running from the wheel about one hundred feet to the stream below, seems to have been but recently made, so little has it been obstructed.

"In this retired spot, the kindly hand of nature has protected and preserved the handiwork of the Huguenots, as it has been kept in no other locality in Oxford. The place is full of interest to the antiquary, and is well worth a visit, not only for its associations, but for its quiet, picturesque beauty."

The views from the French fort present quiet pastoral scenes of exquisite loveliness, environed in the distance by enchanting forest hills; and from the hill sides there is a long extent of beautiful vista, and beyond are distant hills, with Wachusett mountain seen fading away in a fainter blue.

The river winding its silvery way, and its flowery meadows remain the same in view as in the days gone by, and the ripple and rush of the water-way is now the only sound in this enchanting valley, for the "old French mills" have long since fallen to decay.

There is seen the same hazy distance of mountain landscape gilded with the same bright sunshine as when the refugees gazed upon this new wilderness home. "But as generations of men come and go these old ruins look down on many changes."

To-day there is seen in the distance the village street with its churches, rising among them the tower of the Episcopal church, very different in its architecture from the rude French chapel of two hundred years ago, where preached the Rev. Daniel Bondet, ordained at Fullam palace by Bishop Compton of London.

CHAPTER XVII.

The Annals of Oxford.

In 1713 at the close of Queen Anne's war was the settlement of English families commenced in Oxford, the required number of thirty families being obtained. The settlement was made in the good old colony time, when we lived under the queen "when queues were long and patches large."

Richard Moore, Esq., Lieut. John Town and Col. Ebenezer Learned were gentlemen, then good servants to the queen, and were enhancing her most gracious Majesty's interests by endeavoring to increase her government by the settlement of Oxford.

"Oxford was made a town May 16, 1683. In the year 1693 a particular act passed empowering Oxford to send a representative to the 'General Court' as appears by the records in the Secretary's office of this Commonwealth."*

---
* Whitney's History of Worcester County, Mass.

In 1694 an assessment of taxes was made and sent with an order for its collection, to the constable of the French plantation, Andrew Sigourney. The grant for Oxford was made 1681-2.

Mr. John Gore of Roxbury made the survey, and a return of the same being presented to the "General Court," it was accepted, and on May 16, 1683, they granted the plantation and it received the name of Oxford, after a city of that name in England, and was at that time a town in Suffolk county.*

The grant for Oxford had a great prospect of success with such efficient guardians to watch over its interests as Dudley and others of high position in the colony.

Dudley thought the locality of the Oxford grant "capable of a good settlement, with its western part, including many hills, and its eastern section was set apart for a village, being more attractive because of its plains and meadows.† These plains ex-

---

* "Towns were made when there were few, or no inhabitants in them, and when a sufficient number of people had settled in them, a special resolve of court passed to empower them to meet and choose their town officers."

"But in a later date they have been incorporated, named and empowered to hold town meetings by the same act."

July 31, 1716, Town meeting.

Richard Moore chosen moderator, voted in y' affirmative y₍ Lt. John Towne and Inˢⁿ Ebenezer Learned should go to ye Court to search ye Records to see what may be found concerning Oxford being granted for a Township, also to petition the General Court if we may be made a town if it be needful.— *Oxford Records.*

May 28, 1718.

At Great and Gen. Court of Assembly for ye province of ye Massachusetts Bay in New England held at Boston on ye 28 day of May 1718.

On the petition of John Towne Selectman of the town of Oxford June 18, 1718, Read and ordered that a tax may be levied upon the lands of non-residents to enable them to build a meeting-house and settle a minister.

† Now the town Charlton.

tend three miles north and south, the soil of which is a warm sandy loam, and the Nipmuck country was famed for its Indian corn."

Major Gookin said of Manchang (Oxford), "It is situated in a fertile country for good land."

The natural meadows bordering the rivers which ran on either side the plains, were considered the most valuable of all the lands, on account of the quantity of hay they yielded.*

Another attraction presented to the minds of Dudley and Stoughton, favorable for a settlement of the Oxford grant, was that this location was easy of access.

The old Bay road from Boston to Springfield crossed this part of the Nipmuck county, afterward known as the New Oxford settlement, in its northern part, and the old Connecticut road passed through its southern section.

"I gave New Roxbury the name of Woodstock, because of its nearness to Oxford, for the sake of Queen Elizabeth and the notable meetings that have been held at that place bearing the name in England."—*Diary of Judge Sewall of Boston.*

In the time of the Oxford settlement all varieties of animals common to the New England forests were to be found in the woodlands of Oxford. Deer, wolves, wild cats and bears were game for the hunters, and fish abounded in the small lakes and rivers, affording means of subsistence. Deer were numerous and were quite an article of traffic.

---

* "The artificial pond in the eastern part of Oxford, called 'Robinson's pond,' covers what was one of the finest meadows in the vicinity, which has been known from the first history of the town as "Mendon meadow," as Mendon people came here yearly to cut the hay before the settlement of the town.

"As late as at the commencement of the present century, it was a custom every spring, at a certain time, to open the waste-gates at the mill near the south end of the plain, and draw the water from the meadows above, that the crops of hay might grow and be harvested."

One of the town officers chosen annually was a " deer reeve " to protect the deer; these officers were chosen until near the close of the last century.*

Bears were not uncommon in the settlement of Oxford. The last bear in the town was killed by Samuel Davis and John Dana. Mr. Davis resided on the farm now owned by James Lovett, and the adjoining farm was the residence of Mr. —— Dana. Both of these farms are near to a swamp, long known as " Bug swamp." Each of these proprietors had a corn field near the swamp, and adjoining to each other.

Before harvesting, the owners were decided that they were suffering in their corn, by the depredations of some bear concealed in the swamp, which was a most unfrequented place, and its solitude and silence had favored the bear to select the trunk of some hollow forest tree, as they both climb and descend trees with great agility, for his den, or in some natural cavern among rocks.

Mr. Davis, and his neighbor Mr. Dana, decided to appoint a morning, at the early hour of 2 o'clock, to meet and watch for the bear. Mr. Dana was first, upon the time appointed, and soon sighted the bear, and fired his single-barreled heavy shotgun, which wounded the bear. Dana at once sought his safety by refuge in the swamp. The bear came toward him, and

---

*In 1792 Capt. Amasa Kingsbury and Joshua Merrian were the last deer reeves chosen by the town.

Among the early punishments found on the court record of Worcester county, 1748, one having in his possession the flesh of a deer, killed contrary to law, was fined fifty shillings, one-half to the King, and half to the informers, which was paid with costs.

Tradition states at Ballard's grain mill (now Howarth's) that wolves were common. On a winter morning seven wolves were counted on the ice of Angretteback pond.

At the farm of Mr. John Larned, west of the river, in the south-west part of the town, the family would be awakened many a time by the cry of the wolves from the highlands near their home.

when almost within hugging distance, rose on his haunches to throw himself upon Dana, who, perceiving his situation, had gathered in his hands and arms mud and decayed roots, which he threw into the face of the bear, who stopped very leisurely to wipe with his paws the mud from his eyes. Mr. Davis had heard the report of Dana's gun, and arrived at this critical moment, armed with his shot-gun, and fired upon the bear, which now fell dead in a heap before them.

In the History of the Huguenots in France and America, Mrs. Lee, quoting from the manuscript of Mr. John Mayo, of Oxford, narrates:

"I heard Joseph Rockwood, who served in the fort, tell of having got lost in the woods when out for the cows. He heard at a distance the cries of wild beasts, and ascended a tree for safety. He was surrounded during the night by half-famished howling wolves.*

A RECORD OF TROUBLESOME BIRDS.

In a warrant for a town meeting, dated Feb. 19, 1791:

"6th. To see if the town will bid a bounty on the heads of crows that shall be killed within said town by the inhabitants for the year ensuing or act thereon as the town shall think proper. By order of the Selectmen.—*Samuel Harris, Town Clerk.*

"March 7, 1791, at a town meeting; voted, a bounty on the heads of crows, viz., for each old crow one shilling a head, and for each young crow four pence per head, that shall be killed within this town by the inhabitants thereof within one year."

The keeping of sheep in those days was quite an item of profit to the land-holders. All sheep were marked by their owners and entered on record in the town. Among many

---

* Joseph Rockwood was in the English settlement of Oxford, and his plantation was near the French fort, and subsequently was included in the farm lands of John Mayo.

others: "Rev. Elias Dudley marks his sheep with a Swallow Tail on the right ear." — May 14, 1793.

"Mr. James Butler's marking stamp for his Beasts is a capital 'B' thus 'B'" (painted black or red) — January 5, 1795.

In some instances in marking animals humanity was forgotten. "Lt. John Ballard Marks his cattle and Sheep with a crop off the left Ear and the right Ear split of each creature" — Decemr. 1st 1792.

Mrs. Kingsbury (the widow of Capt. Jeremiah Kingsbury) narrated, when in her youth and residing with her father Jonathan Ballard, whose plantation and corn mill included a part of the landed estate of John Nichols, in later time known as Howarth:

The Ballard family, were greatly annoyed by the Indians. When gathering peas and other vegetables from their garden they were obliged to protect themselves with fire-arms. If in any manner they returned to the house leaving the basket, on returning to the garden the basket and peas were gone.

Governor Hutchinson in his history of Massachusetts writes an item in the history of Oxford: "August 6, 1724, four Indians came upon a small house in Oxford, which was built under a hill. They made a breach in the roof, and as one of them was attempting to enter, he received a shot from a courageous woman, the only person in the house, who had two muskets and two pistols charged, and was prepared for all four, but they thought fit to retreat, carrying off the dead or wounded man."

Tradition states the woman placed a feather-bed in the chimney and with a fire and the smoke prevented them from entering the house. The name of this heroine is not preserved, neither the site of her humble dwelling.

Cattle were often taken from the English settlement by the Indians. When looking for cows at pasture fire-arms were required.

Peter Papillon of Boston died in 1733. (John Wolcott of Salem his son-in-law Administrator of his estate, Boston Feb. ye 11th, 1734).

The stock of creatures, etc., on the Farm at Oxford amounted to £85. 11. 0. as by Inventory lodg'd in ye Registrs. Office and which are still on sd Farm to be deducted out of ye first Inventory of £1033. 9. 6½.

One Mare now at Oxford £12. 0. 0.

One can imagine the English planters as they arrive from various settlements in Oxford village, with their wagons containing household goods and pack-horses overburdened, with their cattle and other domestic animals soon following. The pioneers in a new settlement at that period encountered many hardships, to build their log cabins, make roads and lay rustic bridges over the small rivers, as well as the labor of subduing the soil.

The first houses were rude structures, with roofs covered with thatch. In a few years houses of a better order began to appear; they were built with two stories in front and sloped down to one in the rear "leanto style" the windows were small and opened outward on hinges; they consisted of very small diamond panes of glass. The frames of the houses were of heavy oak timber showing the beams inside. These rustic homes all had immense fire-places, where the blazing fire of huge back logs gave cheerfulness to the whole apartment during the long winter evenings, children and servants sitting in the chimney corners, with a high-backed settle on one side for older people.

But for the great blazing fire that was constantly burning in the wide chimney, the family room of the farm-house would have been gloomy. Then there was the floor so neatly sanded, the spinning-wheels and reels were a part of the furniture, and to the children of the family an amusement, as the spinning on a large wheel made a cheery whirring sound as though making woolen garments were the most delightful thing possible.

The young people studied their arithmetic and grammar by the dim light of a candle, and for amusements they played "Blind-man's buff" and "Come Philander, let us be a marching," with many other games but long since forgotten. Then there were the harvest parties and the quilting parties enlivened with a cup of tea that gave social pleasures.* But all these fashions have seen their day "as the family hearth and the great iron crane hangs rusty on its hinges and groans rheumatically when wakened from its long slumbers." The cry of the chimney-sweep is no longer heard in the village street.†

The ancient mile stone at "Sigourney's corner" states the distance of Oxford from Boston to be fifty-three and one-half miles. The village street is a mile and a half in length and more than one hundred feet broad, and almost its whole length is presented at one view.

---

*January 1, 1770. "They are not much esteemed now who will not treat high and gossip about. Tea has now become the darling of our women. Almost every little tradesman's wife must sit sipping tea for an hour or more in a morning, and it may be again in the afternoon, if they can get it, and nothing will please them to sip it out of but china ware, if they can get it. They talk of bestowing thirty or forty shillings upon a tea equipage, as they call it. There is the silver spoon, silver tongs and many other trinkets I cannot name."— *Coffin's* "*History of Newbury.*"

Tea kettles in ancient times held about a pint.

†Whittier writes: "A remarkable custom brought from the old country, formerly prevailed in the rural districts of New England. On the death of a member of the family, the bees were at once informed of the event and their hives dressed in mourning. This ceremonial was supposed to be necessary to prevent the swarms from leaving their hives and seeking a new home."

This antique fashion is continued in some of the country villages within ten miles of Worcester at the present time. It is still regarded as a matter of policy to prevent the bees from deserting their hives.

The old way of telling the bees was for the master or mistress to ap-

The street was silent from noise of carriages in those days; only a few pedestrians were seen on the highway, with now and then a person passing on horseback, with occasionally a lady seated upon a pillion on the same horse.

The broad highway was lined with flocks of gabbling geese, which marched up and down the street in search of mud pools, to the terror of all small children, and this fashion continued long into the present century.

---

proach the hives and rap gently upon them. When the bees' attention was thus secured, say in a low voice that such a person, mentioning the name, was dead.

Another way of telling the bees was for the mistress or some one in her place to drape the hives in black, at the same time softly humming some mournful tune to herself.

TELLING THE BEES — *Whittier*.

"Just the same as a month before,—
  The house and the trees,
The barn's brown gable, the vine by the door,—
  Nothing changed but the hives of bees.

Before them, under the garden wall,
  Forward and back,
Went drearily singing the chore-girl small,
  Draping each hive with a shred of black.

Trembling, I listened; the summer sun
  Had the chill of snow:
For I knew she was telling the bees of one
  Gone on the journey we all must go!

Then I said to myself, 'My Mary weeps
  For the dead to-day:
Happly her blind old grandsire sleeps
  The fret and the pain of his age away.'

But her dog whined low; on the doorway sill,
  With his cane to his chin,
The old man sat; and the chore-girl still
  Sung to the bees stealing out and in.

Josiah Wolcott, Esq., at this time was the owner of a pleasure carriage (a square top chaise) and also of a one-horse chair, both vehicles dating back before 1776. Only a few of the country gentry kept a chair or chaise, which was only "tackled" on Sundays, or occasionally for a journey.*

The present time affords in the town facilities for traveling by railroad, a contrast to the former time.

In 1715, two years subsequently to the English settlement, Bernon gave the stones and irons of the grist-mill to Daniel Elliot on condition a mill should be built in a specified time.†

And the song she was singing ever since
In my ear sounds on;—
'Stay at home, pretty bees, fly not hence !
Mistress Mary is dead and gone!"

* A copy from a note-book of Josiah Wolcott:

1776 May 23   Mr. Joshua Turner

To chaise to Scituate 72 miles at 16 y° mile	5 —	8
To chais to Worcester 11 miles 16 y° mile	2	0 0
Settled	£.8.4.6.	

† [*Gov. Dudley to G. Bernon.*]

ROXBURY, *Apr. 6th*, 1715.

"SIR :

"We are now in a way to thrive at Oxford, and I particularly thank you for what you have done toward a grist-mill in the village, by giving the mill stones to Daniel Elliot, conditionally that the mill should be built to serve the town within a prefixed time, which is now past and nothing done. I desire you to write to him to go forward immediately, so as to finish the mill presently to the satisfaction of the Inhabitants, or that you will order the said mill and Irons to be given to such other person as will go forward in the work, that they may not be starved the next winter.

"I pray you take effectual order in the matter.

"I am your humble servant,

"J. DUDLEY.

"To Mr. Gabriel Bernon, Narragansct."

In his reply, Bernon says he has " ordered Daniel Elliot to finish the crist-mill at Oxford or to let the town have the two mills-town, to set the mill in a convenient place," — " it will be a great blessing to strive [thrive] after so much distorbance." *

Col. Ebenezer Learned of North Oxford built a dam and saw-mill on his estate previous to 1723. This mill was run until 1859 when factories were erected in its place.

The old grass-grown Charlton road, the northerly boundary to the church-yard near the south common, was once the traveled way to Ballard's grain mill; at a later date a lovely highway was made to the mill from the south Charlton road, terminating in a broad wooded avenue, which passes the site (intersecting with the old road) of this ancient mill, and is unequaled by any in the town for good taste and rural beauty, and yet all is arranged for utility; even the stone watering trough is a thing of beauty and humanity. The winding avenue is bordered by the forest trees in all their natural gracefulness, fringing the lake even to the water's edge.†

The late Sterens De Witt and subsequently the late George Hodges, Esq., were both much interested in preserving all its natural scenery.

---

* January 25, 1714, " Voted at a lofel town meten that Danel Elact should build a greust mel for the town use." — *Oxford Records.*

" May 20, 1715, at a town meeting It was also voted to choose two persons to go to Daniel Elliot and discours with him consarning building ye corn mill to see whether he will go on with ye corn mill and accomplish it in a reasonable time. Richard Moore and Benony Twichel were chosen for sd work."

Eliot built the mill on Eliot Mill brook near the crossing of the stream and Worcester road, near the Hawes place adjoining the north cemetery.

† March 11, 1754. Voted " to accept of a highway 2 rods wide begining at the eight rod highway (now Main Street) Running west by the South side of Dr. Holden's House running up on the said Holden's line to the North West corner of the burying place from thence straight to

Mr. Thomas Davis, in 1747, built a grist-mill on the river passing through his estate, where is situated the mill known formerly as belonging to Ebenezer D. Rich. The old French mill was located near this site on the same landed estate once belonging to Gabriel Bernon, the President of the French plantation. Mr. Thomas Davis had received this large and valuable estate from his father, Mr. Samuel Davis, of Roxbury, Mass., subsequently a resident of Oxford.

Improvements in the present time include the item of saving labor. In the olden time to many of the houses in the first settlement of Oxford, would be attached a small shop, with a chimney in one corner, where the father and sons would be engaged in the winter season only in manufacturing shoes, with occasionally apprentices. This would form the entire establishment.

The last shop that recalls those primitive days was located on the late Josiah Russell place.

A great contrast is now noticeable in modern improvements to these isolated little shops of domestic industry.

Large manufacturing establishments have superseded them, controlled by wealthy owners, who not only supply all that is required for home consumption but make large exportations to foreign markets, thus affording employment to many most estimable inhabitants of New England towns and villages.

But finally the carding-machines, the fulling-mills, the clothier's shop and the spinning and weaving at the farm-house were banished from sight, being superseded by manufacturing by machinery. The two manufacturing villages west of the village street and North Oxford, with its long stretch of

---

the foot of the hill by Mr. Manning's fence from thence as will be most convenient near or in the road now trod to the bridge by Mr. Ballard's above his mill dam." This road and the Quaboag lane were the only roads to the south part of Charlton and Sturbridge for many years.

villages on the French river, with the town of Webster, are now to be seen in the places of these few solitary mills.

In Oxford, Charlton and adjacent places in the southern part of Worcester county, before banking had become common, Ebenezer Davis, Esq., of Charlton, and his brother, General Jonathan Davis, of Oxford, became the private bankers of the people who had occasion to secure loans of money. Ebenezer Davis, it is said, did not invest in large amounts; he loaned in small sums to hundreds of individuals in Charlton and vicinity. Through the influence of General Jonathan Davis, of Oxford, the Oxford Bank was incorporated in 1823, and for the first ten years he was its president. It was changed to a National bank in 1865. He was succeeded by Richard Olney, Esq., a gentleman of wealth and great influence, from Providence, R. I., John Wetherell, Esq., Hon. Alexander De Witt, and in more modern times, by Charles A. Angell, Esq., and other distinguished gentlemen.*

Fronting on the south-east corner of the south common there was a little gray school-house, itself " toeing the highway," with its two chimneys, with its capacious hearths for log fires of a winter's day. The benches were of the rudest style, instruments of torture, being very narrow and straight backs. For many years this little country school-house, with small high windows of diamond glass, graced the corner of the village common, weather stained with time, its decayed sills and warped clap-boards " crumbled from its moss-flecked sides."

This first school-house in the town occupied the site of the present residence of Mr. Charles Lamb, and for many years re-

---

* The late Mr. James Freeland, of Sutton, once engaged in commerce with Canada en route for Montreal through the eastern section of New York State, ascertained that the entire site of the present city of Utica could be purchased on very favorable terms. He communicated with Ebenezer Davis, Esq., but failed to interest him in a partnership where so large a fortune could have been attained.

mained fronting upon the common. Tradition states some of its timber is still preserved in the house of Mr. Lamb.*

> "Beside yon straggling fence that skirts the way,
> With blossom'd furze, unprofitably gay.
> There in his noisy mansion, skilled to rule,
> The village master taught his little school.
> A man severe he was and stern to view;
> I knew him well, and every truant knew;
> Well had the boding tremblers learned to trace
> The day's disasters in his morning face;
> Full well they laughed with counterfeit glee
> At all his jokes, for many a joke had he;
> Full well the busy whisper, circling round,
> Conveyed the dismal tidings when he frowned.
>   Yet he was kind, or if severe in aught,
> The love he bore to learning was his fault.
> The village all declared how much he knew,
> 'Twas certain he could write and cipher too:
> Lands he could measure, terms and tides presage,
> And e'en the story ruu—that he could gauge;
> In arguing, too, the parson owned his skill,
> For e'en though vanquished, he could argue still,
> While words of learned length and thund'ring sound,
> Amazed the gazing rustics ranged around;
> And still they gazed, and still the wonder grew,
> That one small head could carry all he knew.
> But past is all his fame. The very spot
> Where many a time he triumphed, is forgot."

Mr. Richard Rogers was the first teacher of a school in Oxford, date 1740. He was the most accomplished teacher of his time, not only in English and Latin, but noted for his unrivaled penmanship. In those days a master had no need of a pen wiper, for they wiped their pens on the hair under their wigs.

---

*The benches and the black walnut ferule used in the first schools in Oxford were brought to Sutton by the widow of Mr. Rogers on her third marriage to Isaac Dodge. The relics were to be seen a few years since.

Town meeting July 29, 1714, voted to build a meeting-house thirty feet square, and to set the house on the west side of the highway near Twitchell's field.

This first church was located near the north-west corner of the south common, separated from the church-yard by the Charlton road, as afterward called, the church fronting on the common.

The churches in New England at this time exhibited a peculiar combination of severe plainness. The eastern boundary of the church was the Worcester road, at present opening from the common; as it appears by records of the town the location of the road was anciently.

"Tradition states in 1748 when a new church was erected Col. Ebenezer Learned gave the land and 'commons' around it (now known as the old north common), one and one-half miles south from his residence," and one mile north of the south common.

The old square church on the north common was built in the center of the twelve thousand acres of land comprising the township of Oxford at that period in the history of the town.

"And the church was at the court end of the town," and had the appearance of once being colored a dingy yellow brown, with three doors in the porch entering on the east and west sides, and south front, with corner pews in the gallery for slaves and negro servants.

March 5, 1749, voted to sell the old meeting-house at a vendue to the highest bidder, and Moses Gleason bid £66. 0. 0, and it was sold to him accordingly.

NOTE.— Sumner Baston (Barston), Esq., a native of Uxbridge, Mass., was the first cashier of the Oxford Bank, a gentleman of great natural endowments and of much refinement, with most affable manners. He had received his education at Brown's University. He became a lawyer of distinction and was highly respected in the county as a gentleman of integrity and candor. He had received the appointment of Brigade Inspector with the rank of Major. He had also been a candidate for Representative to Congress.

Oct. 14, 1751, voted that the selectmen shall inquire after the glass of the old house and give account thereof to the town. In 1752 it was again sold with the church land to Dr. Jabez Holden.*

There was a tything-man, whose duty it was to maintain order during the church service, to drive dogs from the church and to watch over the boys and young people. At any misdemeanor the tything-man would give a sharp rap with his long black staff and levelled like a musket at any offender.

This church had a porch bulging out, with its old-fashioned square wall pews and squeaking seats turned upon hinges. The great feature of this church, especially in the eyes of children, was the huge sounding board above the pulpit, and then their fears should it fall upon the minister's head. The body of the house was filled with long seats or pews opening from the center aisle of the church, with a little shelf-like table on hinges at the head of the pew. The pulpit was high and narrow. When the clergyman entered the church the people remained standing while he ascended the pulpit staircase.

In the old churches there were no fire-places, and it was before the days of stoves, furnaces or steam were used for heating them.

The women carried tiny foot stoves, filled with coals from their own fire-side; then between the church services they would have leave to replenish them from the friendly hearths of their friends near the church or at the village hotel.

The male members would frequent the hotel or old store opposite the common and obtain their "flip" or "gin slings" and then return to the church service.

On Sunday morning, a rude picture is presented, as these habitans of the new settlement are seen passing over the common to church, some on horseback singly, others double with

---

* Some of the timber of this church is still retained as a relic in the Town Hall of Oxford.

saddle and pillion, the wife on the pillion behind her husband, with maybe a little child in her arms, with a small boy on behind, holding on by the crupper.

They all dismounted on the horse-block in front of the church.

Quaint old figures toiling up to the church could be discerned as far as the eye could reach, by the old cocked hat, or many-caped great-coat. The ladies had lovely bouquets of pinks, with some sweet green mint or roses attached to their persons, of a Sunday morning in the summer. During the winter these ladies, many of them, were conspicuous from their fine scarlet broadcloth cloaks and rich sable muffs. The bearskin muff was more common.

For on a Sunday the people put on their best clothes. As wealth increased broadcloth and silk began to take the place of home spun.

The old "meeting-house" and all its surroundings were finally sold at auction, the horse-blocks removed, and all lost to view excepting the lovely common; even the ancient elms with age have disappeared. A new church was erected in 1829, fronting on the South Common.

From the settlement of the town by the English in 1713 there was only one church till 1793. The Universalist church was completed as a place for public service. The society had been formed in 1785. In 1836 the Baptist church was erected at North Oxford.

In 1840 the Methodist Episcopal church was erected. In 1843 it was enlarged by a donation from the late Jonathan Sibley, Esq. A new church has subsequently been erected.

St. Roche Catholic Church is located on Main street opposite the South Common; it commands a fine view. The present site was purchased in 1867 of John O'Shea. Since then the grounds have been improved and extended by additional valuable land purchased of Mr. Peter Butler, of Quincy, by Mr.

Shea, and transferred by him to Rt. Rev. P. T. O'Reilly, Bishop of Springfield.

In 1852 Rev. Napoleon Mignault was placed in charge of this mission by Rt. Rev. John B. Fitzpatrick, Bishop of Boston. Previous to this service was held in private houses; subsequently the present church was erected.

In 1858 Rev. James Quann was appointed rector by Bishop Fitzpatric. The reverend gentleman is a native of British America, is of kindly manners and esteemed by all classes in society. He remained in charge until 1886, when Oxford was erected into a parish by Bishop O'Reilly of Springfield, and a resident clergyman appointed.

More recently a beautiful rectory with ornamented grounds has been purchased of John E. Kimball, Esq., of Oxford, and and is now comprised in the church estate.

Grace Church (Protestant Episcopal) is beautifully located on east side of Main street on the northern portion of the Samuel Hagburn estate, one of the plantations in the first settlement of Oxford. The church rectory is imbedded in its cultivated grounds. The corner-stone was laid with ceremonies September 20, 1864. It was first occupied October 8, 1865. On November 16, following, it was consecrated by Rt. Rev. Manton Eastburn, D. D.

"The whole edifice, externally and internally, is harmonious and elegant. It is an architectural ornament such as few country villages possess." The building is of dark stone.

At the time of the settlement of Rev. Mr. Campbell in Oxford, 1721, all was not luxury and ease. Indians were lurking about. The peace of Utrecht was broken in 1722. As late as August 21, 1723, in the neighboring towns, clergymen carried arms to defend themselves during the church service. It is to be regretted that Mr. Campbell did not leave any diary with allusion to the passing events of this time, and about his journey to Boston in 1722, when he went to be married to

Miss Wheatly. They came to Oxford with two saddle horses. We can trace the Rev. Mr. and Madame Campbell on their bridal route, entertained by the clergymen on whom they called, by the journey of Dr. Parkman, of Westborough, in 1723, the clergyman of that place. He writes that he rode to Westborough from Boston on horseback, leaving Watertown, his first watering-place, at half-past twelve, and reaching Westborough at dark.

Returing to Boston, after he had secured his invitation, he stopped at Hopkinton, where he visited the clergyman and fared sumptuously on roast goose, roast pea-hen, baked stuffed venison, beef, pork. etc.

" After dinner," he adds, " we smoked a pipe and read Gov. Shute's memorial to the king."

Town meeting October 7, 1718, there is found a record stating, that a messenger was chosen to fetch us ye minister Rev. John McKinstry (to accompany him on horseback to Oxford, as was the fashion of the time), Mr. McKinstry, being in Worcester, and a graduate from Edinburgh university. One can easily picture the person of Rev. Mr. McKinstry as he entered Oxford village; his counntenance is surmounted by the large round white wig, with its depth of curls, the three-cornered, smartly-cocked hat with its broad brim with loops at the side.

The nice white necktie or white linen scarf, the end falling loosely on his breast (changed for church service for bands and surplice), his black velvet or satin breeches with the silver knee and shoe buckles, his black silk stockings, the long coat with large buttons and the long waist coat with its deep pockets and fair ruffles falling over his hands.

This style of dress marked the clergyman of olden time.

As in ancient fashion a committee was chosen by the town to confer with a clergyman as to what manner he would choose to come into town, and to wait on him accordingly.

There is no mention made of any escort being provided to accompany the clergyman into town until after the settlement of Rev. Ebenezer Newhall in 1823, on his marriage to Miss Sarah Clarke, a niece of Prof. Stuart of Andover. On the day of their arrival a party of ladies and gentlemen from Oxford proceeded with their fine carriages (yellow-bodied chaises) and fleet horses to the town of Grafton, twelve miles distant, to there wait at the hotel the arrival of the clergyman and his bride; then, as their escort, to accompany them to their pleasant home previously made ready for their reception.

As the line of carriages entered the village they met many people much to the surprise of the bride dressed " in their Sunday best," as on a gala-day, and the people seemed to be all hurrying in one direction. At the head of the village street the white gateway at the parsonage was opened for the reception of the party and groups of people were ready to welcome them to their new home. They were ushered into the house, every apartment furnished, for the furniture had arrived from Boston the week previously, and the ladies of the parish had given every direction for its arrangement.

The party were soon invited to the tea-room for a five o'clock tea with every delicacy suitable for the occasion.

Mrs. Newhall writes, "They were our first people" and "this was our first home, for Mr. Newhall had been invited to a parish in the most beautiful country town in all New England."*

In 1832 the south part of Oxford, taken to form the town of Webster, which contained much of the most valuable water power within its limits, reduced Oxford in her territory and commerce.

---

* Mrs. Elizabeth Stewart Phelps (a cousin of Mrs. Newhall), in her "Sunny Side," published many years since, gives a part of this description as an illustration of the sunny side in a clergyman's life.

The new town has increased to great population, and in its large manufacturing establishments has become a second Manchester, while Oxford is left in a state of quietude and of great beauty and as a country town, ever having been a place of cultivated society. In historic incidents Oxford is not to be surpassed by any town in New England.

CHAPTER XVIII.

NOTABLE OLD HOUSES.

In the English settlement of Oxford there were several garrison-houses in the town for the protection of the inhabitants from an attack from the Indians. The house of Col. Ebenezer Learned in the north section was garrisoned (the house is still standing). There was a garrison at the house afterward known as the Josiah Russell place and the house of Ebenezer Humphrey.*

The house of Col. Ebenezer Learned of North Oxford is one of the most ancient mansions now remaining in Oxford. "Oxford May ye tenth, 1714, laid out to Ebenezer Learned his house lot at or near a place called ye uper fall's." The house is still in good preservation (1890). "A part of the old house is of a more modern construction, having been enlarged many years ago to accommodate his son, Capt. Jeremiah Learned, on his marriage. The interior of the house is modelled in the English heavy massive style of the last century." Col. Learned died in 1772. At his decease in his "will" he places Madame Learned under the care of his son, Capt. Jeremiah Learned, his son affording her "every thing necessary and convenient for her according

---

*Garrison-houses were nothing more than common dwelling-houses surrounded by palisades, and furnished with a supply of fire-arms and ammunition.

to her rank and circumstances,* and my black man Mingo† to wait upon her during their natural lives."

An ancient house is still to be seen near the Eliott Mill brook, once the home of Julia Daily.

In the town records is the following:

"May 20, 1765. The town's house that Mrs. Bixbee lives in it was voted to sell at a vendue and said house was accordingly sett up at a vendue and Capt. James Griffin bid fifty-three pounds old tenor which was the Highest and it was struck off to him accordingly." This house was one of the old garrison-houses in the first settlement of the English in the town, and is known in the present century as the residence of the late Josiah Russell. In ancient time the house was said to be haunted by a treasure being supposed to be buried in the cellar which had been obtained by robbery. It was said every night at midnight a man could be heard digging in the cellar, as Capt. Reading, a retired sea captain had once been a resident on the estate. From an old tomb-stone is the following inscription, "Lieut. James Griffin of Gen. Shirley's regiment died Nov. 17, 1769."

This house was once the home of Rev. William Phipps, a

---

* Ebenezer Learned's lot is allowed by me as to the quntity of 40 acres and the place of being taken up and I Establish him an Inhabitant in Oxford Village.

Witness my hand May ye tenth, 1714.

JOHN CHANDLER.

JOHN TOWNE,
ABIEL LAMB,
BENONEY TWICHELL,
    Committee.

† Mingo was an African slave—his shoes of the largest size. His spoon and his block, on which he used to sit in the corner of the deep fireplace in the old west room of the house, were preserved until a few years since in the family. His place in the chimney-corner was to attend Madame Learned's wood fire.—*Reminiscences of Martha E. Stone.*

retired clergyman of Douglas, who had married Mrs. Abigail Walker, the widow of Mr. Asa Walker of Sutton, a lady possessed of a good dower in a rich landed estate.

Mrs. Abigail Phipps, widow of Wm. Phipps, Esq., died July 31, 1820, aged 92 years.

It was once the home of Peter Shumway, 2d, October, 1791, who came to Oxford on Joshua Chandler's rights.

In the settlement of Oxford the Indians were observed to be lurking about Mr. Hudson's plantation. The family were fearful of an attack, and for safety went to the garrison-house, which was on the site of the late Josiah Russell estate, and remained for two weeks.

On the Hudson place there was a native apple tree of sweet apples, of which fruit the Indians were very fond. This tree was the favorite resort of one Indian in particular, who often regaled himself with the fruit.

A part of the decayed trunk of the tree is still to be seen (1880) embedded in a wall, as stated by the late Mr. Joseph Hudson.

There is no ancient house of more interest than the Hudson house.

The home of the late Captain Humphrey, which tradition states once belonged to Gabriel Bernon. The house by some is called "Bowerwood," so beautifully is it environed by majestic elms and one ancient oak tree that dates back to the French and English settlements and still spreads its branches to shade the traveler.

Capt. Humphrey stated to Dr. Abiel Holmes on one of his visits to Oxford that his father kept the garrison-house in the French re-settlement of Oxford. There were soldiers from Woodstock stationed in Oxford.

It is a tradition that he also kept a garrison-house in the English settlement. The descendants of Captain Humphrey have been in possession of this estate since the first English settlement, and many of the French annals of the town have been preserved by this family that otherwise would have been lost in history.

Capt. Humphrey was in the Revolutionary War and also his brother Arthur Humphrey.

No gentleman was more respected in his time than Capt. Humphrey, both in church and town history. He lived to a very advanced age and his descendants honor his memory.

The house of the late Jasper Brown is an ancient house, and was in its time built in a very superior style. It was in olden time the home of Duncan Campbell, Esq., for many years, from 1748-1778, and afterward of James Butler. The house is wainscotted very beautifully; a buffet ornaments the parlor. The house stands with extensive lands on the west side of the old North Common. "It is covered with the same shaved clapboards, held by the same hand-wrought nails that were attached to it at the time of its erection."* The ancient money coffer, inlaid in the wall on the west side of the south-east room, is still to be found. The Charlton road, which now passes the house on its north side, formerly was located on the south side of the house.

On the south side of the north common at the opening of the Sutton road, there is one of the most ancient houses in the town. It was known for a long time as the home of the late Dr. David Holman, for many years a physician of Oxford. This ancient house is surrounded with much interest. It still retains remnants of its former style; a parlor buffet is preserved, and its ancient rich staircase remains as a relic of the past. The house is

---

*This old mansion, and every house of any pretension, had its "cock loft in the steep gable roof" for its house slaves or negro servants. And then the huge old chimney passing through this spacious attic was found convenient for all the requisites of turning the spit for roasting the meats in the kitchen. The services of the "Jack" were of great utility before mechanical improvements rendered them unnecessary by better methods of turning the spit.

pleasantly located, being retired some little distance from the Worcester road by an avenue, the lovely old common on one side and a once small orchard in front giving a very picturesque aspect to this antique house.

The ancient residence of Mr. Ira Merrimon, at the present time, was formerly the home of Dr. Daniel Fiske. The situation of the house has ever been attractive on an elevated site overlooking the "Oxford lake," but formerly known as "Towne's pond," a name given in honor of the family of that name, as the lake was a boundary of their plantations.*

It is said Dr. Daniel Fiske was a gentleman possessed of great refinement. On the lake he had pleasure boats, which added to the landscape picture, and on the south side of his mansion were terraces stretching one after another into the valley. These terraces were filled with rich border flowers and choice herbs, which have now unfortunately disappeared from rustic gardens.

The residence of Mr. John Mayo commanded, from its site near the ancient French fort, a beautiful view of the valley below and the mountains in the distance. Here was an old-fashioned garden, with old-time fashioned flowers and sweet herbs, with choice peach trees. The flowers were arranged with great neatness. The house of Mr. Mayo, with antique garden and flowers, and its lovely views of surrounding scenery, rendered it the most beautiful spot in the county. Mr. Mayo looked out upon the same quiet valley and wooded hill-sides for nearly ninety years. In the warm spring days Mr. Mayo would be seen sitting on the lawn with a book before him, for he was fond of reading or watching the bees, for in those days there were attached to almost every farm-house garden bee-hives ranged on the sunny side of a wall.

---

* Jacob Towne was the ancestor of General Towne, of Charlton, and Col. Sylvanus Towne, of Oxford.

(The ancient farm-house and the site of the French garrison-house were formerly approached from the village street by two huge gates, one near the entrance of the old Boston road on the Woodstock trail, as it was then designated, and the second gate above, as the farm-house was more nearly approached.)

The house of Mr. Samuel Davis of Roxbury, who came to Oxford soon following its first settlement, is in the style of an English farm-house. The site of this ancient house was selected with much taste. From its height of situation it commands an extensive view, not only of the valley lands, with the village of Oxford, but distant views of great beauty. The windows of the house were originally small and opened outward on hinges. They consisted of very small diamond panes of glass set in leaden casements.

The Samuel Davis house was the last known to have this style of windows in the town. Mr. Samuel Davis had purchased a large tract of land in Oxford of Mr. Gabriel Bernon, a French gentleman who possessed a large plantation. On a large landed estate, situated on the Boston road about two miles from the village street, was the mansion-house of Edward Davis, Esq., and subsequently of his son General Jonathan Davis. The house was built in the style of an English hall. It would appear to have been originally of a brown shade of stone color, with its narrow windows heavily and richly set. The house was ornamented with a terrace in front. There was an air of home comfort and indescribable hospitable aspect about the whole mansion. The interior of the house is richly wainscotted. The south-east parlor, with its sunny aspect, made it a most charming room, and an old buffet was one of the attractions in ancient time. It contained the silver and the daintiest china possible.

In this rich wainscotting in one of the apartments (a tiny room) there are delightful little cupboards and small drawers and over the chimney piece and in the sides of the room of the out of the way corners.

Such cupboards and drawers are all unknown to modern houses.

If a visitor arrived on a winter's day, the hall door opened into a pleasant sunny square room with a cheerful fireside in full view, which not only presented warmth and cheerfulness, but the comforts and luxuries of a country gentleman's home of more than a hundred years ago.

The comfortable kitchen with its enormous chimney and hearth of stone, upon which the embers were rarely if ever extinguished, and at its side the high-backed settle, the cupboards and dressers resplendent with pewter, and so it appears the home of Edward Davis, Esq., possessed every thing that ever modern aestheticism could suggest for a country home.

On the marriage of his son, General Jonathan Davis, who succeeded his father as the owner of this valuable landed estate as utility required, the mansion was enlarged but its architectural beauty was lessened as being strictly an English hall.

Those quaint old homes are being preserved and all the fashions restored.

There is an effort at the present time in the fashion of country residences to have them a perfect reproduction of the best colonial type of architecture, and the landscape gardening has been made to harmonize with it.

"One of the most charming features is the profusoin of old-fashioned flowers, which were so dear to the hearts of our grandmothers, which have never been surpassed in real beauty by their more pretentious successors with botanial names to give them fashion."

The visit of General Lafayette to Worcester is included in the annals of Oxford.

"General Jonathan Davis of Oxford received an invitation from Judge Lincoln to be present at the reception of Gen. Lafayette in Worcester and to extend the invitation to his townsmen."

The morning of Sept. 3, 1824, was pleasant, and the drive promised an agreeable time. Soon after breakfast General Davis, accompanied by several of his friends, all in fine carriages, "the rich one-horse chaise with a yellow body," and stylish horses. But the old Revolutionary soldiers had set out early on foot or in any conveyance at hand to be there to welcome one whom they so well remembered.*

Town meeting, May 21, 1751, voted to build a house for Mr. Rogers, to live in as long as he is our school-master, on the town's land near to the meeting-house.† Sixteen feet long and sixteen feet wide, besides convenient room for a chimney, voted

---

*The visit of General Lafayette to Worcester, September 3, 1824, was the occasion of an enthusiastic demonstration of popular favor. The arrangements were in the charge of a committee of citizens, whose chairman was Judge Levi Lincoln (afterward governor) who entertained the General at his own house. He was met at West Boylston by a company of cavalry under Capt. James Estabrook, and at the town-line by the committee of arrangements. Judge Lincoln met him in a barouche drawn by four gray horses at Clark's tavern, a mile or two from the town. A regiment of light infantry, under Lieut. Col. Ward, was added to the escort. At the entrance to Dr. William Paine's estate, on Lincoln street, an arch of flags was erected over the street; another over Court Hill, decorated by the ladies of the town.

"The children of the public schools were arranged on each side of Main street, and threw bunches of laurel before the carriage of Lafayette. Another arch of flags was erected on Main street near the Worcester Bank. On the arrival of the procession at Judge Lincoln's house, the Judge in behalf of the committee of arrangements, delivered an address of welcome, to which the General replied. A very noticeable part of the honors rendered to General Layayette was connected with the veterans of the Revolution, who had assembled from town and country villages, and formed a line of soldiers in the grounds of the Lincoln mansion house, and as he entered, every soldier extended his hand for a welcome to one they had known and honored on the field of battle. The General returned the greeting with much emotion, addressing them as 'my comrades in arms.'"

† In 1752 this church was removed.

thirteen pounds six shillings and eight pence to defray the charge of building said house.

JEREMIAH SHUMWAY,
JAMES HOVEY,
DUNCAN CAMBELL,
Committee.

This cottage for Mr. Rogers was located on the north-east corner of theSouth Common fronting south. In later times Mr. Rogers' house was known as a part of the Wolcott mansion, it being the small house attached to the north-east corner of the mansion, used for slaves or colored servants in the family.

The ancient well, near the highway to the Wolcott mansion, with its scooped out Indian mortar which in olden time was used for daily bathing was a well belonging to the town and attached to the house of Mr. Rogers.

Very near to the house of Mr. Rogers was the Wolcott mansion fronting on the south common. This house was erected in 1749 (it is said) for the residence of Duncan Campbell, Esq., on his marriage to Elizabeth, the daughter of Thomas Sterne, of Worcester. On the marriage day, accompanied by twelve ladies and gentlemen on horseback as an escort, Mr. and Mrs. Campbell arrived at their home and commenced house-keeping. In 1750-1 Josiah Wolcott, Esq., a gentleman, came to Oxford to take possession of his Freake and Papillon estates. He married Isabella, the daughter of Rev. John Campbell, and purchased this estate of Duncan Campbell.

This Wolcott home was in its time an elegant residence, constructed with much style, the paneled wainscotting very rich and elaborate, its long narrow windows with hoods or cowls, as they were termed, over windows and doors. In the spacious parlor there was a deep fireplace, ornamented with blue and white Dutch tiles, representing scenes from sacred history. On the parlor walls were rich French hangings, representing belle and beau of the past century, the portraits of the ancient

Freake and Wolcott families, painted in the court style of Charles II, portraits also of the Kitchen family, with an ancient portrait of Judge Wolcott with a huge wig, deep ruffles, and in a red velvet mantle, all these portraits representing persons, as the town records state, of land proprietors of Oxford.

A curiously carved buffet, filled with choice Eastern china and heavy silver plate, of such a quantity that an inventory was demanded by government, and is still preserved as a relic.

"And ye sconce a hanging candle stick with a heavy plate glass mirror to reflect ye rays," graced the walls of the elegant old parlor. Rich antique furniture ornamented the apartments.

And in the hall were hung funeral hatchments. "A silent intimation that the rich have been emptying their house and replenishing their sepulchres."

The Earl of Loudoun when he visited the Rev. John Campbell was also entertained at the Wolcott mansion.*

The town had sold the church land on the South Common to Dr. Holden, a residence fronting on the common, and is named in the records of Oxford. It was also the residence of

---

* 1771, Monday, March 11. In town meeting, among other items. "To know the minds of the Town relating to a strip of land lying between the Revd. Mr. Joseph Bowman's (and) Josiah Wolcott Esqrs. land being part of the old Road between their Houses and to do and act thereon as the town shall think proper.

"Voted and granted to the Revd. Mr. Joseph Bowman part of the eight Rod Highway between his house and Josiah Wolcott, Esqr's., which has not heretofore been granted away about four Rod wided to the corner of said Mr. Wolcott's Wall extending North as his Board fence now stands about sixteen Rods from the Revd. Mr. Bowmans South East corner (both residinces fronted south on the south common)."--*Town Records*, p. 144.

It would appear by this conveyance of land that the road, in place of passing on the east side of the residence of Josiah Wolcott, was first on the west side where the street is now located. The highway on the east side is still continued as a private street.

Rev. Joseph Bowman. It was a superior house in its time, and a part of it is still to be seen, though removed from its former site.

This house was the home of several distinguished families. Erasmus Babbitt, Esq., a son of Dr. Babbitt of Sturbridge, or Brookfield, was a lawyer. He was educated at Harvard University, and on his marriage to Mary, a daughter of Thomas Saunders of Gloucester, he became a resident of Oxford, and occupied this ancient mansion. Mary Eliza Babbitt, one of his two daughters, married Elkahau Cushman, and his eldest child was Charlotte Saunders Cushman, the celebrated actress. Erasmus Babbitt was a captain in the army under Col. Rice, stationed in Oxford, in the fall and winter of 1798–1799. It is said Capt. Babbitt died in service during the British war with the United States, in 1812–1815.

It was also at one time the residence of Major Archibald Campbell, a gentleman distinguished in his time. Afterward the old mansion became the home of Mr. John Torrey, of Franklin, Mass. Mr. and Mrs. Torrey were much esteemed in society. Of five sons, two became distinguished lawyers; the eldest son, Ebenezer, was educated at Harvard University, studied law in the office of John Shepley, Esq. Mr. Torrey became distinguished in his profession. In 1849 he was one of the five senators elected at large from Worcester county, and was one of a committee on banks and banking. Hon. Rufus Torrey also was educated at Harvard University. At Mr. Torrey's decease the Mobile *Register* named him as one of the most estimable gentlemen of southern Alabama; he was judge of the County Court of Monroe county; he was chosen to represent the twenty-first district in the State Senate; he died at Claiborne, Alabama, September, 1882.

Harriet, the eldest daughter of John and Sally Richardson Torrey, married Lewis Shumway. Sally R., the second daughter, married Jonathan Dudley of Sutton. On Sept. 13, 1824, "the ladies of Oxford presented an elegant standard to the

'Oxford Invincibles,' commanded by Capt. Andrew Sigourney, Jr.; the standard was presented to Ensign B. Franklin Campbell by Miss Sally R. Torrey. Miss Torrey's address to the soldiers of the 'Light Infantry' was published in the county newspapers and greatly applauded for its merit. Mr. Campbell's reply was quite noted for its gallantry and patriotism. Mr. Campbell closed his address with this sentiment: 'Then, with a soldier's devotion, we would offer the trophies of our arms and the affection of our hearts, a sacrifice to the holy shrine of female virtue.'"

The ancient school-house on the common was abandoned for other localities in different parts of the town, and this ancient building became an English trading-house in Oxford. It was owned by Josiah Wolcott. There are ancient store accounts still preserved, showing its trade to have been of European and India goods. Various kinds of cloth and taffeta are named as items. Then a mug of flip, Bohea tea and other commodities were sold to patrons. This trading-house was continued for thirty years or a longer time. Tradition states that John Wolcott was the proprietor of a store on Sigourney corner 1782-1793.

A store was established in Oxford at the close of the Revolutionary War. It was attached to the residence of James Butler, opposite the North Common. Mr. Butler and his brother in law, Captain Andrew Sigourney, were associated in the business of this country store, which was filled with home-made cloths, linen, tow and woolen fabrics, shoes, with shoe and knee buckles, gentlemen's hats, for such was the demand that a manufactory of hats was included as an item of commerce, as well as the manufacturing of potash; wooden ware was also represented in spinning-wheels, and there were candle sticks and warming-pans, sugar, molasses and tobacco, with codfish. Madeira wine and Jamacia rum were articles of trade, including Bohea and extra Hyson teas.

There were European and India goods, with various small commodities.

They were the first to introduce cotton in this section of the country, at one dollar per pound. Long before Samuel Slater of England had established his mills for manufacturing cotton cloth in Oxford. In ancient time cotton was mixed with flax for domestic fabrics. Specimens of this cloth were taken to Worcester to the calico printing establishment of the Stowells,* and returned to Oxford as dress goods. There are fragments of these prints still treasured by some of the descendants of the Sigourney family.

In 1793, or previously, Mr. Butler remained sole proprietor. Mr. Sigourney removed to the village street, and was located in a store on the corner of the Sutton road.

To the tourist who now passes through the town it presents very little of the appearance that it would a century since. Its lovely lakes still glitter in the bright sunshine. The quiet French river glides along through the green meadows as in days gone by. Rev. Peter Whitney, a quaint historian who visited Oxford one hundred years ago, narrates, 1793: "There are two or three stores of European and India goods and in the town there are all the common artificers, tradesmen and mechanics." (The people being land proprietors.) "There are within Oxford limits three grist-mills, six saw-mills, and two clothiers' works. There are also in the town potash works." Webster was then a part of Oxford.

The residence of Rev. John Campbell was situated a little distance from the South Common, on the Worcester road. After

---

* From the newspaper items of Worcester, January 5, 1793:

"The weavers shop of Cornelius and Peter Stowell was burned. Loss £300.

"They also carried on calico printing and fancy dyeing."

In 1793: "Messrs. Stowel by whom the clothier's business in all its branches is carried on to perfection. They dye fine scarlet and deep blue colors."— *Whitney's History.*

passing the little bridge over the brook there was an avenue to the mansion, with its gambrel roof. The house was superior in its style of building, and its location possessed many attractions, and was regarded as foreign in its style like houses in Scotland.

A modern house has been erected on its site.

It was for many years the residence of Nathan Hall, and his descendants still retain the estate.

On the west side of Main street the next ancient site of a house was on the estate of the late Sternes De Witt. This estate was the plantation of Nathaniel Chamberlain and once the home of the Hamlin family, who removed to Maine. Then it passed into the possession of Mr. James Gleason. The old house was a small square house located just in front of the present mansion. The only attraction of the situation was a fine landed estate beautifully located, with ancient trees.

Near the center of Main street, on the corner of the Charlton road, was the old "red tavern."

It is said to have been in its day a good and sufficient house, with a large chimney in its center giving fire-places to the apartments, fit in all respects for a house of entertainment, with stables of large accommodations for the time. The old house consisted of a large south-east square room, a staircase and a room of a smaller size fronting east on the village street. This large square room, with a small entry and staircase, with a large kitchen annexed, formed the south front on the Charlton road. The house was afterward enlarged with other apartments.

The large south-east room was the "entertaining-room" so-called, for in the north-west corner was the bar, where were displayed the mugs for flip, the keg of beer, gray earthen crocks with sugar and various wines, with Jamaica rum to tempt the traveler or lounger to much dissipation. It is said landed estates were lost and won at this bar for a "mug of flip and a song," and many widows and orphans suffered severely for its existence. The first post-office was in this tavern. The landed estate of the old tavern included the site of the present hotel.

This old red tavern was erected in 1760 by Dr. Alexander Campbell. In 1773 Ezra Bowman became the proprietor and made many improvements; he remained until 1782.

The next old mansion was on the site of the present house of Dr. Cushman. It was anciently the residence of Mr. John Walker, an English gentleman. It was a notable house with its "gamber ruff" (gambrel roof) and its deep lawn upon the street, and its landed estate in back lands, adjacent to the residence, and at the present time it is noticeable for elegance. Its ancient northern boundary included the Town Hall; it was bounded southerly by Quaboag lane, two rods wide, being a road to Charlton and Sturbridge. Mr. Walker married Mary, daughter of Duncan Campbell, Esq. The house was richly furnished with antique furniture, the walls were adorned with family portraits from England. This valuable estate passed into the Russell family, and was afterward owned by Jonathan Sibley, and then followed by Thomas Nichols as owner of the estate.

The mansion-house of Abijah Davis, Esq., was the last residence in Oxford which was built in English style with rich wainscotting. It is beautifully located on South Main street, once a part of the Hogburn estate. The landed estate was very valuable and is so considered at the present time. The house was erected 1795. Col. Rice, while in Oxford, occupied for his quarters the residence of the late Abijah Davis, Esq. It is said "he lived in great style and that Madame Rice required many servants and much waiting upon herself, and that she was dressed in rich silk gowns and her best wig every day."

During the administration of John Adams a detachment of the United States army, consisting of several regiments of infantry, was stationed in Oxford under the command of Col. Nathaniel Rice of Sturbridge from October, 1798, to June, 1800.

On the east side of Main street there was an ancient house on or near the site of the residence of the late William Sigourney. On the corner of Main street and the Sutton road was the trading-house or store of Capt. Andrew Sigourny, Sen. Afterward, on the same site, was erected a new store for his son, Capt. William Sigourney, and in modern times was a post-office, but one hundred years ago there was no post-office in Oxford. On the left-hand entrance to the Sutton road near the store was the quaint old mansion of Andrew Sigourney, Sen. Opposite the store, on the right hand of Main street and on Sutton road, was an old house on the site of the present brick house, once the residence of Andrew Sigourney, Sen. This part of Main street has ever been known as Sigourney corner.

On the east side of Main street, on the site of the present Protestant Episcopal church, there was a house pleasantly situated and roomy; it presented many attractions with its pleasant garden. The last house on the east side of the main street was that of Dr. Alexander Campbell, a gambrel roof, fine old mansion, occupying a site in the rear or on the east side of the mansion of the heirs of the late Israel Sibley. A cottage has been erected on the site of Dr. Campbell's house. The estate originally had extensive grounds in front, reaching to the street, with large elms as shade trees. These grounds are now included with the residence of the Sibley heirs.

The last house on the main street, west side, was the residence of Richard Moore, Esq. This residence was at the south end of what was called the " village street." This ancient house, belonging to the Moore family, was in its day a substantial mansion, built in the style of an English hall, its gables being on the north and south, fronting on the street, but extending westerly, giving a south front, and like every house in those times served as a sundial, for at mid-day the sun shone square upon the south front, and for many years in modern times a leaden sundial was seen attached to one of its south window-sills.

The broad street door opening into one of its apartments was rich and much ornamented in its architecture, as were the houses of the gentry; in its different apartments were large broad-breasted chimneys, occupying space sufficient for a good-sized apartment, with large open fire-places, and then there was in these pleasant rooms rich wainscotting. The house commanded a southern landscape of its own landed estate with a narrow lawn and lovely garden.* This landed estate was a part of the Samuel Hagburn plantation, and was bounded northerly by Quaboag lane. The house was large and elegant. It was the home of Richard Moore, Sen., in his declining years, and also of his son Richard, and also of Marvin, son of Richard.

The giant oak which anciently overshadowed the Moore residence still stands on the lawn as a sentinel on duty and a landmark to direct the traveler. It was a tree of great size and age two hundred years ago, and from one decade of years to another has shaded many groups of children in their childish sports. The old oak could tell many stories of those who have played beneath its shade, and grown old and passed away.†

> "I swear by leaf, and wind, and rain,
>   And hear me with thine ears,
> That I circle in the grain
>   Five hundred rings of years.
>
> "And I have shadowed many a group
>   Of beauties that were born
> In tea-cup times of hood and hoop,
>   Or while the patch was worn." —*Tennyson.*

---

* In New England tall English clocks were uncommon; few were imported, but soon came into general use. In some English church-yards there were sundials of stone and a sundial over the door of a south front on old English churches.

† The late Honorable Ira Moore Barton of Worcester, Mass., often visited the Moore place as the home of his ancestors. The Moore family were originally of Scotch extraction, tracing back their ancestry to the time of William the Conqueror.

Timothy Harris removed to Oxford in 1733, from Watertown, having purchased the old Huguenot mill at the south end of the village street in Oxford, on the road to the French Fort, owned in the French settlement by Gabriel Bernon. This mill lot was once the plantation of Jonathan Tillotson, a planter in the English settlement.

Mr. Harris and his descendants retained this estate for one hundred and fifty years. There was an ancient house on this estate which was regarded with interest into the present century.

A small house with a half acre of land on Main street nearly opposite the Town Hall was the home of Abner Miller, the sexton of the village. There is a tradition that a gentleman resided here as a recluse, boarding at the Red Tavern, and was always engaged in writing. He had received many services from Abner Miller, and on leaving town he placed his house and land in the care of Mr. Miller until his return ; he never appeared and Miller held the estate.

On the Red Tavern estate north on the site of the Town Hall was a small cottage which was erected by the heirs of Dr. Alexander Campbell, who died at his home east of Israel Sibley's house January, 1785, for his widow, who survived him until March, 1816, she having relinquished her dower to favor the heirs in the rich old gambrel-roofed mansion situated easterly of the present estate of the late Israel Sibley estate.

CHAPTER XIX.

ROADS AND MILESTONES.

Milestones.

The old milestone on Lincoln street, Worcester, is of red sandstone, with the following inscription:

42
Miles from
Boston 50 to
Springfield,
1771.

By a Provincial enactment made in Governor Hutchinson's time, this milestone was one of many placed in the year 1771 along on the "New Connecticut road," which way was afterward called the "post road" from Boston to New York and Albany. This road left Boston for Marlborough thence to Quinsigamond (Worcester) and then to Brookfield and so on to Springfield.

In the history of the town of Northborough, once a part of Marlborough, it is stated "The oldest vestige of pioneer life still in existence is doubtless the great road to Worcester, as it is called."

Originally this road in 1672 was only a pathway or trail through the forests, when Marlborough was a frontier settlement with its garrison house. After leaving Marlborough there was no habitation on the Boston road to Springfield until the garrison house was reached at Quabaug (now Brookfield) with the exception in Quinsigamond (Worcester) of a little Indian town of huts on Pakachoag Hill, the highlands of which reach the town of Auburn. On or near the site of this Indian town is now located "Holy Cross College."

This Indian town is described by Gookin:
"This village lyeth about three miles south of the new roadway that leadeth from Boston to Connecticut; it consists of about twenty families. This town is situated upon a fertile hill and is denominated from a delicate spring of water that is there."

Settlement of Worcester. "A tract of land eight miles square was purchased of the Indians for twelve pounds lawful money. The deed bears date July 13, 1674."

Dec. 2, 1675, Increase Mather writes: "This day all the houses in Quonsukamuck (Worcester) were burned by the Indians."

"At what is West Brookfield, near to the south-west end of Wickabaug Pond, on a knoll below the junction of the waters of the pond with Quabaug river, stood Mark's garrison."

Quabaug (Brookfield) became the established English bridle path between the Bay and the Connecticut. "The single horseman or a cavalcade of riders and pack horses was a common sight to the Indians." The Old Connecticut road had in a manner ceased to be used as the most traveled path to Connecticut and was already displaced by the New Connecticut road.

The Old Connecticut road was the inland trail of Massachusetts of which we have the most ancient account. From Cambridge it proceeded to the south-east part of Marlborough, then passed to Hassamamisett (Grafton, a part of the township of Sutton) and thence to Oxford near the French fort, Woodstock and so on to Springfield.

It is stated that in the autumn of 1630 the chief of the Indians of Wabquasset, now Woodstock, visited the English governor at the Bay to establish a trading house, and this Indian trading expedition brought this forest path to the knowledge of the English, who made it their way to travel to the Connecticut Valley.

John Oldham followed this old Connecticut path in 1633, odging in Indian towns all the way. A well-defined trail from Mount Hope and the Narraganset country, known as the Providence path, intersected the Old Connecticut path in or near Woodstock. Another trail, known as the Nipmuck path, came from Norwich to the same point of junction. From here a branch track proceeded to the north-west into Sturbridge, where it separated, one track going westerly past the lead mines, and on to Springfield. Miss Ellen D. Larned, the author of the History of Windham County, writes of this " Connecticut path:" "This rude track became the main thoroughfare between the two colonies, Massachusetts and Connecticut. Hundreds of families toiled over it to reach homes in the wilderness. The fathers of Hartford and New Haven, ministers and governors, captains and commissioners, government officials and land speculators, crossed and recrossed this forest path."

There were milestones placed all the way along this " Old Connecticut road" from Boston to Springfield.

On the southerly front of the site of the house of Col. Woodbury in Sutton stands the queen of all milestones; it is of red sandstone, five feet in height, two feet wide and eight inches in thickness, with this inscription :

<pre>
           48
         ML To
         Boston
          1771
          B W
</pre>

Col. Bartholomew Woodbury of Sutton was the proprietor of a country inn which was with a fine landed estate situated on this " Old Connecticut road." Col. Woodbury offered the commissioners, who were directing the sites of the milestones, if they would make the last mile a little less than its limit, placing it near to his house, that it might attract travellers, he would be at the expense of erecting the milestone, and that it should excel all others en route from Boston to Springfield on this same Old Connecticut road.

At every country inn there was a horse block for the convenience of travellers on horseback — a gentleman in the saddle, may be, and a lady on a pillion behind him. Ladies of high position had a separate horse with a side-saddle, and were escorted by a gentleman or a servant, and to avoid the gaze of travellers wore masks of black velvet, as was the fashion of the time.

Long since the brown house, with its huge cobble stone chimney and oven outside the house, has passed away and only its stately milestone with its companion, the horse block, covered in the summer time with greenery and flowers, remain to mark the site of the "Wayside Inn." There is one notable milestone in Oxford on this Old Connecticut road where the Sutton road enters the village street. It stands on Sigourney corner and was erected by Josiah Wolcott, a resident of Oxford, with this inscription:

$53\frac{1}{2}$
Miles to
Boston
J & W
1771

Milestones were anciently placed along the roads in eastern countries.

It is said by travellers at the present time in Palestine they may be seen here and there in that country.

Milestones were once common in England, viz., the roads leading from London to the large towns.

"'Tis such an easy walk, so smooth and straight,
The second milestone fronts the garden gate."
— "*Retirement*," *Cowper*.

The Bay Path.

In 1673 this highway was established for the use of the country leading from Watertown as the nearest and best way to Marlborough and thence to Quabaug (Brookfield). This new path left the "Old Connecticut path" at "Happy Hollow" (now in Wayland) and passed through Marlborough, Worcester, Oxford in its northern section, Charlton on to Brookfield where it parted, one branch following the old trail or Old Connecticut road to Springfield, and the other leading on through Ware and Belchertown to Hadley.

The late Hon. Salem Towne, of Charlton, stated that remains of the "Old Bay road" were still to be seen lying in the western valley lands of Charlton; vestiges of this "Bay road" are still remaining in Oxford on the Old North Charlton road.

The "Old Bay path" is beautifully described by Dr. Holland in his romance of that name.

"It was a path marked by trees a portion of the distance, and by slight clearings of brush and thicket for the remainder. No stream was bridged, no hill graded, and no marsh drained. The path led through woods which bore the mark of centuries, over barren hills that had been licked by the Indian's hounds of fire, and along the banks of streams that the seine had never dragged."

NOTE.— In July, 1675, Ephraim Curtis was engaged to conduct "Uncas his six men" from Boston home. He says, "I conducted [them] safly while I com in sight of Webquesesne new planting fielde, first to Natuck, from thenc to Marelborrow, thenc to Esnemisco, thenc to Mumchogg [Oxford], thenc to Chabanagon komug, thenc to Mayenecket, thenc over the river to Sencksig, while wee cam nere to Wabaquasesn wher they were willing that wee should leve them."— *Mass. Arch.*, lxvii, 214.

The old Connecticut road or Woodstock path, now the road to Webster, was long since trod by the Connecticut pioneers, Huguenots, and many others. The Shumway house was on this Old Connecticut road.

"It is wonderful what a powerful interest was attached to the Bay path, the rough thread of soil, chopped by the blades of a hundred streams, was the one way left open, through which the sweet tide of sympathy might flow. Every rod had been prayed over by friends on the journey and friends at home. If every traveller had raised his Ebenezer as the morning dawned upon his trusting sleep, the monuments would have risen and stood like milestones."

The late Mr. Samuel Mayo, whose ancestors were in the English settlement of Oxford, stated that the old Connecticut road or Boston road passed near to the French fort in Oxford and could be traced for a considerable distance, it being on the Indian great trail to Woodstock, Ct., passing by or very near the residence of late John Hurd. This old Connecticut road passed near to the mills known for many years as owned by Ebenezer Rich, and then near the residence of Samuel Davis.

"In 1656 the road or bridle-path from Boston to Hadley was to Marlborough, then to Brookfield, the nearest settlement west, and then on to Hadley meadows, guided by blazed or marked trees through the wilderness, to Brookfield in the road of Connecticut.

"The Old Bay path or road crossed the Quaboag at Brookfield, following somewhat the course of this (river), and " Chicuppee to Indian Orchard, thence to Agawam (Springfield)."*

---

*In 1674 Major Gookin states in naming Hassanamesit [Grafton]: " It is near unto the old road way to Connecticut." The most direct route from Grafton to Woodstock, Ct., is through Oxford.

On a plan dated April 1, 1713, in the Massachusetts Archives, of a grant of land to Jethro Coffin, located in Northbridge, there is laid down easterly and westerly, a line designated as the "French road" (to Oxford).—*Plans and Grants*, i, 240.

Marlboro Records, May 21, 1688. There is mention made in view of a line of division between the western and eastern parts of the town. " To be made by a line at the cart-way at Stirrup-Brook, where Connecti-

From the Sutton Records is the following reference to the Oxford road through Sutton: " The road from Oxford to Marlborough, beginning at the farms,* so returning upon the point of compasse to the meeting-house hill, thence to the north side of Elisha Johnson's house to Cold-spring brook, six rods wide from the heads of the proprietors' lotts — laid out March, 1716, by Nathaniel Brewer, Jonathan Draper, Eleazur Daniels."

Elisha Johnson's cabin was situated very near the place now occupied by Samuel Prescott.

In 1713 old roads in the English settlement of Oxford : " A way laid out by the select men beginning att a white oake tree

---

coat way now goeth over" (now within the limits of Northborough, a part of Marlborough).

In 1717 this division line was one of the boundary lines of the town of Westboro.

This way was called in the old records "the great trail," as plainly indicating that it was originally the Indian path --(which passed the French fort in Oxford to Woodstock).

March 30, 1683. There is a record of a petition for a bridge across the "Medfield river."

The court grant the petition. "Whereas, the way to Kenecticut now used, being very hazardous to travellers, by reason of one deep river that is passed fower or five times over, which may be avoided as is conceived by a better and nearer way, it is refered to Major Pynchon to order the said to be laid out and well marked."—*Mass. Col. Rec.*, v, 391.

"Quaboag lane" in Oxford, once an Indian trail to Brookfield, which forded the river near the stone arch bridge entered the Eight-rod way from the west, bounding the north side of the estate of late Abijah Davis, formerly a part of the plantation of Samuel Hagburn.

In 1711 there is a record of land of Major Fitch included in Windham County, Ct., in the northern part of the county where the "Connecticut path" is designated as entering the town of Thompson, near the middle of its northern boundary-line and near to where the "Frenchtown river," as there named, enters the town. This Connecticut path it would appear must have been on the westerly side of Chanbunagungamaug pond and this would indicate that its course was through Oxford.

* "Manchaug Farms" (West Sutton).

on Jonson's plain near Woodstock path running northwardly marked on the west sid to neland's feald on the great plain by the old mill place, from thence marked on the East sid by stake and trees tel it coms to the brooke on the Northwardly sid of peter Shumway's frame of his house, from thence on the West sid of the swamp to and by the ends of the house lots of John Town and Daniel Eloit Juner sd way being Eight rods wide laid out fubruary the sixt 1713-4" — Ibid.; 1 *Village Rec.* This "way" included the present Main street.

May 24, 1716, at a town meeting legally warned Richard Moore, chosen moderator voted in ye affirmative y^t there should be a cast bridg built oner ye brook in ye Eight Rod highway ye brook commonly called ye mill brook.

May 24, 1716, voted y^t there shall be a bridg made passabal for horses ouer ye brook by Jonathan Tillotsons on the four rod way to the fort.

May 24, 1716, voted also y^t there shall be a bridg built ouer ye brook in ye highway near Ollouer Collers on the Sutton road.

The Record of Mr. campbels petison to ye proprietors of oxford village:

oxford, march 16th, 1723.

Gentlemen :

Whereas I haue for the benefit of Trauellers and Inhabitants Turned the eight rod highway opposite to my house and the two rod highway that Leads to the great meadow ; the eight rod highway is Shortened about ten or eleuen rods and the other about so maney as allso it hath saved the making of a bridge of some considerable charges and therefore I humbly Request that you would be pleased to accept of the Turning of the aboue Said ways at your next meeting.

JOHN CAMPBELL.

At a proprietors meeting March 19th, 1723, in oxford uillge the queston being put whether Mr. campbell's Request Should be Granted which was voted in the afirmatiue.

March 11, 1759. " To accept of the county road 4 rods wide from the stone bridge by the Rev. Mr. Campbell's land then through a corner of Mr. Campbell's land and also through Mr. Duncan Campbell's land that he bought lately of Mr. Joseph Rocket straight into the county road west of the barn on said land allowing said Duncan Campbell liberty to shut up four rods of the eight rod road against Dr. Holden's and Mr. Mellins."

Town meeting May 20, 1765, voted to accept of a Bridle road from Mr. William Browns to Mr. John Town's house instead of an open one ; upon consideration that Isaac Town will make and maintain two suitable gates, one at each end of said Road.*

French river, so called by the English, runs through the town. The river runs about three-quarters of a mile west of the great road that leads over Oxford plain, and falls into the Quinebang in the town of Thompson, in Connecticut. Rev. Dr. Holmes writes : In passing the bridge which is at a considerable distance below the village of Oxford (on the Webster road), seeing a boy near the bridge I asked him, " What is the

---

* In 1808, to facilitate travel and for the more rapid communication by mail, the Providence and Douglas turnpike was made through what at that time was almost a dense forest. Another turnpike, which was a continuation of this Providence road, extended from Douglas to Oxford and for many years it was the most direct traveled route from Providence to Oxford and the towns in the vicinity. It passed through a large tract of land in the Douglas woods, including the Streeter farm, so called. This " Gore turnpike " through the woods was built in 1826. The territory lying west of Douglas previously to this date was known as " Oxford South Gore," now Webster, and a road crossing the turnpike in the south part, of the town as the " Gore road !" There were toll-gates on the turnpike road ; each person on horseback or with a chaise was required to pay twelve and a half cents at these gates. At about the close of the last century the Boston and New York turnpike passed through this section of country. There was an immense amount of travel over this road during the War of 1812 from all of the eastern towns.

name of this river?" "French* river," he replied. "Why," I asked, "is it called French river?" "I believe," said he, "there was some French people once here," — pointing up the stream.

The Eight-rod way, so named in the English settlement of the town, commenced south at the junction of the present Thompson and Webster roads at the farm long known as the Jonas Leonard estate, passing northerly over Johnson's Plain, the Great Plain and Towne's Plain, including the Daniel Eliott mill estate on the north.

Upon the Eight-rod way were located mostly the plantations of the English in their settlement of Oxford. On the Great Plain south was the plantation of Samuel Hagburn on the west side; it reached northerly to Quaboag lane; on the easterly side from the Huguenot mill estate on its northern boundary to the Episcopal church, including the site of a house north of this church. Thomas Gleason, a gentleman who possessed wealth, was an original proprietor of a plantation on the south-east corner of Main street and Sutton road, now known as Andrew Sigourney corner. This plantation bounded on the south the Samuel Hagburn estate. The Gleason estate extended on the Sutton road to the brook. Oliver Coller's plantation was on the north-east corner of Main street and the Sutton road; on the Sutton road it extended to the brook and northerly on Main street to the plantation of Joseph Rockwood — which included the Josiah Wolcott estate and joined the estate of Rev. John Campbell. Nathaniel Chamberlain's plantation extended from the South Common to the estate of Benjamin Chamberlain, which included the site of Memorial Hall, Old Red Tavern and extended south to Quaboag lane.

---

*This river was called French river in the early English settlement. It is named as a boundary in Rev. John Campbell's "Will." The Indian name of the French river was the Muanexit. It might ever have been retained by the English as a memento of the Nipmuck Indians.

Towne's Plain — John Towne, one of the original proprietors of Oxford, resided on a part of his plantation which adjoined the North Common, at the present time, 1890, known as the estate of Joseph Stephens. John Towne conveyed this estate to his son Jonathan, who gave the estate to his son John, who was a Captain in the War of the Revolution. Ephraim Towne, son of John Towne, Sen., owned the estate west of the North Common, and with his brother Jonathan, known at present as the estate of late Joseph Brown. Jonathan Towne conveyed to Duncan Campbell in 1748, who erected the present house. Israel Towne was the proprietor of the estate opposite Towne's pond, known once as the Dr. Daniel Fiske estate, later as the estate of Ira Merriam.

In 1749 a road from Jacob Towne's into the old Charlton road north of Towne's pond.

In 1736 the Court of Sessions ordered a cart bridge to be built over the river in the North gore "on the road to Oxford."

The road easterly of the North Common to Sutton was made prior to 1750.

In 1788 a road was made to Sutton past the Lovett farm.

In 1803 a road from present Howarth north to Charlton road was accepted.

July, 1817, from Nichols' mill east and south by the pond to Charlton road; a cart road with bars and gate had been established prior to this date.

1791 a road to Charlton from Gen. Leonard's west, two rods wide, at present time discontinued.

March, 1731, a road from the Eight-rod way on (Towne's Plain) north side of Towne's pond, past the little cedar swamp and crossing the river at Joseph Brown's place, discontinued in 1819.

May, 1793, from North Common west to the bridge intersecting the old road to Charlton, north of Towne's pond, continued to the present time.

A road to Charlton was laid out and completed in 1785 from Lieut. John Nichols', on the Sturbridge road, near the present school-house in the Buffum district, easterly over the river at the present stone bridge, entering the Main street near the tavern at the center.

An old record states, "began four rods south of the house of Ezra Bowman inn-holder on westerly to a popple in Quaboag or town road, thence west to the river and Coburn's land, thence on near John Nichols' house."

"Coming home from Worcester on Tuesday night my horse fell with me and hurt me so that I cannot be at Worcester this court. You will take care of the road with Maj^r Upham if he is needed. You can inform the court that the Town of Oxford maintains seven Bridges over the same river, [French] and this not of any service to the Town, it is thought that it will cost the Town Two hundred pounds if it is accepted. There is one Bridge within less than a hundred rods, there is one other Bridge that is to be built over the same river to come to Town from Elijah Leonard's and that part of the Town it is thought a great burden if it is accepted as the bench is very thin it may be left to put it to August. You can inform the court that the Town are very unanimous in opposing it.

"from yours to serve

"Oxford, June 15th 1797.   SILVANUS TOWN.

"Maj^r JOHN D. DUNBAR."

CHAPTER XX.

TAVERNS AND POST-OFFICES.

Daniel Eliott was the first inn-holder in Oxford, 1714, at the extreme north end of the village, near the crossing of the Eliott mill brook and Worcester road and the Hawes estate, which includes some of the Eliott place.

In 1715 the second tavern was that of Richard Moore, who was licensed on the Samuel Hagburn estate, which he had purchased, subsequently owned by Dr. Alexander Campbell as a residence, late Israel Sibley estate. The house was located a little distance easterly of Main street.

For forty-five years it was the hotel of the village. In 1734 Elijah, son of Richard Moore, succeeded his father and continued until 1760.

Moses Marcy was licensed in 1736 as a tavern-keeper in Oxford, at the most westerly part of the town, now Southbridge.

" Worcester S S Anno R^i R^s Georgij Secundi nunc Magnæ Britaniæ Franciae et Hiberniae Octavo.

Att a Court of Generall Sessions of the peace begun and held at Worcester within and for the County of Worcester on The Second Tuesday of August being the thirteenth day of Said month Annoq Dom 1734" —

" Tavern Keepers and Retailors Lycenced ye year Ensuing & y^t gave bond."

OXFORD
ELIJAH MOORE INHOLDR
1735

" A list of Tavern Keepers and Retailors Lycenced by this Court & ye names of the Suretys."

OXFORD

Mr. Elijah Moore; Capt. Moore principall, Suretys Capt. Flagg & Joe: Crosby.

Mr. Moses Marcy principall — Suretys Capt. Flagg & Jno. Stacy New Medfield.

1636

"A list of Inholders and Retailors lycenced by this Court with ye Names of their Suretys each principall Recognized in fifty pound and Each Surety in Twenty five pounds.

"The following persons are Inholders unless Retailor is added to there names."

OXFORD

Mr. Elijah Moore, Capt. Moore principall Suretys Danl Newhall Joe Crosby.

Capt. Moses Marcy Capt. Flagg principall Suretys Jno Harwood Joseph Dyer.

To keep a tavern "a convenient sign was to be set out at the most conspicuous" place to give notice to strangers. There was a tall staff in front of the South tavern which swung aloft in the wind the creaking sign board. In days away back in the history of the town this hotel was a noted resort, when public meetings, dances, balls and other assemblies of a political, social and business character were usually held in such public houses, and being then famed for athletic games, for the excellency of its flip and punch. It was the gathering place of convival spirits in Oxford and the country around in its vicinity. As for the bar-room itself it was usually filled with village loungers. Samuel Campbell it is said was the proprietor and landlord of this hotel some years. In the olden time before daily papers and mails were established, the neighbors used to gather at the village tavern to learn the news from travelers, and find out about the markets by teamsters from Boston.

Col. Sylvanus Learned, on his return home from the Revolutionary War, after a long service, received $1,500 in Continental money, which one day in the tavern he sold for a mug of flip. Col. Learned considered his payment as worthless and made this disposal as to its value.

It is related that upon a time a "professional" from a distance having heard of Samuel Davis,* known in all the region as a wrestler, came to town to try a match with him.

"News of the affair quickly spread through the village, and a large company assembled at the old tavern on the plain to see the sport. Mr. Davis, who was not personally known to his opponent, kept a little in the back ground, and when the match was "called," his brother Elijah, who was a stalwart man, stepped forward, and grappling with the champion, after somewhat a lengthened contest, was thrown. Samuel, who had watched closely his antagonist for the purpose of learning his game, now walked into the ring, saying: "I am the man you came to Oxford to wrestle with," and very soon demonstrated his superiority."†

"In 1777 Agreeable to an act of court entitled, 'An act to prevent monopoly and oppression,' "Inn-holders for a meal of victuals of their best kind not to exceed 1s. 6d. and of common kind 8d, flip made of the best New England rum pr. mug 8d. and made from West India rum not to exceed 10d."

"For lodging a single person over night, 3¼d. For keeping a horse 24 hours 1s. 3d."‡

---

* Mr. Davis, of Oxford, it is said, was noted as a person of great muscular strength. In person he was tall and broad-breasted, possessed of a fine personal appearance, and was ever fond of all athletic games — in which he excelled. His residence was on the landed estate now owned by Charles Lovett.

† History of Samuel Davis of Oxford and his Descendants.

‡ M^r	Dunbar.	Dr.
To Breakfast, 4	....	6
Dinner, 5.	.......·...................	7
Supper, 1	....	1

268   *The Records of Oxford.*

Major Dunham of Col. Nathan Rice's* Regiment, then quartered in Oxford, delivered an address in January, 1800, to the soldiers, Free Masons and citizens of Oxford, on receiving the announcement of the death of General Washington, who died at his residence at Mount Vernon, Dec. 14, 1799.

The people assembled with crape on their arms, followed by a company of militia with muffled drums. This military and Masonic funeral procession was formed on Oxford plain, including Col. Rice's Regiment, and proceeded as far as the old North

To Lodging...	1	4
Grog...		
Wine...		3
Punch		
Servants...		
Horses		9
Seat in Stage to ———		
	£1 7	4

Received Payment, 1794, March 29,

              EPHRAIM MOWER.

(Capt. Ephraim Mower's tavern was at the corner of Mechanic street, near the spot where Clark's Block now stands, in Worcester.)

*In Oxford, October, 1798, a detachment of the United States Army, consisting of four regiments of Infantry under the command of Col. Nathan Rice, was stationed in Oxford on the high land west of the village street, afterward known as Camp hill. A number of the officers of this army had their headquarters at the two hotels. It is said at the old tavern on the north common that the "money coffer" used by them is still to be seen in the south-east room. Soldiers for disobedience were fastened to the staff which supported the south tavern sign, and received a severe punishment at this whipping-post.

The high land west of the village street, occupied by Col. Rice's Regiment, long retained the name of Camp hill as having been the place of the soldiers' encampment. Opposite this height of land, on the south side of the road leaving Oxford, there are the remains of a ditch made by the soldiers as a punishment for their misdemeanors.

Common. A coffin was borne on a bier and surmounted by a funeral urn.*

"Lt. EVERETT, 5 Mass. Reg.:
"General Washington presents his compliments to Lt. Everett, and requests the favor of his company at dinner tomorrow, 3 o'clock, Tuesday.
"Answer if you please."

This note of invitation is now in the possession of Leonard E. Thayer, a lineal descendant of Col. Everett.

It is said that the soldiers in the army stationed in Oxford in the years 1798, 1799 and 1800 introduced much dissipation into the town.

At the tavern on the village street the barroom was so crowded evenings with soldiers calling for their mug of flip, that the bar-keeper was obliged in taking the red heated logger head from the fire, to brandish it before him to permit himself to enter the bar.

The sale of wine and brandy was immense, and that a large income from it was derived by the proprietor is not to be doubted. At the north tavern there was no bar at this time, and it was no place sought as a resort for the soldiers. It appears there was no bar in this hotel until after the year 1820.

There was an ancient store attached to this hotel on the north side, where Madeira wine was sold, with brandy and Jamaica rum. If any guests wished for the wine, etc., they were furnished from the store or cellar.

There was much boiling, roasting and baking going on in the tavern before the "muster."

The militia trainings, too, made lively days at the village

---

* The following item is found in the Worcester *Spy*, dated June 18, 1800:

"On Tuesday the 10th inst, Gen. Alexander Hamilton and his suite arrived at Oxford to settle the business relative to the discharge of the troops stationed there; and on Friday last he passed through this town on his way to Boston."

tavern, and then the old-fashioned muster (or military review) which came in September, the mustering of all the companies of soldiers in a regiment or brigade for a general training. At sunrise the drums were beating. The general reviewed the soldiers and the military review ended in a sham fight. Each company endeavored to be first on parade to go through with its manœuvres in presence of an admiring crowd of spectators, the fifes playing "Yankee Doodle" and "On the road to Boston," tunes which had animated the hearts of the soldiers of the Revolution.

The uniforms were blue coats with red facings and bright buttons, white pantaloons, caps with tall white plumes tipped with red.

The annual muster (or regimental training) was a great occasion for these military reviews. The companies, infantry and light artillery, riflemen, grenadiers and cavalry or troopers and artillery, with their cannons, assembled together and became the center of attraction. Military officers retired from service welcomed the review by their presence. Men and boys followed them on the public roads. Horse jockeys, gingerbread carts, peddlers of every description, with showmen with wax figures, monkeys and bears, enlivened the day, and all became as a grand carnival. These scenes of gayety sometimes were for two days continued. In Oxford the ground chosen for this military review was selected on the estate of late Andrew Sigourney near the corner of Main street and Sutton road in a large field adjoining his brick mansion house, bounded northerly by the Sutton road. In Sutton the large fields of the late James Freeland's farm were selected.

It is said military trainings were then common in all the country towns. Much rivalship was manifested by the towns to see which could produce the best-drilled, uniformed, armed and equipped companies. The regimental musters or reviews were scenes of great public festivity and enjoyment.

One can picture a village tavern at nightfall. There had arrived travelers on horseback with portmanteaus made of leather, or as substitutes long sacks woven of coarse red and green yarn, with leather tops and bottoms, called saddlebags, into which all their luggage however minute or bulky had been packed.

Ladies as well as gentlemen traveled in this fashion, with side saddles, and children were transported through the country in the same manner, sitting on pillions (little cushions stuffed with feathers) attached to the saddle, with one hand holding to the crupper of the saddle and one clinging to the person in front of them by means of a scarf attached to the waist of the rider, or sometimes when the pillion is occupied by a lady the children are placed in front of the gentleman. Most ladies traveled on horseback, and ladies made long journeys in this way, riding alone or with a friend or servant who was himself on horseback and usually well armed, for the roads were not always safe.

In front of the tavern there stood great carts filled with spinning-wheels for country trade, wagons filled with common household furniture, and all things necessary for a new settlement, peddler's carts of every description, and stock drovers, for that old house once swarmed with guests, but its day is done, and its old "green, spindle-backed arm chairs" have become things of the past. The old tavern well on the opposite side of the Charlton road still remains.*

Formerly there were more public-houses in the country villages than at the present time. Travelers then had their

---

* A few years since the daughter of Samuel Campbell (the innkeeper) revisited Oxford, having been absent over forty years. She said when upon the street she drank water from this old well; that it was all that would recall Oxford to her memory as existing in her childhood, so great had been the change upon the village street, and this well had supplied the village school.

town private carriages of some description, and sought the hostality of the village tavern. There would be seen at its open door at noon or at evening a blue or red painted coach belonging to some family of wealth, low hung and broad wheeled, with its colored coachman, or a stout, large, square-top chaise containing some stylish gentleman, and maybe accompanied by a lady journeying to some distant part of the country. The chaise in these days was called a " hahnsum kerridg."

The last square-top chaise that was seen in Oxford belonged to Charles Sigourney, Esq., of Hartford, Ct., who visited the place with Mrs. Sigourney many years since. The harness was silver mounted and attracted, it was said by the villagers, more attention than the distinguished guests.

Have you heard of the wonderful one hoss shay?

We are told they were made of " the strongest oak that could not be split nor bent nor broke."

> "For the wheels were just as strong as the thills,
> And the floor was just as strong as the sills,
> And the panels just as strong as the floor,
> And the whipple tree neither less nor more,
> And the back cross bar as strong as the fore,
> And the spring and axle and hub encore."
>
> DR. OLIVER WENDELL HOLMES.

Before the Revolution there were vehicles used in Boston at an early date resembling " English road carts," which made so much racket by rattling and pounding through the streets they were called " homespun thunder carriages."*

---

* In Oxford in olden time there were very few of these vehicles. On Sunday, or some special occasion, Edward Davis, Esq., appeared in a "one hoss shay " and also his townsmen, Josiah Wolcott, Esq., and James Butler, all attracting much observation. There was a prejudice against them as they represented certain caste distinction of long ago. It is said that a worthy man in Worcester took an elderly friend of his to church in his chaise. He had just arrived at the church door when a prominent citizen of the upper class of that period thus accosted him,

Taverns and Post-offices.

Prior to the Revolution is styled ancient time, and very few if any, private coaches were used in this country. All travel was confined to horseback riding, and the equipments were styled the furniture of the horse. When Gen. Washington received his family coach from London it was spoken of as an item of interest throughout the country. Coaches were not common at this early date.

It was not uncommon for travelers in these day to take their own provisions with them, and to request the hostess of an inn to furnish them in the waiting-room with cooking utensils to prepare their luxuries for the table. The tea and coffee, with pickled or spiced meats, old fashioned, nice bread, would soon be served and with rich pies, cakes and preserves, gave to all an appearance of comfort. The landlord was compensated for this trouble in the settlement of the bill or for any extras furnished to his guests.

The horses of travelers were stabled, the private coachman and the driver of a freight team ordered and superintended all for the comfort of their tired animals, many times furnishing their own grain. At this time most inland freight was carried by horses, and then there was excitement at the village inns when the stage coach carrying the mails and passengers would

---

with a vehemence of protest that made his shirt ruffles quiver: " Fine times we are coming to, fine times, Mr. E———, when mechanics ride to meeting in chaises."

But in the present time mechanics and artisans enjoy all there is of the luxuries of life, and through their skill and energy we all share them and to them Worcester owes her unrivalled success in population and wealth.

Very soon these gentlemen with their "pleasure carriages," as they were termed, were followed by General Learned and Joseph Hudson. There are those of Mr. Hudson's descendants that can at the present time recall in their early childhood seeing Madam Hudson in her "square-top chase" riding down Long hill [Federal hill] with her milk white horse noted for his fat and sleek condition the country around.

roll by at regular intervals, then the only vehicle of public conveyance, and stage loads stopping to dine. But the railroads of the present time have diverted all this travel and business into new channels. The stage coaches have left the highways. Sometimes in the depth of winter there would be much excitement at the village inn by the arrival of a sleighing party for the evening dance and sometimes by travelers in sleighs journeying to visit their friends in the new settlements of Vermont and other parts of northern New England.

This old South Tavern of Oxford for more than one hundred years was the center of all communication with the outside world and the life of the neighborhood.

Here the balls and the junketings of the olden time were held in an apartment being lighted with candles which would have ordinarily furnished only a dim light if not for the ample chimney with its cheerful wood fire.

Here were assembled the young ladies with dresses of extremely short waists, and hair dressed a la Grecque, with their low stately courtesy.

And the young gentlemen in silk stockings with shoe and knee buckles, their queues laced with ribbons, and with rolling coat collars and high shirt collars half covering the face. These balls were of frequent occurrence. There was the election ball in May. The Thanksgiving ball, the Christmas ball, and one on St. John's day, when the tables were in rustic bowers, then the Masonic lodge figured largely, and on the settlement of a new clergyman an ordination ball would be announced.

The gentlemen will please choose their partners. There was bowing and courtesying and the dancing commenced, minuets, reels and jigs went on.

> "But from the parlor of the inn
> A pleasant murmur smote the ear,
> Like water rushing through a weir:
> Oft interrupted by the din
> Of laughter and of loud applause,
> And in each intervening pause,
> The music of a violin.
>
> "Before the blazing fire of wood
> Erect the wrapt musician stood;
> And ever and anon he bent
> His head upon his instrument,
> And seemed to listen, till he caught
> Confessions of its secret thought,
> The joy, the triumph, the lament,
> The exultation and the pain;
> Then by the magic of his art,
> He soothed the throbbings of his heart,
> And lulled it into peace again."
> — *Longfellow.*

It would appear that a tavern in Oxford occupied the site or was the south part of the present residence of the late Jasper Brown, Esq., at the junction of one of the ancient roads to Charlton, with the Boston road through Marlborough and Worcester to Connecticut, which being *en route* one mile nearer Worcester, interrupted much of the patronage of quiet travelers from Boston to Connecticut.

> "As ancient is this hostelry
> As any in the land may be,
> Built in the old Colonial day,
> When men lived in a grander way,
> With ampler hospitality:
>
> "A kind of old Hobgoblin Hall,
> Now somewhat fallen to decay,
> With weather stains upon the wall,
> And stairways worn, and crazy doors,
> And creaking and uneven floors,
> And chimneys huge, and tiled and tall.

" Round this old-fashioned, quaint abode,
Deep silence reigned, save when a gust,
Went rushing down the country road,
And skeletons of leaves and dust,
A moment quickened by its breath,
Shuddered and danced their dance of death,
And through the ancient oaks o'er head
Mysterious voices moaned and fled." — *Longfellow*.

THE TIME AND MANNER OF TRAVELING AND SENDING COMMUNICATIONS FROM BOSTON TO SUTTON IN 1746 AS CONTRASTED WITH THE SAME IN 1890.

From Records of Sigourney Family, Anthony Sigourney of Boston, was married to Mary Waters of Salem, April 11, 1740. Mrs. Sigourney was an invalid from consumption. Her physician named change to the country hoping for her recovery. Mrs. Sigourney left Boston for Sutton where resided her brother, Richard Waters. She soon became too ill to venture a return to Boston. She survived until winter, 1746. Previously to her decease a message was despatched to Boston to acquaint Mr. Sigourney with the circumstances. No answer was received. The roads were impassable from the deep heavy snows. The funeral services were postponed for two weeks or more, until it was decided there could be no longer any delay from the absence of Mr. Sigourney. During the services he arrived. Having been unable to proceed from saddle-horses furnished him, he had walked most of the distance from Boston to Sutton, by the aid of snow-shoes or rackets. Mrs. Sigourney was buried in the burying-ground belonging to the Waters, Goff and Putnam families, in Sutton, no head-stone, only stone marks.

James Davie Butler on leaving Oxford and becoming a resident of Rutland, Vt., in the year 1787.

His first journeys to and fro were on horseback with a bag of silver on the pommel of the saddle, but he soon accomplished his journeys by driving a pair of horses in this new section of country as it was then termed. He was a merchant of the town for fifty years.

"HONORED SIR — After Due respect to you and your family this opportunity presents itself though (unexpectedly) to inform you that we are all well & throu the protection of a mersefull God we have been so for a year past.

"I have nothing metearial to write at present we have not heard aney inteliageable acount from
you since we left oxford & I wish you to write a letter
& leve at Cambels for M:̄ Cudworth to fetch to me.

"That we may know wheather you are all alive or not. We remember our love to our honored mother & all the family & our friends in general.

So we Remain your afectionate &c.
"JACOB GLYSSON.*
"GREENBUSH, December 21, 1805.
"4 miles north of the village of Troy.

"N. B.— We live within 200 yards of the church where we can have Dutch and English preaching a very steadey set of people to go to meeting and the quer of it is we can have our children Baptized for two shillings per head. But I chuse to keep that money to pay the school master for they go stedy and learn well. They all Remember their Love to cousins.

TRAVELING WEST IN 1817.

Anthony Butler, son of James Butler of Oxford, Mass., in a series of wayside letters to his brother James of Rutland, Vt.,

---

*Jacob Gleason, son of Dr. James Gleason, of Oxford South Gore, born July, 1768, died at Stockton, N. Y., October, 1812, married Mahatable, daughter of Joseph Hudson. Their address, "On the Grants in New York State. "Mrs. Gleason, born 1770, died at Stockton, 1871. On leaving Greenbush, N. Y., he removed with his family to the "Holland Purchase," a part of the Chatauqua county, south-western part of New York.

describes his travels *en route* from his landed estate a few miles distant from Rutland to Cincinnati.

The outfit consisted of two large wagons, one single wagon and five horses. Mr. Butler with his family leaves his home in Vermont Sept. 30, 1817, and arrives at Cincinnati, November 14, after traveling fifty-six days. Three of his letters were mailed at Montgomery, Orange Co., N. Y., Oct. 10, Loudoun, Franklin Co., Pa., Oct. 23, and Pittsburgh, Nov. 12. In his letter from Loudoun Mr. Butler states: "The reason for proceeding so far south is to cross the Alleghany Mountains on a turnpike." He adds, "Our horses are in good style."

In crossing Laurel Ridge, three miles up and four miles down, he found no house, and camped on the summit. In his own words "built a fire against a log, daughters dismayed, night dark and rainy, both dogs on the watch till morning." "Descending the Laurel Ridge, the roads from the heavy rain were almost impassable, the loose rock worn by wagon wheels and horses' feet 10 or 12 and perhaps 15 feet. One horse path three feet lower than the other—at times the horses going frantic with rage. We descended without accident and reached a tavern before night.

"In the vicinity of Pittsburgh, the horses requiring rest, we changed our mode of traveling at Pittsburgh to proceed on to Cincinnati. I purchased a boat for $60, with a deck, fireplace, and other conveniences large enough for to transport ourselves, wagons and horses, and was so fortunate as to secure a good pilot (a man who had been a ship carpenter and a seaman on board a man of war), and we arrived safely at Cincinnati 500 miles from Pittsburgh."

Anthony Butler was a Mason, and thus writes: "In the neighborhood of Pittsburgh I became acquainted with John Grove, the landlord at whose public house we were entertained, I showed him the certificate which Captain Lord had handed me from the Royal Arch Chapter. He went into the city and on his return told me there were $300 in Pittsburgh at my acceptance, and quarters for me and my family in some of their best houses, if I would accept the favor, as my traveling expenses were considered very great. I accepted with thanks the kindness of the gentlemen (Masons) of Pittsburgh, but assured them I had provided for an expensive journey and for winter quarters, and would in the spring receive remittances from Vermont to purchase a landed estate in the State of Ohio.

Post-Houses and Post-Riders.

"Hark! 'tis the twanging horn!"

"He comes, the herald of a noisy world,
With spatter'd boots, strapp'd waist, and frozen locks,
News from all nations lumbering at his back,
True to his charge, the close-pack'd load behind,
Yet careless what he brings, his one concern
Is to conduct it to the destined inn;
And having dropp'd the expected bag pass on." — *Cowper.*

Reminiscences of the Late Archibald Campbell.

Oxford became a post-town in 1801. Samuel Campbell was the first "post-master" of Oxford. The post-house was at the hotel on the corner of the Charlton road and the village street (the present site of the brick store). Major Archibald Campbell was the second post-master, at his residence on the site of the present Episcopal church, Main street. William Sigourney was Maj. Campbell's deputy of the office. One small left-hand drawer in an ancient English desk devoted to the purpose, contained all the letters, papers and mail matter of the Oxford post-house. Maj. Campbell was succeeded by William Sigourney. The post-house was then removed to the old tannery on the Sutton road near the bridge, occupying the currying room. The post-office was then removed to a new store on Sigourney corner, and Capt. William Sigourney was the post-master for many years.

"In olden time the post was carried by a messenger provided with a spare horse, a horn and good portmantles."

"In 1704, the only post on all this continent was that which went east from New York so far as Boston, and west to Philadelphia."

"The mails were conveyed from one town to another by the postman who traveled over the hills and through the valleys on horseback, and made known his approach once a week to each post-village by the winding of a huge horn, which was always carried ready for use." The weekly post-rider, when he came by, was sure to tarry at the village inn a sufficient time not only to distribute whatever papers and letters (and few and far between they were) which he might have to leave there, but also to report such rumors as he might have collected by the way; "for post haste" was with him by no means a descriptive term. In government dispatches, the landlord at the village tavern had the first and surest news in days when armed horsemen did the work now performed by railroad and telegraph. Eager with impatience everybody rushed for the news to the village tavern, and there with a bowl of punch or a mug of flip listened to the last report left behind by some galloping rider, waiting for a fresh steed to take him for a new relay.

Mr. Campbell states, Major Daniel Mansfield, it is said, was the first regular mail carrier from Worcester through Millbury, Sutton, Oxford, and Dudley on to Ashford, Ct., about the years 1810–12.

Previously to this time letters were sent from Worcester in packets to the towns in the vicinity by reliable parties, who were requested to forward them to the inn of the town, and there they were distributed or left to persons to whom they were addressed *en route*.

So slow was the news in reaching Oxford of what transpired in the outside world, that in 1813, when Washington was burnt, some ten days elapsed before the news was received. William Eaton, a sheriff, arrived at the hotel and gave the intelligence. Mr. Campbell, then a child, listened to the announcement.

In 1815 the glad tidings of peace between Great Britain and the United States were received throughout the country with acclamations of joy. Heralds on horseback with government despatches were welcomed by loud peals of bells whenever they entered towns or villages. The citizens of Oxford were witnesses to the scene of the government despatch sent from Washington to Boston passing through Dudley and on the old Dudley road to Oxford. The horse who bore the rider and despatches was covered with foam and blood, and as he reached the several towns en route for a relay bringing the news he sounded his horn and cried with a loud voice "Peace — Peace — Peace!"

Tidings of this treaty reached the United States little more than a month after the battle of New Orleans.*

Abner Cooper was one of the early post-riders between Worcester and Oxford.

"When Cooper the post-carrier weekly arrived in Oxford on horseback with saddle bags containing the weekly papers & (letters) from Worcester, on reaching Towne's pond, a little passed the residence of Dr. Daniel Fiske nearly opposite an oak tree near the potash mound he would sound his horn that people of the north vilage might arrive at the inn and receive the news."

Mr. Cooper's card in the Worcester *Spy*:

"Abner Cooper informs his friends that April next his quarter ends."

An elderly lady being inquired of respecting posting letters in the olden time, replied "We only sent communications to

---

* From the Worcester *Spy*, Wednesday, February 15, 1815:

"When the news of peace reached this town Monday last, it was received by all with the utmost transports of joy."

our friends, or letters of business by reliable persons who were travelling to that section of country where they resided, and of course waited a long time for letters in return." *

In these days stage coaches were used, but a greater speed was reached by those who traveled " post," as it was called ; that is, by relays of horses that were frequently changed.

The President's message was conveyed in this manner, express riders affording great interest to the inhabitants of the several towns through which it passed.

Among the last of these village excitements in Oxford. The bearer of the " President's message " had failed of his relay at his last stopping place (Dudley), and proceeding on the old Dudley road before reaching Oxford, his horse, already over driven, was becoming exhausted. When a mile from the village hotel, near the residence of the late Peter Shumway, he observed a farmer† leading with a bridle a very able nice horse crossing the road, intently observing the movements of the express *sans cérémonie*. The rider came alongside, and leaped upon the farmer's horse and was with his spurs soon out of sight with his fresh relay. As soon as the farmer recovered from his consternation he pursued and found his own horse safe at the hotel with a sufficient remuneration.

It is said the arrival and departure of the Boston mail coach in Oxford was the event of the day more than one half century ago. The driver always wound his horn on the Boston road just after passing the bridge east of the street.

The coach was known to be approaching about sunset by the bugle horn in the distance. As heralds of the approaching coach a group of children would be seen about sunset on the village street or a deep lawn, all at once exclaiming, " There comes the Boston coach ! Don't you see it on the Sutton road ? " as the four horses and the great lumbering vehicle are outlined against

---

* Late Mrs. Francis Sibley of Oxford, aged 93 years in 1884.
† Late Jonas Learned.

the green hedge that borders the old Boston post-road on either side of the highway.

The coach soon ascends "Sigourney hill," as the rising of the ground after crossing the little bridge was called in those days. And the panting horses with distended nostrils rush forward at full speed, the driver sounds his horn for to give notice of his expected arrival at the post-office and the village inn to have all in readiness, and cracks his whip, tightens his grasp on the reins, and with loud clattering of hoofs and rumbling of wheels, the heavily-laden coach with its passengers passes Sigourney corner, burying the brick mansion house beneath a dusty cloud. The country people gathered at the tavern to see the cumbersome vehicle as it came swinging around at the entrance of the Sutton road with the horses galloping in coach horse fashion. After a short stop for passengers, mail, or may be for a little refreshment "from mine host," the horn tooted loudly, and away the heavy old-fashioned yellow stage coach jolted and swung along the level street, with the driver so friendly to all persons he passed.

Though the arrival of the coach from Boston was an occurrence three times during the week, returning on the alternate days, the excitement attending its arrival never lost its charm for old or young.

Many years have now passed away since the mail coaches were to be seen in the village streets. They were drawn by four horses. Sometimes a change was made *en route* of coaches and coachmen, as well as of horses.

The coachmen were usually men of very obliging dispositions. They would go out of their way to bear a message to some shop or dressmaker for to please their lady patrons or leave a newspaper. They did much of the business that is now done by the express companies.

One lady relates that when she was traveling in the mountains of Vermont the coachman would gather her wild flowers, and brought her some petted raccoons or "Vermont kittens," as he termed them, for her amusement at the public house when waiting for a fresh relay.

The Norwich and Worcester railroad is unlaid. The citizens of this quaint village may be seen at early evening waiting at the post-office for the arrival of the Boston mail coach to receive their weekly newspapers and letters. Daily papers were not to be found in inland country towns.

Very few persons in Oxford received a newspaper in those days by the post-man. The Boston *News-Letter* was the paper most read in the country before the War of the Revolution, for modern time is said to have commenced with the Revolution. In this paper, "All valuable Real Estate and Slaves were advertised for sale, with the deaths of noted personages, and Servants, Runaways, or Goods Stole or Lost may have the same inserted at a reasonable Rate; from Twelve Pence to Five Shillings, and not to exceed : Who may agree with Nicholas Boone for the same at his shop, next door to Major Davis's; Apothecary, in Boston, near the Old Meeting house."

"All persons in Town and Country may have said *News-Letter* Weekly upon reasonable terms, agreeing with John Campbell Post Master, (Boston,) for the same." In Revolutionary time and afterward the Massachusetts *Spy* was the newspaper most appreciated throughout the country.

An advertisement in the Boston *News-Letter*, in August, 1742 : "A negro woman to be sold by the printer of this paper; the very best negro woman in town,—who has had the small-pox, and the measles,—is as healthy as a horse,—as brisk as a bird, and will work like a beaver."

"At last the floundering carrier bore
  The village paper to our door."
"Welcome to us its week old news."
"Its corner for the rustic Muse,
  Its monthly gauge of snow and rain,

> Its record, mingling in a breath
> The wedding knell and dirge of death,
> Jest, anecdote and love-lorn tale,
> The latest culprit sent to jail:
> Its hue and cry of stolen and lost,
> Its vendue sales and goods at cost,
> And traffic calling loud for gain."—*Whittier.*

CHAPTER XXI.

CHURCHES.

The first town meeting, July 22, 1713. By warrant from John Chandler, Esquire, one of her Majesty's justices of the peace for the county of Suffolk, for the choice of town officers.

It was then voted that three persons should be chosen for selectmen for the present year.

Chose John Town,
 " Benoni Twitchel, } Selectmen.
 " Joseph Chamberlain,
 " John Town, For Town Clerk,
 " Thomas Huskins, " Constable,
 " Oliver Collier, " Highway Surveyor,
 " Abiel Lamb, " Tything-Man.*

All of whom were sworn before John Chandler, justice of peace.

---

* The office of Tything-men was conferred only on those persons who were of most respectable character, and such as possessed great dignity of manner; their badge of office was a long black staff. They were expected to be constant attendants at church, and to see that all persons who were in attendance should be seated before the church service commenced. All traveling and labor were prohibited by law; and that he would also, by virtue of his office "have an eye" upon all absentees from church.

Tything-men were chosen in Oxford for the benefit of the people into the present century.

In the record of town officers there were tything-men, deer-reeves, "clerk of the market." It is difficult to conceive of the necessity of a clerk of the market in a place where none purchased and few sold any commodities, and yet these various offices were filled for a great many years after the incorporation of the town.

Another officer who was chosen annually for many years, but though a State officer, is now discontinued, was a "warden." The only explanation of this office " that coming from England the English wished to maintain the same customs here as at home."

Town Meeting, November 19, 1713, Voted : "That John Towne, Samuel Hageburn and Benjamin Chamberlain, should be a committee to lay out a Minister's lot and burying-place."

Town Meeting, July 29, 1714, Voted : "That each lot man shall pay his equal proportion of ten shillings a Sabbath, for a quarter of a year, to Mr. John James, for his preaching with us."

July 29, 1714, Voted : "to build a meeting house thirty feet square, and to set the house on the west side of the highway, near Twitchell's field.

At a Great and Gen. Court of Assembly for y' province of y' Massachusetts bay in New England begun and held at boston on y' 28 day of may 1718.

On the petition of John Towne select man of the Town of Oxford in behalf of y' said town In the hous of Representatives June the 18th 1718 Red and ordered that y' select men or assessors, of y' Town of Oxford be Impowered to Levy a tax upon y' lands of y' non Resident proprietors In the said Town after the Rates of twenty Shillings p annum on Each Thousand acres during the whole term of five years next after this present Session That so the Inhabitants may be Enabled to build a meeting house and settle a minister

among Them and the money so arising shall be applied accordingly and no otherwise.
In Council Read and concurred Consented to
SAM. U. SHUTE
a True Copy as of Record
Examined p
J. WILLARD
Secry.

Page 18 of Record.
From the Oxford Records, March 2, 1719. Voted that if the Rev. John McKinstry dos continue preaching the Gospil and settle with us yt he shall be an Equal Proprietor with the rest of the inhabitants of Oxford village.

May 27, 1719. Voted to give to Mr. McKinstry sixty pounds sallery and fifty pounds in building and fencing and breaking up ground and labor and 100 acres of land.

Mr. McKinstry, however, did not comply with the invitations, tradition states, to the great disappointment of the people.

Rev. John McKinstry, a native of Scotland, joined a company of Scotch emigrants from the north of Ireland and arrived in Boston in the summer of 1718.

Mr. McKinstry is said to have been a gentleman of a superior education, and of great natural endowments, with refined manners and of a genial temperament of character. He became the clergyman of the church in Sutton and subsequently of East Windsor, Ct.

He had graduated at Edinburgh University and received a diploma.

A TRANSLATION.

"Be it known to all whom it may concern, that we the Professors of the University of Edinboro' of King James, testify that this youth John McKinstry, of Ireland, after having completed the study of philosophy and human literature with the integrity and modesty of manners which is becoming an ingenious youth, has graduated with us, and is entitled to all the privileges which the course of discipline and the custom of this Academy, is accustomed to confer. And now with the consent of the Faculty and teachers of this college he is declared a Master in the liberal Arts, and entitled to all the privileges which are wont to be conceded to the Masters of the Good Arts, of which fact, that there may be greater faith, we the distinguished governors, Teachers and Patrons of the University of Edinburgh have placed our signatures this 4th Calends of March, 1712."

Datum EDINBURGI.

       JOH. GOODALL, L. S. P.
       ROBERTUS HENDERSON,
        B. & Acad. ab. Archivi.
       GULIEL HAMILTON, N. S. P.
       GULIELMUS LAW, P. P.
       GULIELMUS SCOT, P. P.
       ROBERTUS STOUAOL, P. P.
       COL. DRUMOND, P. P.
       JA. GREGORY, MATH. P.

May 1720, att a town meeting. "They voted that Mr. John Campbell, should be treated with in order to settlement." "Then voted Mr. Israel Town, who resided on the Dr. Fisk farm, opposite Towne's pond, should entertain the minister."

Rev. John Campbell, the first clergyman of the church in Oxford, was from Scotland, having graduated at Edinburgh University. At a Town meeting in May, 1720, Mr. John Campbell's arrival in Oxford is first mentioned. At the above date Ebenezer Learned is authorized by a vote of the town to make an engagement with Rev. John Campbell, for to remain with them as their clergyman for one or two months.

July 15, 1720, a committee of five, of which John Town was chairman, was chosen and instructed to make definite proposals to Mr. Campbell in reference to his settlement. The committee presented the following report:
In the name of the inhabitants of the town :
1st. We called the Rev. John Campbell to be our minister.
2d. We promised to the said Mr. Campbell £60 salary.
3d. That the Rev. Mr. Campbell himself, his heirs, and assigns have freely given them the lot already laid out for the first minister of Oxford, with the rights thereunto belonging, and one hundred acres joining the above, if it can be had ; if not when it can be conveniently had.
4th. That we will give the said Mr. Campbell one hundred pounds settlement in work, as reasonable as others have work for the money in Oxford; twenty-five pounds of it to be paid quarterly as shall be directed by Mr. Campbell, provided he shall be willing to live and die with us in the work of the ministry.

Rev. Mr. Campbell's Answer to the Selectmen of Oxford.

Gentlemen, I have had your call and proposals before me and upon mature deliberation I accept of your call and proposals to me as propounded and hereby promise to be willing to continue with you in the work of the ministry as the Lord shall enable me, provided you continue a ministerial people.

Oxford, *August 12th*, 1720.

JOHN CAMPBELL.

In September, 1720, Lieut. John Town, Abiel Lamb, Samuel Barton and Joseph Wiley, gentlemen, united in their influence to establish a Church of Christ in Oxford, making an appointment to meet on Thursday, October 27, at four of the o'clock post meridian, at the house of Israel Town.

In 1720 the town authorities of Oxford applied to the association of ministers for their advice respecting Rev. John Campbell as a clergyman.

The association replied:

WOODSTOCK, *September* 7, 1720.

" We the subscribers, having had acquaintance with the Rev. Mr. Campbell now of Oxford, do approve of him as a minister endowed with ministerial accomplishments. We hope and believe that, by the blessing of Heaven, he will serve to the glory of God and the spiritual edification of souls, in the place where Divine Providence shall fix him in the gospel ministry.

(Signed.)

JOSIAH DWIGHT.	JOSEPH BAXTER.
JOHN SWIFT.	ROBERT BRECK.
JOHN PRENTICE.	JOSEPH DORR.

" To the select men of Oxford.

The church* was organized Jan. 20, 1720, O. S., with the following members:

John Town and wife,	Israel Town and wife,
Benj. Chamberlain and wife,	Benony Twitchell and wife,
Isaac Learned and wife,	Joseph Wiley and wife,
John Comins and wife,	Samuel Barton and wife,
Absolem Skinner,	David Town and wife,
Ebenezer Learned and wife,	Nat. Chamberlain and wife,
Philip Amidown and wife,	Thomas Gleason, Jr., and wife,
Abiel Lamb and wife,	Collins Moore and wife.

---

* This church adopted no creed at its formation. In the early history of our country articles of belief were promulgated by the higher ecclesiastical bodies, and the Cambridge platform served most of the Congregational churches until near the close of the last century, when, on account of a diversity of opinions, articles of faith in the form of a creed were then introduced to be assented to by those becoming members of the church.

Churches.

The ordination services of Rev. John Campbell were March 1, 1721, and were as follows :

Introductory prayer, by Rev. Joseph Dorr, of Mendon.
Sermon, by Rev. John Prentice, Lancaster, Ephs. vi, 18-19.
Prayer before the Charge, by Rev. Josiah Dwight, of Woodstock.
Charge, by Rev. Joseph Baxter, of Medfield.
Prayer after Charge, by Rev. Joseph Breck, Malborough.
Right Hand of Fellowship, by Rev. John Swift of Framingham.
Benediction, by Rev. John Campbell.

The first church in Oxford was located on the north-west corner of the south common, the old Charlton road separating it from the burying-ground. It fronted on the south toward the common. It was thirty feet square; had double or folding doors in front; the pulpit was on the north side of the house opposite the doors which opened into the aisle of the church; the gallery extended on the east and west sides. The seats in the area of the church were of rude construction, with backs, those upon the east side for ladies, and those upon the west side for gentlemen; this was a Puritan fashion of New England.

January, 1722-3, "Voted in ye affirmative that Capt. Richard Moore may build and have set up a pew on ye west side of ye pulpit of about six foot square for the benefit of himself and his family." * * *

Feby 11 1722-3, At a town meeting legally warned voted to grant a pew to be made for Mr. Campbell and dispose of other places for pews First voted in the affirmative yt Mr. Campbell may build and set up a pew of y' East side of y pulpit from y pulpit to y middle or senter of ye post under y gallery beam extending to y' corner of y' deacons seat to be done at y charge of y town.

March 29, 1724, At the town meeting it was voted that Eng{^n} Ebenezer Learned should have a Room in the East corner of the meeting-house joyning to Mr. Campbell's pew for a pew for him and his family in the meeting house and he is to finish it in the year.

March 4 1734, Voted yt Capt Ebenezer Learned shall have ye pew on the Easterly part of y meeting house behind ye woman's seats for Toon (ten) pound paying his equal proportions towards finishing said meeting house sd pew adjoyning to the duble doors.

March 4 1734, Voted that Mr. Samuel Davis shall have ye pew on the Westerly sid of ye meeting house adjoyning to the duble doors he paying toon pound and his equal proportion towards finishing sd meeting house.

May 16, 1726, At a legal town meeting, Capt. Ebenezer Learned was chosen to go to ye General Court, at a petition Requesting that the lands of ye non-resident proprietors, may be taxed, to inable us to support ye Gospel ministry amongs us.

Oxford, September 4th 1732, "Then Received in full for my sallery from the beginning of my Settlement at Oxford, in y' work of ye Gospels, there to the first of May, one thousand seven hundred and twenty-seven in conformity, to a vote passed by the said Town of Oxford," March 6, 1726-7, per me. John Campbell.

The duty of the sexton in olden time was not only to take charge of the church, keep it swept, have the key in his possession, but to take care of the cushion for the desk.

August 29, 1728, Voted "to take so much of the Interest money belonging to y' town to procure a cushion for the pulpit. Capt. Larned, to be intrusted with the commission."

March 4, 1734. Voted yt Capt. Richard Moore, shall have Liberty to inlarge his pew at his own charge and bearing y cost of turning y pulpit stair-case if Mr. Campbell be willing, and make a door for y deacons seat.

March 4, 1734, Voted Lieut. Isaac Learned, shall have y pew at the North East corner of the meeting-house, joyning to Mr. Campbells pew, paying four pound and bearing his proportion towards finishing said meeting-house.

August 25, 1743, the town voted to build a new meeting-house, which was erected 1747.

July 13, 1748, Voted that the Town shall Build Two Pews one on Each Side the Broad Alley, one behind the men's seats and the other behind the women's seats to accommodate the Gentlemen that have had their Land Taxed towards Building of our New meeting-house, when any of them shall come to our meeting.

Voted that there shall be two pews more built to take up the rest of the room behind the seats to the alleys at each end of the seats to be disposed of by the town. In front of the pulpit were four long narrow pews, two for the deacons, the others for aged persons. The gallery extended round three sides of the church, leaving the high pulpit on the north side; seats back of the galleries in the corners of the church were devoted to slaves or colored servants.

August 22, 1748, Voted Richard Moore, Jun, Collector to gather the tax laid on the non-resident Proprietors lands in Oxford, towards building our new meeting-house by an act of the General Court.

May 17, 1750. Voted one hundred and ten ounces of silver and other money equivalent, to it for the Rev. Mr. Campbell's sallery for this present year.

Sept. 14, 1752, Voted to choose a committee to Dignify and prize the Pews. Mr. David Baldwin, Mr. Duncan Campbell, Mr. Benjamin Davis, Committee Men to Dignify and Prize the pews.

The person who paid the highest tax had the first choice, and so in succession. In many places other than money considerations had influence in "dignifying" the pews.

Sept. 14, 1752 (N. S.), Voted to accept the report of the committee that was chosen to Dignify and prize the Pews.

Nov. 17, 1752, Voted that the pew next to the Pulpit on the East side shall be the minister's pew. Then those that were the highest in the Rates for their Real Estate towards building our meeting-house in Oxford proceeded to draw their pews, and Col. Ebenezer Learned being highest in said Rates, chose No. 3 price £52 16s.

It is believed that the term "dignify," as here used, was to give the preference in the selection of pews to those persons most distinguished in public affairs, and for their liberality in furnishing the means for the erection of the church and the support of public worship.

The "pew spots," as they were called, that is, places where pews might be, were thus disposed of as the society had dignified them. In the Town Warrant, Oct. 4, 1748 — To see how the town will dispose of the Pew Spots in the said meeting-house. In these old-fashioned churches the people were not allowed to make their selection of seats. A committee was chosen to assign seats to the worshippers "according to estate and age annually." This arrangement of seats was termed "seating the meeting-house."

March 20, 1764, Voted and chose Edward Davis, Esquire, (Capt.) Ebenezer Learned and Mr. Josiah Wolcott, committee to treat with the Rev[d]. Joseph Bowman concerning his settling with us and to lay the votes and grants of the church and Town before him in view for his consideration and to give us his answer in due time, and the said committee are impowered to make some further proposals to the said Mr. Bowman concerning his settlement and sallary and report to the town the next town meeting.

24 September 1764, Voted in the Affirmative to Add Sixty Six Pounds thirteen Shillings and four Pence to a former Grant made to Rev. Mr. Joseph Bowman on the 20th Day of March

1764, of One Hundred and Thirty-three Pounds Six Shillings and Eight pence making in the whole Two Hundred Pounds to be Paid, the one-half within One year after his settling with us, in case he accepts of our Choice of him to be our Minister and settle with us.

March 20, 1764, voted & chose Edward Davis, Col. Ebenezer Learned, Josiah Wolcott, a committee.

Warrant October 1, 1764. To grant Money to defray the cost and charge of the ordinations or installment of the Rev'd Mr. Joseph Bowman to the Pastoral Office among us October 15, 1764.*

Rev. Joseph Bowman remained the clergyman of this church until August, 1782. In 1791, April 17, Rev. Elias Dudley necceded the Rev. Joseph Bowman. Rev. Mr. Dudley retired from being the clergyman March 6, 1799. Dr. Emmons of Franklin preached the sermon at the ordination of Rev. Mr. Dudley. His residence while a clergyman in Oxford was the mansion of the late Dr. David Holman.

In the present century there may have been connected with this church no clergyman more distinguished than Rev. Horatio Bardwell, D. D., who was established over the church in 1836 and so continued for many years. He died in Oxford May 5, 1866. His memory is spoken of "as a precious legacy to his church." He received his ordination as a clergyman at Newburyport June 21, 1815, and on the following October 23 he sailed for India in the ship *Dryad*, and on his arrival in India he became a resident of Bombay, and remained as an American missionary in India until 1821, when he returned to this country. While in India, Dr. and Mrs. Bardwell received many kind

---

* October 15, 1764. Edward Davis, Esq., and Deacon Thomas Davis undertook to provide Entertainment for the Council that are to install the Rev. Mr. Joseph Bowman to the pastoral office among us without making it a public charge to the town.

attentions from the English residents and from the officials of government.

At one period during his home in India he was most honorably invited to take the place of a rector in the English Episcopal church, which for a limited time he filled with much acceptance to his English friends. Mrs. Bardwell was a lady of a superior education, as could be discerned in her conversation, and in her extensive correspondence. Her description of her Eastern life, as associated with English residents as well as the poor natives of the country, was in her recital as a picture presented to the view. And like Mrs. Sherwood of England her description was to remain in a life long memory.

One can easily follow Mrs. Bardwell in her Indian home, plainly dressed in white muslin, as ladies in India are obliged to dress from the climate, on her veranda, surrounded by a group of native children, teaching them their daily Bible lessons. On the return of Dr. and Mrs. Bardwell to America they departed from India with regret and with many kind services rendered them from the English governor.*

Two merchant vessels left India for Boston at the time of Dr. and Mrs. Bardwell's passage being engaged. One ship was lost at sea, and was so reported, and left much uncertainty as regarded the safety of Dr. and Mrs. Bardwell. On their arrival in port they hastened to their home in Andover. An escort

---

* Dr. Bardwell was married in 1815 to Rachel, daughter of Simon Forbush, of Andover.

Dr. Bardwell in his manners was courteous and affable, and was styled a gentleman in English society while abroad, as well as one who was distinguished in his judgment and views of the affairs of state government, and with all these endowments he was more distinguished for his most devout Christian life, and as a clergyman he was possessed of large and liberal views toward all evangelical Christians.

The Book of Common Prayer used by Dr. Bardwell in India is still cherished as a relic by Miss Ellen Paine, once a communicant in his church at Oxford, now Mrs. Gilchrist of McGregor.

was at once offered to accompany them to their friends, who proceeded in advance, and announced the safe arrival of the ship and then the safety of Dr. and Mrs. Bardwell and child, and their immediate arrival that morning to the parents of Mrs. Bardwell.

20 May 1765, Voted that Lieut. John Nichols and Mr. Edward Raymond, shall each of them have the Liberty for two persons to sit in the Pew on the West side of the Broad Alley in our Meeting-House that was granted to the non Resident Gentlemen that had their unimproved lands Taxed towards Building our Meeting-House Each of them paying three Pounds old tenor pr year as long as they enjoy said privilege and to give place to any of Said Gentlemen if they should come to our meeting.

That Mr. Josiah Wolcott shall have liberty to use and improve the pew on the East side of the broad alley in our meeting-house filling the said pew.

May 19 1767, Then that behind the womans Seats next to the Broad Alley was set up and Lieut. John Nichols bid twelve pounds eight shillings lawful money which was the highest and it was struck off to him accordingly and he paid two dollars down.

To see if the town will grant liberty to Rev. Mr. Hill and Mr. Amos Shumway and Mr. James Butler and Doct. Daniel Fisk, to take up the two hind seats in the mens and womens body seats and build them four pews for their use and their heirs forever or act thereon as the town shall think proper.

By order of the select men.   SAMUEL HARRIS
Oxford *May* 21 1781.   *Town Clerk.*

July 19, 1781, At a Town Meeting, received the Report of the committee chosen for the sale of the pew ground in the mens and womens body seats, and voted to accept said Report which is as follows:

No. 1, on the womans side of the broad alley, sold to Mr. Anthony Sigourny, for 20½ hard dollars.

No. 2, on the men's side of the broad alley, sold to Mr. James Butler, for 20 hard dollars.

No. 3, on the womans side, on the east side, sold Mr. John Dana, for 17 hard dollars.

No. 4, on the west side of the men's seats, sold to Mr. Jesse Jones for 16½ hard dollars.

Voted that the money coming by the sale of the four pews as before mentioned be applied for the support of the soldiers families and the poor of the town.

In olden time in the churches of New England the sermon was made the principal feature of the service. The Scriptures were not read in the churches until the early part of the last century, and not always were prayers offered in the churches.

As early as 1699, however, Rev. Mr. Coleman of Boston read the Bible in his church, and he even repeated the Lord's prayer, after an introduction of one of his own. "But many were strongly prejudiced against his innovations."

Reading of the Scriptures in the service of New England churches on the Sabbath, is comparatively modern. It was considered in ancient time as partaking too much of the formality of the English church — in many churches not introduced until the middle of the last century.

The Ratio Disciplinae says that in 1726, that "the practice of reading the sacred volume was observed in many churches without giving offence." The church in Medford, in 1759, "voted to read the Bible in the congregation." How early reading of the Scriptures in the church in Oxford was adopted, there is no record.*

---

* With things that have had their day during these long sermons, in some churches, there was an hour-glass standing on the desk to guide the clergyman, and which would claim the attention of his hearers for one

It does not appear from any record in Oxford when the introduction of instrumental music became a part of the church service, or the change in the mode of singing caused any disquietude in the church, even when the pitch-pipe was sounded.

Before the close of the last century the New England version of Psalms and Hymns was the only sacred poetry that was allowed admittance into most of the churches. These were read, line by line, by one of the deacons, when another set the tune, in which the whole congregation were expected to unite.

In England there was annexed to the Book of Common Prayer the version of Sternhold and Hopkins. The first metrical version of the Psalms in English appeared in 1549.

"Thomas Sternhold a court poet, translated 51 Psalms."

John Hopkins a clergyman, 58.

The other contributors were, principally, William Whytingham, Dean of Durham, and Thomas Norton, a barrister.

This version, enlarged, was annexed to the Book of Common Prayer, and was in general use until 1696.*

---

hour. In front of some pulpits was a socket for the hour-glass. An hour-glass was also in the library of the minister, to guide him in preparing his sermons. One of the duties of the sexton was to keep and turn the glass.

* The New England version, or better known as the Bay Psalm Book, was made in 1640, and was the work of Revs. Thomas Weld, John Eliot and Richard Mather, and continued in use for more than 100 years, and was succeeded by the collection of hymns by Dr. Watts, nearly at the close of the last century.

Tate and Brady's collection followed Sternhold and Hopkins' version, and was generally used in the Episcopal church in America and other churches in this country.

The church in Oxford made use of this collection.

There are still copies to be found which were used in church service in Oxford.

"Some of the clergymen attempted a reform in singing — and the notes, fa, sol, la, were by some considered blasphemous." "The new way of singing will make the young people disorderly, and if they go to singing school they will be having frolics."

In the Oxford church those who could sing sat in the "singers' seats." The leader, Mr. Ludden, gave out the tune and the pitch, the singers sounded their parts, bass, tenor, alto and treble, fa-la-sol-fa " singing a fuguing tune, one part following another, till all seem to be lost in a labyrinth of melody, but coming out right at last."

In 1780, many persons objected to new tunes being sung in the churches and were offended at the innovation and absented themselves from church service. At what time a change was made from singing by the congregation to a choir in Oxford does not appear, but previously some one had been chosen to line the hymn when it was sung.*

Before the Revolution the hymns were "lined," the clerk of the church standing in front of the pulpit reading a line and the congregation singing it, and then reading another, and so on through the hymn.

---

* At a meeting in the north parish of Sutton, Feb. 4, 1768, "It was proposed that, if it would not be grievous to any of the Brethren, a Hymn out of Dr. Watts' should be sung at the communion, and if it would be grievous to any they were desired to speak."

"After three or four hymns being read that were pertinent for that purpose no objections appeared, but several spoke agreeable." — From an old town record in the north parish of Sutton.

In 1743 Rev. John Campbell, of Oxford, wrote, "Using Hymns, so as almost to have superseded the Psalms of David and other spiritual Songs. This is a manifest Violation and reproach of the Wisdom and Law of God. . . . I am far from thinking that the good Gentleman [Dr. Watts] whose hymns are mostly used by our giddy Zealots ever intended that composure of his should ever supersede the Psalms of David."— *Campbell's Treatise.*

And then on Sunday, standing in the singers' seats, with a bass-viol to keep them making music that thrilled and delighted the congregation. There was great opposition to viols and violins in the churches. As the years passed not only the viols and violins, but flutes, bugles, horns, clarinets, bassoons and trombones were used as a part of sacred music.*

Funeral Service.

In 1730, a Boston newspaper, in speaking of a funeral, says, "Before carrying out the corpse, a funeral prayer was made by one of the pastors of the old church, which, though a custom in the country towns, is a singular instance in this place, but it is wished may prove a leading example to the general practice of so decent and Christian example.

During the first half of the last century there was often great parade made at funerals, particularly by those of the rich. Gloves, gold rings, hat-bands and mourning scarfs were frequently presented to those gentlemen in attendance. Near friends acted as bearers, carrying the body on a bier on the shoulders, there being relays as occasion required in the procession (in some places males and females did not walk together, but those of the sex of the deceased walked nearest to the remains). Officers with staffs and mourning badges accompanied the procession.

This custom has until very recently been continued in some of the country towns in this county. The town of Sutton

---

* To the time of Luther the psalms of the Bible were mostly used by Christians in devotional service. Among the earliest was, "Lord, thou hast been our dwelling place in all generations," written by Moses.

Clement of Alexandria was an ancient writer of hymns. In the eleventh century, Bernard de Morals, monk of Cluni, made great additions to sacred poetry. A translation from his works is a hymn, than which no more beautiful has been written, "Jerusalem the Golden."

Then followed the sweet hymns of Thomas à Kempis, Luther and Clement Marot.

may be named as one of the last of those towns retaining this tribute of respect.

Oxford Town Records, April 4, 1796. In Town meeting voted that the selectmen provide a wheeled carriage to convey the dead to burial. Previous to this date all funeral processions, whether on foot or on horseback, the dead were conveyed on a bier with relays if the distance required.

Mrs. Eunice (Turner) Eastman's funeral was one of the last in Oxford where the mourners were on horseback, two horses abreast. The funeral service was at the old church on the north common, and a daughter of James Butler was buried in the same manner. The gentleman to whom she was engaged to be married preceded the parents on horseback unaccompanied. Rings were presented to the near friends of the deceased in memory of the departed.

A lady described the funeral of Mrs. Eunice (Turner) Eastman, as the procession wound its way among the tall elms over the north common to the church. It was a cold, gloomy day in December; heavy clouds hung low down in the sky; the air filled with snow. Though the lady were a child sitting at her nursery window, in a deep wide gable of an ancient house, she received her first impressions of death from viewing the sable procession on that mournful day and the measured tread of the horses' hoofs, for there were no carriages following the coffin on the bier, borne by bearers. All the mourners were on horseback two in file. The church-yard near the south common then a common stone wall enclosed its ground — fifty years ago it was choked with briars and fat weeds.

One has to look very carefully to discover those old graves. Their dust should be respected. Sometimes the only inscriptions are the initial letters and the year rudely carved. Then there was the poor corner where were the graves of the friendless.

In many old cemeteries before the year 1700, the head-stones seldom had any name or date. These stones were the common brownstone. In instances a chisel had cut the initial letters of the name of the one entombed.

In the seventeenth century hour-glasses were used as a device on tomb-stones, with this inscription : " As this glass runneth, so man's life passeth."

Upon some ancient head-stones in the burying-ground would be rudely cut the old man Time, with an hour-glass clutched in one hand and a scythe in the other. Angels blowing trumpets with open books, or a skull and cross-bones, would be seen on other head-stones. *

An old record Dec. 1, 1808, It being Thanksgiving Mr. Andrew Sigourney presented the Congregational Chh & Society by the hand of Rev⁴ Mr. Moulton with a large elegant Gilt Bible & Psalm Book to be kept for the use of the desk in the north meeting house in Oxford; on the receiving of which the Chh & Society voted their thanks to Mr. Sigourney the Donor.†

---

* October 24, 1771, It was granted 3 pounds to buy a new Burying cloth.— Town Records.

Oxford Town Records, May, 14, 1798, At a Town-meeting "Mr. Andrew Sigourney, came into the meeting and presented the town with a velvet funeral pall, upon receiving his present the town voted him thanks."

† In families of distinguished birth in these days escutcheons were placed upon the coffin, and hatchments were hung in the mansion house of the deceased.

"Escutcheons with rings and kid gloves were given to near friends, and in some instances suits of mourning, and relatives and servants were put in mourning. Tenants and dependents received gloves as well as intimate friends with their invitation to the funeral ceremony. Gloves were also given to pall-bearers, and sometimes orphans of a surviving parent, deceased, following first after the corpse, were accompanied by a waiting maid and a negro servant. Both were put in mourning as usual."

In an ancient charge of funeral expenses, 11 dozen gloves "for funeral " £20–6 11.

Letchford, writing in 1641, says, " At burials nothing is read, nor any funeral sermon made, but all the neighborhood, or a good company of

In these days and into the present century it was regarded as a breach of etiquette, a downright inhospitality, not to offer wine to the guests, particularly when the minister called.

Even at a funeral the bearers must "take a drink" before they removed their coffined neighbor from his own earthly home.

Marriages in olden time in Oxford were announced by the publication of marriage by banns, or a notice of the intended marriage was posted on the church door or in some other public place.

In about 1750, a statute of the twenty-sixth year of George II enacted that "the banns should be regularly published three successive Sundays in the church of the parish where for the time residing.

Archbishop Secker, the primate between 1758 and 1768, originated the arrangement of special licenses.

During Cromwell's protectorate, the "Little Parliament of 1653, declared that marriage was to be merely a civil contract; forbade the use of the 'Book of Common Prayer,' and interdicted the clergy from performing any of the offices of the church under severe penalties."

The parties professed in the presence of a justice of the peace their mutual desire to be married.

---

them, came together by tolling of the bell, and carry the dead solemnly to his grave, and then stand by him while he is buried. The ministers are most commonly present.

"On the return from the grave a liberal entertainment was served at which wines and intoxicating liquors, pipes and tobacco were liberally provided." The cause of temperance has made wonderful progress during the last half century. "Fifty years ago," says a clergyman (Rev. Dr. Patton of New Haven, Ct.), "funerals were set at three o'clock in the afternoon, and the procession did not move until four; the intervening time was spent in drinking. A great many persons went to funerals then. They went early, and did not leave until the funeral started."

In 1713, Judge Sewall has this record in his diary: "The four churches (in Boston) treated their ministers."

Usually the proclamation was made in the market place by the bellman.

This act continued until 1658, when persons were allowed to adopt the accustomed rites of religion if they preferred them.

The earliest canonical enactment on the subject of marriage banns in the English church, is said to have been made by the Synod of Westminster or London in 1200, which ordered that no marriage should be contracted without banns thrice published in the church, unless by the special authority of the bishop.

Formerly the betrothal ring was worn as at the present time, on the left hand on the finger next to the least.

It is said that women wore the wedding ring upon the left hand, because that hand is a sign of inferiority or subjection.

During the time of the commonwealth the Puritans endeavored to abolish the use of the wedding ring, for the reason it was of pagan invention.

It is now required that a wedding ring should be used at a marriage in the English church. The rubric directs that "the man shall give unto the woman a ring. * * * And the priest taking the ring shall deliver it to the man, to put it upon the fourth finger of the woman's left hand.

During the reigns of George I and George II, the wedding ring, although placed upon the usual finger at the time of marriage, was sometimes worn on the thumb, in which position it is represented in the portrait of Madam Elizabeth Freake, still a relic retained by her descendants in the Sigourney family of Oxford.*

---

*A wedding ring worn upon the thumb dates back to the reign of Charles II.

Anciently a ring was used in betrothals rather than at weddings. The man placed a ring on the finger, which is at the present day pre-

At early English weddings money was thrown over the heads of the bride and bridegroom and distributed at the church door. The Wardrobe Accounts of Edward II state this fashion of the time: "In the tenth year of his reign money to the value £2 10s. was thrown over the heads of Oliver de Bordeaux and the Lady Maude Trussel, during the solemnization of their nuptials, at the door of the chapel within the park of Woodstock, by the King's order." No wedding could be complete without the marriage benedictions of a priest, hence the bridegroom was called a Benedict.

The giving of gloves at weddings is a very ancient fashion. Ben Jonson, in his play of the "Silent Woman," makes Lady Haughty say, "We see no ensigns of a wedding here, no character of a bride ale; where be our skarves and our gloves?" Arnold, in his "Chronicle," in 1521, refers to an inquiry to be made at the visitation of ordinaries to churches, namely: "Whether the curat refuse to do the solemnysacyon of lawful matrymonye before he have gyfte of money, hoses or gloves." Pepys in his "Diary" under date 5th July, 1663, says he was at a wedding and had two pairs of gloves like the rest of the visitors. It is still the custom to give white gloves to the guests at marriages.

"Bride favors were formerly worn by gentlemen in their hats, or on their breasts or arms, for several weeks. They consisted of a large knot of ribbons of various colors. White ribbons were favorites for these adornments. Misson says, 'When the eldest son of M. de Overkerque marry'd the Duke of Ormond's sister, they dispers'd a whole inundation of those little favors.

---

served for the benedictions of marriage; a man who wished to pledge his faith as the future husband of a woman.

In England the ancient marriage ritual recognized the practice of offering money. Thus in the Salisbury Missal. "The man be enjoined to say: 'Wyth this rynge y the wedde, and thys gold and selvir the geve and with all my worldly catel I thee endowe.'"

"Nothing else was here to be meet with, from the hat of the King down to the lowest servant among the citizens and plain gentlemen, which is what they call the gentry. They sometimes give these favors."

"In 1629 Bay was used for garlands and that 'rosemary is almost of as great use as bays as well for civill as physical purposes for civil as all doe know at weddings to bestow among friends.'" See Garden of Flowers, Parkinson.

"In 1634, we are told that 'bay is fit for halls and stately roomes, where if there be a wedding kept, or such like feast, he will be sure to take a place more eminent than the rest.'"

"He is a great companion with the rosemary, which was thought in olden time to strengthen the memory and was worn at weddings and funerals."

The "strewing of herbs, rushes, and flowers from the house of the bride to the church was an ancient fashion in England. At bride ales the houses and chambers were woont to be strawed (with roses) these odoriferous and sweet herbes."

The fashion of strewing flowers before a bride is still retained in some parts of England. The children of the village scatter wild flowers before the bride as she leaves the church after the ceremony.

The wedding party walked or rode in pairs at rustic weddings. Four little bridesmaids carried baskets of buttercups and wild roses to grace the weddings in days by-gone.

Bouquets or nosegays and posies, as they were formerly called, were common appendages to a wedding in olden time.

Primroses and violets are mentioned as flowers used in bridal nosegays. Some old customs are still continued; the departing bride and bridegroom are sometimes saluted with old shoes and slippers, as omens for good luck, and rice is thrown over the bride.

The fashion of introducing orange blossoms into wedding bouquets and wreaths, though an European fashion, is derived from eastern countries, being the emblem of a prosperous marriage.

CHAPTER XXII.

SCHOOLS AND LIBRARIES.

Before the incorporation of Worcester county in 1731, the colonial laws required the towns to have free schools for the education of all the children. The public school system of the colony was fully established. It was enacted that the "General Court of Sessions of the Peace," in each county, should have jurisdiction in regard to schools so far as to hear complaints from the towns which neglected to provide the means of education for all the children according to the requirements of the law. The court exerted its authority in every case, and the towns thus negligent were required to supply school-houses and furnish teachers for their children on pain of fine and costs. In these school-days of only two months during the year many of the scholars were obliged to pass through deep woods by following difficult foot-trails in the summer, or in winter this course was over a hard-beaten path in the snow. The schools were in very desolate places in the midst of an unbroken forest.

SCHOOLS IN OXFORD.

There is a record of a vote upon the town books in 1733, by which the selectmen were instructed to "procure a schoolmaster." In 1736, the town voted to build a school-house 14x20 ft. with a chimney at each end.

1740 May ye 28, Then hired by the Select men of this town Mr. Richard Rogers, to teach school the fifth day of June, from thence to teach at such places as the Select men shall order, the said school-master is to be paid out of the Town's Treasury sixty pounds in "Bils" of Public Credit of the old tenor or the equivalent.

Mr. Rogers being hired to keep the school at £60 per year $200, and he kept the school for twenty-two years in succession.

OXFORD, *May the* 8, 1747.

Then Reconed with the Select men of Oxford and Received Sixty pounds in full for keeping a school in said Oxford from the Begining of the world to this day I say Received for me.

RICHARD ROGERS.*

---

*" May 17, 1750, Voted that the school be kept in four places in the town two at the North End and two at the South End a quarter of a year at a place."

1766, Voted that there be liberty granted to set up a school-house in the south part of the town and liberty granted to set up a school-house in the north part of the town.

It is said Mr. Rogers was a gentleman of superior education, "the best teacher of his time," being an excellent scholar in Latin and excelled every one in his time in penmanship. Tradition states he had no superior in his profession. Oxford was quite at the head of education. He gave instruction to the sons of Rev. John Campbell in Latin either at the school he taught (as was allowed by paying additional school fee to the "Master") or as a private tutor.

The Latin book which belonged to his pupils (Mr. Campbell's sons) is in good preservation, as also specimens of Mr. Rogers' elegant penmanship.

If Latin were taught in a school it was called a grammar school.

Mr. Rogers in 1732 was a schoolmaster in Worcester and taught a school for several years. In 1740 he came to Oxford and was engaged as a teacher until his enlistment in the French War, 1760. In deeds he was styled "scrivener." He died in 1761.

He married Martha, a daughter of Jeremiah Buckman, of Sutton; his widow married in April, 1761, Jonathan Towne, of Oxford, and in a third marriage, December, 1775, Isaac Dodge, of Sutton. Mr. David Dodge, a great grandson of Isaac Dodge, stated that when he accompanied his aunt, Miss Prudence Dodge (who died in Sutton in 1862, at a very advanced age), to Oxford, or passed through the town, that when they were opposite the old common in front of the church-yard, Miss Prudence would call his attention by telling him "here was the house

In 1740 it was voted that twenty families on Prospect Hill might build a school-house and draw their proportion of money for a school.

That those living between "Prospect" and "ye brook that runs between Mr. Campbell's and Joseph Rockets might do the same (and also those south of the said brook)."

In 1760 it appears by record that there were two school-houses at the south part of the town. There was one on the plain fronting north on the South Common. In 1767 there was a second school-house built upon the plain east of the house of Jonathan Fuller on the Six-rod road to Sutton. He had bought the north-west side of Sigourney corner including the old house that was afterward the home of Andrew Sigourney until he built the brick house in 1817 on the south-west corner of the Six-rod road with Main street.

In 1767 a school-house was built on the north part of the town in the lane eastward of the Eight-rod way from Jonas Pratt's, near Towne's pond. Pratt had made a settlement on the west side of the Eight-rod way on Towne's plain. This school-house was removed to the Wolcott estate and not used for a school.†

In 1775 Joseph Hudson, Jeremiah Shumway and others on the hill known as Long or Federal Hill, north-east part of the town, were set off to have a school by themselves.

In 1782 Ebenezer Davis and others in the east part of the town were set off in like manner.

of your grandmother Rogers Dodge." Mr. David Dodge said it was very near the Wolcott mansion house, he thought, some part of the house.

In 1751 a house was built for Mr. Rogers, sixteen by eighteen feet, "inside convenient room for a chimney," at a cost of £13 6s 8d, which he occupied until his decease. This house joined the Wolcott house on the north-east corner.

† When the school-house east of Jonas Pratt's estate was removed another school-house was erected not far from its site, known as James Butler's (North Centre, No. 6 ward).

In 1775 these divisions which were called "squadrons" were called "wards."

In 1803 or in 1804 a school-house was built on the plain on the Charlton road next the Red Tavern and near Mrs. L. Corbin's residence. The one east of Fuller's house on Sutton road was no longer used for a school.

A school record of Oxford from 1780-1787. James Butler stated "he learned grammar from one Shumway, while the other children (his brothers and sisters) were the scholars of a Dr. Walker, who, for fear of betraying his own ignorance, would never let them parse."

The first "Dame School" in Oxford of which there is any tradition was taught by Miss Betty Jerner (Elizabeth Shumway).

Miss Betty's home was about one mile easterly of the old north common; here there was no open road, only a bridle-path passed the house, with gate-ways or bar places for an occasional traveler on horseback to pass through; whenever the sound of a horse's hoof was heard Miss Betty and her pupils presented themselves at the door and passed their salutations. There was a heavy stone chimney to the house and a deep cavern-like fireplace, which in winter presented a cheerful fireside with its heavy log fire. The floor was scoured to whiteness and covered with the finest sand. Her instruction in arithmetic was oral, Miss Betty making the figures on the sanded floor with her rod (for teachers were thus armed in those days), and her pupils with their square pieces of birch-bark and bits of charcoal copying the sums she had given them.

The children having walked a long distance were made very comfortable at the long recess, as their dinners were many times frozen, and sometimes their food required cooking. Miss Betty was devoted in her care for them in preparing their frugal repast. Apples were roasted and nuts were cracked in profusion, and then with their old-fashioned games they had an enjoyable time.

The ancestors of the Hudson, Dana and Pratt families were included in the school.

There is no record of ladies being employed by the town as teachers or school dames in the schools. In the latter part of the last century and at the commencement of the present century, there were ladies who taught the summer schools.

Mrs. Susan Thurston, the widow of Rev. Mr. Thurston of Medway, and in a second marriage to Ebenezer Waters, Esq., of Sutton, was a teacher and taught in the little school-house on the Sutton road, the Oxford plain, so called, very early in the present century, which was the second school-house erected upon Oxford plain, the site of which was on the left hand side of the Sutton road as you leave Main street about opposite to the blacksmith's shop.

Miss Davis, of Roxbury, taught a school in the first Samuel Davis mansion, in the east part of the town. Miss Hudson, of Oxford, taught school in the school-house nearly opposite to Towne's pond, near the old north common. Miss Hudson afterward was married to Mr. John Mayo, of Oxford. She lived to a great age of over ninety years. Miss Mary Turner also taught the school at this same place at a very early date for many summers, and died in Oxford, at a very advanced age, and was the last of these ancient ladies.

Knitting, plain sewing and needle work were taught by all ladies who were employed to teach, and was in those days, before sewing machines were in practice, a part of a female pupil's education. For every pupil, in finishing her school days, wrought a sampler of small size on yellow canvas. Others wrought on a large square of white or yellow canvas, containing the alphabet in Roman and writing letters, with figures, sometimes surrounded on three sides with a wreath of flowers, while underneath were trees and old ruins and churches; and sometimes a basket of flowers, or even birds and beasts, were wrought in many-colored silk, and then the name of the artist was added, with some sentiment of a prose or poetical effusion, as "Industrious Ingenuity may find Noble employment for the female mind."

An antique sampler from England. The embroidery with which it was embellished comprised a portion of a flower-garden, representing tulips and other flowers, with a landscape view ornamented from natural history. Grace Varley, her work, 1796 with Elizabeth Henderson.

A specimen of good manners from the "Young Ladies and Gentleman's spelling book" a century ago: "When you come into a room, or go out of it, or when you meet people on the street, you must make the handsomest bow you can."

"If you ask for any thing you must say, pray, sir, give me such a thing; or, pray, madam, give me such a thing."

"When you are spoken to, you must say, yes, sir; or no, sir; yes, madam or no, madam."

"Your most obedient, Miss Sally, and how do you do to-day?"

"I thank you, Miss Polly, I am very well, and I hope I have the pleasure of seeing you well."

Boys and girls were taught in the "women school" or dame's school, and used the New England Primer or any substitute from which the alphabet and primary reading and spelling could be learned and taught, the catechism. School books were so few that a whole family of children, not of a poor family, would be seen going to school with only one speller. At eleven years of age the pupils of these schools were taught arithmetic, and at twelve years of age they should be taught to make pens.

The catechism was taught in all public schools outside of Boston until the close of the last century, and in some of the dame schools at a still later date.

1767 March 2, to see if the town will pass a vote that each school squadron (Ward) shall be obliged, each person or persons belonging to each squadron to pay toward building their respective schools in the Province Rate.

The school-houses were soon increased as the town was divided into "squares," or "squadrons," or school districts, as they were afterward designated.

The school districts were not designated by the numbers, as at the present time, but were named from some landed proprietor in their vicinity or otherwise, as the North Gore, or South Gore, Prospect, etc.

The first school books to come into use in the colonies from England were the spellers. These were successively, Fenning's, Moore's, Dilworth's and Perry's; were in the schools previous to the Revolution. The two last named retained their place in New England schools until after the commencement of the present century. Dilworth's speller was entitled "A New Guide to the English Tongue," and contained not only a grammar and reading lessons, but several forms of prayer.

A copy published at Hartford, Ct., in 1786, is of the 23d edition. Most of the editions were published in England. The book was obviously intended for the teacher only.

Thomas Dilworth "Schoolmaster of Wapping," England.

The spelling book of William Perry was entitled "The Only Sure Guide to the English Tongue."

The clergymen who were located over New England in these various rural parishes, were in the habit of hearing the recitations of many of the young people in the higher branches of study in an education.

All the youth were guided to a great degree in their reading by the suggestions of the clergymen to good English authors, and then the social intercourse with the clergyman's family was of great advantage, as the society of clergymen's families was of a most eligible character in all its surroundings.

AN EXAMPLE OF HOME INFLUENCE.

The mother of Washington was in the daily habit of reading to her sons from some serious standard book. One of her great favorites was Sir Matthew Hale's "Contemplations, Moral and Divine," and her copy of this book is still preserved among the treasures of Mount Vernon.

Miss Mary Turner, as was the fashion of the time, finished her education under the instruction of a clergyman, becoming the inmate of Rev. Dr. Crane's family of Northbridge, Mass.

Hon. Judge Barton, a native of Oxford, was in his youth directed in his education before entering Brown University by the famous Master Hall of Sutton, Mass., who was extensively known as "learned in the ancient languages." Master Hall was the son of the distinguished Rev. Dr. Hall of Sutton.

Many young men who had little to do in winter went to the village school until they were from eighteen to twenty years of age. So that the winter schools to a certain extent were composed of young men. The school would continue three and sometimes four months. In those days the "committee man" selected the teachers, and the teacher "boarded round" in families where he had scholars. To be sure there was much rusticity in the manners of the children and youth, more than in the present. The boys then took off their hats to all travelers they met upon the streets and roadside, however inelegantly it might be performed, and passed all persons with a noticeable respect.

In parish schools the spelling classes then went "above," the position of the "head of the class" being held but one week, when the head scholar was placed at the foot of the class with the hope of rising again.

As an incentive to good orthography, extra evening "Spelling Schools" were the fashion all through the country towns to pass away the long winter evenings.

Though Washington was extremely dignified, he was kind and polite to all. A very old colored women, who remembered him as a visitor at her master's house, said he was very kind to the servants, and always remembering their names. "Other gentlemen would pass by without a word, but de President — he'd a been President then — he used always to say, 'How's you dis mornin, Katy?' same as if I'd been a lady. But you don't see such gentlemen now a days. They don't teach young folks manners like they used!"

MANNERS OUT OF SCHOOL.

My aunt taught me, her little niece, to move gently, to speak softly and prettily, to say "yes, ma'am" and "no, ma'am," to keep my clothes clean, and knit and sew at regular hours, to go to church on Sundays and make all the responses, and come home and be thoroughly drilled in the catechism.— *Harriet Beecher Stowe.*

The boarding schools for young ladies were very few and of a very high character. Miss L. M. Thayer, of Braintree, Mass., a sister of Col. Thayer, commandant at West Point, and her sisters, were teachers of great celebrity in the early part of the present century, and among other places the young ladies of Oxford were favored with their instruction. Not only were their English studies carefully directed, but in deportment and in drawing, painting and in the most beautiful embroidery, that can scarcely be equaled in the present time, and in all choice needlework.

Ladies did a great deal of embroidery, working most wonderful landscapes and seascapes. The style was of that delightful kind which combined figures with landscapes.

There is still to be found in antique embroidery Arcadia, the ideal country of virtue and happiness. (We need not try to identify with the country formerly so called in the peninsulas of Greece.)

At a time when people had nothing to do but to stroll about or sit in the rural meadows, as a shepherdess leaning on her crook watching her flock of sheep and a shepherd boy piping sweet music with a simple reedy flute and singing of their love for one another.

Many designs from ancient history or heathen mythology were most beautifully executed.

The Misses Saunders and Beach taught a boarding school at Dorchester, Mass. "The young ladies however used pewter spoons which were thought good enough for boarding school girls in that day."

One young lady of the ancient Hutchinson family of Boston on her arrival at the school took out of her "long pocket" a silver spoon and began eating her breakfast. "As long as there are silver spoons in the world," she said in an undertone, "I shall eat with one, and when there ceases to be, I will put up with some inferior metal."

Many years after, when one of her school friends had become an elderly lady, she said of this young lady, "She was really the most generous girl in school," and this Anne Jane Robbins in her brilliant youthfulness was married to Judge Lyman of Northampton.— An extract from "Recollections of my Mother," by Susan Inches Lesley.

For many years the portrait of this young lady's grandmother, Mrs. Elizabeth (Freake) Hutchinson, graced the walls of the Wolcott mansion, and her mother's uncle, Mr. Edward Hutchinson, made Oxford his home, giving his fortune to his niece, who married Governor Robbins. The remains of Mr. Hutchinson were placed in the Wolcott family vault.

"The old-fashioned blank-book — its paper yellow with age — at the 'Ladies Academy,' Dorchester, July 20, 1803." One-half of the book is taken up with sections, as they are called, describing the "Use of Globes." And the fine, large, clear handwriting, the exact definitions of globes, spheres, properties of spheres, climates, circles, declinations and ascensions, together with the perfect spelling, make me believe that the child of thirteen received excellent instruction at the "Ladies Academy." — "Recollections of my Mother," by Susan Inches Lesley.

The school books in these primitive days were few. The reading of the Bible, especially the Psalter, and the study of the catechism, with Dilworth's spelling book. Then there was the sum book, of magic interest in the study of arithmetic. Grammar when mastered Latin was studied. Many assert that the learning of the catechism trained the memory. The effort to understand gave vigor to the mind, precision to habits of thinking and clearness of expression. As an educating expedient, it has been followed by nothing superior in all the excellent compendiums of mental or moral science used in school.

In later times clergymen of the town visited the schools and heard the recitations from the catechism. Dr. Emmons of Franklin, the noted divine of the last century, it appears, was the last to discontinue this practice in the schools of New England, continuing the same into the early part of the present century.

It is said in the present century Dr. Emmons was not in favor of establishing Sunday-schools in the churches, preferring the practice of catechising the children at the village school. It is said the first Sunday-school in Franklin, Mass., "was established almost under the protest of Dr. Emmons" — as he believed many who were taught the catechism in the village schools would not be included in a Sunday-school for instruction.

One of his pupils, still living (1885), states that when Dr. Emmons entered the school-room all the pupils arose from their seats and bowed to him, or made their manners (as then styled), he waving his hand and bowing to them. As soon as he was seated the pupils resumed their seats; the different classes were called out to stand before him while he should question them from the catechism. They all bowed to him at the commencement of the lesson, and again at the close of their examination. After offering prayers in the school the scholars arose while he took his leave of them in the room. These visits to the scholars were made on Saturday every month.

Mrs. Alexander De Witt, one of his pupils, states his manner of catechising the children in the village schools. After they had repeated the words of the catechism, Dr. Emmons would inquire : " Well, Polly (my little maid), let me hear if you understand what you said respecting the commandments of God." Again he would to another pupil say, " Repeat to me the eighth commandment. Now, my little man, do you understand the meaning of this commandment, to respect your neighbor's property?

" Does this commandment allow you to take apples from his orchard, or in any way to take his property without his consent?"

One can easily picture Dr. Emmons as he entered the school-room to catechise the children, and with what awe and respect he was received by the pupils, with his tri-cornered cocked hat held in his hand extended, dressed in a plain black suit with a very long coat and knee-breeches, and black stockings. Knee and shoe buckles set off his dignified person. It is said he wore his hair long in early life and at a later date his hair fell between his shoulders in a ribbon-bound queue, which fashion of dressing the hair followed the powdered wig. Dr. Emmons never changed his style of dress, though he lived into this century.

In the ancient north parish of Sutton and what is now known as the " Old Millbury Common," February 28, 1779, a vote was passed to the effect that all youth under the authority of parents and masters of the congregation (in that parish), should be catechised four times a year by the pastor (Rev. Mr. Chaplin).

Madame Campan.

Madame Campan, a Catholic lady of France, was a French writer upon education in the last century.

She resided at the court of Louis XVI. Her writings were honored by the French Academy. She was at the head of the French bureau of education.

A translation from the French: "In parish schools there should be most assiduous care in the moral education of the young."

"Religion, so powerful over all hearts, and morals, which ought to rule all our thoughts, our affections and our conduct, is the indispensable basis of this particular system of instruction. It is very essential to stifle at an early period the germs of vice in the young.— *Extract from the Memoirs of Madame Campan, French edition.*

Madame Campan states that "all should receive the rudiments of an education, reading, writing and a knowledge of figures, with a strict moral instruction to all classes of society.

"And then a separate course of education should be pursued with the different positions in society — those intended for a professional life should direct their pursuits in learning to that end, and others to mercantile life or as soldiers or artisans" or to cultivate landed estates.

"In the brilliant pensionnet of St. Germain, in the beautiful establishment d'Écouen, these reflections were often presented to my mind. I was still more impressed when I lived in the quiet retreat of a little village, how incomplete was the system of education. A moral instruction and religion will teach a child to respect the authority of his parents and teacher, to respect the laws of his country and to respect the property of his neighbor. The youth should continue to learn the history of the Old and New Testament; that all the words of the Gospel be graven in their hearts as much as in their memory, and follow the instructions of the catechism of their church."

To the young: One cannot repeat too often this ancient and useful maxim: " Idleness is the mother of all vices, falsehood, robbery and other crimes." A respect for the property of others is a tie of all society; all would be confusion and lost in the world without this respect of that which does not belong to ourselves.

Madame Campan gives an illustration : Cartouche, the famous robber of the seventeenth century. He was educated in a college of Paris but he had profited by his studies only to increase his deceptions and vices. He finished his career by becoming an assassin, and by being condemned to be broken alive *sur la place de Grève à Paris.*

Cartouche had occupied the attention of all France by the pains the police had to secure the arrest of his person.

When he ascended the scaffold, his hands pinioned behind his back, he had a calm air. Several of the attendants of the executioner surrounded him; he requested to speak to the vast multitude of people; his request was granted. One of the attendants cried with a loud voice, " Cartouche wishes to speak to the assembly." In an instant a most profound silence reigned in the place. The criminal advanced to the extreme edge of the scaffold and made the following confession :

" I die penitent," said he to the assembly. " I wish to render my death useful to the fathers of families and to the instructors of youth. Parents, tutors and instructors, fulfill your duties in a watchfulness over the morals of the youth. At the age of seven years my parents placed me at a college.

" There was at the gate at the entrance of the college where I was educated a dealer of fruits and sweet-meats. My first robbery was a plum. I took one in going out to walk. In returning I took a second. Unhappy and fatal day. My inexperience hindered me from seeing the first step taken to the scaffold. I continued my petty larcenies for several months without being discovered. My second robbery was that of a roasted pullet exposed for sale at a cook shop near the college. I soon had courage to rob silver. I took six livres from my preceptor, then a louis. I evaded his suspicion. My vacation arrived; I went to the country seat of my father, and I robbed him of twenty-five louis of gold. He would have had me placed in the house of correction of Saint Lazare. I evaded him, I wandered in the country, I slept in a forest, and I became connected with robbers, and in my robberies with this band of brigands, and thus I became an assassin, hoping to shun justice."

Madame Campan enjoins humanity to be taught. It is a necessity to take the life of animals. But all should be regarded in mercy. But to make animals suffer, or to take lives to be amused with their sufferings is an atrocious wickedness, and even without taking their lives it is very blameable to make animals suffer by barbarous games. "Fly from them; they are the school of the greatest cruelty."

In Oxford, many years ago, the study of natural history was introduced into the village school near the old north common in Oxford. Now it is introduced into schools in Europe.

Monsieur de Sailly gave notes of "Teaching Kindness in School." From the mirror that he presented to our view we saw the reflection of his own character, as that of one possessing extreme refinement of mind blended with humanity as one of its crowning Christian elements.

We would hope that our whole system of school education might be modelled from Prof. de Sailly's outline of instructions, as impressions made on the mind during the first fourteen years of life are said to mould the character.

ILLUSTRATION.

"*The Redbreast.*"— One quiet summer's day a redbreast was seen to be hovering near the porch of an ancient New

England school-room, while the teacher and her pupils were engaged in their daily routine of lessons. The attention of the children became riveted to the movements of this strange little visitor. The teacher for a brief interval indulged their childish pleasure, and showed her own sympathy by requesting them to unite with her in giving the redbreast their protection, for in this kind act they would have an illustration of the kindness she had taught them when giving to them lessons from "Natural History." The redbreast became the protégé of the school. She made her nest near to the old porch, where it could be easily reached by the children, and yet she was unharmed. The confidence which this little bird appeared to place in her new friends was shown by her coming daily to the porch for food, and then bringing her young family with her to partake of their share. A lovely picture is thus presented: a group of children listening to words of humanity, with the redbreast and her young birds sharing the lesson.

The children, from the time they became interested in this pet bird, were more gentle and affectionate to each other. Humanity taught them other right principles. They became more kind in their care of domestic animals, abandoning the practice of robbing birds' nests and destroying small birds. They were made sad by the suffering of animals, and suffered themselves by any act of cruelty done them.

The results of this branch of humane education were of a most pleasing character. These young children went forth from the "village school-room" to excite their parents and others to compassion for the poor brute, and with them to love humanity.*
M. DE W. F.

---

* The teacher of this school (the late Mrs. Sternes DeWitt) gave instruction for some years to the same pupils, and the same redbreast returned from year to year for protection.

EARLY LESSONS IN HUMANITY.

When I was a little girl and lived with my father and mother and sister in our home in the country, we had every thing lovely around us; there was our pleasant flower-garden with its rich border flowers that my mother so much loved; at the bottom of the garden, an arbor covered with honeysuckle and trellises with grapevines. Whenever this lovely picture of the home of my childhood returns to my memory, the sweet lessons of Christian faith and humanity taught by my mother, remain, never to be forgotten. They were so blended, the one with the other, that humanity seemed a basis of all excellence. We were not taught that humanity was the only religion, or all of the Christian faith, but we were taught that humanity was a part of the Christian life, and that an act of cruelty, whether to a poor child on the street, or to any brute, was displeasing to God, for every creature shared in His kind care.

An English divine has said that every brute should be made more happy by having a Christian master. At this pleasant country home I was allowed to go to the village academy to recite my Latin lessons. One day, as the school-boys were going to a green field to finish a large map of the world, that the teachers permitted them to sketch on the ground, a part of the turf being left to form the land picture, and the part removed to represent the water, I heard one boy say to another, " Let's have a squirrel hunt," and then produced from one of his pockets a squirrel. It looked so forlorn and hapless that I at once would have taken it to my heart. I hesitated to speak to them of their cruel sport, and I remained standing in silence. All the lessons of my mother came to my mind; I could speak to no one my childish thoughts, my dislike to go alone to a public play-ground for boys only, for I never had brothers of my own. But the school recess would soon be ended, and the squirrel must be saved, even if it met the scorn and rude laugh of the whole school. Away I hastened over the rough stone stiles, regardless of my nicely plaited white dress and the smooth curls of my hair; reaching the play-ground with a disordered dress and flushed face, I stood before the large group of boys and begged the life of the squirrel. My request was granted by all the boys in one voice, "Give her the squirrel." One boy came forward and presented to me the poor little half-starved creature. I was fearful at first to take it, but soon managed to fold it in my dress for safety, and then where to place my prisoner became a question of great interest to my mind, as a child. I passed on with rapid steps from field to meadow, until I came to some shade trees and water, and then I gave my captive its liberty, returning to the school-room just in time to save me from tardiness. I was made happy, in the one thought that my care for one of God's creatures would receive the approbation of my mother. M. DE W. F.

CHURCH LIBRARY.

A church library was the first public library established in Oxford. Rev. Mr. Campbell writes, in 1743: "The Honorable Judge Dudley devised this liberal thing and sedulously promotes it among gentlemen. The Donors' Names are in a Catalogue of the Books in 'Perpetuam Doni memoriam.' I very willingly embrace this opportunity to present my humble thanks to our generous Benefactors who have made a collection of Books for the use of the incumbent minister of this Parish."

JOHN CAMPBELL.

These books included specimens of costly book-making, ponderous volumes. Treatises on the Christian faith, books of sermons and commentaries. A Scripture Commentary, London Edition of 1624, was "the gift of the Rev'd Mr. Benjamin Wadsworth, for the use of the Church or Parish Library of Oxford in the County of Suffolk, 1719." Mr. Wadsworth was the minister of the First Church in Boston, once the President of Harvard University. A volume entitled "Hexaphla" or commentary on Romans. "Roxbury, 3d July 1736. For the use of the Parish Library in Oxford, New England, the Rev. Mr. Cambel being the minister. Given by Paul Dudley. A sermon written by William Morice, Esq., given by Paul Dudley. An Exposition of the Psalms, a large folio in Latin, given by Rev. Dr. Colman of Boston. A volume of Sermons by Samuel Hieron, Given by Samuel Taylor of Boston.

"Social Library," of Oxford, dates back to the time of the Revolutionary War. Its founders were General Jonathan Davis, Dr. Stephen Barton and Josiah Wolcott, Esq., with other influential persons in the town — a most valuable institution of the last century and during the commencement of the present century in Oxford.*

The Catalogue was as follows: British Album, Brown's Elements, Barclay's Apology, Chesterfield Abridged, Clark's Travels, 3 vols., Campbell's Narrative, Dean's Husbandry, Dialogue of Devils, Domestic Encyclopaedia, 5 vols., Domestic Cookery, Encyclopaedia, 18 vols., Franklin's Works, Female Biography, Goldsmith's Works, 6 vols., Grandpré's Voyage, Holmes' Sketches, 2 vols., The Hive, Herriot's Travels, Heathen Gods, Indian Wars, Locke on the Understanding, 2 vols., Life of Washington, 5 vols., Paradise Lost, Memoir of Cumberland, Modern Europe, Prideaux' History of the Bible, 4 vols., Parent's Friend, Pope's Works, 4 vols., Parke's Travels, Porteus' Evidences of Christian Religion, Relly's Works, 2 vols., Rights of Women, Rambler, 4 vols., Rollin's Ancient History, 8 vols., Robertson's America, 2 vols., Seneca's Morals, Self

---

* In 1839, Judge Barton, then of Worcester, presented to the library four large supplementary volumes of the British Encyclopaedia with a volume of plates. In his accompanying note, addressed to Mr. Peter Butler, he says: "In tendering it to your Association I shall only make a small but grateful return for the pleasure and benefit derived in the days of my boyhood from their useful library."

Knowledge, Shakespeare, 6 vols., Spectator, 8 vols., The Task, Thompson's Seasons, Telemachus, 2 vols., Thinks I to Myself, Vicar of Wakefield, Views of Religion, Whitney's History of Worcester County, Mr. Williams' Letters, Winchester's Letters.

The names of the proprietors were as follows: James Butler, Peter Butler, Lemuel Crane, Jonathan Davis, Rufus Davis, Abijah Davis, Nehemiah Davis, Stephen Davis, Jonathan Davis, Jr., William T. Fisk, Asa Harris, Samuel Harris, Jonas Hartwell, Bradford Hudson, Jeremiah Kingsbury, Samuel Kingsbury, Stephen Kingsbury, Sylvanus Learned, Abisha Learned, William Lamson, John Mayo, Richard Moore, Thomas Meriam, Jotham Meriam, John Pratt, John Putnam, Amos Rich, Joseph Stone, William Sigourney, Samuel Ward.

The share of Asa Harris was purchased by Sternes De Witt.

Society Library.

In 1792, the church voted an appropriation of £30 from the Hagburn fund toward a new library.

Rev. Mr. Dudley, the minister with Captain Elisha Davis, John Dana, Esq., and Captain Ebenezer Humphrey, were deputed to purchase books.

The following gentlemen not connected with the church became members: John Ballard, Jonas Eddy, Lemuel Crane, Anthony Sigourney, Simeon Kingsbury, Ebenezer Shumway, Jr., Jesse Stone, of Ward, Allen Hancock, Amos Shumway, Jr., Joseph Hurd, Daniel Kingsbury, Ambrose Stone, Jr., Sylvanus Town.

In 1796, Sigourney sold his share in the library to Elias Pratt.

A prudential committee of five gentlemen was chosen annually to manage the institution, and for the first twenty years,

Ebenezer Learned, Elisha Davis, Samuel Harris, Lemuel Crane, John Ballard, Ebenezer Humphrey, Joseph Hurd, Joshua Turner, John Dana, constituted this committee.

In 1825, the church voted to replenish the library, and the name was changed from " Society Library " to " Second Social Library." Among the valuable additions to the library were Scott's Bible, 6 vols., Rollin's History, several vols., Silliman's Travels, 3 vols., Massillon's Sermons, Kimpton's History of the Bible.

The titles of works first produced were : Gibbon's Abridgment, 2 vols., Robertson's America, 2 vols., Guthrie's Grammar, Morse's Grammar, Dodd's Thoughts, Fordyce's Sermons, Paley's Philosophy, Citizen of the World, 2 vols., Blackstone's Commentaries, 4 vols., Webster's Essay, Paradise Lost, Night Thoughts, Beattie's Evidences, Beattie's Moral Science, Stackhouse's History of the Bible, 6 vols., The Task, Edwards on the Will, Jennyn's View, Mason's Self Knowledge, Watts' Death and Heaven, Ramsay's History, Doddridge's Rise and Progress, Child's Friend, 2 vols., Minot's Insurrections, Keats' Pelew Islands, Vicar of Wakefield, Edwards on Sin, Edwards on Redemption, Gardiner's Life, Blair's Sermons, 2 vols., Boston's Distinguished Characters, Edwards on the Affections, Edwards against Chauncey, The Spectator, 8 vols., Doddridge's Sermons, Christian Theology, Pilgrim's Progress, Martin's Grammar, Newton on the Prophesies, 2 vols., Seneca's Morals, Hopkins on Holiness, Edwards on Virtue, American Preacher, 3 vols., Butler's Analogy, Price's Dissertations, Hervey's Meditations, Bigelow's Tour, 2 vols., Millot's Elements, 5 vols., Locke's Essay, 2 vols., Ferguson's Astronomy.

Some of the entries on the records of fines are quite suggestive of the olden time, as when Mr. Lemuel Crane " greased Blackstone ; " Peter Shumway " dropped tallow on the American Preacher ; " Silas Eddy " dropped tallow on and burnt

Stackhouse;" John Dana, "a drop of the candle on book;" Amos Shumway " blurred (snuff) Josephus." Fines for tallow drops were common.

FREE PUBLIC LIBRARY.

Judge Barton's will, dated 1 June, 1867, contained the following: "One thousand dollars to the inhabitants of the town of Oxford, my native place, toward establishing a Free Public Library in that town, as an inadequate return for the kindness and patronage of their fathers in my early professional life."

This gift was formally accepted by the town in April, 1868.

In November, 1869, on the report of a committee appointed in the preceding April to consider the subject, it was voted to organize a town library under the provisions of the State laws. In 1870 the library was established.

CHAPTER XXIII.

MANUFACTURES AND OLD FASHIONS.

Until 1530 all spinning was done by the distaff and spindle, but in that year a man in Germany invented the spinning-wheel. Queen Elizabeth directed that laws should be passed in England to encourage manufacturing.

In the early settlement of New England every farmer kept a flock of sheep for the wool, and when the wool shearing came round after it was washed and carded, then it was spun and woven into cloth.

The farmer's wife or house-maid took the wool and dyed it in the dye-pot standing in the corner of the fire-place, and when not in use this dye-pot was covered and answered for the purpose of a seat for children or servants.

There was the carding of wool by hand into rolls, spinning then on a large wheel, walking to and fro through the long and weary days, turning the wheel with one hand, and holding the thread with the other. Then the yarn was reeled into skeins, dyed and washed, and put upon the warping-bars, and into the loom.

Then each thread of the warp must be drawn through the "harness" and through the "reed;" then the shuttle was thrown backward and forward, and the thread beaten in by the "lathe."

The flax had been spread upon the green sward to decay during the rains of autumn. It had been bound in bundles ready for the breaking in a winter's day.

It was pulled, dried and swingled by the farm laborer, but the farmer's wife or house-maid combed, spun, wove and bleached until the white linen was ready for family use, and when of extra fineness the linen sheets were packed away in lavender in huge chests for the marriage gift to some young maiden of the household.

When the wardrobe and household linen of a maiden were completed the lover requested the domine to come and marry them.

The mothers and daughters of the farmer or their maids toiled all the day wielding the hand-cards, throwing the shuttle or whirling the wheel, and then the carding, spinning, dying and weaving.

And there was the weaving of linen for the household, the making of linsey-woolsey for gowns, or of all wool cloth for men's garments.

Linsey-woolsey was a fabric made of wool and linen. Portions of the wool in yarn were dyed in colors and plaid, and striped cloths were thus manufactured for female dress, for every lady wore home-spun clothing.

The spinning-wheel was set to humming at an early hour of the day.

Children in olden time were trained in industrious habits; they could wind the quills and turn the reels, while the matrons and daughters or the maids accomplished their "day's work" at the loom or spinning-wheel.

The weaving-room with all its comforts was the apartment in the farm-house resorted to by the children of the family.

The quill-wheel, by which the shuttle-spools were bound with filling, was an attraction.

Any woman who could spin, weave and embroider was considered quite a treasure in those days away back in the first settlement of New England; then the old loom made such a busy sound in the farm-house and cottage for "the farmer's wife or her maids used to run races in 'spinnin' 'and a weavin,' 'for all were master hands at spinnin.'"

Then these industrious persons of a long afternoon (for they dined at an early hour) or of a long evening, for five o'clock teas were fashionable in these days, would spend a considerable piece of time together over their spinning-wheels "for folks spent a heap o' time spinning in these days."

It is not known when the first fulling-mills were set up in Oxford, nor in the country, but they date far back into the last century. For many years in passing through the country towns and villages, one would see standing there deserted mills.

The fulling-mill in its day became a necessity to the domestic manufactures, for it was impossible to full the cloth at the farm in as finished a style as desirable.

Then came the clothier's shop where the fulled cloth was dressed by teazles and shears (fixed on cylinders).

Then there was much attention given to the dying the fabrics, and among the favorite colors which were the fashion of the time a century since were deep blue, brown, snuff color or butternut, and a shade of wine color.

The clothiers felt an ambition in their business and gave a good appearance to the cloth that was sent to them for dress.

About the same time carding-machines, or mills run by water, were established in the country towns. Loads of fleeces went from the farm-houses to the mills and came back handsome rolls, but still the spinning and weaving were done at the farm by the farmer's wife or house-maid on the old-fashioned wheel and hand-loom.

Samuel Slater's object in establishing mills in Oxford (this interior part of the country) was to introduce his yarn for weaving into cloth. The means for effecting this improvement in manufacturing was to consign large quantities of yarn to the country traders, and they introduce the same to the weavers of the farm-house to be woven into cloth. It was considered a great acquisition in families to obtain this yarn for weaving.

Until about the years 1808 to 1810 the manufacture of yarn into cloth was then only done in families upon the hand-loom and in such quantities as domestic necessity required. The mode of weaving yarn into cloth by water power had not at this time been discovered. The farmer raised flax for summer use and bedding, and kept sheep for the product of wool for winter clothing.

This flax and wool were spun into yarn and woven into cloth at the various farm-houses. These weavers had by necessity become skilled in the use of the hand-wheel and the hand-loom. The old life fashion went out of Oxford with the hand-looms.

This business continued from 1812 to 1823. The manufacture of cotton into yarn was commenced in 1813. The power-loom introduced in 1814 did not supersede the hand-loom in this connection until about ten years later.

But the carding, spinning and weaving in families for domestic purposes was not displaced by the power-loom for many years after the factories had ceased to employ the hand-loom for weaving their yarn. The weaving of woolen yarn by the manufacturers of wool cloths by the hand-loom was continued till about 1823, when it was abandoned by substituting the power-loom for weaving these fabrics. In 1814 was commenced in Oxford the making of broadcloths.

In 1812, Samuel Slater had established himself in what was then Oxford,* and Oxford mechanics were employed by him. New enterprises claimed to utilize this experience, and so Oxford mechanics became the leaders in the new direction of labor and kept it until the wooden wheels were superseded by the iron wheels now in use.

Samuel Slater had introduced spinning by power on machines he had made like those he had been familiar with in England. From this beginning, at about 1800, commenced the mill-wright's business. Oxford was "the town of mill wrights; almost every mechanic in the place was a mill-wright."

"Israel Sibley by his energy and capability and business enterprise was at the head of the mechanics of which Oxford was the great center. He was the central figure among these skilled workmen of the town, who did more than any other to win and retain his reputation."

Edward Howard, an Englishman, had commenced the manufacture of woolen goods in Oxford, now Webster, in the interest of Samuel Slater the cotton manufacturer.

"Young Sibley was employed in the fitting up of the establishment, the arrangement of the machinery. Howard did not like some of the mills in use in this country, especially the 'crank fulling-mills.' They used a better mill in England, and they made the best cloth there of any nation on the globe, so he tried to describe to young Sibley how it was made and how it worked. Of course the young mechanic did not understand much of the process of finishing woolen goods, but he could see how a machine could be made to effect the result, and at Howard's suggestion he undertook to build one. The result was after some alteration a success in erecting an entirely new

* Now Webster.

mill, and one that was destined to be the standard mill of his time.

"Had he patented his invention there would have been a fortune in it, as it was, he was contented to let the public have the benefit of the mill without incumbrance.

"The invention of the fulling stocks and fulling-mill began Sibley's successful career as a mill wright and his prominence as a master of mechanics in the country."

Israel Sibley acquired a competency and retired from business with an income from his estate. He purchased a fine landed estate, located on the village street, with a pleasant old mansion house, presenting many attractions, near the site of where once was the residence of Dr. Alexander Campbell. He married Miss Davis, the granddaughter of Elijah Davis, Esq., and he became one of the influential men of the town. He was a stockholder, and for a series of years a director, in the Oxford Bank. He held important town offices, and represented the town in the Legislature. "He was quiet and unpretending in his manners and style of life. He was a man of few words, but of great executive ability, and hardly realized the power he was in the community, and how much he contributed to the prosperity of the town and the advancement of its interests."

In the ancient farm-houses of Oxford there was a large square chamber which was distinguished as the "weaving-room," with its south and south-western windows, which lengthened the hours of the day, and thus favored industry, as the mistress or maid sprung the shuttle and heaved the beam.

This apartment presents itself as a picture of the past. The rooms in old-fashioned houses were of medium height when compared with the present fashion. They were styled "low-browed," the huge chimney giving a fire-place in a corner of this weaving-room. A wood fire added to its cheerfulness and comfort.

Then there were such piles of flannel and linen sheeting, with table-cloths and toweling and coverlets, woven in a variety of patterns of foreign damask, showing great artistic skill.

Then there were the various kinds of cloth and grades needful for family use, heavy woolen cloth for men's wear in the winter, and tow cloth for summer, woolen stuff, linsey woolsey and ginghams for women and children.

There was also great attention given to weaving carpeting, the warp being spun wool of various colors, and the woof made of cast-off winter clothing as a matter of economy, or remnants purchased of the tailors or tailoresses, cut in narrow strips and colored black or butternut brown. These carpets were of great simplicity, but were in good taste. They were closely copied from Venetian carpeting, which was considered priceless for country wear, and then they were durable in their colors and were a combination of beauty and utility.

Coverlets very artistically woven are still preserved as relics, also bed and table linen, domestic chintz, embroidered or plain, for bed hangings, flannel and woolen fabrics.

For coverlets there were regular patterns for weaving. "Summer and winter" was a favorite.

Miss Rebecca Mayo, of Oxford, was a person of no ordinary character or ability. Her presence was commanding, with a noticeable depth of character, not only by her powers of mind, but by her taste for embroidery and every feminine accomplishment of her time.

Miss Rebecca was known to all the community—"such dainty linen as came from her hand, so firm in its texture and then so fine and white." "She had watched the flax in its blue blossoms when it first appeared, she had wound its fibre on the distaff and spun and woven every thread herself, she had spread the web to bleach, and when all was completed it was laid away in the great store-chest."

Bourdillon, the Huguenot named by Captain Humphrey, who remained in New Oxford after the re-settlement of the French, had abandoned the place. A tradition of the Mayo family states he was employed by the English in printing the domestic fabrics used as dress goods for the English families.

Mrs. L. H. Sigourney narrates that in her own warbrobe were included articles of dress of choice domestic fabrics woven at her country home at Norwich, Ct., which she had in her extreme youth worn with more satisfaction than she had since worn brocades, as court costume at presentations of royalty.

Mrs. Sigourney at her own elegant mansion in Hartford, Ct., introduced the spinning-wheel as a gratification to Mr. Sigourney and to her own refined taste. Mrs. Oldboro, the nurse of her children, in days long since, in leisure hours, engaged herself at the spinning-wheel.

Before the Revolution there was little ambition for success in manufacturing extending beyond home consumption in the colonies, as it was the policy of the British government to suppress manufacturing in all its branches beyond its own requirements in the colonies.

But one of the great advantages of the Revolution was claimed the commencement of an industrial as well as a political independence.

During the time of the war of the Revolution Madam Washington's influence in society as to style of dress was of severe plainness. It is said two of her dresses were of cotton, striped with silk, and entirely of domestic manufacture, for in her own home the spinning-wheels and looms were kept constantly going and her dresses were many times woven by her own waiting-maids.

Tradition states General Washington at his first inauguration wore a full suit of fine clothes, manufactured by his own household.

Before the war it appears, by an order sent to his agent in London, that General Washington was an admirer of nice articles of dress for a lady's wardrobe.

Washington was ever mindful of the happiness of those dependent upon him. He had no children of his own, but he was devotedly attached to the children of Mrs. Washington by her first marriage. At one time he sent to Mr. Cory, his agent in London, a long invoice of various matters needed for the large establishment at Mount Vernon. The list ends with "six little books and ten shillings of toys for Master Custis, six years old," and "a fashionably-dressed baby, worth ten shillings, and ten shillings of other toys," for Miss Patty, aged four. On the arrival of the ship which contained these goods there must have been much excitement of the household over the unpacking of the welcome gifts; the childish ecstasy of Miss Patty over her London doll must have been extreme, as well as the pleasure of Madame Washington over an addition to her wardrobe, viz.: the "salmon-colored velvet, with satin flowers," and the "cap, kerchief, tucker and ruffles of Brussels or point, proper to wear with the same." And then the rejoicing of the children, white and black, over the pound of barley sugar and the fifteen pounds of rock candy which were included in the same list. Rock candy was then esteemed a sovereign remedy for a cold, and was also often used to sweeten tea and coffee.

THE FASHIONS OF DRESS IN THE EIGHTEENTH CENTURY.

The ladies wore caps, long stiff stays, and high-heeled shoes.

Their bonnets were of satin or silk, and usually black.

Gowns were extremely long waisted, with tight sleeves, another fashion was, very short sleeves, with an immense frill at the elbow, leaving the rest of the arm naked. A large flexible hoop, three or four feet in diameter, was for some time quilted in the hem of the gown. A long, round cushion, stuffed with hair or cotton and covered with black crape, was laid across the head, over which the hair was combed back and fastened.

It was the fashion for ladies to wear necklaces when in dress. Some of these necklaces were composed of pearls, to which a gold locket would be attached — and others were simply gold beads, thirty-nine in number, about the size of a small pea.

In olden time, in full dress, ladies' shoes were made of satin and damask or of rich brocaded silk, the same as their dresses, with high wooden heels, afterward cork heels.

The shoes were generally fashioned with straps with large silver buckles, which was the fashion of those days for ladies as well as gentlemen. For a more common article of shoes various stuffs were in use, such as leather, woolen cloth, shalloon and russet.

Though the people raised their own flax and wool, and made their own cloth, gentlemen universally purchased a suit of English broadcloth, and ladies purchased a rich brocade or an India chintz for a gown on grand occasions.

Sheep-skins and buck-skins were dressed and made into breeches, as they were then styled, and were of nice quality, and worn by gentlemen.

Gentlemen, in those days, wore hats with broad brims, turned up into three corners, with loops at the side; long coats with large pocket folds and cuffs, and without collars. The buttons were commonly plated, but sometimes of silver, often as large as half a dollar. Shirts had bosom and wrist ruffles, and all wore gold or silver shirt buttons at the wrist, united by a link. The waistcoat was long with large pockets; and the neckcloth or scarf of fine white linen, muslin or figured stuff, broidered, and the ends falling loosely on the breast. The breeches were usually close, with silver buckles at the knees, with long gray stockings, which on holidays were exchanged for black or white silk.

Boots with broad white tops, or shoes with straps and large silver buckles, completed the costume of a gentleman. Clergymen when in dress wore black silk stockings.

All gentlemen who had reached the age of twenty-five or thirty-five years had two wigs; one for Sunday and one for ordinary every-day wear.

The Sunday wig was very expensive and elaborate. The hair was shaven closely, that the wig might be fitted to the head. The dress wig sometimes rose a foot above the head and came down on either side the head to the waist.

All elderly people who wore wigs usually removed them in the church during service, and supplied their place with a plain linen cap, or one knit of cotton or linen and of woolen in the winter; a small tassel on the top of the cap was the only ornament; clergymen when they made visits on their parishioners, removed the wig and hung it upon the pegs or heavy nails on the paneling of the walls; when leaving the cap was laid aside and the wig resumed its place.

Coat, vest, knee-breeches, of the long-waisted, single-breasted, large pocket-flapped kind were counted style in those days. They were made of snuff-brown silk of the quality of Mrs. Vicar Wakefield's wedding gown, that was bound to wear well.

Three-cornered cocked hats, plum-colored, crimson, green and purple velvet coats, embroidered waistcoats, buckles, powdered wigs and pig-tails, all were the going fashion previous to the Revolution. But these fashions were now waning.

Soon after the War of the Revolution the fashion of wearing wigs by gentlemen was discontinued, though some elderly gentlemen wore them till the commencement of the present century.

Gentlemen wore their hair in a queue, the front hair being brushed straight over the forehead.

Tailors and tailoresses went from house to house to make the clothing for men, with their shears and long pockets. The coarse tow cloth was made into rough but durable clothing for workingmen.

Simplicity in dress, manners and equipage characterized these New England homes until quite a number of years after the Revolutionary War. As wealth increased broadcloth and silk began to take the place of home-spun.

Woolen and linen fabrics constituted the clothing. A silk dress then lasted a life-time and descended as an heir-loom from mother to daughter. Furs were quite common as there were so many wild animals. Bear skin muffs were the fashion. Strips of the bear skin were sewed alternately to silk or linen goods, as the skins were too heavy to be used as a whole. Black and white fox skins were in great demand and fine sets of European sable were common.

The visit of Lady Washington was noticed in the newspapers and one of her receptions described.

"Most of the ladies were arrayed in gorgeous brocade and taffeta luxuriously displayed on hoops with comely bodices laced around that ancient armour, the stay, disclosing most perilous waists, and with sleeves that clung to the arm as far as the elbow, when they took a graceful leave in ruffles, their hair all drawn back over cushions and falling in cataracts upon the shoulders, in shoes with formidible point to the toe and high tottering heels painfully cut in wood, with their tower built hats crowned with tall feathers."

In a gentleman's style of dress the ruff gave place to the fashion of the falling collar, which began to increase in size as extravagantly as the ruff had done, until it was as big as a cape, made of the most expensive lace that could be woven. On the restoration of the Stuarts, Charles II and his court resumed the lace collar, but of more moderate dimensions. Gradually the collar became limper and limper until it disappeared, and a wisp of lawn, linen or lace took its place, and when tied loosely in a knot it was quite a graceful fashion, but little by little the plain collar became the style with all its numerous changes of fashion.

During the time of the protector the Round Heads were as well known by their cropped hair and severe simplicity in dress as the Cavaliers had been by the extravagance of their attire. Their rich low collars were doomed to oblivion, and a plain piece of turned-down linen was adopted by the Puritans.

Samuel Slater* may be regarded as the founder of the town of Webster, as through the introduction of his manufacturing establishments of cotton and woolen fabrics, its population has been increased and its commercial celebrity has been established.

On young Slater's arrival in New York, he sought the patronage of Moses Brown of Providence, R. I., a gentleman extensively known in the country, and finally secured a partnership in business with Mr. Almy, the son-in-law of Mr. Brown.

He was styled the father (or founder) of the cotton manufacture of the United States. In October, 1791, some of the yarn first spun, and some of the cotton cloth first made from his yarn in America, was sent to the secretary of the United States to be preserved in the Treasury department.

In the year 1832 the town of Webster was formed from the towns of Dudley and Oxford with the territory of Oxford, known for many years as "Oxford South Gore," and another tract belonging to the Pegan Indians (a remnant tribe of the Nipmucks), which they had received from the town of Dudley for their relinquishment of certain rights to land located on

---

*Samuel Slater was a native of Belper, Derbyshire, England. He left for London September 1, 1789. On the 13th sailed for New York, and, after sixty-six days, arrived in that city. When ready to sail he despatched a letter by the post to his mother, informing her he had left England for the United States, thus avoiding the parting scene. His father died when he was but fourteen years of age. Samuel Slater was born June 28, 1768. He died in Oxford (now Webster) April 20, 1835.

Dudley hill, which was part of the land known formerly as 'Black, James & Co.'s Grant," surveyed to them in 1684.

This reservation was equal to about five miles square, made by the ancestors of these Indians in their deed procured by Hon. William Stoughton and Joseph Dudley, agents of the colony.*

Through the introduction of both cotton and woolen manufacture its chief prosperity and population has been introduced.

It is a subject of historical interest to ascertain by what means Mr. Slater became acquainted with the water-power at this place.

Mr. James Tiffany, of South Brimfield (now Wales), in Massachusetts, in often visiting Providence and Pawtucket, formed an acquaintance with Samuel Slater and his cotton manufacture at Pawtucket. Mr. Slater became interested in the young sons of Mr. Tiffany who were well educated for the time.

Mr. Tiffany recognizing Mr. Slater's superior business talents, requested him to take his sons and educate them for a mercantile position. On the father's recommendation alone Mr. Slater consented that one of the sons should be sent to him on trial. Soon after the eldest, Lyman, made his appearance at Pawtucket, and soon proved himself to be all the fond father had recommended, and became a favorite in Mr. Slater's family.

Bela, a second son of Mr. Tiffany, soon followed his brother in Mr. Slater's care, and proved himself capable and satisfactory in the performance of the trust confided to him.

---

* "Six years after the close of the war, Eliot could claim but four towns in the State." One of these was Chaubunagungamaug (now Webster).— Drake, 179.

Rev. John Eliot, 1688, gives the name of the large pond as "Chabanakongkomun." The nearest approach to a translation of the word is found in a collection of the Connecticut Historical Society (documents) by I. H. Trumbull, and was given as "The boundary fishing place," as the lake formed the boundary between the Nipmucks and Mulhekans, and was resorted to by both nations.

Mr. Slater to effect his plans, manufacturing establishments were to be erected in the country; he had made inquiry as to some suitable locations, when his friend Tiffany described to him the valuable water-power afforded by the outlet of the Chabanakongkomun pond.*

Mr. Tiffany, in his journeyings to and from Pawtucket and Providence, passed and repassed this outlet, which at that time was the principal way of travel, the more direct roads having since been opened for travel.

With the recommendation of this water-power by Mr. Tiffany, Mr. Slater despatched young Tiffany, then in his employ, in May, 1811, who, having examined the premises, writes Mr. Slater as follows:

FRANKLIN, *May* 27, 1811.
Mr. SAMUEL SLATER:

DEAR SIR.—I was very much disappointed when I arrived at Mr. Rud's in Uxbridge, for I had no information of the cause why you were not there. True the letter came Friday night, but through mistake, being brought after I had retired, was put into the post-office, and when I returned on Sunday morning (having been up to the pond), it was taken out of the office, and fortunately I found it; but I thought it best to pursue the intended journey, by which I could in some measure satisfy myself, which is as follows:

Buildings—Large two-story house unfinished inside, built for two families; grist-mill with two run of stones, tolerably good; a very good saw-mill, and a trip-hammer shop in good repair, 11 with about 13 or 14 acres of land, one-half of which is swamp of very little value, and the rest not very good. With regard to water and fall, there is no doubt enough to

---

* Lake Chabanakongkomun is a beautiful lake which extends over an area of 1,200 acres of land. The shores and its heavily wooden islands add much to the beauty of scenery.

answer any purpose we should want, and so situated that a mill may be erected with as little expense as in any place I have seen; it is convenient to the road, and I believe quite secure from inundation.

The principal objection, in my opinion, is that it is the most benighted part of the globe, 4 miles from Oxford, 3 from Dudley, 6½ from Thompson, where the corners of the three towns intersect each other.

Terms are as follows : Four thousand dollars are the lowest terms; one thousand dollars down, in two years one thousand more, and then one thousand yearly until balance is paid or if at the expiration of one year the residue is paid that is the three thousand dollars, a deduction of one hundred will be made, which I consider no object. I have the refusal at the above stipulation until the 20th of June, but he said it would oblige him if we could determine soon, as two men were expected to look at the place the 20th instant, who had seen it before and solicited him to join them and erect a mill but he said he preferred to sell right out, as a farm life would be most agreeable to himself and family, and says that if I will sell my farm he will look at it, and did it suit him, give a fair price, which will be some advantage to me, because it will almost pay him for the privilege. There is a farm adjoining the mill site of about 220 acres of land, a dwelling-house and barn, for sale, for about $3,000, which, if it should be wanted, may be had, and which may be worth very near that money. If you feel desirous to have the place, you will please write me, for I told him he should hear from me within that time, one way or the other.

Your obedient servant,
BELA TIFFANY.

This valuable water-power afforded by the outlet of Chabanakongkomun lake was purchased by Samuel Slater.

With Mr. Slater's approval of purchasing this water-power and some adjoining lands, the purchases were made in Mr. Tiffany's individual name; bought of three different parties — 9½ acres in two parcels, of Elisha Pratt, for the consideration $3,700.

One of these parcels of four acres contained a dwelling-house and barn, grist-mill and saw-mill, a trip-hammer shop, coal-house, and an old building formerly a grist-mill.

The date of this first is "January 6, 1812," and, as expressed in this deed, the land was located partly in each, Dudley and Oxford.

The second purchase was 203 acres, situated in the towns of Dudley and Oxford, bought of Asa and Samuel Robinson, with the buildings, for the consideration of $3,500, by deed dated "January 28, 1812."

A third lot was bought of Josiah Kingsbury, of 56 acres, with a dwelling-house, and clothing-mill thereon, for the consideration of $1,800, by deed dated "May 4, 1812."

The three purchases contained 268½ acres of land, with the aforesaid buildings and mills, giving the entire control of the outlet and water-power connected with the large pond before named, were secured, for the total sum of $9,000. Mr. Bela Tiffany sold to Samuel Slater five-sixths of all this estate at the precise cost to him, $7,500, making a joint-interest to be held in common and undivided, he reserving one-sixth for himself. This deed is dated "11th of December, 1812," and witnessed by Samuel A. Hitchcock and Lorin Tiffany, who were at that time there acting in the capacity of clerks for Slater & Tiffany.

The cotton-factory, known as the "Green mill," was erected during the year 1812, and the manufacture of cotton into yarn was first begun here in 1813.

It appears that the dye and bleaching buildings were built at the same time, and placed under the care of Mr. John Tyson from England, who, it appears, held a joint interest in the business. Mr. Tyson continued connected with the dye-house business from seven to eight years — his health became impaired, and after one or more voyages to Bermuda for relief, he died of consumption August 2, 1821.

In about 1814 Samuel Slater commenced the woolen manufacture. At this time was commenced the making of broadcloths under the charge of Edward Howard, who came from England.

Edward Howard it is said or believed was among the first — if not exclusively so — to introduce the manufacture of American broadcloth.

Mr. Slater's business here had been confined to the water-power connected with the Chabanakongkomun pond, at the East village, but this year, 1821, associated with Mr. Howard, he made a location upon the French river, now known as the South village.

Messrs. Slater & Tiffany, besides the management of the cotton manufacture and dying and bleaching business, a store was added, and thus further purchases of real estate continued. The great depression in the cotton manufacture which followed the close of the war between Great Britain and the United States, December, 1814, consequent upon the large importation of English manufactures, caused Mr. Tiffany to sell all his interest in this business to Mr. Slater. The date of deed " November 27, 1816."

Mr. Bela Tiffany, after retiring from his partnership with Mr. Slater, entered upon the commission sale of American cotton and wool manufactures in Boston and New York, and after retiring from business he became a resident of Southbridge, became interested in forming the Southbridge bank, and many public improvements. He died June 29, 1851, aged 65 years.

July 18, 1821, Edward Howard bought land of William Wakefield and Gibbs Dodge, executors of Solomon Wakefield. Another tract of William Wakefield. And a third tract from David Wakefield, and a fourth tract, a wood lot; bought of Daniel Mansfield a tract of land.

Manufactures and Old Fashions. 347

This embraced several mills and buildings, where the woolen works are now located.

The business was now conducted here in the name of Slater & Howard. Slater & Howard purchased tracts of additional land.

Slater & Howard purchased the village factory estate, Nov. 6, 1824. Dana A. Braman, William M. Benedict and Jason Waters. Together with the village factory, dwelling-houses and the water privilege belonging to the cotton, woolen and linen manufacturing company, reference being had to the deed of Samuel Waters, and others to above village factory company.

Village Factory Sale.

To this estate was added additional purchase, in which was included the Peter Pond wood lot of about twenty acres, on the west side of French river.

The style of this firm was Slater & Howard. January 2, 1829, Edward Howard sells to Samuel Slater of Oxford, George B. Slater and Horatio Nelson Slater, his one undivided half of the property of the woolen manufacturing company.

This includes all the water power supplied by the French river within the limits of Webster.

"It may be said that Bela Tiffany, John Tyson and Edward Howard were the chief managers in executing the plans of Mr. Slater, in founding the principal business of Webster, and that which furnishes its chief prosperity and growth as a town."

It appears that after the Revolutionary War Rev. Samuel Waters and other Baptist clergymen preached occasionally. In 1790 the east part of the town was the principal place of holding services. In 1798 a reorganization of this church took place in the east part of Dudley, which subsequently became the town of Webster, and Solomon Wakefield was ordained as their minister. Its principal members were Joseph Wakefield, William Wakefield, Paul Robinson, Silas Robinson.

CHAPTER XXIV.

THE INTER-COLONIAL WARS.

I. *King William's War.*

There is found, dated April, 1690, a quaint old agreement among the "Bernon Papers." Gabriel Bernon,* the president of the Huguenot settlement of Oxford, enters upon an agreement with one Jean Barre, a fellow refugee, promising to furnish him with "one fire-lock muskett of three pounds valen, one pistoll of twenty shillings price, one Carthuse Boxe of three shillings one hatchet of two shillings," and other necessaries, besides three pounds in money, "for his now intended voyage on Board the good shipp called the *Porkepine*, Capt. Ciprian Southack, commander, now bound to sea in a war farcing voyage." Captain Southack was a Boston skipper, who became noted at a later day for his success in breaking up piracy.

The "good ship *Porcupine*" belonged to the fleet that was then getting ready to sail from Boston harbor, under Sir William Phipps; and the "war farcing voyage" in question was the expedition for the capture of Port Royal, in Nova Scotia, which Massachusetts sent forth in the spring of the year 1690, preliminary to the enterprise then on foot for the conquest of Canada.

The expedition for the capture of Port Royal was thoroughly successful, and it awakened eager hopes in Boston for the more important undertaking of which this was but the first step — the attack about to be made upon Quebec.

None were more keenly interested in these movements than the newly-arrived Huguenots in Boston.

During King William's War in 1690, in the winter, most of

---

* Gabriel Bernon, the founder of Oxford, Mass.

the frontier settlements in Maine and New Hampshire were destroyed by the French and Indians, and in other parts of the country.

Sir William Phipps commanded a small fleet from Massachusetts Bay, and captured the old French settlement of Port Royal in Nova Scotia.

Rev. Grindal Rawson* went as a chaplain with the fleet, " receiving his appointment from the Governor, confirmed by both houses, July 31, 1690," to accompany the general and forces to carry on the worshipping of God in that expedition."

A translation of a letter written in French in 1691 :

"Our fleet," wrote Benjamin Faneuil, in great glee, on the 22d of May, to Thomas Bureau in London, "which we sent out from here to take Port Royal, has sent back a ketch, which has arrived this day, with news of the taking of the place. On capitulation they have seized six ketches or brigantines, loaded with wine, brandy and salt, together with the governor and seventy soldiers, and have demolished the fort. They have also taken twenty-four very fine pieces of cannon and thirty barrels of powder. We expect them hourly. Our fleet, which was composed of six vessels, one of which carried forty guns, will be re-enforced with a number of strong ships, and will be sent with twelve hundred men and some Indians to take Canada. I hope it will succeed." †

In 1696 Gabriel Bernon, son of the refugee, was engaged in trade between Boston, Portsmouth and Port Royal with Charles de La Tour, who resided at Port Royal.

De La Tour, in November or December of that year, " was arrested when about to proceed from Portsmouth to Acadia

---

* Rev. Grindal Rawson was the son of Edward Rawson (Secretary of State) and the ancestor of John Rawson, who became a resident of Oxford (now Webster) in 1774.

† Sir William Phipps commanded this fleet, and it is said returned to Boston, having " obtained considerable booty."

or Nova Scotia — just then under British rule — and his sloop was condemned as a lawful prize, under charge of having violated one of the provisions of the oppressive navigation laws, as well as a recent enactment of the colonial legislature of Massachusetts, that prohibited all commerce between that colony and Nova Scotia. This enactment, which had been inspired by the suspicion that the French — then at war with England — obtained supplies at Port Royal, bore very heavily on the Acadians, who depended so greatly for subsistence upon their dealing with New England."

"You can well see," wrote young Bernon to his father, then in England, "from the manner in which this people treat us, that it will be impossible for us to live any longer among them without strong recommendation to the governor, who is expected soon. They commit the greatest possible injustice toward the inhabitants of Acadia; for whilst they assume to take them under their protection, they pass laws that condemn them to perish with cold and hunger; and if they do any thing contrary to the interests of the English, they punish them as subjects of the king of England." — *Bernon Papers.**

II. *Queen Anne's War.*

The peace of Ryswick did not long continue. In 1702 England declared war against France and Spain, and the American colonies were engaged in the contest called in America Queen Anne's War. After continuing eleven years this was closed by a treaty made in 1713 at Utrecht, a town in Holland.

III. *The Spanish War.*

In October, 1739, after some quarter of a century had passed, England and Spain were engaged in war with each other.

During the contest England called upon her American colonies to furnish soldiers to aid an English fleet, and in captur-

---
* Huguenot Emigration, vol. 1, p. 140.

ing Spanish settlements in the West Indies. Four thousand men were furnished from the colonies.

The enterprise terminated disastrously to the English, and but a few hundred men ever returned to their homes.

There is no record of men furnished for this war.*

IV. *King George's War.*

The Spanish War of 1739 had merged into King George's War. The capture of Louisburg, situated on the island of Cape Breton, from the French, was the most important event of this war, as it commanded the entrance to the Gulf of St. Lawrence.

In the summer of 1745 it was taken by an army from New England under command of Sir William Pepperell of Maine, aided by an English fleet that sailed from Boston.

King George's War ended in 1748 by the treaty of Aix-la-Chapelle.

The French held a strong line of posts from the St. Lawrence to the mouth of the Mississippi. The French were strongly allied with the Indians, and announced their claims by nailing to the trees and sinking in the earth leaden plates bearing the arms of France.

This State contributed forces to the army which laid siege to Louisburg. Oxford and the neighboring towns shared in the excitement which prevailed in the colonies. April 7, 1745: "This day is a fast day to implore of God his mercy and smiles on our expedition to Cape Breton against Louisburg, the stronghold of the French on that island." July 18: A public thanksgiving was held " on ye occasion of ye taking of Cape

---

* Ebenezer Waters, son of Richard Waters, Esq., formerly of Salem, subsequently of Manchung farm, adjacent to Oxford, now in Sutton, was on this expedition under Admiral Vernon, and died at Cuba. At his decease a valuable gun belonging to him was returned to his friends, and is still retained as a relic with a descendant of the Waters family.

Breton." On the return of the army to Boston the soldiers were received with transports of joy.

French and Indian War.

Early in the spring of 1755 General Braddock landed in Virginia with two British regiments. He had been appointed commander-in-chief of all the forces in the provinces. Four expeditions were planned. These were to be sent against Fort Duquesne, Nova Scotia, Crown Point and Niagara.

The force which went against the French on the Ohio was led by Braddock himself, Colonel Washington acting as an aide-de-camp. The British general was ignorant of Indian warfare, yet too self-confident to heed the prudent counsels which Washington gave him. When within a few miles of Fort Duquesne, his army was surprised July 9 by a small party of French, with their Indian allies, and routed with terrible slaughter. Braddock was mortally wounded.

Capt. Ebenezer Learned, a son of Lieut.-Col. Ebenezer Learned of Oxford, in 1756, with his company of soldiers, marched to the seat of war, and as a part of Col. Ruggles' regiment was in camp Sept. 9 at Lake George.

At this time in Oxford there were two companies of militia, commanded, respectively, by Edward Davis and Samuel Davis, brothers, from both of which soldiers were furnished in a new company under Capt. Learned.

While preparations for the northern expedition were in progress Col. Chandler wrote to the authorities at Boston as follows:

"WORCESTER, *April* 22, 1756.

"The bearer, Capt. Ebenezer Learned, is to have command of a company of men in Col. Ruggles' regiment, and as guns and stores will be wanted for his company he will engage to bring them up if you please. * * * What Learned engages to do will be faithfully done." *

---
* Massachusetts Archives, LXXV, 536.

The following are the names of soldiers from Oxford:
Ebenezer Learned, captain ; Elisha Rich (Sutton), lieutenant; Elijah Towne, sergeant. Privates: Joseph Baker, Solomon Smellige, Ebenezer Davis, John Barnes, Elijah Curtis, Hezekiah Eddy, Samuel Manning, Jonathan Eddy, Isaac Learned, Jr., Caleb Barton, Jr., Stephen Shumway, Samuel Baker, Josiah Kingsbury, Jr.

Philip Richardson's company, August, 1756, in Ruggles' regiment : Enoch Jones, sergeant ; Noah McIntire ; Philip McIntire ; Captain Dresser, Charlton District.

Tradition states that Rev. John Campbell was styled " Old Col. Campbell " at this time, and was much interested in Capt. Learned and his soldiers who left Oxford to join Col. Ruggles' regiment stationed at Lake George, and personally had ably seconded Capt. Learned by his knowledge of the science of military tactics.

Mr. Campbell was called " as great a swordsman as he was a gownsman." He was also a proficient in fencing.

Fort William Henry taken August 3, 1757. Marquis de Montcalm laid siege and compelled its garrison to surrender.

The prisoners were promised safe escort to the English fort, held by Gen. Webb, but the savages fell on them as they began their march, and the French officers were unable to prevent them from being plundered, and some of them were massacred. The militia of Massachusetts hastened to their rescue.

August 10. Detachments from the two Oxford companies marched as far as Sheffield, one hundred and five miles, and were out sixteen days.

First detachment, date of roll, August 18 : Edward Davis, captain ; John Edwards, lieutenant ; Jeremiah Learned, ensign ; Jedediah Barton, sergeant ; Joseph Edwards, sergeant ; John Town, sergeant ; Phinehas Ward, corporal ; Moses Town, corporal ; Alexander Nichols, Jacob Comins, Ebenezer Eddy,

John Wiley, William Eddy, Joseph Phillips, Jr., Israel Phillips ("detached and sent to Stockbridge"), Daniel Fairfield, John Duncan, Hezekiah Merriam, Jr., Jonathan Phillips, Silas Town, Samuel Larned, Ebenezer Gale, Jr., Joseph Gleason, Samuel Eddy, Jr., Elisha Gleason, Moses Gleason, Jr., Joseph Goggins ("detached and sent to Stockbridge"), Josiah Wolcott, Aaron Parker, Edmund Town, Joseph Pratt, Jesse Pratt, Nathan Shumway, David Pratt, privates.

The second detachment: Samuel Davis, captain; John Larned, captain; Elisha Davis, sergeant; John Nichols, sergeant; Amos Shumway, sergeant; William Parker, sergeant; Jeremiah Shumway, corporal; John Davis, corporal; Thomas Town, Isaac Larned, Jonas Coller, John Shumway, William Nichols, John Barton, Jonathan Fuller, Ichabod Town, Joseph Pratt, Jr., Stephen Jewett, Joseph Davis, Benjamin Hudson, John Marvin, Isaac Town, Adams Streeter, Arthur Humphrey, Peter Shumway, Joseph Kingsbury, Jeremiah Kingsbury, Roger Amidown, Abijah Harris, Zebulon Streeter, John Dana, Samuel Manning, John Watson, John Robbins, John Coburn, John Shumway, Jr., William Comins, William Learned, Joseph Wilson, John Moore, privates.

The company were mounted and marched under Capt. Davis to Springfield, and thence to Sheffield under Capt. Larned.

In October, 1757, Capt. John Larned with twenty-nine men, of whom twelve were of Oxford, called the "Minute Expedition," marched as far as Westfield, being out from October 20 to November 11 — three weeks and two days.

Roll: John Larned, captain; Jonathan (?) Nichols, lieutenant; Jacob Cummins, sergeant; Jeremiah Shumway, corporal; Joseph Davis, John Duncan, Ebenezer Fish, Nathan Moore, Ebenezer Eddy, William Lamb, John Nichols, Elijah Larned, Arthur Humphrey, privates.

A roll of Capt. Joshua Meriam, North Gore, September 26, 1758, gives: Joshua Meriam, captain; Uriah Stone, clerk;

Isaac Hartwell, Robert Meriam, Hezeziah Eddy, Elijah Curtis, Ebenezer Lock, Paul Wheelock, —— Wheelock, Jonas Hammond, Ebenezer Hammond, John Thompson, David Wheelock, corporal; Nehemiah Stone, corporal; Jesse Smith, Elijah Stoddard, Aaron Thompson, Uriah Ward, Simon Mory, Zenas Mory, Asa Jones, Malachi Partrige, Peter W——n, Joseph Parker, Job Weld.

These were in service 1757, marched to relieve the province forts, went to Sheffield, were out eight days and returned.

SHEFFIELD, *August* 15, 1757.

Capt. MERRIAM — Upon fresh advice from Gen. Webb your further Proceeding on your march appears innecessary, and the Exigency of the affairs of many of your Company urge their Return home. You are hereby ordered to march them to ye country Gore, all except Zenas Moréy, and Discharge them unless you Receive Counter orders afterwards, for which this shall be your sufficient Warrant.

GARD'R CHANDLER, *Major*.

Feb. 6, 1760. Capt. Jeremiah Learned's company includes the following: Jeremiah Learned, captain; Jonathan Holman of Sutton, lieutenant; William Lamb, Samuel Learned, Reuben Barton, corporals; David Pratt, Jr., Thomas Eddy, Edward Davis, Jr., Hezekiah Meriam, Jr., Samuel Manning, Jr., Ebenezer Lamb, privates. All of Oxford.

This company, most of the members of which were from Charlton and Sutton, was in 1760 at Ticonderoga.

Other Oxford men, known to have been in the service, were: Israel Whitney, in Cape Breton expedition, 1745; Jonas Gleason, Cape Breton expedition, January, 1752; William Campbell, in Louisburg expedition, 1758; Naphtali Streeter, 1759; Richard Rogers, 1760; Edmund Barton, Samuel Call (Jacob and Josiah Towne, sons of Jonathan Towne, were at

Fort Edward 1755; Jacob died at Fort Edward, and was buried in the woods by his brother Josiah. John Streeter died November, 1756, at Sheffield), Benjamin Davis (Lieut. Samuel Jennison, 1756, not from Oxford).

On a roll of Capt. McFarland's company, February 3, 1761: Abijah Gale, Micah Pratt, Abraham Pratt, Nathaniel Smith, Reuben, son of Oliver Shumway, William Lackey and Joseph Goggins. All of Oxford.

1758. A return of men enlisted in John Chandler's regiment for the invasion of Canada, under Gen. Amherst: John Boyle, Elijah Town, Abraham Pratt, William Lackey, sergeant; Joseph Goggins, Moses Town, Solomon Comings, Samuel Streeter, Abijah Gale, John Duncan, Nathan Moore, David Towne, John Ballard, Abel Levens, Peter Shumway, Jonathan Phillips, Elijah Larned, Richard Moore, 3d, Zebulon Streeter. All of Oxford.

In 1759 the following men of Oxford were enlisted in the expedition against Crown Point: Samuel Davis, Capt. John Learned, Capt. Elisha Davis, Sergt. John Nichols, Sergt. Amos Shumway, Sergt. Wm. Parker, Sergt. Jeremiah Shumway, Corp. John Davis, Corp. Ebenezer Learned, Elijah Town, John Wiley, Jr., Hezekiah Eddy, Jonathan Eddy, Stephen Shumway, Caleb Barton, Jr., Ebenezer Davis, Samuel Manning, Solomon Smiledge, Isaac Learned, Jr., John Barnes, Wm. Simpson, George Alverson, Caleb Barton, Peter Shumway, Elisha Blandin, Francis Blandin, Jonas Blandin, Ezekiel Coller, Solomon Cook, Ebenezer Robbins, Joseph Philips, Josiah Kingsbury, Joseph Bacon, Elisha Ward, Arthur Daggett, Elijah Kingsbury.

On a roll of Capt. Newhall's company, Leicester, are Joseph Goggins, Joseph Kingsbury, Israel Phillips, Zebulon Streeter. All of Oxford.

Joseph Goggins was in Capt. White's company, and served through the campaign.

July, 1758, Canada surrendered. A large fleet aided the army of Gen. Amherst, who was sent to capture Louisburg. The fortress was won by the English. The whole island of Cape Breton was reduced, for Louisburg, the key of the Canadas, was taken.

In July, 1759, Niagara yielded, and a few weeks later Ticonderoga was surrendered and Crown Point abandoned.

September 13, Gen. Wolfe's victory at Quebec.

September 6, 1760, Gen. Amherst assembled a large force before Montreal, and two days later French dominion in Canada ended, and " all that magnificent structure which the genius of Champlain and the patient labors of the French Jesuits had devotedly raised, vanished."

In 1755 the expedition against Acadia, or Nova Scotia, captured the French forts in that province, and the entire country east of the Penobscot became subject to the British authority. But this success was disgraced by cruelty. Several thousands of these French colonists were accused of disloyalty to the English, and were driven on board ships by British soldiers. These unfortunate people were taken from their homes, and many were separated from their friends never to meet again.

These French prisoners were scattered throughout the colonies. Many families came to Worcester county, and some were consigned to Oxford and other towns.

On June 2, 1757, Duncan Campbell of Oxford represented to the General Court " that the selectmen of Newton bound out to him five children of some of the late inhabitants of Nova Scotia ; that on his placing them at Worcester their parents followed them there, and as the result they all went away." Asking allowance, on which was voted him 42 shillings, 3½ pence.

In November Mr. Campbell presented another memorial setting forth that : " Last May session [he] preferred a petition to the honorable court that £17, 13s. 4d. might be allowed [him] for transporting from Cambridge to Oxford and keeping some

French neutrals, * * * from which [he] hath never received any profit or service, they refusing to work — that upon said petition said court was pleased to allow [him] no more than 42s. 3½d. — that the honorable board have sent your petitioner's servants to the town of Dedham, and so he is deprived of any service from them until this time, notwithstanding the great expense he was put to in maintaining them. * * *"

He prays he may be allowed the remainder of his account, "or that he may have an order from the honorable court to take those that were bound to him from Dedham and compel them to work."

The chief item in his bill was for boarding the family at Capt. Thomas Sterne's, Worcester. Upon this petition, on March 20, 1758, in the House of Representatives, £5, 9s. and 4 pence were ordered paid, but the council non-concurred.

On August 26, 1757, a warrant was drawn to pay from the treasury of the colony £15, 6s. 6d. to the selectmen of Oxford for the support of "French from Nova Scotia sent there."

A family named LeBlanc came to Oxford. Supplies from March 10, 1758, to May 24, 1759, were furnished them by Dr. Alexander Campbell, for which he sent a bill of £21 to the Legislature. From May, 1759, to March, 1760, Edward Davis, Esq., provided for them at an expense of £18. This family, father, mother and nine children, later removed to Brimfield.

A petition had been sent to his excellency, the governor-general of the province of Massachusetts Bay, in New England, and to the honorable gentlemen of the council, that in these French families parents and children should not be separated. "That houses be provided for each family, so they may keep together."

After the close of the war, in the first regiment, Worcester county militia, March, 1763, were officers from Oxford as follows: Edward Davis, major; First Oxford Co., Elisha Davis, captain; John Nichols, lieutenant; William Larned, ensign;

Second Oxford Co., Jeremiah Learned, captain ; Jedediah Barton, lieutenant; John Towne, Jr., ensign. In 1771 : Edward Davis, major; First Oxford Co., Elisha Davis, captain; Ephraim Ballard, first lieutenant; William Watson, second lieutenant; Thomas Towne, ensign ; Second Oxford Co., Joseph Phillips, captain ; Samuel Eddy, lieutenant ; Isaac Putnam, ensign.

NOTE.— PROVINCE OF THE MASSACHUSETTS BAY.

SPENCER PHIPS, ESQ., *Lieutenant-Governor and Commander-in-Chief, in and over His Majesty's Province of the Massachusetts Bay, New England, etc.*

[SEAL]

To SAMUEL DAVIS, *Gentleman*, greeting:

By virtue of the Power and Authority, in and by His Majesty's Royal Commission, to Me granted, to be Lieutenant-Governor over His Majesty's Province of the Massachusetts Bay aforesaid, and Commander-in-Chief during the Absence of the Captain-General, I do (by these Presents), reposing especial Trust and Confidence in your Loyalty Courage and good Conduct, constitute and appoint You, the said Samuel Davis, to be Second Lieutenant of the Foot Company in the Town of Oxford, under the command of Lieut.-Col. Ebenezer Learned, in the the first Regiment of Militia in the County of Worcester, whereof John Chandler, Esq., Colonell.

You are, therefore, carefully and diligently to discharge the Duty of a Second Lieutenant in leading, ordering and exercising said Company in Arms, both inferiour Officers and Soldiers, and to keep them in good Order and Discipline; hereby commanding them to obey you as their Second Lieutenant, and yourself to observe and follow such Orders and Instructions as you shall from Time to Time receive from Me, or the Commander-in-Chief for the Time being, or other your Superiour Officers for His Majesty's Service, according to Military Rules and Discipline, pursuant to the Trust reposed in You.

> Given under my Hand and Seal at Arms, at Boston, the Eighth Day of November, In the Twenty-Sixth Year of the Reign of His Majesty, King George the Second, *Annoq Domini*, 1752.

S. PHIPS.

By Order of the Honourable the Lieutenant-Governor.

I. WILLARD, *Secretary.*

NOTE.— Brigadier-General Learned of Oxford, and Col. Jonathan Holman of Sutton, had both been veterans in the British service in Canada during the "French War." It is said that General Learned and Colonel Holman suffered much while in this service, particularly in the vicinity of Lake George and Ticonderoga.

Holman and Learned each retired from service in the French and Indian War with a commission of Major.

In the French and Indian War Capt. Ebenezer Learned was appointed by the Crown to weigh out the gold and silver bullion to make payments to the soldiers.

CHAPTER XXV.

REVOLUTIONARY WAR.

The Stamp Act was passed by the Parliament of England in 1765.

The Assembly and people of Massachusetts, being regarded by the authorities of England as most active in their disloyalty to their sovereign, two regiments were sent to Boston.

The troops arrived in the autumn of 1768, and landing, marched into town with offensive parade.

The following ancient account exhibits the sentiments of the people of Boston on their arrival:

"On Friday, Septr. 30th, 1768, the Ships of War, Armed Schooner, Transports, etc., came up the Harbour and Anchored round the Town; their cannon loaded, a spring on their Cables as for a regular Siege."

"At noon on Saturday, October the 1st the fourteenth and twenty-ninth Regiments a detachment from the 59th Regt. and train of Artillery with two pieces of Cannons landed on the Long Wharf; there Formed and Marched with Insolent Parade, drums beating, fifes playing, and Colours flying up King Street. Each soldier having received 16 rounds of Powder and Ball."

The fleet consisted of ships *Beaver, Senegal, Martin, Glascow, Mermaid, Romney, Launceston* and *Bonetta*.

The wharf at the right or north of Long wharf is Hancock's wharf; the north battery is shown at the extreme right.

The dedication in the lower right-hand corner is as follows:

To the Earl of Hillsborough,

His Majest⁸. Ser. y of State for America.

This view of the only well Plan'd Expedition formed for supporting ye dignity of Britain and chastising ye insolence of America.

Humly Inscrib'd.

A view was taken of part of the town of Boston in New England and British ships of war landing their troops 1768.

Engraved, printed and sold by Paul Revere, Boston.*

In September, 1774, the report of various disturbances in Boston aroused the whole country. Powder stored in Cambridge by the patriots was removed to Boston by a detachment of troops under orders from Gov. Gage. The people immediately rushed out in great excitement loudly denouncing the act and demanding the restitution of the powder.

"In the clamor and confusion a report was somehow started that the British fleet and garrison had commenced hostilities, and swift-footed messengers caught this rumor, and hurried with it in various directions. It was afterward asserted that this story was sent out by patriot leaders for the express purpose of showing the British government the temper and spirit of the colonies. If this were so they gained their end. The rumor flew on three great traveled routes, gaining in flight."

"Southward, it came to Esquire Wolcott of Oxford, who forthwith posted his son John Wolcott, off to Boston, 'to learn the certainty,' but receiving further confirmations of the great news at Grafton, the young man turned back, and took it straightway to Curtis' tavern in Dudley. One Clark, a trader, caught it up and hurried it on to his father in Woodstock.

---

* One of these engravings (now very rare) is in the possession of George W. Sigourney, Esq., a descendant of Capt. Andrew Sigourney of Boston, afterward of Oxford.

Capt. Clark in hot haste bore it on to Captain Keyes of Pomfret, and he at 11 A. M., Saturday, Sept. 3, brought it to Col. Israel Putnam. Hitherto the news had gone from mouth to mouth like the highland war cry:

> 'Boston our Boston is in need!
> Speed forth the signal : patriots, speed.'

"But now Putnam gave it a more tangible form by scrawling off the following to Capt. Aaron Cleveland of Canterbury:

"'CAPTAIN CLEVELAND. — Mr. Keyes has this A. M. brought us the news that the Men of War and troops began to fire on the people of Boston last night at sunset, when a post was sent immediately off to inform the country. He informs that the artillery played all night, that the people are universally (rallied from Boston) as far as here in arms, and desires all the assistance possible. It (alarm) was occasioned by the country people's being robbed of their powder from (Boston) as far as Framingham, and when found out the people went to take the soldiers and six of our people were killed on the spot, and several were wounded. Beg you will rally all the forces you can and be on the march immediately for the relief of Boston and the people that way. — I. P.'

"'Fast as hoof could fly' this was carried to Cleveland, countersigned by him, and sent by express 'along to Norwich and elsewhere.' Reaching Norwich at 4 P. M., it was forwarded by Capt. John Durkee, at New London. It was indorsed by Richard Law, Nathaniel Shaw, and Samuel Parsons, and hurried on to New Haven and New York.

"Gaining credence and fresh signatures at every stopping place it speeded southward ; and at nine o'clock Tuesday morning, just seventy hours from Pomfret, it was laid before the Continental Congress, just assembling in Philadelphia. Thus from Boston to Pennsylvania the whole country had been aroused. From the great centres the news had spread in every quarter.

The hour of conflict had come. Boston was attacked and all were summoned to her relief. Never was rallying cry more effective. Coming from Putnam and endorsed by prominent and responsible men, it was everywhere received and obeyed.

"'To arms,' was the quick response, and thousands hurried to the rescue. A thousand men took up arms in the three lower counties of Delaware, twenty-thousand were reported *en route* in Connecticut. The summons coming on Sunday it had the effect of putting that Puritan Colony 'into alarm and motion on the Lord's day.' Col. Putnam's missive was read publicly in most of the congregations, and furnished the text for many a stirring exhortation.

"In many of the more distant towns the messenger brought the tidings to the meeting-house in the midst of divine service, and worthy members of the church militant left the sanctuary for the battle-field. Even ministers were said, to have left their pulpits for the gun and drum, and set off for Boston.' In Norwich, Putnam's letter was 'printed off, and circulated through the town in hand bills,' and on Sunday morning over four hundred men, well armed and mostly mounted upon good horses, started for Boston under command of Major John Durkee.

"Two hundred ardent volunteers, well armed and mounted, left Windham at sunrise, and bodies of men were despatched from all the other towns of Windham County. Putnam having sent the despatch, set out himself with four comrades for the scene of action, and had proceeded as far northward as Douglas when he heard 'that the alarm was false and Massachusetts forces returning.' He immediately turned back and after a sixty-mile ride reached home at sunrise, and 'sent the contradiction along to stop the forces marching or rallying'

"The Norwich troops were met seven miles from their town with the intelligence *via* Providence that the report was without foundation. The Windham men marched on to Massachusetts line before receiving counter tidings. This revelation that the great mass of the people were ready to take up arms whenever occasion called them greatly cheered the patriot leaders, and stimulated them to farther resistance."*

The report of this uprising excited much interest at home and abroad " Words cannot express," wrote Putnam and his committee in behalf of five hundred men under arms at Pomfret, " the gladness discovered by every one at the appearance of a door being opened to avenge the many abuses and insults which those foes to liberty have offered to our brethren in your town and province. But for counter intelligence we should have had forty thousand well equipped and ready to march this morning. Send a written express to the foreman of this committee when you have occasion for our martial assistance." The rapid transmission of the news was considered very remarkable. On Nov. 12 it reached England and the report on its reception there comes back to New York on January 20.

OXFORD IN THE REVOLUTION.

The proceedings of Oxford during the Revolution are a representation of the acts in other towns in the State.

In almost every town there was a " Committee of Correspondence, Inspection and Safety," whose office was to give information of the proceedings of the American Congress, the state government and that of other towns.

September 29, 1774, the people of Oxford resolved, " That we ever have been, and will be true and loyal subjects of our most gracious Sovereign George III, King of Great Britain, so long as we are permitted the free execution of our charter rights."

At the same meeting, Voted, " Dr. Alexander Campbell and Capt. Ebenezer Learned to attend the Provincial Congress, at

---

* History of Windham County, by Miss Ellen Douglas Learned.

Concord, on the second Tuesday of October next, or at any other town in the province that shall be agreed upon."

The Continental Congress, which was then in session at Philadelphia, resulted in the publication of a " Bill of Rights," which was submitted to the people. One article of high practical importance was the " Non-Importation Compact." They agreed, and associated themselves and their constituents, under the sacred ties of virtue, honor and the love of liberty, not to import or use any British goods after the 1st day of December, 1774, particularly the article of tea. Committees were to be appointed in every place to see that this agreement was observed, and those who violated it were to be denounced as enemies to the rights of their country.*

Of the great men who composed this Congress, Lord Chatham remarked in the British Parliament as follows:

" That, though he had studied and admired the free states of antiquity — the master spirits of the world — yet, for solidity of reasoning, force of sagacity, and wisdom of conclusion, no body of men could stand in preference to this Congress; in the presence of their own peculiar difficulties did not forget the cause of suffering humanity, but made, with other resolutions, one by which they bound themselves, not to be in any way concerned in the Slave Trade."

---

*In November a meeting was called "to hear some Resolves of the Grand Congress," and also of the Provincial Congress, and act thereon. At this meeting Edward Davis was moderator. Adjourned to December 16. "Then met" and voted "that the Province Tax in the hands of the Constables be paid into the town treasury, and the town will protect said Constables," and chose Lieut. William Campbell, Daniel Phillips and Lieut. Samuel Eddy a committee of inspection to see that the association of the Continental Congress be duly observed. These articles of association were adopted in Continental Congress October 24, 1774. By them the members, for themselves and their constituents, "under the sacred ties of virtue, honor and love of country," agreed not to import or use English goods, not to import or purchase slaves,

January 12, 1775, Voted and chose Col. Ebenezer Learned to meet with the Provincial Congress at Cambridge on the first day February next, or sooner if needed.

March 6, 1775, At the town meeting, Voted, That there shall be ten stands of fire arms fixed with bayonets provided by the Select men at the cost of the town and kept for those men that are not able to find themselves arms.

"Voted that we will in all reasonable ways and means whatso-

---

or tea brought from the East Indies, but to encourage the growing of wool and the raising of finer breeds of sheep, to favor frugality, economy and industry, and promote agriculture, the arts and manufactures among the people; to discourage dissipation, horse-racing, gaming, shows, etc., to wear no mourning for deceased friends excepting crape on the hat, or black ribbons and necklaces for ladies, and to furnish no gloves at funerals; to take no advantage of a scarcity of an article to raise the price thereof, and to withdraw fellowship and patronage from all who did not adhere to the scales of prices which might be adopted. They also recommended that in every State, county and town committees be appointed to see that these articles be observed.

On June 29, 1775, Provincial Congress sent to the towns for army supplies thirteen thousand coats, which had been promised, one each to the eight-months' soldiers. On August 30 the selectmen sent to public stores five shirts, five pairs of breeches and nine pairs of stockings. On October 16, thirty-seven coats. "As thro' want of flax we could not send our proportion of shirts, etc., but we have a prospect of getting our proportion of coats sometime in October, that was set upon Oxford." "We have provided thirty-seven coats, containing one hundred and thirty-nine yards and one-half — making thirty-seven coats, 4s. per coat, £7. 8s. Total value, £47. 1s. 9½d. The average price of cloth was about 5s. per yard. James Brown, the tailor, cut these coats and made twenty. Supplies in the line of shoes, stockings, shirts, etc., could not be had on contract as at the present day. Requisitions were therefore made for them on the towns as for men. Some orders sent to Oxford were: January 20, 1777, fourteen blankets; June 17, 1778, shoes, stockings and shirts — twenty-eight each; June, 1779, shoes, stockings and shirts — twenty-eight each; May, 1780, shoes, stockings and shirts — twenty each and ten blankets; June, 1781, shoes, stockings and shirts — nineteen each.

ever strive to maintain our Charter Rights and privileges in all constitutional measures even to the risque of our lives and property."

May 24, 1775, At a town meeting, chose Edward Davis, Esquire to meet with the Provincial Congress at Watertown on May 31, for six months as their representative.

1775, The Freeholders and other Inhabitants of the Town of Oxford duly qualified to vote and act in Town affairs are hereby Required in His Majesty's Name to meet at our Meeting-house in Oxford on Mondy the 20th day of March current at one o'clock afternoon. (The last warrant issued in his Majesty's name.)

October 12, 1776, The style of notice is changed. "The freeholders, etc., are notified and warned, in the name of the Government of the people of this State, to meet," etc.

Oct. 12, 1776, is the date of the transition from the town's allegiance to the King of Great Britain to the new government of the State, appears.

Before the intelligence had reached the town of the Declaration of Independence at Philadelphia, July 4,

July 8, 1776, Voted : " To advise our representative in the General Court, That if the honorable Congress should, for the safety of the colonies, declare themselves independent of the Kingdom of Great Britain, to concur therewith; and the inhabitants of this town do solemnly engage with their lives and fortunes, to sustain this measure."

In 1777, " The town voted to add to the bounty offered by the American Congress and this State, the sum of £14 to each man who shall enlist in the town as a private soldier for three years, or during the war, before any draft be made."

At the same meeting, it was voted " to raise £1,000, to be assessed on the polls and real estate in the town, to complete the quota of soldiers now sent for to reinforce the Continental army."

In 1778 the town voted "concurrence with the articles of confederation proposed by the American Congress" and at the same meeting voted to pay £800 into the State Treasury.

August 25, 1779, the town chose Ebenezer Learned, Esq., and Ezra Bowman, delegates to the State convention at Cambridge, to act in forming a constitution of government for this State.

20 Day of October, 1779, Voted to impower the Treasurer of the Town of Oxford to borrow a sum of money not exceeding Four Hundred Pounds for the supply of the soldiers families, and other necessary charges arising in the Town.

November 8, 1779, Voted that Samuel Harris, Town Treasurer be empowered to Borrow a further Sum of Money not exceeding Three Hundred Pounds on the same condition and Manner, and for the ends as is expressed in the vote of the 20th of October Last.

March 6, 1780, The Town voted and chose Capt. John Nichols, Capt. Elias Pratt a committee to Supply the Soldiers' Families, and that their expenses shall be made good when they receive their pay of the Town.

March 5, 1781, Chose a committee to provide for the poor, and the soldiers families, viz. Capt. John Nichols, Ephraim Russell, Lt. Levi Davis.

Supplementing the different installments of aid afforded to the families of soldiers in 1780. The town voted to provide 5960 pounds of beef for the army, August 27, 1781.

Voted and granted Ninety pounds hard money for to purchase the beef required of this time by a resolve of the General Court, passed June 22, 1781.

The Committee, Ezra Bowman, Reuben Lamb, John Dana, Amasa Kingsbury.

May 13, 1774, General Thomas Gage, the newly-appointed English Governor, arrived in Boston and occupied the town with four regiments of British soldiers.

April 19, 1775, Gov. Gage sent a detachment of British

soldiers to destroy the military stores at Concord; and on their way occurred the battle of Lexington, from which the opening of the Revolution may be dated.

During the early night of April 18, 1775, Paul Revere made his now famous ride. Before day-break, that memorable day-break of Wednesday, the 19th of April.

Wednesday, April 19, 1775, Somewhere about nine o'clock A. M. the Watertown committee started Israel Bissell to convey the news through the country. At noon he entered Worcester shouting, "To arms, to arms, the war is begun!" He had ridden thirty-six miles; his white horse bloody with spurring, and exhausted, fell as he reached the church door (the old south church on the common). Immediately another was procured, the Watertown despatch was indorsed and Israel Bissell was off again, due south for Brooklyn, Connecticut, thirty-eight miles more. This for some reason, he only reached at eleven the next morning. But General Putnam quickly heard the news, left his plow in the furrow, and he too was off. Norwich, twenty miles more, was reached at four o'clock P. M. New London (thirteen miles) at seven P. M.

Here he had also reached the Boston post-road, by Providence; but the British had stopped the exit from Boston, and he must carry his news to Saybrook (twenty miles more) in order to meet the New York rider. At four A. M. of Friday he was there. It is one hundred and thirty-seven miles to New York. A new rider now mounts (quite possible the veteran Hurd whose route it was). That same day at noon he was at Branford, seven miles from New Haven. At eight o'clock P. M., on Saturday, Jonathan Sturges signed this despatch at Fairfield; Sunday the twenty-third at noon, Isaac Low signed it at New York and at four P. M. forwarded it to Philadelphia.*

---

* This first Revolutionary despatch is now in the Historical rooms at Philadelphia.

The intelligence of the breaking out of hostilities was immediately followed by circulars from the Massachusetts committee of safety, calling out the militia.

April 20. One addressed to the towns urged them "to hasten and encourage by all means the enlistment of men to the army," to send them forward without delay. "Our all," it reads, "is at stake. Death and devastation are the certain consequences of delay. Every moment is infinitely precious. An hour lost may deluge your country and entail perpetual slavery upon the few of your posterity that may survive the carnage."

Before thirty days had passed after the battle of Lexington, Oxford and the towns in the immediate vicinity had raised a full regiment of ten companies, all volunteers, and they were on the march to the battle-field.

In 1775, soon following the battle of Lexington, Colonel Ebenezer Learned, with his regiment, reported for service at Cambridge, and with Colonels Prescott and Warren, was ordered to join General Thomas at Roxbury, where they arrived more than two months before Washington came to take command of the army.

May, 1775. The following enrollment and organization of the regiment of Col. Ebenezer Learned is from Force's Archives, Vol. 11, 4th series, p. 823:

"Col. Learned's regiment: J. Danforth Keys, Lieut. Colonel; Jonathan Hollman, Major; —— Barrister, Adjutant Captains: Peter Harwood, Adam Martin, John Granger, Joel Greene, Samuel Billings, William Campbell, Arthur Daggett, Nathaniel Nealey, Samuel Curtis, Isaac Bolster. Lieutenants Asa Danforth, Abel Mason, Matthew Gray, David Pronty, Barnabas Lean, Reuben Davis, Jonathan Carrier, Salem Town, Samuel Learned, John Haselton. Ensigns: Benjamin Pollard, Benjamin Felton, Stephen Gorham, Thomas Fisk, John Howard, William Powdry."

"In Provincial Congress, Watertown, May 23d, 1775.
"Resolved that commissions be given to the officers of Col. Learned's regiment agreeable to the above list."

Soon after the arrival of Col. Learned's regiment at Roxbury occurred the famous battle of Bunker Hill, " all of which it saw a part of which it was," although it was not actually engaged in the fight on the hill. It formed a part of the right wing of the army, under the command of Gen. John Thomas, which was stretched round from Dorchester, through Roxbury, to Boston line, to prevent the enemy from breaking through and making a flank movement.

This regiment enlisted for eight months; from May 1, 1775, till January 1, 1776. The regiment was in service in and around Boston. When their time expired the men were regularly discharged.

The battle of Bunker Hill took place June 17, 1775.

In the victory to the Americans the British were dispirited, who had boasted that a few regiments could conquer the whole country.*

Gen. Washington left Philadelphia June 21, 1775, to assume command of the American army at Cambridge. At New York he received news of the battle of Bunker Hill. At Brookfield, July 1, he was met by a company of horsemen from Worcester, commanded by Capt. James Chadwick, who escorted him into town.

Dec. 10, 1775, " On Sunday last the lady of his excellency General Washington, and the lady of General Gates, with their attendants, passed through this town (Worcester) on their way to Cambridge."

General Washington, as commander-in-chief arrived in Boston July 2, 1775, after the battle of Bunker Hill, and

* There is at the Town Hall in Oxford a cannon ball of twenty-four pounds weight, brought by Col. Ebenezer Learned as a relic from the battle-field of Bunker Hill.

reached Cambridge, the headquarters of the American army. He found there a large body of Provincials not accustomed to disciplined warfare, destitute of arms and ammunition. He at once commenced organizing the soldiers and subjecting them to military service. And the Provincial allies became the Continental Army.

Washington erected a line of batteries from Winter Hill near Mystic river, through Cambridge, Brookline and Roxbury as far as Dorchester Heights. He held the British forces besieged in Boston until March, when they set sail for Halifax and the war was transferred to other States.

Thomas and Jonathan Amory with Peter Johonnot who have at the earnest entreaties of the inhabitants through the Lieutenant-Governor, solicited a flag of truce for this purpose.

JOHN SCOLLEY,
TIMOTHY NEWALL,
THOMAS MARSHALL,
SAMUEL AUSTIN.

This paper was received at the lines at Roxbury by Col. Learned who carried it to headquarters; and in return, the next day, wrote to the messengers as follows:

ROXBURY, *March* 9, 1776.

GENTLEMEN: — Agreeably to a promise made to you at the lines yesterday, I waited upon his excellency General Washington, and presented to him the paper handed to me by you from the selectmen of Boston. The answer I received from him was to this effect: "That, as it was an unauthenticated paper, without an address, and not obligatory upon General Howe, he would take no notice of it." I am with esteem and respect, gentlemen,

Your most obedient servant,
EBENEZER LEARNED.

To Messers Amory and Johonnot.

The British commander was now reduced to the alternative of either dislodging Washington's forces or the evacuation of the place.

The British General, Lord Howe, then resolved to evacuate the towns without delay. He commenced very early in the morning of Sunday, March 17th, the embarkation of his army. About nine o'clock the garrison left Bunker Hill. Two men were sent forward to reconnoitre, found the fortress was left in charge of wooden sentinels, and immediately gave the joyous signal that it was evacuated.

A detachment soon took possession of it. General Putnam ordered another detachment to march forward and take possession of Boston, while the remainder of the troops returned to Cambridge.

Meanwhile General Ward arrived with about five hundred troops from Roxbury, under the immediate command of Colonel Ebenezer Learned of Oxford.*

Col. Learned, accompanied by a crowd of loyalist refugees, marched in through the deserted gates, having unbarred them with his own hands.

After the evacuation Learned, with his command, remained about two weeks on the highlands south of the town, where he could observe the movements of the British fleet. On March 20 Gen. Greene issued the following order: " Col. Learned is directed to man six whale boats every night while the enemy remain in the harbor, whose duty it is to row about and make discoveries of any movement of the enemy, that the garrison may be apprised thereof." On April 2 Learned and his regiment were relieved from duty at Dorchester Point, and were soon after ordered with the main body of the army to the defence of New York.

As soon as the British fleet had put to sea, the American army proceeded by divisions to New York, where it arrived April 14. The disastrous affair of Long Island, August 27.

---
* Army Record.

Washington withdrew his forces from the island April 28, at night. Soon afterward he removed his army to Harlem Heights in the northern part of New York island. Washington was obliged to evacuate New York on Sept. 15, then to Kingsbridge the army moved toward White Plains, and here took place the battle of White Plains. Washington then changed his position. Fort Washington on York island was taken and its garrison made prisoners. Washington then retreated to New Jersey. Then followed the battles of Princeton and Trenton. In July, 1777, Gen. Howe embarked his forces and proceeded against Philadelphia.

Sept. 10, the battle of Brandywine was fought and the Americans defeated.

Sept. 26, 1777, Lord Howe entered Philadelphia with his army. While the British were in the possession of Philadelphia Washington endeavored to cut off their supplies for the army.

Washington then distributed his soldiers into winter quarters at Valley Forge. In June, 1778, the British evacuated Philadelphia, the position being considered dangerous by the position France was about to take in the war.

At the siege of Yorktown, Sept. 28, to October 9, 1781, Lord Cornwallis surrendered.

After the battle of Bunker Hill Col. Learned received injuries at Roxbury which disabled him from service for a time.

In April, 1777, he was commissioned a Brigadier-General in the northern army.*

THE BATTLE OF BEMIS HEIGHTS, SEPT. 19, 1777.

General Gates made preparations for resistance. Brave officers and determined soldiers in high spirits were gathered around him, and the latter were hourly increasing in numbers. The counsels of General Schuyler and the known bravery of General Arnold were at his command and he felt confident of victory, aided by such men as Poor, Learned, Stark, Whipple,

* From Boston Records.

Paterson, Warner, Fellows, Baily, Glover, Wolcott, Bricketts and Tenbroeck with their full brigades.

General Arnold resolved to do what he could with those under his command, which consisted of General Learned's brigade and New York troops. Arnold led the van of his men and fell upon the foe. By voice and action he encouraged his troops, but the overwhelming numbers of the enemy for a time repulsed them. It was now three o'clock in the afternoon; for an hour the Americans had disputed the ground inch by inch, but the crushing force of superior numbers pressed them back to their lines. Both armies retained their position until October 7. The British general determined to make one more trial of strength with his adversary.

Neilson in describing this battle of September 19, says:

"Toward the close of the day Gen. Learned's brigade and another regiment were principally engaged on a rise of ground, west of the cottage (Freeman's), with the British grenadiers and a regiment of British infantry, and bravely contested the ground till night."

On September 26 Gen. Gates issued the following:

"The public business having so entirely engaged the General's attention that he has not been properly at leisure to return his grateful thanks to Gen. Poor's and Gen. Learned's brigades, to the regiment of Riflemen, Corps of Light Infantry, and Col. Marshall's regiment for their valiant behavior in the action of the 19th inst., which will forever establish and confirm the reputation of the Arms of the United States."

THE BATTLE OF SARATOGA.*

The following account of this brilliant affair of October 7,

---

* Sir Edward Creasy, M. A., in a book published in London, in 1872 and entitled the Fourteen Decisive Battles of the World, from Marathon to Waterloo, singled out the battle of Saratoga as the decisive battle of the Revolution.

1777, is given in Thatcher's Military Journal, published in New York at the time.

"I am fortunate enough to obtain from our officers a particular account of the glorious event of the 7th inst.

"The advanced parties of the two armies came into contact at two o'clock on Tuesday afternoon, and immediately displayed their hostile attitude. The Americans soon approached the royal army, and each party in defiance awaited the deadly blow. The gallant Colonel Morgan at the head of his famous rifle corps, and Major Dearborn, leading a detachment of infantry, commenced the action with such intrepidity, that the works were carried and their brave commander Colonel Breyman was slain.

"The Germans were pursued to their encampment, which, with all the equipage of the brigade, fell into our hands. Nightfall put a stop to our brilliant career though the victory was most decisive, and it is with pride and exultation that we recount the triumph of American bravery.

"This was indeed a signal victory."

The troops of Poor and Learned marched steadily up the gentle slope of the eminence on which the British grenadiers* and part of the artillery under Ackland and Williams were stationed, and true to their orders not to fire until after the first discharge of the enemy, pressed on in awful silence towards the batallions and batteries.

Arnold assaulted the works occupied by the light infantry under Earl Balcarras, and at the point of the bayonet drove the enemy from a strong abatis, through which he attempted to force his way into the camp. He was obliged to abandon the effort, and dashing forward to the right flank of the enemy, exposed to the cross fire of the contending armies, he met Learned's brigade advancing to make an assault upon the British works at an opening in the abatis between Balcarras' light infantry

---
* The grenadiers were the flower of the British army.

and the German right flank defense under Col. Breyman. The Germans, who fled, finding the assault general, threw down their arms and retreated to the interior of the camp, leaving their commander, Col. Breyman, mortally wounded. Burgoyne endeavored to rally the panic-stricken Germans.

Personal differences with Gates had led to Arnold's removal from command since the battle of the 19th., and he had remained in camp, and though without any regular command, Arnold was the animating spirit in the last conflict. Gates sent an aid to recall him. "But Arnold, keeping out of the way of the messenger, placed himself at the head of one brigade, and then another, and led them on with a reckless daring, to attack the enemy, with good judgment and undaunted courage. The British line was already breaking as he entered the field. Under his impetuous assaults with Patterson and Glover's brigades, and then with Learned's, the enemy gave way everywhere in confusion."*

The Hessians received the first assault of Arnold's brigades upon the British centre with a brave resistance, but when upon

* "Arnold rode to the front of Learned's brigade, which had been so recently under his command, and dashed into the fight. He was cheered as he rode past, and like a whirlwind the regiments went with him upon the broken British lines. Fraser fell mortally wounded in this assault, and swiftly behind the half-crazy volunteers came Ten Broeck with a force nearly double that of the whole British line. That line was now in full retreat. Phillips and Reidesel, as well as Burgoyne, in person exhibited marvellous courage in an hour so perilous, but nothing could stop Arnold; wheresoever he found troops he assumed command, and by the magnetism of his will and passion he became supreme in daring endeavor. With a part of the brigades of Patterson and Glover he assaulted the intrenchments of Earl Balcarras, but was repulsed. To the right of Balcarras the Canadians and Royalists were posted under cover of two stockade redoubts. There again Arnold met Learned's brigade, took the lead, and with a single charge cleared these works, leaving the left of Breyman's position entirely exposed."—*Notes of Gen. Carrington.*

a second charge he dashed furiously among them at the head of his men, they broke and fled in dismay. Gen. Fraser was killed. Burgoyne now took command in person, but could not keep up the sinking courage of the men. The whole line gave way and fled precipitately within the intrenchments of the camp.

At length "the Americans press forward with renewed strength and ardor, and compel the whole British line, commanded by Burgoyne himself, to yield to their deadly fire, and they retreat in disorder. The German troops remain firmly posted at their lines; these were now boldly assaulted by Brigadier-General Learned and Lieutenant-Colonel Brooks at the head of their respective commands.

"Here General Learned, mounted on his powerful horse, which at first refused to proceed, was forced by soldiers on with his rider through the opening of the abatis filled with the dead and wounded."[*]

Gen. Wilkinson, who was Gates' adjutant, and on the field, says:

"About sunset I perceived Gen. Learned advancing toward the enemy with his brigade in open column * * * when I rode up to him. On saluting this brave old soldier he inquired, '*where can I put in with most advantage?*' I had particularly examined the ground between the left of the Germans and the light infantry, occupied by provincialists, from whence I had observed a slack fire. I therefore recommended to Gen. Learned to incline to his right, and attack at that point; he did so with great gallantry; the provincialists abandoned their position and fled; the German flank was by this means uncovered; they were assaulted vigorously, overturned in five minutes and retreated in disorder, leaving their commander, * * * Breyman, dead on the field. The night

---

[*]Reminiscences of David Stone, who was in service under Gen. Learned.

was now closing in. The victory of the Americans was decisive."

Before dawn Burgoyne removed the whole of his army camp and artillery, meditating a retreat to Fort Edward. On the morning of the 8th of October the Americans took possession of the evacuated British camp. Burgoyne on the 9th of October quietly retreated to Saratoga. Gates followed the enemy. Morgan, Poor and Learned threatened their rear on the west. Burgoyne sent a flag of truce to the American commander.

EXTRACTS FROM A LETTER OF REV. JOSEPH BOWMAN OF OXFORD, DATE OCTOBER 23, 1777, TO BRIGADIER-GENERAL LEARNED, " IN YE NORTHERN ARMY."

" The most particular accounts, yt we have had of affairs in your quarter yt we could depend upon have been in your letters to Mrs. Learned, one of which was published in ye Worcester Paper; viz yt which gave an account of an action of y 19th of Sept. I do not know how it is, but seems yt our printers have no correspondence in y Army & consequently few particulars and those collected from one, and another, are vague and uncertain & sometimes unintelligible and some accounts contradicted by others so yt we knew not what to believe.

" Most of ye intelligence that I rely upon has come from you by y way of Mrs. Learned this summer; and I hope you will continue to give as circumstantial an account of things as you can as I shall still hope to gain some knowledge by yt means thro' her kindness, even tho' you should not write to me in particular which would be peculiarly acceptable if you could find leisure time enough for such a thing, amidst a multitude of care and Business which I know must lie upon your hands your family and friends here are all well. Sylvanus has got Bravely again and thinks of Returning to you soon please to give my love to all our oxford Friends with you when you shall see them, and you may tell them that their Friends here are all well it has been remarkably healthy with us this summer past and fall hitherto ye season has been good and very fruitful we have plentiful crops (thro Divine goodness) tho' every thing is excessive dear our privateers bring in many prizes tho' not so many as they did last year from ye Southward we have had various reports since ye battle at Brandywine sometime yt General How has got Philadelphia at others that he has not.

"yt action of y 19th of Sept. you gave us ye most particular account of than any yt we have had but yt of y 7th Instant, your account is general & short, I was about to have added something further, but having just now received authentic intelligence of a most important Event viz ye surrender of ye whole British Army commanded by General Burgoyne to ye American forces I therefore stop short to congratulate you on this most singular, important and happy Event may all our hearts be filled with a grateful sense of ye Divine goodness in this nost interesting affair and may we have grace to ascribe unto ye Lord of Hosts ye God of Armies all ye praise and glory yt is Due to His Great Name and may we never forget His Benefits."

Note.—   GEN. LEARNED'S LETTER.

"STILLWATER, *Sept.* 25, 1777.

"On Thursday the 18th instant marched about 4 miles at 5 o'clock A. M. in order to attack the enemy on the right flank on their march; but they not marching according to expectation prevented our doing any thing of considerable consequence.

"We attacked a small party about 60 or 70 rods from the enemy's front, killed some, said to be five or six, took and sent in that day, as I was informed after my return, 36 prisoners. We all returned about sunset, without the loss of one man killed or wounded.

"The next day (September 19th), we were early alarmed, being informed the enemy were on their march towards our Camp. Agreeable to a result of Council of War, the Riflemen and Infantry from the left of our army went and attacked the Enemy's right Wing, or rather their front guard about 5 minutes before one o'clock. The enemy gave way, we took some prisoners. The enemy reinforced, which caused us to do the same; which was alternately done by the enemy and on our part of the Army till the battle became almost General between the Enemy and our Division.

"I was ordered to send out one Regiment at first, and the rest in succession, except the last.— I then received orders to march to the attack. We marched on briskly and came up to the Enemy's right wing, which was endeavoring to surround our left. A most severe fire lasted till the cover of the night prevented further action. We went back to our camp, and the enemy have encamped near the ground where the battle was fought. We are near neighbors. Our lines and those of the enemy are but about a mile and a quarter from each other. Both armies are fortifying, but time only can determine the further event. The effect of this battle is that we have lost two Lieut.-Colonels killed, with a number of other officers of different ranks. In the whole our killed, wounded and missing are about 318. By the best accounts the enemy's loss, killed and wounded, amounts to a thousand. These are facts. Capt. Wiley is wounded. Our army are in high spirits. We took eighty on the day of battle.

P. S.— On the day of battle, and since, two of our Captains were taken Prisoners, also one Lieut. and 27 privates. This is an exact account of the Prisoners sent by Burgoyne to Gen. Gates, each man's name specified in the list."

NOTE.—In the *Massachusetts Spy* of October 16, 1777, Isaac Pratt gave notice that he was about to start for the army, and would carry letters and bring returns at one shilling postage.

General Learned was esteemed a brave and humane soldier. He survived the Revolution about twenty years, and was much honored after his retirement from the army.

It is said that in personal appearance General Learned was tall and strongly built, being six feet and two inches in height, "his frame being capable of enduring great fatigue. His countenance expressed gentleness and calmness, and yet there were depicted dignity and command. He was endowed by nature with a sound judgment and discerning mind.

"His step and bearing were peculiar to himself, his tread was heavy and measured. In conversation all were impressed with awe in his presence. General Learned was a judge of a horse and rode a very good one in his army campaigns. In the Revolutionary War he rode a high-mettled young black horse of wonderful endurance. His fine appearance on horseback, with his calm courage, and with the peculiar tread of the horse was ever recognized by the soldiers in the distance."

In the War of the Revolution, Captain Jeremiah Kingsbury's company from Oxford was included in Colonel Jonathan Holman's regiment, Massachusetts Fifth, or the Sutton regiment.

Capt. Jeremiah Kingsbury's company, Col. Jonathan Holman's regiment, Providence, January 20, 1777, roll: Jeremiah Kingsbury, captain; Silas Town, lieutenant; Jonas Pratt, Levi Davis, Jonas Eddy, Allen Hancock, sergeants; William Hudson, John Pratt, Amos Shumway, Ebenezer Shumway, corporals; Zaccheus Ballard, John Rawson, Joseph Kingsbury, John Allen, John Larned, Josiah Shumway, Curtis Dixon, Sampson Marvin, John White, Amos Wakefield, Thomas Wolcott, Jesse Gleason, Nathan Pratt, Reuben Eddy, Jonathan Coolidge, Elisha Town, Sylvanus Learned, Jesse Pratt, Jesse Merriam, Samuel Stone, Joseph Sparhawk, Aaron Parker, Jonathan Merriam, Jonas Davis, Benjamin Hovey, William Lamb. Time in camp, forty-three days.

A detachment of this company was again in service when the " Militia " marched to reinforce Gen. Gates' army.

Sept. 27, 1777, the following men from Oxford were members of Capt. Jeremiah Kingsbury's company and Colonel Jonathan Holman's regiment :

Jeremiah Kingsbury Capt., John Ballard, Lieut., Ebenezer Coburn, Sergt., Haynes Learned, Sergt., Jonas Eddy, Corp., Allen Hancock, Corp., John Learned, Aaron Parker, Joshua Pratt, Joseph Rockwood, Joshua Merriam, William Nichols, Nathan Pratt, John Rawson, Ambrose Stone, Jonas Davis,

David Stone, Ambrose Fitts, Amos Shumway, Anthony Sigourney.

The following served nine months in 1778, in Captain Jeremiah Kingsbury's company and Colonel Holman's regiment:

Jeremiah Kingsbury, Capt., Eleazer Stockwell (or Stowell), David Chamberlain, Uriah Carpenter.

The regiment was then honorably discharged from service.*

The following men belonged to the company commanded by Capt. William Campbell in Col. Ebenezer Learned's regiment, and marched to Cambridge April, 1775 : William Campbell, Capt., Thomas Fish, Lieut., John Campbell, Sergt., Sylvester Town, Sergt., James Learned, Corp., Abner Shumway, Drum., Abraham Mansfield, Timothy Sparhalk, Paul Thurston, Samuel Baker, John Fessenden, Josiah Eddy, Moses Kneeland (or Knowland), Negro Will, Moses Coburn, Jonathan Marsh, Thomas Bogle, Frost Rockwood, Daniel Sabins, John Hudson, Thomas McKnight, Jason Collar, Arthur Humphrey, David Dana Town, James Hambleton Parker, John Conant, William Bogle, William Foster, Richard Ferrars.

---

*Another regiment was soon organized, called the Massachusetts Fifth or Sutton regiment, composed of men coming from Sutton, Oxford, Sturbridge, Charlton and Dudley, including adjacent lands, and placed under the command of Col. Jonathan Holman of North Sutton.

The following entry is found in the journal of the Massachusetts Council, Feb. 7, 1776: "In the House of Representatives: The house made choice by ballot of the following gentlemen for field officers of the Fifth Regiment of Militia, in the county of Worcester, viz.:

"Jonathan Holman of Sutton, Colonel, Daniel Plympton, Lieut.-Colonel, William Learned of Oxford, First Major, Jacob Davis of Charlton, 2nd Major. 'In council: Read and concurred.' This regiment was known and styled as the Sutton regiment."

"The Sutton regiment was included in the army of Gen. Wash-

The following belonged to Capt. John Town's company and marched to Cambridge, April 19, 1775: John Town, Capt., Daniel Hovey, Lieut., Thomas Fish, Lieut., Richard Ferrars, Sergt., Samuel Manning, Sergt., Arthur Humphrey, Corp., Phineas Allen, William Foster, Joshua Turner, Allen Hancock, John Hudson, Robert Manning, Elias Pratt, Ebenezer Shumway, John Ballard, William Bogle, John Campbell, Daniel Sabin, Abijah Harris, Timothy Sparhawk, David Dana Town, James Pratt, Jr., Haynes Learned, Abraham Mansfield (Merrifield) Amasa Allen, Samuel Baker, Anthony Sigourney.

"The two companies commanded by William Campbell, Captain, and John Town, Captain, include many of the same men. It would appear that the two companies were merged and the rolls at the State House from which the above lists have been copied taken at different times."

The list of men here given has been obtained from the office for the payment of pensions to Revolutionary soldiers and from the recollection of the aged inhabitants of the town:

Brig.-Gen. Ebenezer Learned, Capt. William Moore, Capt.

ington at Cambridge. Soon following the evacuation of Boston they marched with him first to Rhode Island, where they were stationed some two or three months, from thence proceeding to Long Island, where they were in an engagement with the enemy; thence up the Hudson river to White Plains, where the American army had a severe battle, in which this same Sutton regiment bore a distinguished part.

"After the battle of White Plains the Sutton regiment, under Col. Holman, was ordered to Bennington, Vermont, where it remained several months to guard the country against Gen. Burgoyne's army. After the famous battle of Bennington, the regiment of Col. Holman was next ordered to join the army of Gen. Gates near Saratoga. In the battle that ensued, Col. Holman's regiment was actively engaged, and that they acquitted themselves bravely may be justly inferred from the fact that after the battle this regiment was designated "to take possession of Fort Edward, and to hold it, until the dispersion of Burgoyne's army, which they did."

John Nichols, Lieut. Benjamin Vassall, Lieut. Ebenezer Humphrey, Lieut. Jacob Town, Jason Collier, David Lamb, Frost Rockwood, Ebenezer Pray, William Simpson, George Alverson, Caleb Barton, John Learned, David Town, Allen Hancock, Peter Shumway, Abijah Kingsbury, Joseph Hurd, James Merriam, Elisha Blandin, Francis Blandin, Jonas Blandin, Sylvanus Learned, Arthur Daggett, Elisha Ward, David Stone, Ebenezer Robbins, —— Sewall, Sylvester Town, Levi Davis, Elijah Learned, Richard Coburn, Jacob Learned, Silas Eddy, Solomon Cook, Elijah Kingsbury, Ezekiel Collier.

In May there was a reorganization of troops. William Campbell, previously in Capt. Craft's cavalry company, Sturbridge, was made captain of the Oxford company, and the following additional names appear that year on its rolls: Sylvanus Town, sergeant, from Craft's company, Abner Shumway, drummer, Moses Coburn, Jonathan Marsh (S. Gore), Thomas Bogle (took the place of Asa Larned, discharged), Frost Rockwood, Thomas McKnight, Jason Coller, James H. Parker, John Conant, John Fessenden, Josiah Eddy, Moses Knowland (S. Gore), Paul Thurston, from Craft's company, Will (a negro, servant of Campbell [?], discharged Oct. 5, 1775).

In Col. Learned's regiment, April, 1775, were also in Craft's company of cavalry, Sturbridge, William Campbell, lieutenant Levi Davis, Joseph Hurd, Sylvanus Town, Paul Thurston, John Walker, William Moore.

In Capt. Curtis' company, 1775, Robert Manning, corporal (transferred from Town's company), Stephen Griffith, corporal, died July 31, 1775; Daniel Griffith, Isaac Pratt, Joseph Streeter, Moses Town, Elias Town, John Mellen, Samuel Learned, Phinehas Allen, Benjamin Edwards.

In Capt. Healey's company, 1775, William Moore, sergeant, transferred from Craft's company, Curtis Dixon, Aaron Wakefield, Amos Wakefield.

In Capt. Green's company, October, 1775, Asa Meriam,

Samuel Stone. At Dorchester, 1775, for three months, in Dike's regiment, Richardson's company, Ebenezer Fish, Samuel Kingsbury.

In Tyler's regiment, Ferrer's company, December, 1776, Daniel Fisk.

The following enlisted early in 1777 for three years or during the war; Benjamin Wakefield, Josiah Eddy, corporal, John Hudson, corporal, Joseph Cody, corporal, Peter Shumway, drummer, Moses Knowland, Richard Moore, William Jordan, David Town, all in Capt. Moore's Co. In Webb's company, Sylvanus Learned, sergeant, Noah Harkins, sergeant, John Harvey, David Manning.

Jesse Stone, of Oxford, was captain of a company which marched on the "Bennington Alarm," and was out from July 19 to August 29, 1777. There were no Oxford men in the ranks.

The following served three months in 1776 in the company commanded by Jonathan Carriel and Colonel Josiah Whitney's regiment: Sampson Marvin, Corp., Wm. Jordan, Jedediah Blaney, Richard Moore, Moses Town, Elisha Town, Amos Putnam, Moses Knowland.

Elisha Livermore served as a bombardier three months in 1776 in Captain William Todd's and Colonel Craft's artillery regiment. Nathaniel Wyman, in the same year, served a little over a month in Captain Aaron Guild's company and Colonel Whitney's regiment.

The following served in Dorchester in 1778 in Captain March Chase's company in Col. Nathan Sparhawk's regiment: Jesse Hill, Isaac Anibell, David Smith.

The following were drafted in 1778: Jonathan Fuller, John Jewell, Eleazer Stowell.

The following served six months in 1779 in Captain Thomas Fish's company and Col. Nathan Tyler's regiment in Rhode Island: Thomas Fish, Captain, Ebenezer Coburn, Lieut., Abisha Shumway, Jacob Weeks, Samuel Atwood.

The following served six months in the Continental army 1780: Thomas Walcott, Samuel White, James Atwood, Samuel Wiley, Elisha Town, Jacob Nichols, Jacob Winslow, Moses Baker, Joseph Atwood, Benjamin Turner, Noah Dodge, David Town, Samuel Kelly.

The following served three months in 1781 in Capt. Reuben Davis' company and Col. Luke Drury's regiment: William Tucker, Corp., John M. Jewell, James Atwood, Ebenezer Stone, Phinehas Jones, Jonas Cummings.

Lemuel Cudworth served in Rhode Island in 1781, in Captain Joseph Elliot's company and Colonel William Thomas' regiment.

The following enlisted in 1781 to serve three years in the Continental army: Sylvanus Learned, Sergt., Noah Hoskins, John Harvey, David Manning.

Besides the above the following Oxford men were in the service at various times: Nathan Atwood, Elijah Shumway, John Brown, Benjamin Rider, Adams Sulley, William Stowell, Cupp Donnings, William Lewis, John Quick.

LEICESTER, *December y^e* 27, 1781.

This may certify that I have received from the town of Oxford their full Quota of Men to fill up the Continental army.

SETH WASHBURN, *Superintendent.*

(From the original receipt recorded per Samuel Harris, town clerk.)

FROM THE OXFORD TOWN RECORDS.

Capt. Fish discharge resignation and Reccommendation.

May it please your Honor. I should take it as a favor if you could give me a discharge from the Service as I think myself much injured in my Rank as I can neither have what I think is my rank nor even a board of Gentlemen to sit to settle a dispute of Rank between Capt.

Webb and I both of one Regiment though I have requested it of Col. Shepard commanding the Regiment and at this time the Brigade to which we both belong.

T. FISH, Cap.
COL. SHEPARD, <i>Reg.</i></div>

PROVIDENCE, June 15, 1779.

To the Honorable Maj.-Gen. GATES, Head-Quarters, Providence, June 17, 1779.

Capt. T. Fish being desirous to Quit the service is hereby discharg'd the Army of the United States of America by order of Maj.-Gen. Gates.

ISAAC PEIRCE, A. D. Camp.

THE NAMES OF SOLDIERS IN THE CONTINENTAL ARMY FROM OXFORD NEAR THE CLOSE OF THE WAR.

Richard Moore, Jedediah Adams, Zacheus Ballard, Josiah Eddy, William Foster, John Florey, John Fessenden, Jesse Forsyth, Adonijah Gleason, John Hudson, William Jordan, Moses Knowland, Sylvanus Learned, Samuel Putney, Ebenezer Robbins, Peter Shumway, David Scanning, William Stuart, Moses Town, David Town, Jr., Samuel White.

George Robinson, son-in-law of Gen. Learned, was in his brigade, and was killed at the battle of Saratoga.

Reuben Robinson was also in the service, and died of fever in 1776.

Joseph Kingsbury was drafted in 1777, and Samuel, his son, went in his stead, and was in the Saratoga battles.

Josiah, son of Jeremiah Kingsbury, joined the army at sixteen years of age in 1775, and served till the close of the war; was acting quarter-master under Arnold at West Point, and ensign when discharged.

Others were as follows: James Hovey Davis, Samuel Jennison, lieutenant and quartermaster of Nixon's brigade at Saratoga battles; David, son of John Barton, sick at Richmond after Cornwallis' surrender; William, son of Benjamin Eddy, Parley, son of William Eddy, six months; Jacob Fellows, Abijah, son of Abijah Gale, Brewer's regiment, died in service; Jesse Gale, his brother, killed March 24, 1780; Hezekiah Larned, marched from Upton on Lexington Alarm; Abijah Conant, son-in-law of Capt. John Nichols, went as servant to Nichols, died in service; John Twichell, Gideon Sibley, from Sutton, on Lexington Alarm; Abijah and Elihu, sons of David Thurston, in the same company, and both killed in the same battle August, 1777; Jedediah Adams, seven months in Wiley's company, killed; Phinehas Barton, Capt. John Nichols, joined the army 1777; Andrew Sigourney, in battle at White Plains and others, commissary, with rank of captain;* Anthony Sigourney, in same regiment; Nathan Atwood, Elijah Shumway, John Bowers, Benjamin Rider, Adams Sully, William Stowell, Joseph Phillips.

On September 29, 1777, Ezra Bowman was appointed by the Legislature adjutant of the Fifth regiment and entered the service, continuing until April, 1781, at least.

A reinforcement for Gates, in service from August 1 to November 29, 1777, was commanded by Abijah Lamb, under Col. Cushing. Abijah Lamb, captain; Ebenezer Humphrey, Sylvanus Towne, lieutenants; Elijah Larned, Arthur Humphrey, sergeants; Dana Towne, Timothy Sparhawk, corporals; Thomas Baker, Jonathan Coolidge, Jason Coller, Ebenezer Davis, John Fitts, Joseph Hurd, Isaac Larned, Jonathan Merriam, Samuel Stone (commissary), Elias Towne, Isaac Larned, Jr., privates. This reinforcement was in the Saratoga battles.

Tradition states that Isaac Larned was bombardier in Capt. Todd's artillery company in 1776.

Capt. Ebenezer Humphrey, Col. Jacob Davis. Company

---

* Col. Holman's regiment.

marched July 30, 1780, to Rhode Island "on the alarm." Ebenezer Humphrey, captain; Levi Davis, lieutenant; Joshua Turner, 2d lieutenant; Joseph Hurd, Ebenezer Humphrey, Jr., John Campbell, Amos Shumway, sergeants; Benjamin Shumway, Jonathan Coburn, David Stone, Samuel Stone, corporals; Samuel Cudworth, fifer; Philip Ammidown, Ezekiel Coller, Thomas Campbell, Solomon Covel, Jonas Davis, Simon Gleason, Nathaniel Hamlin, Jonathan Harris, Gideon Hovey, Jeremiah Kingsbury, Reuben Lamb, John Nichols, Jonas Pratt, Thomas Parker, Nathan Pratt, Ebenezer Redding, Moses Rowell, Timothy Sparhawk, Josiah Shumway, Sylvanus Towne, Archibald Todd, Ambrose Stone, privates. Isaac Larned was in this expedition — in another company. Time of service about thirteen days.

LEARNED TO GEN. WASHINGTON.

"Sir, with regret I must humbly represent my case, Being so indisposed in body that I am absolutely rendered unfit to serve the much injured and distressed publick with the alacrity and usefulness I could wish, or the importance of the cause requires; yet my hearty and greatest wish is that your Excellency may receive renown, and the United Colonies' arms still be distinguished with success and victory, and in God's own time every worthy member in the struggle return to and enjoy his own habitation in peace. But at present must request to absent myself from the Army in the manner your Excellency shall prescribe; and if it should be thought most expedient I should be dismissed the Continental service, if my past conduct is equal, should pray I may be dismissed with honor and supported home. In obtaining this I shall have fresh instances of your Excellency's favor; and lay me under new obligations ever to remain your very humble servant.

EBENEZER LEARNED."

Addressed
  To the Hon. His Excellency,
    GEO. WASHINGTON, Esq.

Col. Ebenezer Learned on April 2, 1777, received his appointment from Congress of brigadier-general. He accepted the offer, and soon joined the northern army under General Schuyler.

His first service under his new commission was at Fort Edward, whence he proceeded to Fort Ticonderoga, where he secured and removed valuable stores before that fort was taken by Burgoyne in his progress southward. On July 8, 1777, he was in command at Fort Edward, at which date he addressed the following to Gen. Schuyler:

"Hon*d* and Dear S*r*:

"I have the agreeable Tidings that our Men at Fort Ann are full of Resolution to Defend the Place and I am Supplying every Request from there yesterday after Noon the Enemy appeared in sight our People out and attacked them and Drove them 3 miles — Saw them carrying off Dead & Wounded — the Enemy consisted of Hessians, Canadians, & Indians we had 1 man Killed 3 Wounded —

"From Fort George we are informed that the Enemy have made appearance 7 miles from there on an island — 3 bateaux and 1 canoe — and Since we are drove to the great Necessity to Defend ourselves in this bare handed and confused Situation we are struggling to do it in the best manner we can. Have but very little Artillery and that unmounted — but very little lead Balls — but very few Tools for fortifying — no Tents more but few Kettles &c &c — but in the midst of these Difficulties we find the great Importance of Defending this last security of our Country which God Grant we may never give up though at Present are very Defenceless — I would ask your Particular Orders and advice in this Critical Time — I have made all Dispatch to remove the most valuable stores from Fort George not with any Design to leave it — but find the Necessity to save what few Medicines &c we have left.

"This moment received from Fort Ann: the Enemy made an attack very near the Fort drove our People into the Fort — have heard no more

"S*r* your very Humble Serv*t*

"Eben*a* Learned B.: G.

Hon*d* Gen*l* Schuyler.

"This moment heard there were a firing on Lake George we had boats sent down &c."

Fort Stanwix was saved, and Arnold and Learned marched to the Hudson.

"During their absence the battle of Bennington had been fought, and Schuyler had been superseded by Gen. Gates. Burgoyne was preparing for an advance on Albany, and to oppose his progress Arnold and Kosciusco had selected a position to fortify called Bemis' Heights, a rise of ground peculiarly appropriate for the purpose, lying between the river (near which was the highest portion) and Saratoga Lake, about six miles from it. On this ground, on the 19th of September, occurred the first of two hard-fought battles, and from the best evidence we have, Arnold was a leading spirit in the day's contest, and Learned, who commanded the centre brigade, acted a very important part under him.

WASHINGTON TO HEATH.

The next mention we find of him is in a letter of Gen. Washington to Gen. Heath at Boston, bearing date January 9, 1778, at Valley Forge, which contains the following:

"I beg you will carefully forward the enclosed letters to Brigadiers Glover and Learned. They contain orders for them to join their respective brigades, with which they are much wanted."

Gen. Heath replied, saying these letters had been forwarded as requested. Upon the receipt of Washington's order Learned proceeded to Boston and laid open his case to Gen. Heath, who, on Feb. 7, 1778, wrote as follows to Gen. Washington:

[Extracts from Gen. Heath's Reply.]

Brig.-Gen. Learned called upon me a day or two since and requested that I would transmit your Excellency the enclosed certificates, and represent his present state of health. He has proposed to resign his commission, but the Hon. Mr. Hancock and myself have persuaded him to delay for the present, as in a summer campaign he may render his country essential service. He is anxious to know your Excellency's pleasure.

On February 27, 1778, Gen. Washington replied as follows:

"Considering Gen. Learned's ill state of health, I think his resignation had better be accepted of, more especially as from the nature of his complaint it does not appear that he can ever be able to bear the fatigues of a campaign. I would therefore advise him to make his resignation, with the reasons for so doing, to Congress, who are the proper body to receive it."

GEN. LEARNED'S LETTER TO GEN. WASHINGTON.

"BOSTON, *March* 12, 1778.

"MOST HON^d PR.:

"I have served in this warfare since the beginning as a Col. of a Regt. till May 1776 when by indisposition by reason of certain fatigues in the army I found myself unequal and resigned the service.

"Since I recovered a little the Honorable the Continental Congress on the second day of April 1777 appointed me to the command of a Brig.-Genl.

"I immediately took the field, proceeded to Fort Edward, and at the evacuation of Ticonderoga had great fatigue in securing the remains of our stores that way. Directly on that marched my brigade to the relief of Fort Stanwix.

"Immediately on return we had the satisfaction of reducing Burgoyne's army with much fatigue and was personally and brigade in the severe but victorious actions of Sept. 19 and Oct. 7, and after that army was imprisoned we took a forced March to Albany to stop the progress of the enemy that way.

"All which brought on my former difficulties and by the advice of Doct. Potts I took a furlough of Gen. Gates to retire from the army till I was well; the receipt of which with my surgeon's certificate I have enclosed.

"And I find I am quite unequal to act vigorously in my country's cause in the field and to eat the Publick's bread and not do the service I am not disposed. And I think I am better able to serve in a private or civil than in a military character.

"All of which considered I think it my duty to myself and my family, and country to pray your Honor the Congress to discharge me from the service.

"And I shall remain as before
 " Your Honor's
  " Very Humble Serv't.
   "EBENEZER LEARNED, B.: G."

In Congress, March 24, 1778, it was resolved that this resignation be accepted.

NOTE.— The Saratoga battle-field, in 1885, still retains relics to recall the memories of scenes enacted on its site in the War of the Revolution.

"The breastworks which surrounded Reidesel's Brunswickers, and at the south-eastern extremity of which the Hanau artillery, under Capt. Pausch, was placed (enclosing an area of, perhaps, twenty acres), are yet easily traced, being still two, and in some places five feet high; and in the midst of a dense wood is seen the old camp well used by this portion of Burgoyne's army.

"A large portion of the British camp, after the action of the 19th, was on the site of that battle.

"The house which was the headquarters of Generals Arnold, Learned and Poor, before, during and after the two actions, is still standing in excellent preservation.

"The 'Ensign House,' which received a portion of Burgoyne's wounded, together with the tall Dutch clock, which ticked off the numbered minutes of the dying, still remain.

"Among other souvenirs of similar interest, may be mentioned the 'Lovegat House' of Coreville, in which Burgoyne and his staff rested for one night, both on the advance and on the retreat, and which is rendered additionally interesting from its having been the starting point of Lady Ackland, when, accompanied by Parson Brudewell, she set out in a frail boat, and in the midst of darkness and a cold autumnal storm, to rejoin her husband, then lying wounded in the American camp. The house remains exactly as it was at the time of Burgoyne's visit, and with the same old poplar standing in the door-yard."

CHAPTER XXVI.

War of 1812; Mexican War; The Civil War.

The war of 1812 was caused by aggressions upon the commerce of the United States, and the impressment of seamen from American vessels by the English. The American government decided to declare war against England, June 18, 1812. General Henry Dearborn was commander-in-chief.

The war of 1812 continued until the battle of New Orleans, January 8, 1815.

In 1813 the Americans planned to invade Canada with three armies. The Army of the West, commanded by General William Henry Harrison, was collected near the western end of Lake Erie. The Army of the Centre, under General Dearborn, was at Sackett's Harbor and on the Niagara frontier. The Army of the North assembled on the shores of Lake Champlain, with General Wade Hampton as commander.

Abijah, son of Dr. Daniel Fisk, died in 1813, of camp fever, at Greenbush; John, son of George Alverson, killed in battle; J. Prentice, son of Levi Lamb, died in service; Sylvanus, son of Col. Sylvanus Towne, in regular army on western frontier, from 1800 to 1820, returned and died in Oxford; David Wait served at Fort Warren; Tisdale Atwood and Hovey Bounds, wounded at Queenstown; Russell White and George Blandin died in service; Jesse Briggs, Rufus Briggs, William Stiles, Edward Shumway and Joseph Lamb, musician.

Capt. John Butler during the war of 1812 served in the regular army. The Army Register (p. 107) sets him down second lieutenant, August 14, 1813, and on March 17, 1814, first lieutenant, in the Twenty-fourth infantry. His captain was Robert Desha, and his colonel, E. P. Gaines.

He was stationed at Fort Osage, Jackson Co., Missouri, founded 1808, 300 miles up the river and near the present site of Kansas City. It is described by Brackenbridge in 1811. (Louisiana, p. 217.) Penned in by Indians, his command had no rations but potatoes, while buffaloes were roving before their eyes. They were at last obliged to burn the fort and escape down the river in boats. Among his other stations were St. Charles, Bellefontaine and Fort Clark. In January, 1814, he was acting adjutant at Newport, Ky., keeping guard over 400 British prisoners. He writes from Detroit, May 14, 1814, that he had marched thither from Newport across the State of Ohio; that 400 regulars were in Detroit, and that 400 militia had just pushed on to establish a post ninety miles above. His force reaching St. Joseph, July 20, destroyed it, and also British stores at St. Mary's, arriving at Mackinaw, July 26. On August 4, 900 Americans landed, were attacked by Indians in thick bushes, and fought there forty minutes, losing 87 killed or wounded; they returned to their boats. In Lieutenant Butler's company the captain, Desha, was shot through the thigh, the third lieutenant, Jackson, and six privates were killed; Butler's own sword belt was cut by a bullet. General Cullum's account of the action is as follows (p. 200): "Aug. 4. Our land force attempted an attack from a height in the rear of the fort, which resulted in a sharp conflict, chiefly with Indians in a thick wood, and the retreat of our troops."

Capt. Butler in his person was not a large man, but of uncommon strength and agility. In youth he was a celebrated wrestler.

During the war there were conflicts on the ocean. The sloop-of-war *Hornet*, Captain James Lawrence, compelled the British brig *Peacock* to strike her colors after an engagement continuing but fifteen minutes. Lawrence was promoted to the command of the *Chesapeake*.

James Butler Sigourney of Boston was a sailing master in the United States Navy; entered as midshipman, March —, 1809; was a favorite pupil of Lawrence, on board the *Wasp*. Was sailing master of the *Nautilus* when captured, June 16, 1812; was carried to Halifax, June 28, by the *Shannon;* he soon came back to the States, and was invited to the same station on board the *Hornet,* by his old master, but was unable to accept, because the *Hornet* sailed before his exchange was ratified by our government. He was ordered to the southern station and commanded the schooner *Asp.* July 14, 1813, he was attacked in the Potomac by three British barges, which he successfully repelled, but an hour afterward was overpowered by a force of fifty men, in five boats, who boarded, exclaiming, *no quarter.* Of the *Asp's* crew, twenty-one in all, some threw themselves overboard; the rest (except two) were put to death. Sigourney kept his station, and was cut down when only three men were left on deck, one of whom begged in vain for *quarter.*— *Boston Gazette, August 9,* 1813.

On the 1st of June, 1813, Lawrence, with his vessel ill-equipped and ill-manned, put to sea from Boston, to engage the British frigate *Shannon,* which, with a well-disciplined crew, was lying off the harbor inviting an attack. The action was short, but very furious. In a few minutes the *Chesapeake* became exposed to a raking fire, and her chief officers were killed or wounded. Then the enemy boarded her and hauled down the colors. Lawrence, after he was mortally wounded, gave his last heroic order: "Don't give up the ship." This was the most memorable sea-fight of the year.

Perry's victory on Lake Erie, in capturing British vessels, was a great achievement. General Harrison hastened to profit by this victory of Perry on Lake Erie. Embarking his troops on board of Perry's fleet, he crossed to Canada. Harrison pursued the enemy and overtook them, October 5th, waiting to give battle. He charged upon the English, broke their ranks, and caused them to surrender.

The savages made a brave resistance, but Tecumseh[*], their leader, was soon slain, and they were forced to take flight.

The victories of Perry and Harrison brought the war to an end on the north-western frontier.

---

[*] Tecumseh was a noted Indian warrior; he was chief of the Shawnees and had taken part against the Americans in many conflicts.

Owen Quinn, in the war of 1812, a native of Ireland, had been impressed into the British service when at his home in Ireland, in early youth. His recollections of that home were of his mother standing at the gate of her cottage taking her last leave of him, as he was hurried away, with the sound of drum and fife, to join in the Peninsula war in Spain. He fought against the French, was stationed at the Straits of Gibraltar, and from his tall figure he was a grenadier while in service. In 1813 his regiment was ordered from Spain to the United States to fight against the Americans. Owen Quinn was in the British blockade on the Atlantic coast, which was stationed at the Penobscot river in Maine.

While on board of the British man-of-war he was detailed to go on shore to collect wood for the ship. While on shore he fled to the American camp, was pursued as a deserter, but just escaped being made a prisoner and shot. In sympathy for American liberty he enlisted in the United States service to the end of the war. He knew by deserting he lost all hope of his pension from the British government, as he was promised, if he were disabled or retired with an honorable discharge from service. He became a resident of Oxford (now Webster). He died in Sutton, Mass., December, 1871, aged 82 years.

Captain William Googings of Oxford, it is said, was a native of Maine, born in 1768; in his youth went to Nantucket, where he continued for thirty two years a sailor and whaleman; later in the merchant service, and became part owner and captain of a vessel. In the war of 1812 his vessel, with a valuable cargo, of which he was also part owner, was captured by French privateers, and he was taken to France. A few years after his return he came to Oxford, and resided in a cottage on the old Charlton road near the river, west from the north common. Captain Googings died June, 1832.

Close of the War.

In December, 1814, a fleet of over 10,000 troops arrived from England to capture New Orleans.

On the 8th of January, 1815, the British, under Sir Edward Pakenham, made an attack upon the intrenchments a few miles below New Orleans, but failed of success — General Jackson obtaining a great victory for the Americans in this engagement.

The war had now continued for more than two years and a half before the battle of New Orleans.

A treaty of peace was signed at Ghent, in Belgium, December 24, 1814, by American and British Commissioners.

News traveled slowly in these days.

THE MEXICAN WAR.

President Polk's administration was most notable by the war with Mexico, which resulted from the annexation of Texas. Permitting Texas to join the Union was received by the Mexicans as an act of hostility.

While war was impending, General Taylor received orders from government to advance into Texas with a body of American troops to repel a threatened invasion of the Mexicans. In August, 1845, he formed his camp at Corpus Christi, just within the boundary of the disputed territory. The early part of the following year, having received orders to advance, he moved to the Rio Grande, opposite Matamoras.

Now on the east bank of the river, he commenced building a fort (Fort Brown). Before arriving at the Rio Grande he established at Point Isabel a place of deposit for supplies.

May 8, on returning from Point Isabel, he met General Arista with the Mexican army, and gained a victory over the Mexicans on the plains of Palo Alto. The next day, May 9, General Taylor advancing again met the Mexicans at Resaca de la Palma, and totally defeated them. On the 18th of May

Taylor crossed the river Rio Grande and took possession of Matamoras. In a few months General Taylor moved his army of about 6,600 men against Monterey, and on the 24th of September, after a siege of four days and a series of assaults, the city was surrendered to the Americans. In January, 1847, a large part of General Taylor's best troops were withdrawn to aid General Scott, who had been ordered to invade Mexico by way of Vera Cruz.

Santa Anna, general-in-chief of the Mexican forces, collected 20,000 troops, and made an attack upon Taylor and Wool in a narrow mountain-pass, near the plantation Buena Vista. The battle commenced in the afternoon of the 22d of February, 1847, and continued the next day till night, when Santa Anna retreated. This victory terminated the war in that part of the country held by Taylor's forces. From this time the Mexicans made efforts to resist the invasion which General Scott was to make to the very centre of her power. General Scott had landed his army near Vera Cruz, March 9, 1847, and soon had completely invested the city. After a furious bombardment of four days from the army and fleet, Vera Cruz and the strong castle San Juan d'Ulloa surrendered. A few days afterward Scott began his march toward the city of Mexico. At the mountain-pass of Cerro Gordo he met Santa Anna, who had collected another army. On the 18th of April the Americans totally routed the Mexicans.

The victors continued their march to Pueblo, which was surrendered by the Mexicans. The fortified camp of Contreras, twelve miles south of Mexico, was assaulted and carried. This success was followed by the brilliant victory of Cherubusco. On the 8th of September General Worth led his column against the forces of the enemy in a strong stone structure. "The battle fought on that day was the most bloody of the war, but the position was won."

Five days later the Americans stormed the rock and castle

of Chapultepec, the last strong defense of the capital, and routed the whole Mexican army.

September 14, 1847, the Americans entered the city of Mexico and raised the "stars and stripes" over the national palace. The fall of the capital was the close of the war.

The United States gained by their brilliant victories in Mexico a large territory stretching to the Pacific coast.

A treaty was concluded in February, 1848, and peace was proclaimed by President Polk the following July.

Gen. Nelson Henry Davis of Oxford was distinguished in the Mexican war.

"Nelson H., son of Col. Stephen Davis of Oxford, studied at Leicester Academy, appointed upon nomination of Levi Lincoln (then representative to Congress from fifth Massachusetts district) as cadet at West Point, where he entered July 1, 1841, was graduated 1846, went the same year into the Mexican war under Gen. Taylor at Monterey, joined at Tampico the forces of Gen. Scott, under whom he served through the war; was in the siege of Vera Cruz, the battle of Cerro Gordo, the storming of Contreras, the taking of Chernbusco, and in later engagements in the valley of Mexico, and the taking of the capital. He left Mexico with the army in June, 1848, and in November of that year sailed from New York with troops around Cape Horn, arriving in April at Monterey, Cal. There he served until December, 1853, first as commissary and later with his company at remote stations in the Indian country, where subsistence was difficult, and with the Clear Lake and the Russian River Indians had two notable and successful engagements under the brave captain, later General, Nathaniel Lyon. This was said to have been one of the most brilliant Indian campaigns in the army service.

"His health having been impaired by exposure he obtained leave of absence, and in 1853 visited China and the Sandwich Islands. In January, 1854, he returned to New York, and

for a year was on recruiting duty at Boston. In the fall of
1855 he went into frontier service at Forts Leavenworth, Randall, Ridgely, Ripley, and on field duty in the Indian country,
continuing until the spring of 1861, when he was ordered east
to engage in the late civil war. At the first battle of Bull
Run he was acting major of the 'Regular Battalion,' and on
September 4, 1861, was by Gov. Andrew commissioned as
colonel of the 7th Regt., Mass. Vols., which office he held until November 12, when he was appointed assistant inspector-general of the army, ordered to other duties and resigned his
colonel's commission.

"As assistant inspector-general he served in the field, in the
"Army of the Potomac," at the head quarters of Sumner,
McClellan, Hooker and Meade, and was in all the battles in
which these commanders were engaged while he served under
their commands, and was specially efficient at the battle of
Gettysburg. Later he was ordered to the department of New
Mexico as general inspecting officer. The duties in this field
required almost constant traveling through a vast extent of
wild country infested with hostile Indians, the climate, embracing extremes of heat and cold, rendering the service severe.
Many movements were made at night to avoid the enemy.
"On one of these campaigns, after repeated night marches in
which several Indian Rancherias were captured, * * * a
forced march was made at night over a high range of mountains to the reported camp of the Indians. * * * Near
the summit the escort was divided into two detachments, a
third having been left behind in a cañon to guard the pack-train. These detachments, which were about five miles apart,
attacked simultaneously at dawn two camps of the Apaches,
who were completely surprised." A short and sharp contest
ensued, resulting in large loss to the Indians. This was the
first severe chastisement they had received for many years,
and in recognition of his services in this affair the Legislature

of Arizona passed Davis a vote of thanks, and the United States government conferred on him the rank of colonel in the army.

"Later he was for several years inspecting officer of the Department of the Missouri, to which the District of New Mexico was then attached. From this service he was assigned to special duty under the War Department, with station at New York city, for three years, his duties covering inspections in the Western States and Territories to Alaska. He was next inspector-general of the Division of the Atlantic, under Gen. Hancock, until July 1, 1881, when he was assigned to the same duty in the Division of the Missouri, under Gen. Sheridan, with station at Chicago. On the death of Gen. D. B. Sacket, chief inspector-general of the army, Gen. Davis in March, 1885, was promoted as his successor, assuming the duties of that office at Washington.

"On September 20, 1885, by the operation of the law he was retired from active service as brigadier-general.

"Gen. Davis held every grade of rank in the army from second lieutenant to brigadier-general, and head of the Inspector-General's Department; was brevetted for services in the Mexican War, the War of the Rebellion and Indian fights, and traveled on duty in each and every State and Territory of the Union.

"His services in the Civil War were of the highest importance, and as acting inspector he undoubtedly had a more complete knowledge of the conditions of the 'Army of the Potomac' in its details than any other official in the country.

"Later Gen. Davis resided in New York city, and was several years president of the Colorado Smelting Co., with an office in New York. He died suddenly of apoplexy at Governor Island, N. Y., May 15, 1890."

The Civil War.

On the 15th of April, 1861, the day following the evacuation of Fort Sumter, President Lincoln called for seventy-five thousand troops to serve for three months.

The national troops, only a few thousand in all, were stationed on the remote frontiers, while most of the war ships were dispersed in distant seas.

Friday, April 19, witnessed the contest between the Sixth Massachusetts Regiment and the Baltimore mob.

It was on this eventful evening that gentlemen in Oxford assembled with great enthusiasm to make arrangements for the immediate organization of a volunteer company of soldiers. Hon. Alexander De Witt, president on the occasion.— In a few days a sufficient number of volunteers were obtained to assure the success of a company. The company was organized May 4, under the militia laws of the State, and in honor of Col. Alexander De Witt, was called the "De Witt Guards."

The town provided for the members of the company, procuring uniforms and aiding families. On June 1, an excursion was made to Worcester, where the company were entertained. When passing through Sutton the company halted at Freeland Place, the residence of the late Captain Freeland. On June 28, the company went into camp at Worcester, and was attached to the Fifteenth Regiment, Massachusetts Volunteers, and designated as Company E. Camp duty was continued until August 8, when under the command of Col. Devens, the regiment left en route for Washington, and arrived on the 10th. An encampment was made on the 12th, at Meridian Hill, under the name of Camp Kalorama.

Note.— In November, 1861, the town voted to pay board bills of soldiers not exceeding $267.85. Of this, $132 were paid to L. A. Presby, tavern-keeper. The amount paid by the town to the "De Witt Guards" for drilling was $2,084, and for uniforms $1,043. The bounties paid before the spring of 1862 amounted to $10,650. The amount paid to soldiers' families in the fiscal year ending 1862 was $1,707; 1863, $4,283; 1864, $4,904; 1865, $6,708; 1866, State aid, $2,691. [Town Reports.]

Through the efficiency of Lament B. Corbin, first selectman, as recruiting officer, all demands for men were promptly met. In June, 1864, the town by a unanimous vote expressed its thanks to him "for the energetic, faithful and patriotic manner" in which he had performed the duties.

April, 1864, the following appeared in the Worcester *Spy:* "The town of Oxford considers itself the banner town of the county, having filled all quotas with four or five men in the field in excess, and all have been raised without war meetings, extra bounties or purchases of men out of town."

The following names are found registered as the De Witt Guards: Watson, capt., Nelson Bartholomew, 1st lieut., Bernard B. Vassall, 2d lieut., Luther C. Torrey, 1st sergt., Leonard E. Thayer, student. Henry W. Arnold, Albert Prince, George B. Works, Peleg F. Murray, Charles A. Bacon, Amos H. Shumway, Pliny Allen, John M. Norcross, Loren C. Hoyle, Sutton, Joseph N. Williams, George N. Carr, Patrick Moore, Oscar L. Guild, musicians, Elias B. Ellis, Kensington, Ct., Charles Sutton, wagoner.

Ithiel T. Johnson went August 1, 1861 with Co. E, 15th Regt., as attendant of Lieut. Bartholomew. Feb. 6, 1865, went again and was news agent in Hancock's Veteran Corps.

OXFORD IN THE CIVIL WAR, 1861–1865.

Company E, Fifteenth Regiment.

Peleg F. Murray, sergt., Amos H. Shumway, sergt., John A. Thurston, sergt., Lieut. Nelson Bartholomew, Edward Booth, George W. Cross, George P. Davis, James H. Davis, Alfred W. Davis, Antonio Phillips, Francis C. Pope, Lyman Phipps, Vernon F. Rindge, Edward Ennis, Patrick Elliot, Herbert N. Fuller, Henry Hock, Cyrus Learned, Elliot F. McKinstry, Francis A. Fletcher, Chester I. Smith, Estes E. Baker, James D. Adams, James O. Bartlett, Valentine Suter, Edward

Cudworth, Henry C. Hayden, Charles F. Wheelock, George S. Williams, Albert L. Williams, Patrick Holden, Rufus Vicers, Christopher Vicers, Pliny Allen, corp., Simon Carson, corp., Horace P. Howe, corp., Anthony Murphy, corp., John Toomey, corp., Nathaniel Viall, corp., Joseph H. Williams, corp., Andrew B. Yeomans, corp., Oscar L. Guild, musician, Charles A. Bacon, Matthew Brennan, Patrick Brennan, Samuel A. Clark, Daniel Cobb, Otis Coburn, Edward Cudworth, F. L. Kirby, Leander T. Kirby, James H. Davis, Horatio C. Dodge, Caleb F. Dudley, James Duffy, Frank Dupré, John Eckersley, Joseph E. Fellows, Patrick Feighan, Herbert N. Fuller, Joseph M. Green, George W. Gunston, Joseph E. Haskell, John W. Humphrey, James Hilton, Joseph Jennison, Thomas King, Edward Lovely, Edwin E. Rindge, George O. Raymond, Jerome P. Southwick, Bernard Schmidt, Felix Sherbino, Edwin A. Martin, Julius N. Bellows, Josiah C. Brown, Daniel V. Childs, John Dore, Amos P. Newton, Jr., William Robbins, Albert Foskett, George Bacon, William Ronan, Leonard E. Thayer, Albert S. Moffitt, Margins E. Steere, Timothy Moynahan, Anthony Murphy, William Y. Woodbury, Alexander Thompson, Thomas Thompson, Samuel Thompson, John Tully,— Mac Lynch.

Battles in which Company E, Fifteenth Regiment, Massachusetts Volunteers was engaged. Ball's Bluff, Oct. 21, 1861; Siege of Yorktown, April 5 to May 5, 1862; Fair Oaks, May 31, 1862; Savage Station, June 29, 1862; White Oak Swamp, June 30, 1862; Glendale, later, same day; Malvern Hill, July 1, 1862; Vienna, Sept. 2, 1862, on retreat from Fairfax; South Mountain, Sep. 14, 1862; Antietam, Sept. 17, 1862; Fredericksburg, Dec. 11 to 16, 1862; second Fredericksburg, May 34, 1863; Gettysburg, July 2, 3, 4, 1863; Bristow Station, Oct. 14, 1863; second Bull Run, Oct. 15, 1863; Mine Run or Locust Grove, Nov. 27, 28, 29, 1863; Wilderness, May 5 to 9, 1864; Laurel Hill, May 10, 1864; Farna Hill,

May 11, 1864; Spottsylvania, May 12, 13, 18, 1864; Cold Harbor, June 3 to 11, 1864; before Petersburg, June 18 to 22, 1864.

Gen. George B. McClellan, who had just conducted a successful campaign in West Virginia, was summoned to Washington to take command of the troops on the Potomac. This army soon became immensely strong, but made no general advance until the next year. Some months were spent in organizing and disciplining the grand army. On the 1st of November McClellan succeeded the aged chieftain, Scott, as general-in-chief of the armies of the United States.

In the autumn a severe action took place at Ball's Bluff, on the Potomac, above Washington. Nearly two thousand Union troops sent across the river from the Maryland side by Gen. Stone, the commander in that vicinity, were defeated in a battle, October 21, with heavy loss. Col. Baker, a national senator from Oregon, and the leader of the expedition, was among the killed.

Joseph Jennison, Jr., and James Hilton were killed; Bernard B. Vassall, lieutenant, prisoner; John M. Norcross, Nathaniel A. Viall, Joseph H. Williams and Patrick Moore (both wounded), corporals; privates Amidon, Daniel Cobb, Coburn, Thomas Conroy, William Conroy, Geo. P. Davis, William M. Davis, Dockham, Duffy, Eckersley, Emerson, Fellows, Feighan (wounded), McIntire, McKinstry, Moffit (wounded), Moynahan, Phipps (wounded), Vernon F. Rindge, Schmidt were taken prisoners; 5 officers, 22 privates; total, 27. The number of men of the regiment who crossed was about 625, of these only one-half returned.

McClellan moved forward toward Richmond, and establishing his base of supplies at White House, on the Pamunkey, threw the left wing of his army across the Chickahominy, a very few miles from the rebel capital. This wing was attacked May 31, 1862, near Fair Oaks and Seven Pines. The battle lasted part of two days, and at its close the Confederates fell back to Richmond. The loss was very severe on each side. Gen. Joseph E. Johnston, the Confederate commander, was severely wounded, and Gen. Robert E. Lee was afterward assigned to command in his place.

McClellan had been expecting to be re-enforced by McDowell, who was at Fredericksburg, in command of over forty thousand men. To keep the way open for McDowell to join him, he had sent forward a column under Gen. Fitz-John Porter, who routed a body of the enemy at Hanover Court House, four days before the battle of Fair Oaks. But a bold enterprise performed by the Confederate Gen. Jackson, popularly known as "Stonewall" Jackson, prevented the junction of McDowell and McClellan.

On July 1, 1862, occurred the battle of Malvern Hill, the last of the Richmond battles, in which the Confederates were repulsed at every point. The Fifteenth Regiment was engaged, but the loss was small.

The fighting continued during seven days, known as the Seven Days before Richmond, ending in a bloody repulse of the Confederates at Malvern Hill. The other principal battles had been fought at Mechanicsville.

September 17, was fought the great battle of Antietam, which raged from dawn till dark, and left both armies greatly shattered; but Lee was forced to recross the Potomac.

This was one of the great battles of the war. Each army numbered about one hundred thousand men, and the contest continued from morning till night. During the night the Confederates retreated. In this struggle the Fifteenth lost heavily. The casualties in Company E were : killed, Serg. Amos H. Shumway (buried on the field); Alfred W. Davis, died of wounds Sept. 22 ; John H. Curran, James H. Davis, Alexander Thompson, Conrad Amptaeur, Charles H. Wheelock, with many wounded.

On December 13, 1862, occurred the first battle of Fredericksburg (Gen. Burnside being in command), in which the Fifteenth was engaged. The Confederates fought behind intrenchments and the Unionists in the open field, with great loss. One, Edward Lovely, wounded, and one, Emory F. Bailey, missing, in Company E. A note (in Company E Records), dated December 11, says: " Regiment marched across the river to Fredericksburg — in active service till the 16th — then ordered to old camp near Falmouth."

On the 3d crossed to Fredericksburg and joined, under Gen. Hooker, in the second attack on the Confederate works. Failing in the attempt, it recrossed the river the same night, and for four days acted as picket guard and support of a battery near the river. "On the 8th, " moved back to the hill opposite the Lacy House," where an encampment was made, continuing about five weeks.

1863. In Virginia, Gen. Hooker superseded Burnside, and was severely beaten at Chancellorsville (May 2, 3) by Lee, who soon after set out for a second invasion of the loyal States. General Meade superseded Hooker, beat Lee in the great and decisive battle of Gettysburg (July 1, 2, 3), and pursued him into Virginia.

In a *Spy* editorial, July 23, 1864, occurs the following:*

Gen. Lee, thinking the Union lines weakening, precipitated upon their left center his reserve of eighteen thousand of his best troops, intending to sweep the field. The Union veterans were equal to the emergency, met the assault with coolness and bravery, forced back the attacking column, and decided the fortunes of the day.

---

*The next day (July 3) the battle was renewed. The shock was terrible. Late in the afternoon, when the rebel lines showed signs of wavering, the colors of the Fifteenth were ordered (by Gen. John Gibbon) to advance. The remnant of the regiment rallied to their support, and as if by one impulse the whole line pushed forward with a shout and carried the position. The rebel army was defeated."

Of Company E, privates Geo. W. Cross and Michael Flynn were killed, and Capt. Prince, Corp. Anthony Murphy and Owen Tonar, Robert Lusty and Thomas King, privates, wounded. Flynn was on detached service in a Rhode Island battery, and is said to have been among the bravest.

1863. The Federals, under Rosecrans, were defeated at the Chickamauga (September 19 and 20), and besieged in Chattanooga. The siege was raised, and the enemy thoroughly defeated by Grant in a three days' battle, beginning November 23. Soon after the Confederates were repulsed before Knoxville by Burnside.

Gen. Meade still held command of the Army of the Potomac, which had the task of conquering Lee's army. Lieut.-Gen. Grant had his head-quarters with the Army of the Potomac, and took the general direction of military affairs.

This army crossed the Rapidan, May 4, 1864, and the next day Lee hurled his heavy columns upon it, in the region known as the Wilderness.* There a terrific battle raged for two days, at the close the Confederates withdrawing behind their intrenchments. These were too strong to be assaulted. Grant,

---

* Of the battle of the Wilderness, a recent writer has said: "It was the most strange and indescribable battle in history. A battle which no man saw, and in which artillery was useless. A battle fought in dense woods and tangled brake, when manœuvre was impossible, where the lines of battle were invisible to the commanders, and whose position could only be determined by the rattle and roll and flash of musketry, and where the enemy was also invisible." Another says: "Nothing can be stranger or more difficult to understand and picture mentally than this death grapple between 200,000 men in virtual darkness, this desperate struggle, costing from 12,000 to 15,000 lives, fought out without perception on either side of the entities that were moving rifle-trigger and gun-lock. The firing was guided wholly by the flashes of the opposing volleys. No men were to be seen. Yet death was everywhere. In no battle of the war could the courage of the combatants have been so severely tried as here."—*N. Y. Tribune, June* 22, 1888.

resolving to go on, therefore made a flank movement, but again found his foe before him at Spottsylvania, where the rival armies had a long, fierce struggle. Another flank movement was followed by a fight at the North Anna, and another by the bloody Federal repulse at Cold Harbor. Whenever Grant made a flanking advance, Lee fell back rapidly, and behind breastworks again confronted him.

The great battles of the Civil War were Gettysburg, Spottsylvania, Wilderness, Antietam, Chancellorsville, Chickamauga, Cold Harbor, Fredericksburg, Manassas, Shiloh, Stone River and Petersburg. Gettysburg was the greatest battle of the war; Antietam the bloodiest. The largest army was assembled by the Confederates at the seven days' fight; by the Union, at the Wilderness.

On the 5th and 6th of May was fought the battle of the Wilderness, with many losses and no decided advantage to either side. On the 9th, after three days' hard fighting, the Confederates retreated with 13,000 loss. On the 11th and 12th occurred the battle of Spottsylvania, when 4,000 Confederates were captured.

General Wilson, with thirteen thousand horsemen, sent out by General Thomas, was making a great raid through the heart of Alabama, capturing cities, and destroying railroads and other property useful to an enemy. General Stoneman, from East Tennessee, was also making a great raid with cavalry in South-western Virginia and the western part of North Carolina.

General Sheridan, with near ten thousand troopers, bursting through the Shenandoah Valley, had fallen again upon the little army of Early, and captured most of it. Then he destroyed the canal west of Richmond, and tore up the railroads north of the city. Sweeping around easterly, he joined the Union army before Petersburg.

Grant opened the final campaign on the 29th of March.

On the morning of that day he set in motion strong columns of his army to pass around the end of the intrenchments south-west of Petersburg, so as to get to the enemy's rear. Fighting began on the same day, and on the 1st of April, Sheridan, in command of these flanking columns, thoroughly defeated part of Lee's army, at the cross-roads called Five Forks.

Early in the next morning Grant made a general assault upon the whole line of intrenchments before Petersburg, and carried it, driving the Confederates to their inner works. Jefferson Davis and his Cabinet fled from Richmond. Lee's army abandoned the cities which they had so long and so bravely defended, and hurried westward, aiming to unite with Johnston's army in North Carolina. April 3 the Union troops occupied both Petersburg and Richmond.

The saddest story of all the war is that which tells of the cruel treatment of Union prisoners in the South. We would not here describe, if we could, the terrible sufferings which the captives had to endure in Libby prison, on Belle Isle, and above all, in that great prison-pen at Andersonville, from heat, cold, hunger, from diseases which should have been prevented, and from outrages committed by brutal guards.

NOTE.— The government sent expeditions for the capture of Fort Sumter and Charleston. Early in April, 1863, Admiral Du Pont, with a fleet of iron-clads, assailed the defenses of Charleston Harbor, but he was soon obliged to retire. Afterward land and naval forces, under General Gillmore and Admiral Dahlgren, attacked these defenses. In July Gillmore seized part of Morris Island, and tried to take Fort Wagner, on the other part, by storming it, but failed with sad loss. By a siege, the Confederates were at length forced to abandon this fort. Fort Sumter was bombarded and made a heap of ruins, but the garrison still held it, and Charleston also withstood the long siege, although Gillmore threw shells into the city from Morris Island.

NOTE.— The 1st of February, 1865, saw Sherman again on the march. Moving northward, he easily brushed aside the small bodies of the enemy which offered any annoyance, and on the 17th occupied Columbia, the capital of South Carolina. On the same day Charleston was abandoned by its garrison, whose safety was now threatened by Sherman's movements. On the following day, February 18, Gillmore's troops raised the national flag over Fort Sumter, and took possession of the city.

Oxford Soldiers.

Tenth Regiment.

Co. E: Francis E. Cadwell. Charles S. Knight, corp.

Twelfth Regiment.

Co. C: Abellino S. Burt, disability, lost an arm, May 5, 1864, at Wilderness. Thomas J. Cummings. Co. F: John H. Wellman. Co. C: Daniel F. Bacon. Co. H: George Bacon, July 14, 1863; wounded May 6, 1864, at Wilderness; d. June 6, 1864, at Alexandria, Va. Samuel C. Smith, k. June 21, 1864, at Petersburg, Va. Co. I: James Boyce.

Fifteenth Regiment.

Co. A: George H. Stevens, serg., July 12, 1861; trans. July 29, 1861, to Co G; wounded May 12, 1864, at Spottsylvania; July 28, 1864; d. June 9, 1884, at Oxford, æ. 39. Edward G. Gee, Aug. 14, 1862; March 26, 1864, to re-enlist for Leominster; trans. July 27, 1864, to 20th Reg. Co. C: George O. Raymond, Aug. 8, 1862; d. of wounds at Gettysburg, July 22, 1863. Co. D: Elbridge Acker, Aug. 11, 1862; Feb. 11, 1864, to re-enlist; trans. July 27, 1864, to 20th Reg. Charles H. Lamb, July 12, 1861; Feb. 4, 1864, to re-enlist; trans. July 27, 1864, to 20th Reg. Fred. T. Maple, Dec. 26, 1863; trans. July 27, 1864, to 20th Reg. James E. White, July 12, 1861; deserted March 3, 1863. William M. Blodgett, for Worcester, July 12, 1861; k. at Fair Oaks, May 31, 1862. Co. G: Adam McKnight, July 28, 1863; trans. July 27, 1864, to 20th Reg. Co. H: Nathan A. Seaver, July 25,

1861; July 28, 1864. Co. I: Franklin Hovey, musician; June 20, 1861; trans. July 27, 1864, to 20th Reg. Henry S. Dealing, June 20, 1861; disc. 1862. James Mahoney, July 31, 1861; Nov. 1, 1862, disability [see 1st Reg. Cav.]. Antoine Phillips, May 20, 1861; May 12, 1862, disability [see 51st and 57th Regs.]. Michael Powers, Aug. 1, 1861; disc. 1861, minority. Co. K: Patrick Elliott, Aug. 8, 1862; Sept. 28, 1863; wounded; d. Dec. 4, 1863, at Oxford [Mem. tablets]. Unassigned, James Burke, Aug. 1, 1862; deserted.

Seventeenth Regiment.

Co. G: Patrick O'Dwyer, Sept. 2, 1864; June 30, 1865. Unassigned, Geo. W. Farrington, Aug. 8, 1864; was in 2d H. Art.; trans. to 17th, Jan. 17, 1865.

Eighteenth Regiment.

Co. E: John M. Badger, Aug. 24, 1861; Dec. 13, 1862, disability. Co. G: Edward I. Willis, July 14, 1863; trans. Oct. 1, 1864, to 32d Reg.

Nineteenth Regiment.

Co. A: Orrin B. Chaffee, Feb. 11, 1865; June 30, 1865. Co. E: George H. Davis, March 25, 1865; May 6, 1865.

Twentieth Regiment.
(All transferred from the Fifteenth Regiment.)

Co. E: Otis Coburn, serg., Jan. 4, 1864; June 12, 1865; d. March 18, 1888. Edward Cudworth, serg., Dec. 25, 1863; July 16, 1865. Elbridge Acker, Feb. 11, 1864; July 27, 1865. Joseph E. Fellows, Dec. 25, 1863; d. March 29, 1865, at Andersonville. Herbert N. Fuller, Feb. 26, 1864; d. Feb. 20, 1865, at Andersonville. Co. G: Fred T. Maple, musician, Dec. 25, 1863; July 16, 1865. Charles H. Lamb, Feb. 4, 1864; July 16, 1865. Adam McKnight, July 28, 1863; July 16, 1865. Unassigned, Franklin Hovey [see 15th Reg.].

Twenty-first Regiment.

Band: A. Dorr Wood. William F. Hervey, Aug. 23, 1861; Aug. 11, 1862. Co. A: Samuel P. Hall, Aug. 23, 1861; Jan. 2, 1862, disability. Co. E: Clifford Micer, Aug. 23, 1861; Dec. 4, 1862, disability. Josiah G. Sawyer, Jan. 2, 1864; trans. to 56th Reg. Co. F: Josiah Redfern, Aug. 19, 1861; Jan. 1, 1864, to re-enlist [see 56th Reg.]. Henry C. Wister, Aug. 19, 1861; deserted.

Twenty-fourth Regiment.

Co. I: William J. Lamb, Jan. 2, 1864; Jan. 20, 1866.

Twenty-fifth Regiment.

Co. B: Charles W. Adams, Dec. 18, 1863; July 13, 1865. Co. C: James D. Thompson, Aug. 12, 1864; July 13, 1865. Co. D: Benjamin F. Barnes, March 6, 1865; July 13, 1865. James O. Bartlett, Sept. 27, 1863; Jan. 2, 1864, to re-enlist; served to July 13, 1865; d. May 1, 1866, at Charlton, of wounds at Cold Harbor [credited to Douglas on Adj.-Gen. Rep.]. Benjamin B. Bartlett, Sept. 27, 1861; Jan. 18, 1864, to re-enlist; served to July 13, 1865. Charles E. Grover, March 6, 1865; July 13, 1865. William H. Morris, Oct. 21, 1861; June, 1862, disability. John A. Taft, Oct. 14, 1861; Oct. 20, 1864. Nathaniel E. Taft, Oct. 14, 1861; Feb. 15, 1864, disability. John F. Turner, March 6, 1865; July 13, 1865. Co. F: Calvin S. Aldrich, June 5, 1862; Jan. 2, 1864, to re-enlist; re-enlisted at Webster; served to July 13, 1865. John Gleason, June 5, 1862; Jan. 18, 1864, to re-enlist; served till July 13, 1865. Co. G: Valentine Suter, Sept. 18, 1861; k. Feb. 8, 1862, at Roanoke Island. William C. Wiswall, Oct. 16, 1861; Oct. 20, 1864. Co. H: Charles W. Adams, Sept. 14, 1861; Dec. 17, 1863; re-enlisted in Co. B. James D. Adams, Sept. 14, 1861; Dec. 17, 1863, to re-enlist; served to June 3, 1864; d. Sept. 4, 1864, of wounds at Cold Harbor.

Co. K: Otis D. Cooper, Sept. 21, 1861; Dec. 17, 1863, to re-enlist; served to June 11, 1865. Alfred J. Kirby, Sept. 21, 1861; Oct. 20, 1864. John B. Moulton, Sept. 21, 1861; served to May 16, 1864. Sereno Newton, Sept. 16, 1861; April 23, 1864, disability. Unassigned, George H. Kirby, July 31, 1862. Joshua Evans, July 31, 1862.

Twenty-seventh Regiment.

Co. B: Daniel W. Larned, son of Zenas M., for Athol, serg.; Sept. 24, 1861; re-enlisted Dec. 23, 1863; sec. lieut. June 4, 1864; lieut. Sept. 29, 1864; capt. May 15, 1865; disc. June 26, 1865; was wounded three times; went to Kansas, 1878; clerk of District Court of Hodgeman county, 1882 to 1886; notary public and justice of the peace; resided 1888, at Jetmore, Kansas.

Twenty-eighth Regiment.

Co. I: John O'Donnell, Dec. 16, 1861; Dec. 19, 1864.

Thirty-second Regiment.

Co. A: A. J. Copp, for Grafton, Nov. 13, 1861; d. Oct. 5, 1862, Sharpsburg, Md. Co. B: Michael Fisher [sub. for Emory E. Harwood], Dec. 6, 1864; June 6, 1865. Co. E: John H. Wellman, July 14, 1863; June 29, 1865 [see 12th and 39th Regs.]. Co. L: Edward I. Willis, July 14, 1863; June 30, 1865 [see 18th Reg.].

Thirty-fourth Regiment.

Co. A: George A. Clapp, serg., July 13, 1862; sec. lieut. March 12, 1863; served to June 16, 1865. Patrick Powell, July 7, 1862. Edwin Albee. Michael Riley, Nov. 25, 1863; trans. June 14, 1865, to 24th. Nathaniel C. Walsh, July 13, 1862; July 16, 1865. Co. C: Estes E. Baker, Aug. 2, 1862; d. Aug. 24 [May?], 1864, at Andersonville. Co. F: Horace

W. Walsh, serg., Aug. 2, 1862; June 16, 1865. Franklin W. Carson, July 31, 1862; Nov. 17, 1862, disability. Patrick Casey, Nov. 25, 1863; trans. June 14, 1865, to 24th. Co. G: Oscar E. Adams, Aug. 5, 1865; June 16, 1865. Charles C. Trask, for Westfield, July 31, 1862; trans. Jan. 25, 1864, to V. R. C.; d. July 10, 1890, at Spencer. Horace J. Williams, Sept. 2, 1864; June 16, 1865.

Thirty-fifth Regiment.

Co. K: Alfred J. Kirby.

Thirty-sixth Regiment.

Austin Davis, 1st lieut., Aug. 22, 1862; capt. Nov. 13, 1864; served to June 8, 1865. Co. C: William A. Smith, son of Sanford J., for Worcester; Aug. 11, 1862; d. at Nicholasville, Ky., Sept. 27, 1863. Co. F: Edwin A. Martin, corp., Aug. 9, 1862; k. June 3, 1864, at Cold Harbor. Andrew M. Blanding, Aug. 2, 1862; June 8, 1865; d. 1886, at Boston. John Dore, Aug. 5, 1862; trans. 31 March, 1864, to V. R. C.; d. Sept. 15, 1865, at Oxford. Chester J. Smith, Aug. 6, 1862; d. of wounds, June 3, 1864, at Washington, D. C. Co. G: Warren T. Blanding, Aug. 15, 1862; June 8, 1865. Peter Frazer, Aug. 14, 1862; deserted Sept., 1862. Henry Grimley, Aug. 11, 1862; Jan. 20, 1863, disability; d. June 21, 1890, at Togus, Me. William Jesman, Aug. 14, 1862; deserted 1863. Co. I: Russell Arnold, serg., Aug. 2, 1862; June 8, 1865. Julius N. Bellows, Aug. 5, 1862; d. of wounds, May 12, 1864, at Falmouth, Va. Josiah G. Brown, Aug. 1, 1862; d. July 26, 1863, at Milldale, Miss. Oscar H. Brown, Aug. 6, 1862; trans. Aug. 3, 1864, to V. R. C. Daniel V. Childs, Aug. 2, 1862; k. May 6, 1864, at Wilderness. Jacob L. Childs, Aug. 2, 1862; d. April 4, 1864, at Covington, Ky. Truman Marble, Aug. 6, 1862; Feb. 7, 1865, disability; d. Aug. 1, 1870, æ. 26. Co. K: Josiah Redfern, Jan. 2, 1862; trans. to 56th

Reg. Francis A. Fletcher; d. Dec. 6, 1863, at Falmouth, Va.; mem. of 36th Reg. [Mem. tablets]. The Adj.-Gen. Rep. gives Francis Fletcher, Sutton, Aug. 6, 1862; d. Dec. 8, 1862; Co. I, 36th Reg.

Thirty-ninth Regiment.

Co. D: John H. Wellman, July 14, 1863; trans. June 2, 1865, to 32d Reg. [see 12th Reg.].

Fortieth Regiment.

Co. C: James A. Cummings, serg., Sept. 1, 1862; June 16, 1865.

Forty-second Regiment.

Co. E: John Brown, for Millbury, Nov. 3, 1862; Aug. 20, 1863. Co. F: Orrin B. Chaffee, for Brookfield, July 15, 1864; Nov. 11, 1864. Albert W. Cargel, for Leicester, Sept. 30, 1862; Aug. 20, 1863. Co. G: Danford Johnson, for Worcester, July 21, 1864; Nov. 11, 1864. Co. K: Charles M. Tiffany, for Auburn, Nov. 1, 1862; Aug. 20, 1863.

Fifty-first Regiment (nine months).

Co. C: Bowers Davis, Sept. 25, 1862; July 27, 1863. J. Edward Nichols, Sept. 25, 1862; July 27, 1863. Henry W. Putnam, Sept. 25, 1862; July 27, 1863. Co. E: William A. Copp, for Grafton, Sept. 25, 1862; July 27, 1863. Co. G: Thomas D. Kimball, capt., Sept. 30, 1862; July 27, 1863.* John Harwood, 1st serg., Sept. 30, 1862; July 27, 1863. Lewis T. Emerson, serg., Sept. 30, 1862; July 27, 1863; d. July 23, 1886, at Oxford, æ. 49. Charles H. Burleigh, serg., Sept. 30, 1862; re-enlisted June 1, 1863.* John Grady, corp., Sept. 30, 1862; re-enlisted June 1, 1863.* Charles O. Taft, musician, Sept. 30, 1862; re-enlisted June 1, 1863.* Luke Bergen, Sept. 30, 1862; July 27, 1863. Peter Black, Sept.

* Re-enlisted in 2d Reg., Heavy Artillery.

30, 1862; July 27, 1863. Philip Cain, Jr., Oct. 15, 1862; July 27, 1863. William A. Campbell, Sept. 30, 1862; July 27, 1863 [see 2d Cav. Reg.]. Timothy Carney, Sept. 30, 1862; Oct. 28, 1862. Charles L. Cummings, Sept. 30, 1862; re-enlisted June 1, 1863. John Daley, Sept. 30, 1862; July 27, 1863. Edwin Davis, Sept. 30, 1862; Feb. 25, 1863, disability. George L. Davis, Sept. 30, 1862; July 27, 1863. Stephen Eager, Sept. 30, 1862; July 27, 1863; d. Nov. 28, 1864, at New Berne, N. C.* William S. Forrest, Sept. 30, 1862; July 27, 1863.* Albert G. Foskett, Sept. 30, 1862.† Daniel Foskett, Sept. 30, 1862; July 27, 1863. James Grady, Sept. 30, 1862; July 27, 1863. Thomas Hurst, Sept. 30, 1862; July 27, 1863. George H. Keith, Sept. 30, 1862; July 27, 1863. James H. Kennedy, Sept. 30, 1862; July 27, 1863; Daniel Lucy, Sept. 30, 1862; July 27, 1863; d. Jan. 24, 1882, at Oxford. Martin Maher, Sept. 30, 1862; July 27, 1863. Austin W. Martin, Sept. 30, 1862; Oct. 22, 1862, disability. Patrick Murphy, Sept. 30, 1862; July 27, 1863. John P. Newton, Sept. 30, 1862; July 27, 1863. Amasa Phetteplace, Sept. 30, 1862; Oct. 4, 1862. Antonio Philip, Sept. 30, 1862; July 27, 1863 [see 57th Reg.]. Fred A. Presby, Sept. 30, 1862; July 27, 1863. William Sabin, Sept. 30, 1862; July 27, 1863. Daniel Shea, Sept. 30, 1862; July 27, 1863. John Welsh, Sept. 30, 1862; deserted. Jason West, Sept. 30, 1862; re-enlisted June 1, 1863. In Reg. Cornelius P. Davis, son of Reuben; d. July 1, 1863, at New Berne.

Fifty-fourth Regiment.

Co. F: Eugene T. Williams, Nov. 28, 1863; Aug. 20, 1865; Unassigned, Daniel P. Peters, Sept. 1, 1864; trans. to 55th Reg.

---

* Re-enlisted in 2d Reg., Heavy Artillery.   † Died in service.

Fifty-fifth Regiment.

Co. C: Daniel P. Peters, Sept. 1, 1864; Aug. 29, 1865 [see 54th Reg.].

Fifty-sixth Regiment.

Co. B: Josiah Redfern, Jan. 1, 1864; July 12, 1865 [see 36th Reg.]. Co. I: Josiah G. Sawyer, Jan. 1, 1864; July 12, 1865 [see 21st Reg.].

Fifty-seventh Regiment.

Co. A: Martin Maher, Jan. 4, 1864; July 30, 1865. Asa M. Ray, Jan. 4, 1864; July 30, 1865. John Tulley, Jan. 4, 1864; d. of wounds, May 18, 1865, at Alexandria, Va. Co. B: Eugene Smith, musician, Jan. 4, 1864; July 30, 1865. Daniel V. Adams, Jan. 4, 1864; July 30, 1865. Loring J. Adams, Jan. 4, 1864; Nov. 2, 1864, disability. Henry C. Hayden, Jan. 4, 1864; d. of wounds received June 17, before Petersburg, July 4, 1864, at Annapolis. Amos P. Newton, Jan. 5, 1864; k. May 27, 1864, at North Anna river. Antonio Philip, Jan. 4, 1864; d. Sept. 3, 1864, at Andersonville [see 15th and 51st Regs.]. William Robbins, Jan. 11, 1864; k. at Wilderness, May 6, 1864. Josiah Sawyer, æ. 44, Jan. 4, 1864, rejected. Edwin H. Smith, Jan. 4, 1864; trans. to V. R. C. Co. D: Maurice Welch, musician, Jan. 25, 1864; July 30, 1865. James Cowden, Jan. 25, 1864; July 13, 1864, disability. Edwin Cudworth, Jan. 25, 1864; k. March 25, 1865, at Fort Stedman, near Petersburg. Co. H: Joshua Evans, Jan. 11, 1864; May 12, 1865. William H. Rice, Jan. 11, 1864; May 12, 1865.

Sixty-fifth Regiment.

Co. G: Mowry J. Gibson, March 15, 1865; July 12, 1865.

First Regiment Cavalry.

Co. C: Francis G. Elliot, Jr., Sept. 17, 1861; May 4, 1862, disability.

Second Regiment Cavalry.

Co. A: Joseph Spring, March 20, 1865; July 20, 1865. Co. B: Horace A. Pope, March 16, 1865; July 12, 1865. Co. F: Fred F. Johnson, March 15, 1865; July 20, 1865; d. Dec. 4, 1870, at Oxford. Co. G : George Benway, March 20, 1865; July 20, 1865. George Doubleday, March 10, 1865; July 20, 1865. Co. K: James G. Forrest, March 20, 1865; July 20, 1865. James Mahoney, Jan. 26, 1863; Nov. 6, 1863, disability [lost an arm; see 15th Reg.]. Co. M: George H. Baker, March 20, 1865; July 20, 1865. Unassigned, William A. Campbell, March 16, 1865; May 16, 1865 [see 51st Reg.].

Fourth Regiment Cavalry.

Co. E: Elisha C. Taft, corp., Jan. 27, 1864; Nov. 14, 1865; d. Feb. 26, 1869, at Oxford. Co. F: William D. White, serg., March 1, 1864; Nov. 14, 1865. William Kibbe, March 1, 1864; Nov. 14, 1865. Austin W. Martin [see 51st Reg.], Jan. 27, 1864; Nov. 14, 1865; d. Jan. 21, 1884. John Munroe, Aug. 9, 1864; Nov. 14, 1865. Thomas Murphy, Sept. 3, 1864; May 22, 1865. Co. G: Vernon Chaffee, for Webster, Jan. 27, 1864; May 28, 1865.

Second Regiment Heavy Artillery.

Thomas D. Kimball [see 51st Reg.], capt., Sept. 18, 1863; Sept. 3, 1865; major, Sept. 18, 1865. Co. A: Charles H. Burleigh [see 51st Reg.], 1st serg., Aug. 4, 1863; Sept. 3, 1865. Co. B: John Grady [see 51st Reg.], corp., July 28, 1863; Sept. 3, 1865. Co. D: Patrick O'Dwyer, Sept. 2, 1864; trans. Feb. 9, 1865, to 17th Reg. Charles O. Taft [see 51st Reg.], Aug. 22, 1863; Sept. 3, 1865. William Wiggin, Aug. 22, 1863; Sept. 3, 1865. Co. E: James O'Brien, Oct. 5, 1863; Sept. 3, 1865. Stephen Eager, Oct. 8, 1863; d. Nov. 28, 1864, at New Berne. Co. F: Andrew Darling, Oct. 8, 1863; Sept. 3, 1865. Co. G : William Biggs, Dec. 7, 1863; d. July 21, 1864, at Andersonville. William H. N. Cady, Dec. 7, 1863; d. Nov. 1, 1864, in prison. Patrick Hogan, Dec. 7, 1863; d. Aug. 27, 1864, at Andersonville. Patrick Holden, Dec. 7, 1863; d. Aug. 25, 1864, at Andersonville. Joseph Piper, July 19, 1864; Sept. 3, 1865. John C. Steere, Dec. 7, 1863; rejected. Co. G : Christopher Vicars, Dec. 7, 1863; d. Aug. 30, 1864, at Charleston, S. C.; prisoner. Rufus Vicars, Dec. 7, 1863 ; d. Oct., 1864, at Florence, S. C.; prisoner. Co. H: George W. Farrington, Aug. 8, 1864; trans. Jan. 17, 1865, to 17th Reg. George Hastings, Aug. 6, 1864 ; deserted Sept., 1864. Co. K : William S. Forrest [see 51st Reg.], corp., Dec. 22, 1863 ; Sept. 3, 1865 ; d. Nov. 21, 1889, at Oxford. David N. Harris, Dec. 22, 1863; Sept. 3, 1865 ; d. Nov. 26, 1887, at Oxford. Daniel Toomey, Dec. 22, 1863; June 1, 1865 ; d. Jan. 4, 1882, at Oxford. Albert W. Blanding, Dec. 22, 1863; Sept. 3, 1865. Unassigned, Samuel P. Jones, Sept. 13, 1864 ; Oct. 21, 1864, disability. James Milford, Aug. 6, 1864. William Daniels, not in service.

Third Heavy Artillery.

Co. C: Patrick O'Day, Aug. 14, 1863; deserted May 1, 1864.

First Battalion, Heavy Artillery.

Co. C: Lowell A. Beckwith, Nov. 28, 1864; Oct. 20, 1865. Co. D : Lewis Seymour, June 6, 1863; deserted Oct. 20, 1863.

Tenth Battery, Light Artillery.

Algernon P. Follett, Sept. 5, 1864; June 9, 1865.

Third Battalion, Riflemen.

Co. B: Sereno Newton, May 19, 1861; Aug. 3, 1861.

Forty-second Regiment (100 days).

Co. E: Vernon T. Wetherell, July 22, 1864; Nov. 11, 1864. Co. G: William S. Hurd, July 21, 1864; Nov. 11, 1864.

Nineteenth (Unattached Co.) Infantry.

William S. Hurd, Nov. 25, 1864; June 27, 1865.

Veteran Reserve Corps.

Elix Bulley, Sept. 5, 1864; Nov. 17, 1865. Samuel Meeker.(?)

Regular Army.

David Barton, Nov. 26, 1862; asst. q. m., rank of captain, at Hilton Head, S. C., until resignation on account of ill health, 1864. Samuel R. Barton, Dec. 4, 1862; May 3, 1865; hospital steward at Washington, D. C.

The following from Oxford are given as in Massachusetts regiments, but we do not find them on the Adjutant-General's Report.

Thirty-sixth Regiment.

Welcome Miller.

Fifty-seventh Regiment.

Peter Lamont, disc. Joseph Peake, deserted.

William A. Emerson has served in 51st Reg. and was disc.; was drafted from Oxford in 1864, and served from Aug. to Dec., 1864; unassigned.

George Tiffany, substitute for Braman F. Sibley, served nine months at Boston Harbor.

Dr. Charles W. Lynn enlisted in Co. H, 25th Reg., Sept., 1861 [credited to Thompson]; served 18 months in the ranks, and was detailed to hospital service, continuing until his disc., Oct., 1864.

First R. I. Cavalry Regiment.

Michael Mullen, Dec. 14, 1861; Nov. 15, 1864. Patrick Mullen, Dec. 14, 1861; Aug. 3, 1865. Samuel C. Willis, Jr., Dec. 16, 1861; Aug. 3, 1865; quar. mas. serg. of Co. G, May 10, 1862; reg. com. serg., May 18, 1864; first lieut. and commander, Co. F, Nov. 1, 1864. George F. Cummings, Dec. 14, 1861; Aug. 3, 1865; corp. [given as "Frank Cummings" in Town Rep.]; serg., May 1, 1865; credited to Auburn. Nathaniel Smith Emerson, served in this reg.; Nov. 14, 1861; July, 1862; credited to Worcester. He later went as officer's servant to New Orleans, where he died. Jacob H. Pickett is given as of this reg. in Town Rep.; his name is not on the official list.

Seventh R. I. Regiment.

Co. I: Emory Humes, Aug. 4, 1862; June 9, 1865.

Second N. H. Regiment.

Co. H: John A. Elliot, May 21, 1861; deserted June 10, 1863.

Eleventh Conn. Regiment.

Co. B: William W. Schofield, Sept., 1861; wounded March 14, 1862, at New Berne; disc. for dis. Feb., 1864.

Sixteenth Conn. Regiment.

George R. Kimball, serg., July 29, 1862; July, 1865.

Fourth Vermont Regiment.

Co. I: George H. Amidon, Aug. 21, 1861; July 13, 1865; sec. lieut., Jan. 19, 1862; first lieut., Co. G, July 19, 1862; capt. Co. E, Sept. 23, 1862; brevet major, June 9,

1865; wounded May 5, 1864, at Wilderness, and Oct. 19, 1864, at Cedar Creek; left the service an invalid; d. Jan. 4, 1871, at Oxford.

First Vermont Cavalry.

Co. C: P. Merrick Moffitt, Sept. 20, 1861; wounded Sept. 20, 1863, at Grove Church, Va.; re-enlisted Dec. 28, 1863; disc. Aug. 9, 1865.

Twenty-fourth Wisconsin Volunteers.

Co. B: Albert G. Underwood, Aug., 1862; June, 1865; clerk under Howard, Rosecrans and Sheridan; d. Dec. 22, 1882, in Florida.

Twenty-sixth N. Y. Regiment [U. S. C. T.].

Co. B: John R. Smith, Dec. 28, 1863; Aug. 28, 1865.

U. S. Navy.

Benjamin Dyer, Jr., was acting volunteer lieut. on storeship *Fredonia*, at Arica, Peru, Aug. 13, 1868, the vessel being in the harbor. An earthquake destroyed the town and a tidal wave following wrecked the vessel. She sunk with all on board, including Dyer and his wife.

George Whitley, substitute for Benjamin W. Childs, served from Dec. 7, 1864, to the close of the war.

U. S. Engineers.

Howard Carson.   Leander A. Poor.

The Civil War.
Chronological Review.

"Lincoln became president in 1861. He entered upon a second term in 1865, but, April 14, was assassinated, and Vice-President Johnson succeeded to the presidency.

"During these administrations the most formidable rebellion known to history was subdued, and slavery in the United States was abolished by an amendment of the Constitution.

1861.

"The Rebels attacked Fort Sumter, and compelled Major Anderson to evacuate it, April 14. The president called for troops. Jefferson Davis offered to commission privateers, and a blockade of the southern ports was established. Four more slave States joined the Confederacy.

"The Federals, in Virginia, were disastrously defeated at Bull Run (July 21), and in the autumn at Ball's Bluff. In West Virgina, General McClellan, in July, gained victories over the Confederates at Rich Mountain and Carrick's Ford, and before the end of the year that region was nearly cleared of armed Confederates.

"In Kentucky, the Confederates, in September, seized and fortified Columbus, and the Union troops, under General Grant, then occupied Paducah.

"In Missouri, Lyon captured a camp of disloyalists near St. Louis, in May, but lost the hard-fought battle of Wilson's Creek (August 10).

"On the Atlantic coast the Federals captured the Confederate works at Hatteras Inlet (August 29), and those at Port Royal Entrance, November 7.

Mason and Slidell were taken from the British steamer *Trent.*

1862.

" The Federal government prohibited slavery in the territories, abolished it in the District of Columbia, and authorized the enlistment of colored troops.

" In the West, east of the Mississippi, the Federals gained a victory at Mill Spring (January 19); captured Fort Henry and Fort Donelson, and occupied Nashville; were victorious, under General Grant, at Shiloh (April 6 and 7), and, under General Halleck, compelled the enemy to evacuate Corinth (May 29). In autumn, the Federals, under General Rosecrans, defeated the enemy at Iuka, and at Corinth. The Confederates fell back after the battle of Perryville (October 8), and at Murfreesboro' they were beaten by General Rosecrans in a three days' battle, which began December 31.

" West of the Mississippi, a Union victory was won at Pea-Ridge (March 7 and 8), and nine months afterward, another at Prairie Grove.

The Confederate posts on the Mississippi, as far as Vicksburg, successively yielded to the Federals, and Admiral Farragut opened the river from its mouth to New Orleans (April 25), of which city General Butler took military possession.

" On the Atlantic coast General Burnside and Commodore Goldsborough captured Roanoke Island, and before the end of April nearly the whole coast of North Carolina was at the mercy of the Federals, who also had reduced Fort Pulaski. The Confederate ram *Merrimack* after a day's havoc among the Union vessels in Hampton Roads (March 8), was driven back to Norfolk by the *Monitor*.

" In Virginia, the Army of the Potomac, under McClellan, compelled the Confederates to evacuate Yorktown, beat them at Williamsburg, repulsed them near Fair Oaks and Seven Pines (May 31). Meanwhile Stonewall Jackson drove the Federals from the Shenandoah Valley, and then joined General Lee before Richmond. Lee then, in a seven days' campaign of almost constant fighting, raised the siege of the Confederate capital, pursuing McClellan to the James, where the latter repulsed the Confederates, with great loss, at Malvern Hill (July 1). The Confederates next moved against the Army of Virginia, commanded by General Pope, and, after a series of conflicts, beginning at Cedar Mountain and ending at Chantilly (September 1), compelled Pope to fall back within the defences of Washington. Lee next invaded Maryland. McClellan gained a victory over him at South Mountain, and by the great battle of Antietam (September 17) forced the Confederates, who had meanwhile captured Harper's Ferry, back to Virginia. Burnside superseded McClellan, and was badly defeated, at Fredericksburg (December 13).

" During the summer the Sioux War broke out. It was suppressed the next year.

1863.

" President Lincoln signalized the opening of the year war by issuing the Emancipation Proclamation.

" In Virginia, General Hooker superseded Burnside, and was severely beaten at Chancellorsville (May 2, 3) by Lee, who soon after set out for a second invasion of the loyal States. General Meade superseded Hooker, beat Lee in the great and decisive battle of Gettysburg (July 1, 2, 3), and pursued him into Virginia.

" Vicksburg was surrendered to General Grant (July 4), and a few days later Port Hudson to General Banks.

" The Federals, under Rosecrans, were defeated at the Chickamauga (September 19 and 20), and besieged in Chattanooga. The siege was raised, and the enemy thoroughly defeated by Grant, in a three days' battle, beginning November 23. Soon after the Confederates were repulsed before Knoxville by Burnside.

1864.

"Among the earlier events were the expedition to Meridian, the Fort Pillow massacre, the Red River expedition, and a Federal defeat at Olustee, Florida.

"Grant was appointed to the chief command of the Union armies, and, crossing the Rapidan with the Army of the Potomac (May 4), met the enemy in bloody conflicts in the Wilderness, at Spottsylvania, the North Anna, and Cold Harbor. Then crossing the James (June 14), joined by Butler from Fortress Monroe, he laid siege to Petersburg and Richmond. The Confederates made a third invasion of Maryland. They were soon obliged to retreat, but hovered near the Potomac till General Sheridan, in a brilliant campaign, ending in the victory of Cedar Creek (October 19), closed the war in the Shenandoah Valley.

"In the west, General Sherman made his famous march to the sea. Setting out (May 6) from Chattanooga, he fought heavy battles, the severest being at Resaca, Dallas, and Kenesaw Mountain, and captured Atlanta (September 2); then sweeping through Georgia to the sea, he carried Fort McAllister by assault, and took Savannah (December 21). Meanwhile the Confederates had been successfully resisted at Franklin, and disastrously routed at Nashville (December 15 and 16) by General Thomas.

"In June the notorious privateer *Alabama* was captured. In August Admiral Farragut won a victory in Mobile Bay.

1865.

"Fort Fisher, North Carolina, was captured (January 15). Sherman swept northward through South Carolina; drove the Confederates from Columbia; compelled them to evacuate Charleston; then pressing forward into North Carolina, beat them at Averysboro' and at Bentonville, and entered Goldsboro' (March 23).

www.ingramcontent.com/pod-product-compliance
Lightning Source LLC
Chambersburg PA
CBHW051739300426
44115CB00007B/625